Penguin Education

Peasants and Peasant Societies

Edited by Teodor Shanin

Penguin Modern Sociology Readings

Peasants and Peasant Societies

Selected Readings

Edited by Teodor Shanin

Penguin Books

Penguin Books Ltd, Harmondsworth,
Middlesex, England
Penguin Books Inc., 7110 Ambassador Road,
Baltimore, Md 21207, U.S.A.
Penguin Books Australia Ltd,
Ringwood, Victoria, Australia

First published 1971
This selection copyright © Teodor Shanin, 1971
Introduction and notes copyright © Teodor Shanin, 1971

Made and printed in Great Britain by
C. Nicholls & Company Ltd
Set in Monotype Times

To Nancy, quarrelsomely . . .

Contents

Introduction

One can barely speak of discoveries in the social sciences, yet time and again social issues strike the scholar's eye with all the dramatic force of the apple which fell at Newton's feet. The last few years have seen a somewhat paradoxical rediscovery of peasants. In our rapidly expanding world, the character, livelihood and fate of massive majorities in the world's poorest and potentially most explosive areas have come to be seen as one of the most crucial issues of our time. Suddenly, behind the newsmen's headings about glib politicians, corrupt administrators, vicious landlords and fiery revolutionaries, the great unknown of the peasant majority was 'detected' as one of the major structural determinants which make the so-called developing societies into what they are. After a quarter of a century in obscurity the 'peasant problem' came back with a bang – as the dominant issue of war and peace, Vietnam's battlefields and India's hunger, and reflected in the 'super state' policies, campus revolts and ghetto riots of the other 'civilized' world.

Rural sociology as a discipline in its own right emerged in the United States at the turn of the century, preceding its introduction into Europe. It was, however, focused on the sociology of farming as an occupation rather than on peasants as a social entity (Galeski, 1971). The systematic study of peasantry originated in Central and Eastern Europe; not surprisingly, because in those societies a rapidly 'Westernizing' intelligentsia was faced by a large peasantry – the poorest, most backward and numerically the largest section of their nations. The issue of the peasantry became closely entangled with, and impelled forward by, the ideologies of modernization and by the rediscovery of the national self by people suppressed by the Russian, Austrian, German and Turkish Empires. Subsequently, political leaders, social scientists and scores of amateur ethnographers turned their attention to the peasant.

Since the 1920s European research into peasantry has encountered adverse conditions. Nationalist ideologies, military dictatorships and Russian collectivizers did not favour specific studies of peasantry. The few studies of peasantry published in English remained individual ventures. Furthermore, Western social scientists found themselves conceptually handicapped by the prevailing typology – pre-industrial versus industrial (or modern) societies. Such analyses were, on the whole, related to an ethnocentric preoccupation with industrialization and parliamentary democracy as self-evident ways of progress. Peasants 'disappeared', lumped together with neolithic tribesmen, Chinese gentry, and so on, in the common category of pre-industrial or primitive societies.

The growth of interest in peasant societies has coincided with new developments in anthropology. Western anthropologists, clearly, have been running short of small tribes and closed 'folk' communities. Kroeber's re-conceptualization (see below, p. 14) has drawn attention to the peasantry. Considerable resources and numerous topic-hungry students, especially in the US, were launched into the study of peasant societies, generating a wave of monographs, a number of analytical contributions as well as some rediscoveries of truths long known outside the autarky of the English-speaking world.

In view of the rapidly increasing number of peasant studies there is something amusing, if not grotesque, in the failure of scholars as yet to reach even a general agreement on the very existence of peasantry as a valid concept. To many scholars the unlimited diversity of peasants in different villages, regions, countries and continents makes any generalization 'spurious and misleading'. Moreover, to a large number of scholars, peasant societies, which appear to disintegrate under the impact of the modernizing forces of industrialization and urbanization, do not seem worthy of forward-looking scholarly attention.

The existence of peasantry as a realistic (and not purely semantic) concept can be claimed for both empirical and conceptual reasons. Firstly, it is sufficient to read concurrently a sequence of peasant studies originating in countries as far removed in their physical and social conditions as Russia, Hungary, Turkey, China, Japan, India, Tanzania, Colombia, and so on, to note numerous similarities. There are, of course, important differences which are only to be expected in view of the varied historical experience, etc., but what is striking is, to quote Erasmus, 'The persistence of certain peasant attributes' in societies so far removed (Erasmus, 1967, p. 350). Or in Redfield's words: there is 'something generic about it' (Redfield, 1956, p. 25).

Conceptually, a tendency to treat peasantry as a bodyless notion can be countered on grounds related to the essence of sociology – to the trivial but often forgotten truth that *a sociological generalization does not imply a claim of homogeneity, or an attempt at uniformity*. Quite the contrary, a comparative study implies the existence of both similarities and differences, without which a generalization would, of course, be pointless. In pursuing 'a generalizing science' a sociologist always lays himself open to the outrage of the adherents of those disciplines in which the study of uniqueness is central, and easily develops into a canon of faith. Much of it is based on misunderstanding. Some if it simply illustrates the limitations of the sociologist's trade, and of any conceptualization of an unlimitedly unique reality. In Max Weber's words, 'sociological analysis both abstracts from reality and at the same time helps us to understand it', and, consequently ... 'the abstract character of sociology is responsible for the fact that compared with actual historical reality they [i.e. sociological concepts] are relatively lacking in fullness of concrete content' (Weber, 1925, p. 109–12).

In a framework of thought which accepts both the brief of sociology as 'a generalizing science' and the existence of peasantry as a specific, world-wide type of social structure, we can discern four major conceptual traditions which have influenced contemporary scholarship: the Marxist class theory, the 'specific economy' typology, the ethnographic cultural tradition, and the Durkheimian tradition as developed by Kroeber and allied in its theory of social change to functionalist sociology.

The Marxist tradition of class analysis has approached peasantry in terms of power relationships, i.e. as the suppressed and exploited producers of pre-capitalist society (Marx and Engels, 1950). Contemporary peasantry appears as a leftover of an earlier social formation, its characteristics reinforced by remaining at the bottom of the social power structure. The second tradition

2.) has viewed peasant social structure as being determined by a specific type of economy, the crux of which lies in the way a family farm operates. This approach, too, can be traced to Marx, but was first made explicit by Vasil'chakov (1881) and fully developed by Chayanov (1925). The third tradition, which stems from European ethnography and from traditional Western **3)** anthropology, tends to approach peasants as the representatives of an earlier national tradition, preserved as a 'cultural lag' by the inertia typical of peasant societies. The fourth tradition, originating from Durkheim, has followed a rather complex path. The basic dualism accepted by Durkheim and his generation (Tönnies, Maine, etc.) divides societies into the 'traditional' (divided into social segments – uniform, closed and cohesive) and the modern or 'organic', based upon a division of labour and **4)** necessary interaction of the units (Durkheim, 1960). Kroeber later placed peasant societies in an intermediate position as 'part societies with part cultures' – partly open segments in a town-centred society (Kroeber, 1948, p. 284). The peasant 'part-segments' were turned by Redfield into the cornerstone of a conceptualization accepted by the majority of American anthropologists, with the consequent tendency to become reified into self-evident truths by the sheer volume of monotonous repetition.

Sociological definitions and models resemble two-dimensional sketches of a multi-dimensional reality. Each carries partial truth, each reflects necessarily only part of the characterized phenomenon. The reality is richer than any generalization, and that holds particularly true for peasant societies, highly complex social structures with little formal organization. Yet, without conceptual delineation of peasants and peasant societies as a type of social structure, this Reader would turn into a ghost story.

We shall delimit peasant societies by establishing a general type with four basic facets. A definition of peasantry by one, single determining factor would, no doubt, be neater, but too limiting for our purpose. The general type so defined would include the following:

1. *The peasant family farm as the basic unit of multi-dimensional social organization.* The family, and nearly only the family,

provides the labour on the farm. The farm, and nearly only the farm, provides for the consumption needs of the family and the payment of its duties to the holder of political and economic power. The economic action is closely interwoven with family relations, and the motive of profit maximization in money terms seldom appears in its explicit form. The self-perpetuating family farm operates as the major unit of peasant property, socialization, sociability and welfare, with the individual tending to submit to a formalized family-role behaviour.

2. *Land husbandry as the main means of livelihood directly providing the major part of the consumption needs*. Traditional farming includes a specific combination of tasks on a relatively low level of specialization and family-based vocational training. Food production renders the family farm comparatively autonomous. The impact of nature is particularly important for the livelihood of such small production units with limited resources.

3. *Specific traditional culture related to the way of life of small communities*. Specific cultural features (in the sense of socially determined norms and cognitions) of peasants have been noted by a variety of scholars. The pre-eminence of traditional and conformist attitudes, i.e. the justification of individual action in terms of past experience and the will of the community, may be here used as an example. At least part of these cultural patterns may be related to characteristics of a small village community, life in which may be accepted as an additional defining facet of peasantry.

4. *The underdog position – the domination of peasantry by outsiders*. Peasants, as a rule, have been kept at arms' length from the social sources of power. Their political subjection interlinks with cultural subordination and with their economic exploitation through tax, *corvée*, rent, interest and terms of trade unfavourable to the peasant. Yet in some conditions, they may turn into the revolutionary proletariat of our times.

The definition of a 'general type' leads to a further delineation of *analytically marginal groups* which share with the 'hard core' of peasants most, but not all, of their characteristics. In general, such differences can be presented on quantitive scales of more/

less. Analytical marginality does not here in any sense imply numerical insignificance or some particular lack of stability. The major marginal groups can be classified by the basic characteristics which they do not share with the proposed general type, e.g. an agricultural labourer lacking a fully fledged farm, a rural craftsman holding little or no land, the frontier squatter or the armed peasant who at times escaped centuries of political submission along frontiers or in the mountains (e.g. the Kozaks or the Swiss cantons). Analytically marginal groups may also be either a product of different stages of economic development or, alternatively, of different contemporary State policies towards agriculture. (For example, pastoralists, peasant-workers in modern industrial communities, or the members of a Russian *kolkhoz*.)

Like every social entity, peasantry exists only as a process, i.e. in its change. Regional differences among peasants reflect to a large extent their diverse histories. The typology suggested can be used as a yardstick for historical analysis, types of peasants can be approached as basic stages of development. One should beware, however, of the pitfalls of forcing multi-directional changes into neat and over-simplified schemes which presuppose one-track development for peasantries of every period, area and nation.

Some of the dynamism evident in peasant societies does not lead to structural changes and may be cyclical in nature. On the whole, however, the attention of scholars has been drawn to structural changes and especially to those leading to the increasing integration of peasants into national and world society. The social mechanisms involved in such changes are closely linked and can once more be related to the general type suggested. The diffusion of market relations, the increasing significance of exchange and the advent of a money economy, gradually transform the peasant family farm into an enterprise of a capitalist nature, entailing the disappearance of its peculiar characteristics. Professionalization reflects an increasing division of labour which gradually transforms the agricultural and occupational functions of the peasant. Urbanization, acculturation, and the spread of mass culture through the countryside destroy the specific characteristics of peasant culture and the relative closeness and homogeneity of the villages. The impact of State policy on peasant social structure finds expression in agricultural reform and collectivization. Yet, identifying the factors of social change does not necessarily mean that such change takes place. If simultaneously operating social mechanisms resist it, a reinforcement of peasant social structure, in some conditions, may appear. This has happened at times in some contemporary societies, especially under the influence of agrarian reform. Nevertheless, the definition of peasantry which views it as representing an aspect of the past surviving in the contemporary world seems, on the whole, to be valid. Yet, to discard peasantry as a result seems manifestly wrong: even in our 'dynamic' times, we live in a present rooted in the past, and that is where our future is shaped. It is therefore worth remembering that – as in the past, so in the present – peasants are the majority of mankind.

This Reader focuses upon the generic characteristics of peasant societies viewed as qualitively distinct types of social organization. This kind of approach seems particularly important for Western readers unfamiliar with peasantry. Further treatments stressing the diversity of peasant societies and analysing their historical roots are no doubt necessary, and an attempt has been made to keep 'the other side of the coin' in sight. (See, for example, the contribution by Ortiz, p. 322.) Indeed, the major scholarly controversy which seems to run across each of the possible subdivisions of the field is the gulf between those who tend to concentrate on the specific features of peasant social characteristics (and consequently consider special theoretical constructs necessary), and those who tend to support the opposite view.

The internal division of the Reader is made by topic (and not geographical region), and is related to the 'general type' of peasant society already outlined. The low institutional differentiation typical of peasant societies makes any division of selected articles somewhat arbitrary; many of them could, no doubt, appear under more than one heading. Individual chapters should therefore be viewed as an analytical focus rather than as a watertight compartment. In order to avoid a conservative sociological tradition in which some chapters on 'social structure' are followed by a chapter on 'social change' (and with it an implicit image of a non-changing social structure), all the chapters include both a structural and a dynamic analysis.

In the selection of contributions an attempt has been made to draw the reader's attention to the classical roots of the relevant sociological tradition, and to break linguistic barriers which have hitherto prevented widespread appreciation of many of the European studies of peasantry. Finally, the selection of studies has not here been limited to what sociologists have written, but violates – and rightly so – some of the interdisciplinary barriers.

The contributions in section A of Part One focus on the basic units of peasant social organization: the family farm, the village community, peasant regional groups as well as their internal differentiation, mobility and structural change. Section B indicates some existing types of rural society, and, in particular, the differences between peasant society proper and a number of 'analytical marginal groups' of peasants: Latin American peons, African tribalists, peasant workers, etc. Part Two focuses on forms of production and exchange typical of peasant society. Part Three brings together a number of contributions on the political sociology of peasantry, approached as a class. Part Four discusses peasant cultural patterns in the Wright Mills sense of 'the medium through which men see, the mechanisms by which they interpret and report what they see' (Wright Mills, 1962, p. 406). These include peasant cognition of reality, customs, religion, aesthetics, entertainment and 'acculturation'. The fifth and last part includes some examples of the attitudes and policies towards peasantry in the contemporary world.

The inevitable limitations imposed on the size of a publication of this sort formed, no doubt, the most frustrating part of the editing process. After all, Znaniecki's 2000 pages reflect not verbosity, but the 'richness' of the issue (Thomas and Znaniecki, 1918). Areas like 'Peasantry as history' or the 'Polit-economy of peasantry' (in particular the social impact of land tenure) could only be cursorily treated. The reading list is a partial attempt to rectify this. A true solution, however, can be found only in a further increase in both the number and in the conceptual variety of relevant publications; an increase large enough to match the complexity and the importance of the issue.

References

CHAYANOV, A. V. (1925), *Organizatsiya krest'yanskogo khozyaistva*.
Translated as *The Theory of Peasant Economy*, D. Thorner, R. E. F.
Smith and B. Kerblay (eds.), Irwin, 1966.

DURKHEIM, E. (1960), *The Division of Labor in Society*, Free Press.

ERASMUS, C. (1967), 'The upper limits of peasantry and agrarian reform:
Bolivia, Venezuela and Mexico compared', *Ethnology*, vol. 6, no. 4.

GALESKI, B. (1971), *Rural Sociology*, Manchester University Press.

KROEBER, A. L. (1948), *Anthropology*, Harrap.

MARX, K., and ENGELS, F. (1950), *Selected Writings*, vol. 1,
International Publishing House, Moscow.

REDFIELD, R. (1956), *Peasant Society and Culture*, University of
Chicago Press.

THOMAS, W. I., and ZNANIECKI, F. (1918), *The Polish Peasant in
Europe and America*, Dover Publications, 1958.

VASIL'CHAKOV, A. (1881), *Selskii byt i sel'skoe khozyaistvo v Rossii*
(partly developed in an earlier study published in 1876), St Petersburg

WEBER, M. (1925), *The Theory of Social and Economic Organization*,
Free Press, 1964.

WRIGHT MILLS, C. (1962), *Power, Politics and People*, Ballantine
Books.

Part One
The Social Structure of Peasantry
A. The Basic Units

Part One is devoted to consideration of the basic social units and patterns of interaction typical of peasant societies. Section A examines the fundamental components of what may be termed a general type of peasant society, which represents the specific and generic aspects of these social entities. It begins with an analysis of the peasant family and marriage taken from Thomas and Znaniecki's classic study which, in many respects, initiated systematic sociological research into peasant societies. It is followed by Shanin's and Stirling's contributions on the peasant family and village community respectively, with Ayrout's little anecdote, acting as a rejoinder to Stirling's study. Wolf's study of Mexico advances the issue of the internal divisions within such communities, especially with regard to their patron–client networks and their relationship with the national political structure. Pearse's paper completes the section, shedding light on the basic dynamics of disintegration of peasant social structures initiated by the impact of the urban–industrial complex on rural society. The last two papers stress in particular the position of peasants in relation to society in general.

Some relevant issues like peasant extra-village social networks, the wider kinship organizations (clans, etc.) and the socio-economic differentiation and social mobility (in many cases cyclical in character and reinforcing the stability of the existing social system) have not been systematically covered. The 'Further Reading' will suggest some relevent references.

1 William I. Thomas and Florian Znaniecki

A Polish Peasant Family

Excerpts from William I. Thomas and Florian Znaniecki,
The Polish Peasant in Europe and America, Dover Publications, 1958,
pp. 89–112. First published in 1918.

The family is a very complex group, with limits only approximately determined and with very various kinds and degrees of
relationship between its members. But the fundamental familial
connexion is one and irreducible; it cannot be converted into any
other type of group-relationship nor reduced to a personal relation between otherwise isolated individuals. It may be termed
familial solidarity, and it manifests itself both in assistance rendered to, and in control exerted over, any member of the group
by any other member representing the group as a whole. It is
totally different from territorial, religious, economic or national
solidarity, though evidently these are additional bonds promoting
familial solidarity, and we shall see that any dissolution of them
certainly exerts a dissolving influence upon the family. And again,
the familial solidarity and the degree of assistance and of control
involved should not depend upon the personal character of the
members, but only upon the kind and degree of their relationship; the familial relation between two members admits no
gradation, as does love or friendship.

In this light all the familial relations in their ideal form, that is,
as they would be if there were no progressive disintegration of the
family, become perfectly plain.

The relation of husband and wife is controlled by both the
united families, and husband and wife are not individuals more
or less closely connected according to their personal sentiments,
but group-members connected absolutely in a single way. Therefore the marriage norm is not love, but 'respect', as the relation
which can be controlled and reinforced by the family, and which
corresponds also exactly to the situation of the other party as

member of a group and representing the dignity of that group. The norm of respect from wife to husband includes obedience, fidelity, care for the husband's comfort and health; from husband to wife, good treatment, fidelity, not letting the wife do hired work if it is not indispensable. In general, neither husband nor wife ought to do anything which could lower the social standing of the other, since this would lead to a lowering of the social standing of the other's family. Affection is not explicitly included in the norm of respect, but is desirable. As to sexual love, it is a purely personal matter, is not and ought not to be socialized in any form; the family purposely ignores it, and the slightest indecency or indiscreetness with regard to sexual relations in marriage is viewed with disgust and is morally condemned.

The familial assistance to the young married people is given in the form of the dowry, which they both receive. Though the parents usually give the dowry, a grandfather or grandmother, brother, or uncle may just as well endow the boy or the girl or help to do so. This shows the familial character of the institution, and this character is still more manifest if we recognize that the dowry is not in the full sense the property of the married couple. It remains a part of the general familial property to the extent that the married couple remains a part of the family. The fact that, not the future husband and wife, but their families, represented by their parents and by the matchmakers, come to an understanding on this point is another proof of this relative community of property. The assistance must assume the form of dowry simply because the married couple, composed of members of two different families, must to some extent isolate itself from one or the other of these families; but the isolation is not an individualization, it is only an addition of some new familial ties to the old ones, a beginning of a new nucleus.

The relation of parents to children is also determined by the familial organization. The parental authority is complex. It is, first, the right of control which they exercise as members of the group over other members, but naturally the control is unusually strong in this case because of the particularly intimate relationship. But it is more than this. The parents are privileged representatives of the group as a whole, backed by every other member in the exertion of their authority, but also responsible before the group for their actions. The power of this authority is really great; a rebellious child finds nowhere any help, not even in the younger generation, for every member of the family will side with the child's parents if he considers them right, and everyone will feel the familial will behind him and will play the part of a representative of the group. On the other hand, the responsibility of the parents to the familial group is very clear in every case of undue severity or of too great leniency on their part. [. . .]

The Polish peasant family, as we have seen, is organized as a plurality of interrelated marriage-groups which are so many nuclei of familial life and whose importance is various and changing. The process of constitution and evolution of these nuclei is therefore the essential phenomenon of familial life. But at the same time there culminate in marriage many other interests of the peasant life, and we must take the role of these into consideration.

The whole familial system of attitudes involves absolutely the postulate of marriage for every member of the young generation. The family is a dynamic organization, and changes brought by birth, growth, marriage and death have nothing of the incidental or unexpected, but are included as normal in the organization itself, continually accounted for and foreseen, and the whole practical life of the family is adapted to them. A person who does not marry within a certain time, as well as an old man who does not die at a certain age, provokes in the family-group an attitude of unfavorable astonishment; they seem to have stopped in the midst of a continuous movement, and they are passed by and left alone. There are, indeed, exceptions. A boy (or girl) with some physical or intellectual defect is not supposed to marry, and in his early childhood a corresponding attitude is adopted by the family and a place for him is provided beforehand. His eventual marriage will then provoke the same unfavorable astonishment as the bachelorship of others. [. . .]

The family not only requires its members to be married, but directs their choice. This is neither tyranny nor self-interest on the part of the parents nor solicitude for the future of the child, but a logical consequence of the individual's situation in the familial group. The individual is a match only as member of the group and owing to the social standing of the family within the community and to the protection and help in social and economic matters given by the family. He has therefore corresponding responsibilities; in marrying he must take, not only his own, but also the family's interests into consideration. These latter interests condition the choice of the partner in three respects.

1. The partner in marriage is an outsider who through marriage becomes a member of the family. The family therefore requires in this individual a personality which will fit easily into the group and be assimilated to the group with as little effort as possible. Not only a good character, but a set of habits similar to those prevailing in the family to be entered, is important. Sometimes the prospective partner is unknown to the family, sometimes even unknown to the marrying member of the family, and in this case social guaranties are demanded. The boy or girl ought to come at least from a good family, belonging to the same class as the family to be entered, and settled if possible in the same district, since customs and habits differ from locality to locality. The occupation of a boy ought to be of such a kind as not to develop any undesirable, that is, unassimilable, traits. A girl should have lived at home and should not have done hired work habitually. A man should never have an occupation against which a prejudice exists in the community. In this matter there is still another motive of selection, that is, vanity. Finally, a widow or a widower is an undesirable partner, because more difficult to assimilate than a young girl or boy. If not only the future partner, but even his family, is unknown, the parents, or someone in their place, will try to get acquainted personally with some of his relatives, in order to inspect the general type of their character and behavior. Thence comes the frequent custom of arranging marriages through friends and relatives. This form of matchmaking is intermediary between the one in which the starting-point is personal acquaintance and the other in which the connexion with a certain family is sought first through the *swaty* (professional matchmaker) and personal acquaintance comes later. In this intermediary form the starting-point is the friendship with rela-

tives of the boy or the girl. It is supposed that the future partner resembles his relatives in character, and at the same time that the family to which those relatives belong is worth being connected with. But this leads us to the second aspect of the familial control of marriage.

2. The candidate for marriage belongs himself to a family, which through marriage will become connected with that of his wife. The familial group therefore assumes the right to control the choice of its member, not only with regard to the personal qualities of the future partner, but also with regard to the nature of the group with which it will be allied. The standing of the group within the community is here the basis of selection. This standing itself is conditioned by various factors – wealth, morality, intelligence, instruction, religiousness, political and social influence, connexion with higher classes, solidarity between the family members, kind of occupation, numerousness of the family, its more or less ancient residence in the locality, etc. Every family naturally tries to make the best possible alliance; at the same time it tries not to lower its own dignity by risking a refusal or by accepting at once even the best match and thereby showing too great eagerness. Thence the long selection and hesitation, real or pretended, on both sides, while the problem is not to discourage any possible match, for the range of possibilities open to an individual is a proof of the high standing of the family. Thence also such institutions as that of the matchmaker, whose task is to shorten the ceremonial of choosing without apparently lowering the dignity of the families involved. The relative freedom given to the individuals themselves, the apparent yielding to individual love, has in many cases its source in the desire to shorten the process of selection by shifting the responsibility from the group to the individual. In the traditional formal *swaty* is embodied this familial control of marriage. The young man, accompanied by the matchmaker, visits the families with which his family has judged it desirable to be allied, and only among these can he select a girl. He is received by the parents of the girl, who first learn everything about him and his family and then encourage him to call further or reject him at once. And the girl can select a suitor only among those encouraged by her family.

3. A particular situation is created when a widow or widower with children from the first marriage is involved. Here assimilation is very difficult, because no longer an individual, but a part of a strange marriage-group, has to be assimilated. At the same time the connexion with the widow's or widower's family will be incomplete, because the family of the first husband or wife also has some claims. Therefore such a marriage is not viewed favorably, and there must be some real social superiority of the future partner and his or her family in order to counterbalance the inferiority caused by the peculiar familial situation. A second marriage is thus usually one which, if it were the first, would be a misalliance.

With the disintegration of the familial life there must come, of course, a certain liberation from the familial claims in matters of marriage. But this liberation itself may assume various forms. With regard to the personal qualities of his future wife, the man may neglect to consult his family and still apply the same principles of appreciation which his family would apply – select a person whose character and habits resemble the type prevailing in his own family, a person whose relatives he knows, who comes perhaps from the same locality, etc. Therefore, for example, immigrants in America whose individualization has only begun always try to marry boys or girls fresh from the old country, if possible from their own native village.

A second degree of individualization manifests itself in a more reasoned selection of such qualities as the individual wishes his future mate to possess in view of his own personal happiness and regardless of the family's desire. This type of selection prevails, for example, in most of the second marriages, when the individual has become fully conscious of what he desires from his eventual partner and when the feeling of his own importance, increasing with age, teaches him to neglect the possible protests of his family. It is also a frequent type in towns, where the individual associates with persons of various origins and habits. The typical and universal argument opposed here against any familial protests has the content: 'I shall live with this person, not you, so it is none of your business.'

Finally, the highest form of individualization is found in the real love-marriage. While a reasoned determination of the qualities which the individual wishes to find in his future mate permits of some discussion, some familial control, and some influence of tradition, in the love-marriage every possibility of control is rejected *a priori*. Here, under the influence of the moment, the largest opportunity is given for matches between individuals whose social determinism differs most widely, though this difference is after all usually not very great, since the feeling of love requires a certain community of social traditions.

2 Teodor Shanin

A Russian Peasant Household at the Turn of the Century

Excerpt from Teodor Shanin, *The Awkward Class*, Clarendon Press, 1971.

Peasant households form the basic nuclei of peasant society. The specific nature of peasant households seems to constitute the most significant single characteristic of the peasantry as a specific social phenomenon and to give rise to the generic features displayed by peasantries all over the world.[1] A peasant household is characterized by a nearly total integration of the peasant family's life and its farming enterprise. The family provides the work-team for the farm, while the farm's activities are geared mainly to production of the basic consumption-needs of the family plus the enforced dues to the holders of political and economic power.

The Russian peasant household (*dvor*) at the turn of the century closely corresponded to the general type described. 'The family and the farm appear as almost synonymous' testified Mukhin (1888, p. 151) in his compilation on peasant customs at the end of the nineteenth century. A volume of a Russian encyclopedia published in 1913 (*Novyi Entsiklopedicheskii Slovar*, vol. 18, p. 519) described the bulk of peasant households as 'consumer–labour enterprises, with the consumer needs of the family as their aim and the labour force of the family as their means, with no or very little use of wage labour'.

A Russian peasant household consisted, in the majority of cases, of blood relatives of two or three generations. However, the basic determinant of household membership was not a blood-tie but total participation in the life of the household or, as the Russian peasants put it, 'eating from the common pot' (Chayanov, 1925, p. 54). This unity implied: living together under the

1. For discussion of the generic features of the peasantry in different countries and periods see, for example, Redfield (1956).

authority of a patriarchal head, social organization and division of labour on traditional family lines and basic identification of the member with the household.[2] Consequently, one who joined the household through marriage or adoption (*primaka, vlazen'*) was considered a member with full rights, while a son of the family who set up a household on his own was viewed as an outsider.

The peasant household operated as a highly cohesive unit of social organization, with basic divisions of labour, authority and prestige on ascribed family lines. Generally, the head of the household was the father of the family or the oldest kin-member. His authority over other members and over household affairs by peasant custom implied both autocratic rights and extensive duties of care and protection. The household was the basic unit of production, consumption, property holding, socialization, sociability, moral support and mutual economic help. Both the social prestige and the self-esteem of a peasant were defined by the household he belonged to and his position in it, as were his loyalties and self-identification.

Women, in spite of their heavy burden of labour (both housework and fieldwork), and their functional importance in a peasant household, were considered second-rate citizens and nearly always placed under the authority of a male. However, even the essentially accepted equality of male members should be seen in the framework of a patriarchal structure, involving extensive rights of the head over his household. The strong cohesion of the family and the family property meant submission and lack of any tangible property for junior male members.

'The life of a family is the life of a farm' (Makarov, 1917, p. 71). A typical peasant farm in Russia in the period under consideration was a small agricultural enterprise (five to fifteen acres of sown land), based on centuries-old agricultural techniques and types of equipment.[3] Grain-growing dominated both

2. The word 'traditional' is used here in the wide sense adopted by Weber (1925, pp. 324–423) as the conceptual opposite of 'rational-legal'.
3. Mainly variations of the three-field system of land-use, dependent on a traditional communal crop-rotation and in a majority of cases on the horse-drawn *sokha*. See Aleksandrov (1967, pp. 17–99).

peasant field production and diet (Den, 1925, pp. 188, 211). The Russian peasant economy displayed strong autarkic tendencies characteristic of pre-industrial rural societies. The scope of market relations was limited by largely consumption-determined production objectives, low rates of surplus, limited use of money and a low level of professional specialization among and diversification of the rural population.

The household's production activities primarily consisted of strenuous efforts by its members to make ends meet, i.e. to feed the family and to meet dues and taxes. Serious rural underemployment (both total and seasonal) was partly tempered by peasants' supplementary employment in crafts and trades (*promysly*); competition with growing urban industry was made possible by natural exchange and desperately low earnings. 'When the brief agricultural season did not yield a living for the peasant family, the work for less than subsistence through the long winter months was better than to be altogether idle – and perhaps to be buried in the spring.'[4] However, the main occupation of Russian peasants consisted of performing a wide variety of rather non-specific tasks combined to make up what may be called traditional farming. Peasant family life was the main force of occupational training for the younger generation, while tradition acted as the main occupational guide. The consumption-determined aims, the traditional methods of production, the use of family labour, the low marketability of the product and the lack of checking and control by systematic book-keeping in money terms made the peasant household a production-unit very different from a 'rational' capitalist enterprise. Nature was, in addition, a major determinant of peasant economic life; the smallness of peasant resources magnified its impact. The difference between a good agricultural year and a very bad one was the difference between prosperity and famine, if not death. If it was family history which determined, to a great extent, the development of a farm, it was the modes and seasons of traditional farming which prescribed the pattern of everyday life of the peasant family. The nature and development of the family

4. Robinson (1932, p. 104). The meaning of 'subsistence' was of course far from absolute and varied among areas, households and periods.

made for a peculiarly deep-rooted cyclical rhythm of life on the peasant family farm.

Family property, as accepted by customary peasant law, was the major legal reflection of the character of the Russian peasant household. Unlike private property, family property limited the rights of the formal owner (*khozyain*); he acted as the head administrator of the property (*bol'shak*) rather than as a property-owner in the sense adopted outside peasant society.[5] An extreme expression of this feature was the legal possibility and actual practice of removing the head of a household from his position in some cases of 'mismanagement' or 'wastefulness' and appointing another member of the household instead. On the other hand, unlike in cases of group property, participation in family property did not assume any definable shares of the property or the profits except in terms of rights to share in collective consumption.

The road to self-emancipation for a peasant male was along a traditional path by reaching successive stages of maturity. The peasant proceeded through certain ascribed positions: childhood, pre-marital adolescence, marriage, becoming a head of one's own household and, eventually, retirement and death. Only by becoming a head of a household was it possible to rise to the full status of a man within the peasant community. The only alternative road to self-emancipation for the peasant involved his leaving the peasant community altogether by emigration. Marriage became, in these conditions, 'an absolute postulate' a crucial pre-condition of social maturity necessitated by the character of the farming.[6]

The very existence of a peasant household necessitated the existence of a farm, i.e. some property expressed in holdings of land and equipment. The passing of property from one generation to another was therefore a major issue of everyday peasant life and peasant customary law.

Within the framework of family property, the very notion of inheritance as developed in non-peasant societies failed *sui*

5. For example, in the contemporary Russian Civil Code, which was, however, limited to the non-peasant minority of the population.

6. This explains the early age of marriage typical of the Russian peasantry. See Pisarev (1962, p. 178).

generis to appear. The passing of property from generation to generation did not necessarily involve the death of a parent and was approached legally as a partitioning of family property between its members. Partitioning (or apportionment to set up a junior male) was, in fact, frequently carried out before the death of the head of the household – corresponding closely with the growth of nuclear families and their requests for independence. The head of the household took the decision (partly established by custom) as to when to partition his farm, when to make apportionment to a son, and when to retire. Partitioning led, on the whole, to an equal division of household property between all its male members.[7] In cases of the deaths of all male members of the household, the property was generally taken over by the peasant commune. A typical new household would therefore begin as a young couple with a few young children, on a small farm. The farm would consist of a limited amount of land, one or two horses and little equipment shared out from or by a 'maternal' unit in process of partitioning.

The growth of the family created additional consumption pressures. The head of the new household tried to expand his farm and income by buying or renting additional land and equipment and, at times, employing his family's labour in crafts and trades (*promysly*). The growing-up of children gave additional labour to the farm but also created new consumption needs and problems of employment. It also posed the problem of providing a dowry for daughters and equipment for setting up new farms for sons, which asked for apportionment. After each such apportionment or sometimes upon a partitioning following the death of the head of the household, the same cycle started over again on a new small farm managed by a new young couple.

The Russian State's policy before 1906 supported the stability and cohesion of the peasant household by imposing on it collective responsibility for the payment of taxes and dues and for the 'good behaviour' of its members, in addition to its many other

7. Russian peasant law made an exception for an individual female's property which could include cutlery, cloth, etc. This 'female property' was, in fact, the only private property in the peasant household and could consequently be left by will and/or unequally divided

functions. The State has also legally confirmed the head of the household's wide disciplinary powers over its members.[8] Stolypin's policy, after 1906, greatly reduced the legal powers of heads of households over their members while, at the same time, in many cases making heads of households into unlimited owners of household property (see Robinson, 1932, chs. 11 and 12). From the turn of the century, moreover, the impact of the capitalist developments in urban Russia had been felt increasingly in the countryside. However, a decade of Stolypin policy had failed to produce a decisive change in the social character of the Russian countryside – at least as far as peasant households went. Capitalist farms (or even farms well integrated into the market economy) remained, on the whole, exceptional.[9] The revolution and civil war of 1917–21 swept away the Stolypin Reforms and re-established the essentials of nineteenth-century peasant customary law. Yet even the impact of the revolution on the character of peasant households was modest. The Russian peasant household retained its basic characteristics during the whole of the period under review, i.e. 1890–1929.

References

ALEKSANDROV, V. (ed.) (1967), *Russkie*, Moscow.
BOLSHAKOV, A. (1925), *Sovremennaya derevnya v tsifrakh*, Leningrad.
BROKGAUZ and EFRON (eds.) (1913), *Novyi entsyklopedicheskii slovar*, St Petersburg, 2nd edn.
CHAYANOV, A. (1925), *Organizatsiya krest'yanskogo khozyaistva*. Translated as *The Theory of Peasant Economy*, D. Thorner, R. E. F. Smith and B. Kerblay (eds.), Irwin, 1966.
DEN, V. (1925), *Kurs ekonomicheskoi geografii*, Leningrad.
MAKAROV, N. (1917), *Krest'yanskoe khozyaistvo i ego interesy*, Moscow.
MUKHIN, V. (1888), *Obychnyi poryadok nasledovaniya krest'yan*, St Petersburg.

8. Robinson (1932, p. 66). Until 1906 the head of the household could, on the whole, have a member of his household arrested, sent back to his village under an escort or flogged by simple application to the peasant court.

9. This broad generalization would not hold true for some regions, in particular for the less densely populated south and some of the *Guberniyas* of the north-west, though it did remain valid for the majority of the Russian peasant population.

Pisarev, I. (1962), *Narodonaselenie SSSR*, Moscow.

Redfield, R. (1956), *Peasant Society and Culture*, University of Chicago Press.

Robinson, G. T. (1932), *Rural Russia under the Old Regime*, London.

Weber, M. (1925), *The Theory of Social and Economic Organization*, Hodge, 1947.

3 Paul Stirling

A Turkish Village

Excerpts from Paul Stirling, *A Turkish Village*, Weidenfeld & Nicolson, 1965, pp. 26–35, 290–93.

One major problem in giving or following any ethnographic description is the order of presentation, since an adequate understanding of any one institution presumes a knowledge of other institutions in the same society. I hope I have overcome this difficulty by offering my summary here instead of at the end.

The village itself is the most striking social group. No village forms part of any larger indigenous organization. All the villages in the area, and indeed in most of Turkey, are self-contained clusters of buildings, separated from each other by stretches of unfenced land. To walk from one to the next may take half an hour or two or more hours. There were two villages within half an hour of Sakaltutan, and another nine within one and a half hours.

Each village is composed of distinct patrilineal, patrilocal households. Although several households often occupy one block of buildings, the physical and social boundaries between them are never vague. Village and household are the main social units. Newly married women apart, everyone must belong at one time to one and only one village, and to one and only one household.

Every village is divided into a number of quarters or wards (*mahalle*). These have no clear boundaries and are not corporate. People acknowledge loyalty to their quarters, and may speak of fights in the village as fights between quarters. Because close neighbours often intermarry, and close agnates and sometimes other close kin live near each other, these quarters often have some kinship unity as well. In Elbaşı, several quarters were actually called after lineages. Close neighbours, whether kin or not, will tend to form informal groups for recreation and conversation.

Last of the important groups in the village is the lineage. This group consists of a number of households, the heads of which are descended patrilineally, i.e. strictly through males only, from a common ancestor generally three or four generations back. These households normally form local clusters. The rights and duties of membership are not precisely defined, and the degree to which members are committed varies greatly between individuals. The main function of the lineage is the protection of members from aggression by supporting them in quarrels. Yet not all household heads are members of lineages, nor do all lineages that could be defined genealogically constitute significant social groups. Most of those who are not committed lineage members are among the poorer and less powerful strata of village society.

Apart from membership of these groups, a person's position in the network of interpersonal relationships is mainly determined by the obvious factors – sex and age, kinship, occupation and wealth; and to a lesser degree by piety and learning, by personal honour, and for a man, by the range and strength of his urban contacts.

The sexual distinction is, as one would expect in an Islamic society, strongly emphasized, and for most normal social life the sexes are sharply segregated. Age is not a criterion for any formal groups, but it carries respect and authority.

Kinship relations are both the most intimate and intense and the commonest type of social relations. The personal kin ties of men through men form the core of the lineage groups. Extra lineage kin ties form strong and numerous relationships between both households and individuals. This kinship network extends from village to village and provides vital channels for all sorts of activities – economic, political, religious – and for the arranging of marriages which will in turn forge new kin ties.

Distinctions of wealth are not conspicuous. All households in both villages appear at first sight to live in much the same way. All who can, work. There are no permanent rentier households, though one or two elderly men are supported largely by their sons, womenfolk and share-croppers. The wealthiest and most urbanized households have a comfortable sufficiency, while the poor are badly housed and clothed, and underfed in all but good years. But though differences in wealth are not conspicuous in the way of life, they are of great social importance. The rich are the leaders of the village; they receive deference, carry weight in village counsels, employ their neighbours, and are able, by gifts and loans, to exercise influence and even direct control, especially among their own kin.

Religious learning carries high prestige in the villages. Many village boys receive some kind of special religious training either informally from kinsmen, or from special schools in the towns. A few of these may become village *imams*; others live a normal agricultural life, but with a special reputation for learning and piety. How far a man succeeds in exploiting this prestige for gaining power and wealth seems to depend on personality and circumstances.

Other non-agricultural occupations and skills are structurally of minor importance. Most specialists are part-time, owning or at least wishing to own land; there are no social groups based on occupations such as the castes of Indian society, nor are craftsmen treated as outsiders.

Urban contacts have probably always conferred great influence and prestige in the villages, chiefly, of course, because they imply influence with officials, an influence often overestimated by villagers. Traditionally, it is likely that the main channels for social promotion lay through the official religious hierarchy. Nowadays, in a village like Elbaşı, and even in many poorer ones, people have sons, brothers or affines who are traders or officials, sometimes of fairly high standing, in the urban world. These links give great prestige in the village. Where they exist in numbers as in Elbaşı, they seem to be leading to the beginning of a class structure in the village.

But only the merest beginnings. Village society seems in the past to have had a highly mobile ranking system, with a marked absence of inherited rank. In every generation, each household split, dividing its land at least among the sons, sometimes among both sons and daughters. The richer a man, the more wives and therefore the more heirs he would be likely to have, so that in general there was a tendency for each young married man to find himself on his father's death with a fairly modest amount of land and thus bound to start building up afresh on his own account. In a situation so open, one would expect that occasionally a particular man by skill and luck would establish considerable personal pre-eminence, and stories about the great villagers of the past are current in most villages. But it seems equally true that the successful men did not found dynasties. Their sons normally began again with, at the most, a short lead over rivals.

Village Solidarity

People belong to their village in a way they belong to no other social group. On any definition of community, the village is a community – a social group with many functions, not all of them explicit, and to which people are committed by birth or marriage, and bound by many ties.

None of the geographical or administrative units larger than a village is in any way comparable. The villagers do, of course, see themselves as belonging to a vaguely defined district, and to the Province of Kayseri. Men in the army or working away in the cities often form friendships and groups along the lines of locality of origin, but the actual units of administration, *nahiye*, *kaza* and *vilayet* as such have no social relevance outside their administrative functions.

The virtues of the village are an eternal topic of conversation with outsiders, and of banter between men of different villages. Every village has the best drinking water, and the best climate. One village, which stored winter snow in large deep wells, and drank all through the summer the stagnant water which resulted, pleaded the superiority of their water as an argument for my moving in at once. Every village is more hospitable, more honourable, more virile, more peaceable, gives better weddings, than any of its neighbours. Other villages are savage, mean, dishonourable, lying, lazy, cowardly. Neither Sakaltutan nor Elbaşı found my choice of themselves surprising, but everyone else found it quite incredible.

Each village possesses a territory, recognized by the State as its administrative area, over which it exercises *de facto* pasture rights.

Villages normally own common land, and sometimes meadow or crop land which can be let; but in the Civil Code it has no rights to land within its territory owned by individuals, and unoccupied land belongs to the State.

For the village, this territory is much more than an administrative area – it is a symbol of village identity (de Planhol, 1958, p. 340). If any other village attempts to use land lying within the village boundaries, people mobilize rapidly and are quite prepared to fight, with fire-arms if necessary. Even incursions by other villages' flocks or herds cause at the very least militant indignation. On one occasion, Sakaltutan animals crossed the frontier to Süleymanli, and the Süleymanli headman who happened to be passing on a horse, struck the shepherd in charge with his whip. Many Sakaltutan men talked of immediate armed attack. However, they were restrained by wiser counsel. I never witnessed mobilization of this kind, but it is clear that all members are expected to defend the village regardless of the quarrels which constantly divide them. Not even lineages cross village frontiers, so that the village from the outside presents a solid front of loyalty. Its members are ready at all times to defend both its reputation and its territories.

This outward solidarity is matched by what one might call internal intensity. Village populations are highly stable. Almost all men and more than half the adult women in a village were born there. If we could measure the intensity of social relationships in terms of emotional strength, of the number of rights and duties involved, and of the frequency of contact, we would find that all residents except the more newly arrived wives had their more intense social relationships almost exclusively inside the village. Of course, many indispensable and controlling economic and political relationships lie outside, but these are not intense in the same way. Even beyond their own immediate circle, all the villagers belong to one another. Even enemies inside the village are intimate enemies.

Village Organization

Since the village is a community – a group with a multitude of functions and involvements for its members – it is not surprising that a number of offices and corporate rights and duties are attached to it. Roughly, these are of two kinds, the formal institutions laid down by the State, and the informal institutions run by the village for its own purposes to meet the actual needs of its members. [. . .]

Administratively and legally, the village is ruled by a headman, elected every four years up to 1950, now every two, nominally by secret ballot; all persons over eighteen can vote. He is expected to receive all public visitors, especially officials; to help keep order and bring criminals to justice; to take care of public property – for example the school; to draw up electoral lists; to countersign all official applications for government seed, bank loans and such; to see to the registration of births, deaths and marriages; to report the arrival of strangers, the occurrence of epidemics, and other untoward events, and so on. He is in short the agent, guarantor and communication channel for all village business with government. This post is not sought after.

The council of elders is elected with the headman, and its size depends on the number of the inhabitants. Sakaltutan had four councillors, Elbaşı six. Each council is covered by a like number of reserves, also elected, who take the place of the full members if they are unable to attend meetings. The elder who receives most votes in the election is automatically deputy headman, and so on down the list. The council is supposed to meet at least every month and to discuss all village business.

It would be rash to state that these councils never meet. The council in Sakaltutan did not meet during my stay, and the only function attributed to it by villagers was the supervision of the assessment of contributions to the village chest. People said the Elbaşı council did meet, but it did not do so regularly, and it did not to my knowledge supervise assessment. Certainly the councils did not function as the main decision-making body of the villages. No one took the slightest interest in their election, or attached any importance to their activities. Instead, when something called for corporate action in a matter which the villagers considered important, the senior heads of households and lineage segments assembled either spontaneously, or on the initiative of any leading villager with sufficient prestige. Such a meeting has no formal standing, no constitution, no procedures, and no responsibilities. It can only occur if the matter is important enough to draw together important people. It serves as a means of thrashing out public issues, and letting the headman know what people think, but the interpretation of what is said and the tactical assessment of what is possible and desirable remains in his hands.

Every village is compelled by law to levy a local tax, *Köy Salması*, and to raise a fund, the village chest, *Köy Sandığı*. Out of this, the headman draws a small allowance for entertaining visitors, and meets other expenses, such as keeping school equipment and other village property in order, and clothing and sometimes paying the village watchman. The village households are divided into four tax assessment classes. This assessment is mainly based on the amount of land held, but other circumstances – the number of animals owned, the number of grown working men and the number of mouths to feed – are also taken into account. The poorest households are excluded altogether.

In Sakaltutan the assessment of the four classes were T.L.15, T.L.12, T.L.8 and T.L.5 per annum respectively, in Elbaşı T.L.15, T.L.11, T.L.7 and T.L.4. This fund is the only officially imposed institution which arouses real interest, and, with the offices of headman and watchman, comprises the only area of genuine overlap between village institutions and State-imposed ones. It is the subject of continual argument and accusation, and very difficult to collect. In 1953, many headmen were still not literate, so that even those who wished could hardly keep adequate records. Accusations of cheating the village chest are therefore inevitable, universal, impossible to disprove, but undoubtedly wildly exaggerated, and probably often unfounded.

Villagers claimed that even if the council of elders did nothing else, at least it met to assess the contributions to the chest. Obviously, where the assessing authority, the headman, is a neighbour of no particular eminence or authority except for his temporary office, individuals who feel over-assessed are likely to argue, and any obvious anomaly will arouse jealousy and protest. But I have a strong impression that, once established, the assessment was changed little from year to year, and that changes were normally left to the headman. In general, the headman consults members of the elected council if they are friends of his, if they can actively assist him, or if they represent sections of the village capable of making trouble if not consulted. But very much the same applies to any leading villagers, whether council members or not.

In almost all cases I came across, headman and elders were young or middle-aged men. Senior and outstanding men did not hold office themselves, though very often their sons and younger brothers might.

All villagers must also by law appoint a watchman, a *bekci*; he is a sort of policeman, supposed to act under the orders of the headman. He is also expected by the authorities to act as a messenger, and is continually going back and forth between the District Office and his village. He is chosen by the headman, for a year at a time, on so lowly a salary (T.L.300–100, £37 10s. downwards, in 1949–52) that only the poorest and most incompetent villagers will normally take on the office. The watchman in most villages acts as a servant to the headman, and is often to be found making his coffee, running his errands or even chopping his wood. The Sakaltutan watchman collected his dues in kind himself, household by household.

Apart from this legally required set of institutions, every village has a number of its own officers and servants to meet the needs of a farming community, mostly herdsmen. Two or more special watchmen are usually appointed to guard the harvest for the village as a whole. These are expected to, and do, run foul of the herders, whose animals frequently maraud the standing crops. Elbaşı also appointed two men to supervise the allocation of water during the months of June and July when demand is high and supplies are low. Most of these are chosen by village elders, among whom the current headman has the most say. But the shepherds are appointed by leading sheep-owners. All are paid directly in cash or kind, household by household.

The village is then a corporation, with both official and unofficial servants, and an official and in a sense an unofficial income. The State-imposed general village fund is clearly alien, and so far the traditional arrangements for traditional village servants have not been brought into the new scheme. The traditional method has the advantages that village servants are responsible for collecting their own dues, and that people pay in proportion to their use of the services.

People still regard themselves as dependent politically on the village for defence against other villages, although the vastly increased efficiency of the national maintenance of order has largely rendered this dependence obsolete. But if political dependence is minimal, economic dependence on the village is still very real. Shepherds and watchmen and common pastures are indispensable. Refusal to allow a man to use them would cripple him. Moreover, the annual switch from one side of the village territory to the other ties all the villagers to the alternate year of fallow. The introduction for example, of a revolutionary crop cycle is impossible without disrupting the whole village farming system. Meanwhile, the legal freehold of land is subject to the *de facto* common right of the village to pasture flocks and herds on it every other year. [...]

Other Villages

Differences of prestige among neighbouring villages did not prevent a great deal of social intercourse. People visit, hire craftsmen, seek advice on religious or technical problems, commission magical services, borrow money or food, search for oxen to buy, buy up animals for market, take grain to be milled. In the past, before the petrol engine, longer journeys, especially journeys to town, compelled the traveller to put up for the night with kinsmen or friends on the road. Now people congregate in the villages which serve as boarding points for lorries and buses to Kayseri, gossiping and often visiting as they pass through. The villages are too similar in production for intense economic exchange between them, but social contact is nevertheless constant and lively.

Beyond the occasional conflict over territory, and some traditional enmities, political relations between villages as groups are unimportant. In this area, all the villages were Sunni- and Turkish-speaking, so that the issue of ethnic or language differences did not arise. No one village nowadays has the slightest hope of dominating others, whatever may have been the case in the past. Fighting is rapidly suppressed by the gendarmerie. Feuds did not seem ever to be pursued between whole villages. [...]

Pressures and Change

Peasants are proverbially conservative. The reasons for this are plain. They live normally in societies in which many of their main contacts are with people like themselves who share their values. They are bound to put more weight upon the good opinion of their kin and neighbours with whom they are in daily relations, and on whom they depend for essential help in times of stress or crisis, than upon the values of people superior in standing but remote from the village.

In these Turkish villages the social controls are as strong as one would expect. Any signs of unusual conduct will immediately lead to detailed and widespread discussion. If people take, as they are almost certain to do, the view that the innovation is malicious, pretentious, dangerous, impious or absurd, the innovator, if he persists, has to face criticism, ridicule or even ostracism.

The importance of this conservatism is two-fold. First, it slows down directly the acceptance of most, but not all, technical improvements such as hygienic habits, improved agricultural techniques, and so on. Secondly, in so far as people's ideas about the behaviour appropriate to the various roles in village society is reinforced, the traditional social structure is prevented from adapting itself to changes in the larger world of which it is a part. Traditional relationships persist in social situations to which they are no longer appropriate.

But the forces for change are stronger still. The very great increase in communications with the outside world is at the root of the changes. Increase in law and order makes it possible for anyone to go to town for political or economic purposes with no danger of physical attack. Lorries and buses make possible much cheaper and more rapid transport between town and village not only of people but also of goods in quantity. The vast new market for casual labour draws a constant stream of men out of the rural area sending them back armed with much information and some new ideas. At the same time the national government is concerned for national reasons with village productivity and welfare, and sends an increasing stream of officials to the village to impose unfamiliar rules of conduct for a host of different purposes.

The villages I visited were tightly knit communities. But once they must have been a great deal tighter. Not long ago, individual villagers only approached officialdom with the special protection of their village superiors, or in the company of the headman. The village rulers ruled largely by a monopoly of contact with State sources of power, which both conferred and depended on a dominant position inside the village. Almost every man in those days was dependent on his father's land for his daily food, and if people did leave the village to seek their fortunes, they did not write, nor send money through the post office, nor turn up in person at frequent intervals. It was possible for the village to lead a much more isolated and autonomous life, and virtually to ignore its obvious inferiority to the town.

The effect of the vastly increased contact between town and village which I have just described is two-fold. By greatly increasing the range of social relations even the poorer villagers have with people outside the village, it has decreased the solidarity of the village, weakening the strength of the social controls on which village conservatism is founded. The villagers are no longer necessarily dependent on their leaders. At the same time they come to depend on the goodwill of a host of other people outside the village with different assumptions and ideas. The village community is pulled apart by multiplying relations between its members and the outside world. This process so far is no more than begun, but it has already brought the village into the nation in a much more definite and inescapable way. Even if he pays his taxes without argument and keeps out of the way when involved in violence, the villager can no longer hope to ignore the authorities. He is constantly, through the radio, reminded that he and his village are a part of a much larger social unit, the nation. He has become aware also that the village is despised by townsmen, and that most villagers have a vastly lower standard of living than the urban educated. The village is all too clearly at the bottom of the national hierarchy. Once the village was a social foothill to the distant urban peaks, proud in its semi-autonomy and more or less able to ignore them by looking the other way. Its social world was centred on itself. Now it is acutely aware that it is only the peripheral lower slopes, uncomfortably forced to face or evade the constant stream of interference and scorn which pours down from the urban peaks of national power.

The old attitudes are not gone. The village is still proud; each village still knows itself to be the best of all communities and, like most rural communities, at times writes town society off as corrupt and decadent. But contradictions are a normal part of any society, and the opposite is heard even more often – that the village is backward, uncouth, poor, dirty and violent. Such contradictions can, of course, live more or less permanently in a society. But though I have no empirical first-hand evidence of the village attitudes two generations ago, I am confident that its pride and independent spirit are declining and its diffidence and sense of inferiority increasing.

Changes in this direction are inevitable, and serve humanitarian as well as national ends. A higher standard of living can only come with more technical efficiency, more controls, more education, more taxes, more intervention by national organizations in local politics, and so on. Eventually the full weight of all this may narrow the gap, and by destroying the tightness of the local community, integrate its members more effectively in the nation. But the initial effect of attempts at reform and betterment, by their more or less unintended transformation of the social structure, is likely to be an increase of tension between the villagers and their urban rulers, both local and national.

Reference

PLANHOL, X. de (1958), *De la Plaine Pampaglienne aux Lacs Pisidiens,* Paris.

4 Henry Habib Ayrout

The Village and the Peasant Group

Excerpt from Henry Habib Ayrout, *The Egyptian Peasant*, translated
by John Alden Williams, Beacon Press, 1963, p. 87. First published in 1938.

The fellah should really be referred to in the plural, for he lives
as the member of a group, if not of a crowd. In the fields, as
tenant or owner, he toils with his family; as a day laborer he
works in a gang.

Within the limited confines of the village, he lives and works
more in the open than in his house. Nowhere is there privacy.
The women fetch water in groups, children swarm everywhere;
the daily life is collective and communal. The village or its quarter, not the house, makes up the entity, a community more important in many ways than the family or clan. It happened that
the author once drew on the blackboard of one of our village
schools the outline of a hut, as a test of observation, and asked:

'Now, my children, what must we add to make a real home?'

'A door!' 'Windows!' 'Stairs!' they began to call.

We thought the house complete, and were ready to erase it,
when a little girl cried: 'No, it needs something more.'

'And what is that?'

'The neighbors!' (*al-giran*).

5 Eric R. Wolf

Aspects of Group Relations in a Complex Society: Mexico[1]

Eric R. Wolf, 'Aspects of group relations in a complex society: Mexico', *American Anthropologist*, vol. 58, 1956, no. 6, pp. 1065–78.

Starting from simple beginnings in the twenties, anthropologists have grown increasingly sophisticated about the relationship of nation and community. First, they studied the community in its own terms, taking but little account of its larger matrix. Later, they began to describe 'outside factors' which affected the life of the local group under study. Recently they have come to recognize that nations or 'systems of the higher level do not consist merely of more numerous and diversified parts,' and that it is therefore 'methodologically incorrect to treat each part as though it were an independent whole in itself' (Steward, 1950, p. 107). Communities are 'modified and acquire new characteristics because of their functional dependence upon a new and larger system' (Steward, 1950, p. 111). The present paper is concerned with a continuation of this anthropological discussion in terms of Mexican material.

The dependence of communities on a larger system has affected them in two ways. On the one hand, whole communities have come to play specialized parts within the larger whole. On the other, special functions pertaining to the whole have become the tasks of special groups within communities. These groups Steward calls horizontal socio-cultural segments. I shall simply call them nation-oriented groups. They are usually found in more than one community and follow ways of life different from those of their community-oriented fellow-villagers. They are often the

1. Parts of this paper were read before a meeting of the Central States Anthropological Society at Bloomington, Indiana, on 6 May 1955. I am indebted for helpful criticisms to Julian Steward and Oscar Lewis of the University of Illinois, and to Sidney Mintz of Yale University.

agents of the great national institutions which reach down into the community, and form 'the bones, nerves and sinews running through the total society, binding it together, and affecting it at every point' (Steward, 1950, p. 115). Communities which form parts of a complex society can thus be viewed no longer as self-contained and integrated systems in their own right. It is more appropriate to view them as the local termini of a web of group relations which extend through intermediate levels from the level of the community to that of the nation. In the community itself, these relationships may be wholly tangential to each other.

Forced to understand the community in terms of forces impinging on it from the outside, we have also found it necessary to gain a better understanding of national-level institutions. Yet to date most anthropologists have hesitated to commit themselves to such a study, even when they have become half-convinced that such a step would be desirable. National institutions seem so complex that even a small measure of competence in their operations seems to require full-time specialization. We have therefore left their description and analysis to specialists in other disciplines. Yet the specialists in law, politics or economics have themselves discovered that anthropologists can be of almost as much use to them as they can be to the anthropologist. For they have become increasingly aware that the legal, political or other systems to which they devote their attention are not closed systems either, but possess social and cultural dimensions which cannot be understood in purely institutional terms. They have discovered that they must pay attention to shifting group relationships and interests if their studies are to reflect this other dimension of institutional 'reality'. This is hardly surprising if we consider that institutions are ultimately but cultural patterns for group relationships. Their complex forms allow groups to relate themselves to each other in the multiple processes of conflict and accommodation which must characterize any complex society. They furnish the forms through which some nation-oriented groups may manipulate other nation-oriented or community-oriented groups. The complex apparatus of such institutions is indeed a subject for specialists, but anthropologists may properly attempt to assess some of their functions.

Eric R. Wolf   51

If the communities of a complex system such as Mexico represent but the local termini of group relationships which go beyond the community-level, we cannot hope to construct a model of how the larger society operates by simply adding more community studies. Mexico – or any complex system – is more than the arithmetic sum of its constituent communities. It is also more than the sum of its national-level institutions, or the sum of all the communities and national-level institutions taken together. From the point of view of this paper, it is rather the web of group relationships which connect localities and national-level institutions. The focus of study is not communities or institutions, but groups of people.

In dealing with the group relationships of a complex society, we cannot neglect to underline the fact that the exercise of power by some people over others enters into all of them, on all levels of integration. Certain economic and political relationships are crucial to the functioning of any complex society. No matter what other functions such a society may contain or elaborate, it must both produce surpluses and exercise power to transfer a part of these surpluses from the producing communities to people other than the producers. No matter what combination of cultural forms such a society may utilize, it must also wield power to limit the autonomy of its constituent communities and to interfere in their affairs. This means that all interpersonal and intergroup relationships of such a society must at some point conform to the dictates of economic or political power. Let it be said again, however, that these dictates of power are but aspects of group relationships, mediated in this case through the forms of an economic or political apparatus.

Finally, we must be aware that a web of group relationships implies a historical dimension. Group relationships involve conflict and accommodation, integration and disintegration, processes which take place over time. And just as Mexico in its synchronic aspect is a web of group relationships with termini in both communities and national-level institutions, so it is also more in its diachronic aspect than a sum of the histories of these termini. Local histories are important, as are the histories of national-level institutions, but they are not enough. They are but local or institutional manifestations of group relations in continuous change.

In this paper, then, we shall deal with the relations of community-oriented and nation-oriented groups which characterize Mexico as a whole. We shall emphasize the economic and political aspects of these relationships, and we shall stress their historical dimension, their present as a rearrangement of their past, and their past as a determinant of their present.

From the beginning of Spanish rule in Mexico, we confront a society riven by group conflicts for economic and political control. The Spanish Crown sought to limit the economic and political autonomy of the military entrepreneurs who had conquered the country in its name. It hoped to convert the *conquistadores* into town dwellers, not directly involved in the process of production on the community level but dependent rather on carefully graded hand-outs by the Crown. They were to have no roots in local communities, but to depend directly on a group of officials operating at the level of the nation. The strategic cultural form selected for this purpose was the *encomienda*, in which the recipient received rights to a specified amount of Indian tribute and services, but was not permitted to organize his own labor force nor to settle in Indian towns. Both control of Indian labor and the allocation of tribute payments were to remain in the hands of royal bureaucrats (L. B. Simpson, 1950, esp. pp. 123, 144; Zavala, 1940).

To this end, the Crown encouraged the organization of the Indian population into compact communities with self-rule over their own affairs, subject to supervision and interference at the hands of royal officials (Zavala and Miranda, 1954, pp. 75–9). Many of the cultural forms of this community organization are pre-Hispanic in origin, but they were generally re-patterned and charged with new functions. We must remember that the Indian sector of society underwent a serious reduction in social complexity during the sixteenth and seventeenth centuries. The Indians lost some of their best lands and water supply, as well as the larger part of their population. As a result of this social cataclysm, as well as of government policy, the re-patterned

Indian community emerged as something qualitatively new: a corporate organization of a local group inhabited by peasants (Wolf, 1955a, pp. 456–61). Each community was granted a legal charter and communal lands (Zavala and Miranda, 1954, p. 70); equipped with a communal treasury (Chávez Orozco, 1943, pp. 23–4; Zavala and Miranda, 1954, p. 87–8) and administrative center (Zavala and Miranda, 1954, pp. 80–82); and connected with one of the newly established churches. It was charged with the autonomous enforcement of social control, and with the payment of dues (Zavala and Miranda, 1954, p. 82).

Thus equipped to function in terms of their own resources, these communities became in the centuries after the Conquest veritable redoubts of cultural homeostasis. Communal jurisdiction over land, obligations to expend surplus funds in religious ceremonies, negative attitudes toward personal display of wealth and self-assertion, strong defenses against deviant behavior, all served to emphasize social and cultural homogeneity and to reduce tendencies toward the development of internal class differences and heterogeneity in behavior and interests. The taboo on sales of land to outsiders and the tendency toward endogamy made it difficult for outsiders to gain footholds in these villages (Redfield and Tax, 1952; Wolf, 1955a, pp. 457–61).

At the same time, the Crown failed in its attempt to change the Spanish conquerors into passive dependents on royal favors (Miranda, 1947). Supported by large retinues of clients (such as *criados*, *deudos*, *allegados*, *paniaguados*, cf. Chevalier, 1952, pp. 33–8), the colonists increasingly wrested control of the crucial economic and political relationships from the hands of the royal bureaucracy. Most significantly, they developed their own labor force, in contravention of royal command and independently of the Indian communities. They bought Indian and Negro slaves; they attracted to their embryonic enterprises poor whites who had come off second best in the distribution of conquered riches; and they furnished asylum to Indians who were willing to pay the price of acculturation and personal obligation to a Spanish entrepreneur for freedom from the increasingly narrow life of the encysting Indian communities. By the end of the eighteenth century, the colonist enterprises had achieved substantial independence of the Crown in most economic, political, legal, and even military matters. Power thus passed from the hands of the Crown into the hands of local rulers who interposed themselves effectively between nation and community. Effective power to enforce political and economic decisions contrary to the interest of these power-holders was not returned to the national level until the victory of the Mexican Revolution of 1910 (Wolf 1955b, pp. 193–5).

Alongside the Indian villages and the entrepreneurial communities located near *haciendas*, mines or mills, there developed loosely-structured settlements of casual farmers and workers, middlemen and 'lumpenproletarians' who had no legal place in the colonial order. Colonial records tended to ignore them except when they came into overt conflict with the law. Their symbol in Mexican literature is *El Periquillo Sarniento*, the man who lives by his wits (cf. Yañez, 1945, pp. 60–94). 'Conceived in violence and without joy, born into the world in sorrow' (Fernando Benítez, 1947, p. 47), the very marginality of their origins and social position forced them to develop patterns of behavior adapted to a life unstructured by formal law. They were thus well fitted to take charge of the crucial economic and political relationships of the society at a time when social and cultural change began to break down the barriers between statuses and put a premium on individuals and groups able to rise above their traditional stations through manipulation of social ties and improvisation upon them.

The transfer of power from the national level to the intermediate powerholders, and the abolition of laws protecting the Indian communities – both accomplished when Mexico gained its independence from Spain (Chávez Orozco, 1943, pp. 35–47) – produced a new constellation of relationships among Indian communities, colonist entrepreneurs and 'marginals'. The colonists' enterprises, and chief among them the *hacienda*, began to encroach more and more heavily on the Indian communities. At the same time, the Indian communities increasingly faced the twin threats of internal differentiation and of invasion from the outside by the 'marginals' of colonial times.

Despite the transcendent importance of the *hacienda* in

Mexican life, anthropologists have paid little attention to this cultural form. To date we do not have a single anthropological or sociological study of a Mexican *hacienda* or *hacienda* community. Recent historical research has shown that the *hacienda* is not an offspring of the *encomienda* (Zavala, 1940, 1944). The *encomienda* always remained a form of royal control. The *hacienda*, however, proved admirably adapted to the purposes of the colonists who strove for greater autonomy. Unlike the *encomienda*, it granted direct ownership of land to a manager-owner, and permitted direct control of a resident labor force. From the beginning, it served commercial ends (Bazant, 1950). Its principal function was to convert community-oriented peasants into a disciplined labor force able to produce cash crops for a supracommunity market. The social relationships through which this was accomplished involved a series of voluntary or forced transactions in which the worker abdicated much personal autonomy in exchange for heightened social and economic security.

Many observers have stressed the voracity of the *hacienda* for land and labor. Its appetite for these two factors of production was great indeed, and yet ultimately limited by its very structure. First, the *hacienda* always lacked capital. It thus tended to farm only the best land (Gruening, 1928, p. 134; Tannenbaum, 1929, pp. 121–2), and relied heavily on the traditional technology of its labor force (Simpson, 1937, p. 490). *Hacienda* owners also curtailed production in order to raise land rent and prices, and to keep down wages (Gama, 1931, p. 21). Thus 'Mexico has been a land of large estates, but not a nation of large-scale agriculture' (Martínez de Alba, quoted in Simpson, 1937, p. 490). Second, the *hacienda* was always limited by available demand (Chávez Orozco, 1950, p. 19), which in a country with a largely self-sufficient population was always small. What the *hacienda* owner lacked in capital, however, he made up in the exercise of power over people. He tended to 'monopolize land that he might monopolize labor' (Gruening, 1928, p. 134). But here again the *hacienda* encountered limits to its expansion. Even with intensive farming of its core lands and lavish use of gardeners and torch bearers, it reached a point where its mechanisms of control could no longer cope with the surplus of population nominally under its domination. At this point the *haciendas* ceased to grow, allowing Indian communities like Tepoztlán (Lewis, 1951, p. xxv) or the Sierra and Lake Tarascan villages (West, 1948, p. 17) to survive on their fringes. Most *hacienda* workers did not live on the *haciendas*; they were generally residents of nearby communities who had lost their land, and exchanged their labor for the right to farm a subsistence plot on *hacienda* lands (Aguirre and Pozas, 1954, pp. 202–3). Similarly, only in the arid and sparsely populated North did large *haciendas* predominate. In the heavily populated central region, Mexico's core area, large *haciendas* were the exception and the 'medium-size' *hacienda* of about 3000 hectares was the norm (Aguirre and Pozas, 1954, p. 201; also Simpson, 1937, p. 489).

I should even go so far as to assert that once the *haciendas* reached the apex of their growth within a given area, they began to add to the defensive capacity of the corporately organized communities of Indian peasantry rather than to detract from it. Their major innovation lay in the field of labor organization and not in the field of technology. Their tenants continued to farm substantial land areas by traditional means (Aguirre and Pozas, 1954, p. 201; Whetten, 1948, p. 105) and the *hacienda* did not generally interfere in village affairs except when these came into conflict with its interests. The very threat of a *hacienda's* presence unified the villagers on its fringes in ways which would have been impossible in its absence. A *hacienda* owner also resented outside interference with 'his' Indians, whether these lived inside or outside his property, and outsiders were allowed to operate in the communities only 'by his leave.' He thus often acted as a buffer between the Indian communities and nation-oriented groups, a role similar to that played by the *hacienda* owner in the Northern Highlands of Peru (Mangin, 1955). Periodic work on the *haciendas* further provided the villagers with opportunities, however small, to maintain aspects of their lives which required small outlays of cash and goods, such as their festive patterns, and thus tended to preserve traditional cultural forms and functions which might otherwise have fallen into disuse (Aguirre and Pozas, 1954, p. 221; Wolf, 1953, p. 161).

Where corporate peasant communities were ultimately able to establish relations of hostile symbiosis with the *haciendas*, they confronted other pressures toward dissolution. These pressures came both from within and without the villages, and aimed at the abolition of communal jurisdiction over land. They sought to replace communal jurisdiction with private property in land, that is, to convert village land into a commodity. Like any commodity, land was to become an object to be bought, sold, and used not according to the common understandings of community-oriented groups, but according to the interests of nation-oriented groups outside the community. In some corporate communities outsiders were able to become landowners by buying land or taking land as security on unpaid loans, e.g. in the Tarascan area (Carrasco, 1952, p. 17). Typically, these outsiders belonged to the strata of the population which during colonial times had occupied a marginal position, but which exerted increased pressure for wealth, mobility and social recognition during the nineteenth century. Unable to break the monopoly which the *haciendas* exercised over the best land, they followed the line of least resistance and established beachheads in the Indian communities (Molina Enríquez, 1909, p. 53). They were aided in their endeavors by laws designed to break up the holdings of so-called corporations, which included the lands of the Church and the communal holdings of the Indians.

But even where outsiders were barred from acquiring village lands, the best land of the communities tended to pass into private ownership, this time of members of the community itself (Gama, 1931, pp. 10–11). Important in this change seems to have been the spread of plow culture and oxen which required some capital investment, coupled with the development of wage labor on such holdings and increasing production for a supra-community market. As Oscar Lewis has so well shown for Tepoztlán, once private ownership in land allied to plow culture is established in at least part of the community, the community tends to differentiate into a series of social groups, with different technologies, patterns of work, interests, and thus with different supracommunity relationships (Lewis, 1951, pp. 129–57). This tendency has proceeded at different rates in different parts of

Mexico. It has not yet run its course where land constitutes a poor investment risk, or where a favorable man–land ratio makes private property in land nonfunctional, as among the Popoluca of Sayula in Veracruz (Guiteras Holmes, 1952, pp. 37–40). Elsewhere it was complete at the end of the nineteenth century.

The Mexican Revolution of 1910 destroyed both the cultural form of the *hacienda* and the social relationships which were mediated through it. It did so in part because the *hacienda* was a self-limiting economic system, incapable of further expansion. It did so in part because the *hacienda* prevented the geographic mobility of a large part of Mexico's population. The end of debt bondage, for example, has permitted or forced large numbers of people to leave their local communities and to seek new opportunities elsewhere. It did so, finally, because the *hacienda* blocked the channels of social and cultural mobility and communication from nation to community, and tended to atomize the power of the central government. By destroying its power, the Revolution reopened channels of relationship from the communities to the national level, and permitted new circulation of individuals and groups through the various levels (Iturriaga, 1951, p. 66).

The new power-holders have moved upwards mainly through political channels, and the major means of consolidating and obtaining power on the regional and national level in Mexico today appear to be political. Moreover – and due perhaps in part to the lack of capital in the Mexican economy as a whole – political advantages are necessary to obtain economic advantages. Both economic and political interests must aim at the establishment of monopolistic positions within defined areas of crucial economic and political relationships. Thus political and economic power-seekers tend to meet in alliances and cliques on all levels of the society.

The main formal organization through which their interests are mediated is the government party, the Revolutionary Institutional Party or, as someone has said, 'the Revolution as an institution' (Lee, 1954, p. 300). This party contains not only groups formally defined as political, but also occupational and other special-interests groups. It is a political holding company representing different group interests (Scott, 1955, p. 4). Its major function is to establish channels of communication and mobility from the local community to the central power group at the helm of the government. Individuals who can gain control of the local termini of these channels can now rise to positions of power in the national economy or political machine.

Some of the prerequisites for this new mobility are purely economic. The possession of some wealth, or access to sources of wealth, is important; more important, however, is the ability to adopt the proper patterns of public behavior. These are the patterns of behavior developed by the 'marginal' groups of colonial times which have now become the ideal behavior patterns of the nation-oriented person. An individual who seeks power and recognition outside his local community must shape his behavior to fit these new expectations. He must learn to operate in an arena of continuously changing friendships and alliances, which form and dissolve with the appearance or disappearance of new economic or political opportunities. In other words, he must learn to function in terms which characterize any complex stratified society in which individuals can improve their status through the judicious manipulation of social ties. However, this manipulative behavior is always patterned culturally – and patterned differently in Mexico than in the United States or India. He must therefore learn also the cultural forms in which this manipulative behavior is couched. Individuals who are able to operate both in terms of community-oriented and nation-oriented expectations then tend to be selected out for mobility. They become the economic and political 'brokers' of nation–community relations, a function which carries its own rewards.

The rise of such politician-entrepreneurs, however, has of necessity produced new problems for the central power. The Spanish Crown had to cope with the ever-growing autonomy of the colonists; the central government of the Republic must similarly check the propensity of political power-seekers to free themselves of government control by cornering economic advantages. Once wealthy in their own right, these nation–community 'brokers' would soon be independent of government favors and rewards. The Crown placed a check on the colonists by balancing their localized power over bailiwicks with the concentrated power of a corps of royal officials in charge of the corporate Indian communities. Similarly, the government of the Republic must seek to balance the community-derived power of its political 'brokers' with the power of other power-holders. In modern Mexico, these competing power-holders are the leaders of the labor unions – especially of the labor unions in the nationalized industries – and of the *ejidos*, the groups in local communities who have received land grants in accordance with the agrarian laws growing out of the 1910 Revolution.

Leaving aside a discussion of the labor unions due to limitations of time and personal knowledge, I should like to underline the importance of the *ejido* grants as a nationwide institution. They now include more than 30 per cent of the people in Mexican localities with a population below 10,000 (Whetten, 1948, p. 186). A few of these, located in well-irrigated and highly capitalized areas, have proved an economic as well as a political success (Whetten, 1948, p. 215). The remainder, however, must be regarded as political instruments rather than as economic ones. They are political assets because they have brought under government control large numbers of people who depend ultimately on the government for their livelihood. Agrarian reform has, however, produced social and political changes without concomitant changes in the technological order; the redistribution of land alone can neither change the technology nor supply needed credit (Aguirre and Pozas, 1954, pp. 207–8; Pozas, 1952, p. 316).

At the same time, the Revolution has intensified the tendencies toward further internal differentiation of statuses and interests in the communities, and thus served to reduce their capacity to resist outside impact and pressure. It has mobilized the potentially nation-oriented members of the community, the men with enough land or capital to raise cash crops and operate stores, the men whose position and personality allows them to accept the new patterns of nation-oriented behavior. Yet often enough the attendant show of business and busy-ness tends to obscure the fact that most of the inhabitants of such communities either lack access to new opportunities or are unable to take advantage of such opportunities when offered. Lacking adequate resources in land, water, technical knowledge and contacts in the market, the majority also lack the instruments which can transform use values into marketable commodities. At the same time, their inability to speak Spanish and their failure to understand the cues for the new patterns of nation-oriented behavior isolate them from the channels of communication between community and nation. Under these circumstances they must cling to the traditional 'rejection pattern' of their ancestors, because their narrow economic base sets limits to the introduction of new cultural alternatives. These are all too often non-functional for them. The production of sufficient maize for subsistence purposes remains their major goal in life. In their case, the granting of *ejidos* tended to lend support to their accustomed way of life and reinforced their attachment to their traditional heritage.

Confronted by these contrasts between the mobile and the traditional, the nation-oriented and the community-oriented, village life is riven by contradictions and conflicts, conflicts not only between class groups but also between individuals, families or entire neighborhoods. Such a community will inevitably differentiate into a number of unstable groups with different orientations and interests.

This paper has dealt with the principal ways in which social groups arranged and rearranged themselves in conflict and accommodation along the major economic and political axes of Mexican society. Each rearrangement produced a changed configuration in the relationship of community-oriented and nation-oriented groups. During the first period of post-Columbian Mexican history, political power was concentrated on the national level in the hands of royal officials. Royal officials and colonist entrepreneurs struggled with each other for control of the labor supply located in the Indian communities. In this struggle, the royal officials helped to organize the Indian peasantry into corporate communities which proved strongly resilient to outside change. During the second period, the colonist entrepreneurs – and especially the owners of *haciendas* – threw off royal control and established autonomous local enclaves, centred on their enterprises. With the fusion of political and economic power in the hands of these intermediate power-holders, the national government was rendered impotent and the Indian peasant groups became satellites of the entrepreneurial complex. At the same time, their corporate communal organization was increasingly weakened by internal differentiation and the inroads of outsiders. During the third period, the entrepreneurial complexes standing between community and nation were swept away by the agrarian revolution and power again returned to a central government. Political means are once more applied to check the transformation of power-seekers from the local communities into independent entrepreneurs. Among the groups used in exercising such restraint are the agriculturists, organized in *ejidos* which allow the government direct access to the people of the local communities.

Throughout this analysis, we have been concerned with the bonds which unite different groups on different levels of the larger society, rather than with the internal organization of communities and national-level institutions. Such a shift in emphasis seems increasingly necessary as our traditional models of communities and national institutions become obsolete. Barring such a shift, anthropologists will have to abdicate their new-found interest in complex societies. The social psychological aspects of life in local groups, as opposed to the cultural aspects, have long been explored by sociologists. The study of formal law, politics or economics is better carried out by specialists in these fields than by anthropologists doubling as part-time experts. Yet the hallmark of anthropology has always been its holistic approach, an approach which is increasingly needed in an age of ever-increasing specialization. This paper constitutes an argument that we can achieve greater synthesis in the study of complex societies by focusing our attention on the relationships between different groups operating on different levels of the society, rather than on any one of its isolated segments.

Such an approach will necessarily lead us to ask some new questions and to reconsider some answers to old questions. We may raise two such questions regarding the material presented in the present paper. First, can we make any generalizations about the ways in which groups in Mexico interrelate with each other over time, as compared to those which unite groups in another society, such as Italy or Japan, for example? We hardly possess the necessary information to answer such a question at this point, but one can indicate the direction which a possible answer might take. Let me point to one salient characteristic of Mexican group relationships which appears from the foregoing analysis: the tendency of new group relationships to contribute to the preservation of traditional cultural forms. The Crown reorganized the Indian communities; they became strongholds of the traditional way of life. The *haciendas* transformed the Indian peasants into part-time laborers; their wages stabilized their traditional prestige economy. The Revolution of 1910 opened the channels of opportunity to the nation-oriented; it reinforced the community-orientation of the immobile. It would indeed seem that in Mexico 'the old periods never disappear completely and all wounds, even the oldest, continue to bleed to this day' (Paz, 1947, p. 11). This 'contemporaneity of the noncontemporaneous' is responsible for the 'common-sense' view of many superficial observers that in Mexico 'no problems are ever solved', and 'reforms always produce results opposite to those intended'. It has undoubtedly affected Mexican political development (Wolf, 1953, pp. 160–65). It may be responsible for the violence which has often accompanied even minor ruptures in these symbiotic patterns. And one may well ask the question whether both processes of accommodation or conflict in Mexico have not acquired certain patterned forms as a result of repeated cyclical returns to hostile symbiosis in group relationships.

Such considerations once again raise the thorny problems presented by the national character approach. Much discussion of this concept has turned on the question of whether all nationals conform to a common pattern of behavior and ideals. This view has been subjected to much justified criticism. We should remember, however, that most national character studies have emphasized the study of ideal norms, constructed on the basis of verbal statements by informants, rather than the study of real behavior through participant observation. The result has been, I think, to confuse cultural form and function. It seems possible to define 'national character' operationally as those cultural forms or mechanisms which groups involved in the same overall web of relationships can use in their formal and informal dealings with each other. Such a view need not imply that all nationals think or behave alike, nor that the forms used may not serve different functions in different social contexts. Such common forms must exist if communication between the different constituent groups of a complex society are to be established and maintained. I have pointed out that in modern Mexico the behavior patterns of certain groups in the past have become the expected forms of behavior of nation-oriented individuals. These cultural forms of communication as found in Mexico are manifestly different from those found in other societies (see especially Carrión, 1952, pp. 70–90; Paz, 1947, pp. 29–45). Their study by linguists and students of kinesics (Birdwhistell, 1951) would do much to establish their direct relevance to the study of complex societies.

A second consideration which derives from the analysis presented in this paper concerns the groups of people who mediate between community-oriented groups in communities and nation-oriented groups which operate primarily through national institutions. We have encountered several such groups in this paper. In post-Columbian Mexico, these mediating functions were first carried out by the leaders of Indian corporate communities and royal officials. Later, these tasks fell into the hands of the local entrepreneurs, such as the owners of *haciendas*. After the Revolution of 1910, they passed into the hands of nation-oriented individuals from the local communities who have established ties with the national level, and who serve as 'brokers' between community-oriented and nation-oriented groups.

The study of these 'brokers' will prove increasingly rewarding, as anthropologists shift their attention from the internal organization of communities to the manner of their integration into larger systems. For they stand guard over the crucial junctures or synapses of relationships which connect the local system to the larger whole. Their basic function is to relate community-oriented individuals who want to stabilize or improve their life chances, but who lack economic security and political connexions, with nation-oriented individuals who operate primarily in terms of the complex cultural forms standardized as national institutions, but whose success in these operations depends on the size and strength of their personal following. These functions are of course expressed through cultural forms or mechanisms which will differ from culture to culture. Examples of these are Chinese *kan-ch'ing* (Fried, 1953), Japanese *oyabun-kobun* (Ishino, 1953) and Latin American *compadrazgo* (Mintz and Wolf, 1950).

Special studies of such 'broker' groups can also provide unusual insight into the functions of a complex system through a study of its dysfunctions. The position of these 'brokers' is an 'exposed' one, since, Janus-like, they face in two directions at once. They must serve some of the interests of groups operating on both the community and the national level, and they must cope with the conflicts raised by the collision of these interests. They cannot settle them, since by doing so they would abolish their own usefulness to others. Thus they often act as buffers between groups, maintaining the tensions which provide the dynamic of their actions. The relation of the *hacienda* owner to his satellite Indians, the role of the modern politician-broker to his community-oriented followers, may properly be viewed in this light. These would have no *raison d'être* but for the tensions between community-oriented groups and nation-oriented groups. Yet they must also maintain a grip on these tensions, lest conflict get out of hand and better mediators take their place. Fallers (1955) has demonstrated how much can be learned about the workings of complex systems by studying the 'predicament' of one of its 'brokers', the Soga chief. We shall learn much from similar studies elsewhere.

References

AGUIRRE BELTRÁN, G., and POZAS ARCINIEGAS, R. (1954), 'Instituciones indígenas en el México actual', in A. Caso *et al.*, *Métodos y resultados de la política indigenista en México*, Memorias del Instituto Nacional Indigenista, no. 6, Mexico.

BAZANT, J. (1950), 'Feudalismo y capitalismo en la historia económica de México', *Trimestre Económico*, vol. 17, pp. 81–98.

BENÍTEZ, F. (1947), 'México, la tela de Penélope', *Cuadernos Americanos*, vol. 6, pp. 44–60.

BIRDWHISTELL, R. L. (1951), *Kinetics*, Foreign Service Institute, US Department of State.

CARRASCO, P. (1952), 'Tarascan folk religion: an analysis of economic, social and religious interactions', *Middle American Research Institute Publications*, vol. 17, pp. 1–64.

CARRIÓN, J. (1952), *Mito y magia del Mexicano: México y lo mexicano*, Porrúa y Obregón, Mexico.

CASO, A., *et al.* (1954), *Métodos y resultados de la política indigenista en México*, Memorias del Instituto Nacional Indigenista, no. 6, Mexico.

CHÁVEZ OROZCO, L. (1943), *Las instituciones democraticas de los indígenas mexicanos en la época colonial*, Ediciones del Instituto Indigenista Interamericano, Mexico.

CHÁVEZ OROZCO, L. (1950), 'La irrigación en México: ensayo histórico', *Problemas Agricolas e Industriales de México*, vol. 2, pp. 11–31.

CHEVALIER, F. (1952), 'La formation des grands domaines au Mexique: terre et société aux XVIe–XVIIe siècles', *Travaux et Memoires de l'Institut d'Ethnologie*, no. 56.

FALLERS, L. (1955), 'The predicament of the modern African chief: an instance from Uganda', *Amer. Anthrop.*, vol. 57, pp. 290–305.

FRIED, M. H. (1953), *Fabric of Chinese Society*, Praeger.

GAMA, V. (1931), *La propiedad en México – la reforma agraria*, Empresa Editorial de Ingeniería y Arquitectura.

GRUENING, E. (1928), *Mexico and its Heritage*, Century.

GUITERAS HOLMES, C. (1952), *Sayula*, Sociedad Mexicana de Geografía y Estadística, Mexico.

ISHINO, I. (1953), 'The *oyabun-kobun*: a Japanese ritual kinship institution', *Amer. Anthrop.*, vol. 55, pp. 695–707.

ITURRIAGA, J. E. (1951), *La estructura social y cultural de México*, Fondo de Cultura Económica, Mexico.

LEE, E. (1954), 'Can a one-party system be democratic?', *Dissent*, vol. 1, pp. 299–300.

LEWIS, O. (1951), *Life in a Mexican Village: Tepoztlán Restudied*, University of Illinois Press.

MANGIN, W. (1955), '*Haciendas, comunidades* and strategic acculturation in the Peruvian sierra', paper read before the American Anthropological Association, Boston, 18 November.

MINTZ, S. W., and WOLF, E. R. (1950), 'An analysis of ritual co-parenthood (*compadrazgo*)', *Southwestern J. Anthrop.*, vol. 6, pp. 341–68.

MIRANDA, J. (1947), 'La función económica del encomendero en los orígenes del régimen colonial de Nueva Espana, 1525–31', *Anales del Instituto Nacional de Antropología e Historia*, vol. 2, pp. 421–62.

MOLINA ENRÍQUEZ, A. (1909), *Los grandes problemas nacionales*, Imprenta de A. Carranza e Hijos, Mexico.

PAZ, O. (1947), 'El laberinto de la soledad', *Cuadernos Americanos*.

POZAS ARCINIEGAS, R. (1952), 'La situation économique et financière de l'Indien americain', *Civilisations*, vol. 2, pp. 309–29.

REDFIELD, R., and TAX, S. (1952), 'General characteristics of present-day Mesoamerican Indian society', in S. Tax (ed.), *Heritage of Conquest*, Free Press, pp. 31–9.

SCOTT, R. E. (1955), 'The bases of political power in the Caribbean', lecture delivered at the University of Illinois, January.

SIMPSON, E. N. (1937), *The Ejido: Mexico's Way Out*, University of South Carolina Press.

SIMPSON, L. B. (1950), *The Encomienda in New Spain: The Beginning of Spanish Mexico*, University of California Press.

STEWARD, J. H. (1950), 'Area research: theory and practice', *Social Science Research Council Bulletin*, no. 63, New York.

TANNENBAUM, F. (1929), *The Mexican Agrarian Revolution*, Brookings Institution, Washington.

WEST, R. C. (1948), 'Cultural geography of the modern Tarascan area', *Institute of Social Anthropology*, vol. 7, Smithsonian Institution.

WHETTEN, N. L. (1948), *Rural Mexico*, University of Chicago Press.

WOLF, E. R. (1953), 'La formación de la nación: un ensayo de formulación', *Ciencias Sociales*, vol. 4, pp. 50–62, 98–111, 146–71.

WOLF, E. R. (1955a), 'Types of Latin American peasantry: a preliminary discussion', *Amer. Anthrop.*, vol. 57, pp. 452–71.

WOLF, E. R. (1955b), 'The Mexican *bajío* in the eighteenth century: an analysis of cultural integration', *Middle American Research Institute Publication*, vol. 17, pp. 177–200.

YAÑEZ, A. (1945), *Fichas Mexicanas, Jornadas*, no. 39, El Colegio de México.

ZAVALA, S. (1940), *De encomiendas y propiedad territorial en algunas regiones de la América Española*, Robredo, Mexico.

ZAVALA, S. (1944), 'Orígenes coloniales del peonaje en México', *Trimestre Económico*, vol. 10, pp. 711–48.

ZAVALA, S., and MIRANDA, J. (1954), 'Instituciones indígenas en la colonia', in A. Caso *et al.* (1954), *Métodos y resultados de la política indigenista en México*, Memorias del Instituto Nacional Indigenista, no. 6, Mexico, pp. 29–112.

6 Andrew Pearse

Metropolis and Peasant: The Expansion of the Urban –
Industrial Complex and the Changing Rural Structure[1]

Based on a paper for the Latin American Seminar, Royal Institute
of International Affairs, 30 October 1968.

This paper is concerned with the problem of the small-holding
peasant rather than the estate tenant or worker, that is to say,
the peasants belonging to communities the majority of whose
member-families live by agricultural production on lands to
which they have access rights. This sector, though it probably
constitutes more than half of the agricultural population of the
mainland countries, must be considered, in many ways, as
marginal in Latin America. The reason for this is that within the
agrarian structure itself, the estate was the prevalent form of
the economic organization, and the occurrence of large zones occupied by smallholders usually signified the non-existence or the
decay of conditions as regards land and markets in which the
great estate could prosper. Thus the quality and location of the
smallholders' lands are both marginal, and offer an indifferent
basis for a competitive market agriculture, either because they are
poor, unwatered and hilly, or because they are too small to allow
much beyond family subsistence or because they are too distant
from a suitable market for their products. They are marginal in the
sense that the juridical institutions, elaborated for the regulation
of the great property, offer instruments which are much too
unwieldy or otherwise unsuited to the regulation of small properties, and consequently give place to custom and illegality. The
smallholder may be said to be marginal in the sense that his

1. This paper arose in the course of preparing a field study of ten peasant
neighbourhoods in Chile when the author was working for the Food and
Agricultural Organization of the United Nations, and attached to the
Institute for Training and Research for Land Reform in Santiago. He is
indebted to his colleagues Andrés Pascal, Christopher Scott and David
Benavente, for their parts in the development of the ideas.

participation in the general social system has been that of a dependent powerless element, disposed of by decisions of others, isolated by illiteracy from the circuit of ideas current in the society, rudimentary transport systems and cultural difference, and contractually inferior in his market relations. And whatever his local situation may be, one of his obvious economic functions in the national systems has been that of providing a labour reserve for the occasional and seasonal needs of estate and plantation agriculture.

As a contribution to the study of the changes taking place in rural Latin America and in problems of development, this paper draws attention to the expansion of the core of the great industrial (developed) societies, as the most important single factor in the alterations of rural life and social structure, laying down new conditions in which peasants make their decisions. It refers to a supra-political force of intervention which goes beyond and embraces those actions carried out by states and interest groups with specific intentions, such as the banning of the pill or a counter-revolutionary *golpe*; it is a 'vegetable' force with patches of intentionality. It is not aimed at peasants as such or under-development as such, but at this stage of history it is reaching out into the rural areas of the underdeveloped world just as at an earlier period, and in a different manner, it set off transformations in the fabric of rural life in the now developed countries.

I arrived at a conviction of the importance of this approach from the rural pole of the axis rather than the metropolitan one, simply by seeing the acceleration and intensification of the im-pulses arriving at the periphery from the centre, and by being conscious that I was carried on one of these impulses myself, that in addition to trying to see the problem objectively I was a precise part of it as well as a UN expert in various technical assistance programmes.

We shall, then, take as our starting point the existence of an accelerating movement, emanating from the industrial urban centres of our society and making for the incorporation within its systems of the hitherto unincorporated, wherever it can gain access. In reaching the peasantry in Latin America, it is mediated by the national and regional capitals, which are in part local transmission stations and in part boosters of these impulses, adding their own force to the process. The most important driving force is the market complex, seeking out even marginal sellers of raw materials and cheap labour, as well as buyers for factory-made goods and for services. The stream is augmented by the natural expansiveness of bureaucracies, whether these be the national civil service, churches, health and education programmes, political parties, bilateral and multilateral aid agencies, missions and pilot schemes, or charity hand-outs, all competing hotly for clients, converts, 'natural' leaders, branch secretaries, and likely human types as material for training courses.

The great alterations taking place in agrarian structure, and in the values and behaviour of country people, must be seen as elements in a complicated process whereby the rural, social and economic systems respond to these exogenous impulses.

The 'incorporative drive', as we might call it, requires as a precondition the intensification of interaction between the local neighbourhood and the urban centres of the great society, made possible by improved transport, and the circulation between country and town of people, ideas and manufactured goods. It implies direct attachment of local production, exchange and consumption to the national market system (market incorporation), and the establishment, by the side of local customary institutions and traditional means, of standard national institutions (institutional incorporation). It results in modifications and transformations of values and the cultural goals which are in harmony with them, and in modifications and transformations of the social structure of neighbourhoods and rural localities, and of the structural relations between those and the larger society.

We shall now discuss the penetration of zones in which production for family use is the mainspring of the peasant economy, that is to say, where the subsistence system prevails. The elaboration of this process of commercial penetration must not, of course, be taken to imply a simple continuum from isolated economic autarchy moving chronologically ever closer to complete integration in a market economy. During the historic period in Latin America there have always been communities of families each with functioning productive organizations linked directly to consumers by market relations and making use of money as a means of exchange. Coexisting with those, there have been isolated groups maintaining themselves with a minimum of exchange relations with local and national markets. But for historical reasons, the market linkage of communities of small producers working in relative independence (as also of estates in which small producers were organized under compulsion) has been intermittent rather than continuous. The rise and decline of heavily populated mining centres, the development of a new form of transport or periods of excessive demand in the metropolises for a particular natural product, such as gold, silver, sugar, hides, indigo, cotton, rubber, quinine, wheat, cacao, bananas, etc., have been typical inductors of market relations.

The present period is characterized by rapid growth of cities, and with them a growing internal market, rising population and the general extension of transport, bringing cheap manufactured consumer goods and agricultural elements of production to the rural zones, in exchange for money, and a much greater and more consistent demand for agricultural products, rather than random invasions, answering the rationality of mercantile or industrial capitalism, but not that of the dependent colonial or national economy, and still less of the producing regions. Thus, it is now possible to speak about a persistent process of penetration and incorporation of the rural areas in the system of market relations. But incorporation in the larger market system is partial and does not lead to an evenly distributed economic development, involving increased productivity, income and capital formation.

The response to the incorporative drive is of course varied. In certain communities where a solidary system of collective defence against the larger society has been institutionalized, the response may be near zero, but there is usually a clearly identifiable reaction which may be radical in the alterations it produces, and depends on internal factors connected with the configuration and dynamics of the community as well as the intensity of the incorporative drive.

Local semi-autarchic economic systems, in which direct exchange of a variety of goods and of labour keep the circulation of specie to a minimum, are upset by the coming of cheap manufactured goods and the diffusion of certain kinds of machines. Manufacture for home consumption and arrangements for the exchange of labour fall into disuse. Money increases in importance, for the purchase of manufactured and processed necessities. As a consequence, there is an increase in the relative importance of commerce, transport and credit, and of those who manage or control them. Production does not advance generally, since both additional labour and technical inputs require cash or credit, which is not economically available to the majority. There is less acceptance on the part of the younger men of the obligation to work for their fathers in exchange for subsistence, and more temporary migration for wage work, as well as permanent migration towards centres of urban or industrial employment. Thus, the labour available at busy times is less than previously. Failing a really lucrative cash crop, the more accessible markets do not offer a secure and substantial return which could make possible a radical change of system, and most families are obliged to cling to subsistence agriculture for security.[1] The labour force available is devoted to securing a harvest of cereal or potatoes which will provide for the basic food requirements of the family, plus other items whose sale will provide the cash necessary for subsistence purchases the year round. A further obstacle to the commercial development of the smallholders' economy is the marketing mechanism. On account of the contractual inferiority of the peasant, and the usual concentration of three commercial functions in the hands of single individuals (purchaser of produce, supplier of credit and vendor of consumption goods), any surpluses developed by the little economy tend to be transferred to the middleman rather than remain available for reinvestment.

1. The schematic answer to queries about why the subsistence orientation of family productive units should survive is simple enough: the peasant does not perceive the existence of a secure system of distribution of goods and facilities necessary for family livelihood based on money-exchange, and his perception generally corresponds to the real situation. The crisis is not in the long life of the subsistence systems, but in the dysfunctional straddle between these and a reliable money-market system.

Full incorporation in the market would imply the establishment of competitive commercial farms. This requires certain additions to the peasants' assets of land, labour and traditional techniques, such as access to credit, knowledge of improved methods of production and the addition of some powered machines. It also would seem to imply a very difficult social transformation, namely the abandonment of a life guided by a network of community rights and obligations and its replacement by economically motivated activities in which neighbours and kin are manipulated like any other input. The traditional gearing of productive roles to family relationships must be modified by the submission of the latter to commercial exigencies.

Under these conditions, the commercial agriculturalist does not necessarily emerge directly from the peasantry, since the accumulation of the qualifications for success, namely technical know-how, credit and commercial ability, can only be acquired during a period following escape from an occupational status which carries with it continual dedication to manual labour, and from a social status which carries with it a network of particularistic obligations within the community and contractual inferiority in relations with the market. The commercial farmer may be the peasant migrant who returns from an industrial or commercial occupation to lands already in the possession of his family or which he acquires. He may be an outsider attracted by the productive and commercial opportunities of a community which are not perceived or not realizable by its members. Or he may be a member of the peasant community who has been able to establish himself in commerce or transport, and who has been exposed to urban socialization without necessarily living in the town. The outsider already lives within a circuit of ideas in which market intelligence and improved methods have currency, and he remains in contact with this circuit even if he now lives in the rural community, though his rural neighbours are not necessarily able to 'plug in' to it. And his economic behaviour suffers little restraint or control by this community, since he retains his urban reference-group. The other two types of modernizers will adopt free competitive economic behaviour in proportion to the decline of their community obligations and the growth of their identification with town reference-groups and other modernizers.

An alternative mode of change may be seen in which no commercial farmers emerge within the peasants holdings, but in which entrepreneurs in modern inputs associate with the peasant, raising his productivity but securing his dependence and the lion's share of his surpluses. A current example of this mode of change can be given from a rather remote Bolivian estate which was appropriated by the Land Reform. Prior to the reform, its income was derived from the production for the market of high quality potatoes, requiring chemical manures. After expropriation, the peasants became owners of the land, but within a comparatively short time came to rely on a group of commercially minded people (peasants, traders and lorry-owners) from a more prosperous zone, who brought them the manure necessary for planting and received payment of half the crop at harvest time. In effect, the lot of the traditional peasant is tied to the decline in the relative importance of the factors land and (unpowered) labour in the productive process, and the relative devaluation of recompense in respect of them.

The drive towards incorporation brings to neighbourhoods and rural localities a set of formally organized institutions (some a part of the State apparatus and some not) which are characterized by national standardization, conformity to urban cultural norms and developmental aims, such as schooling, public health, agricultural development, provision of credit, education of adults, mobilization of peasants in community organizations or as voters or in political associations, in football and sports clubs, as converts and as the recipients of charity. While market incorporation is a blind process in which individual agents and groups pursuing economic ends provide the motor, institutional incorporation contains a coherent aim-content, and is to some extent an instrument deliberately used by the state to fit out the 'lagging' peripheral subcultures for their prescribed roles in the national economy and society, though the degree of intentionality should not be exaggerated, however prominent the explicit aims are. Institutional incorporation offers partial alternatives and palliatives to the dilemmas of commercialization.

Andrew Pearse   75

Education can be expected to diversify skills and prepare country people for easier acceptance of innovation. It undoubtedly facilitates the integration of migrants to the cities. The process of acculturation which accompanies institutional incorporation and the intensification of interaction with the larger society, diminishing the cultural differences between town and country people, also removes one of the props on which the contractual inferiority of the peasant is based. The implantation of the national institutions, organized at least formally on the basis of secondary relationship and standard norms, provides experience in leadership and membership through which local pressures may be exercised and local demands represented. Development agencies offering credit and technical services can be expected to provide some alternatives to local monopolies. Co-operatives may lead to the strengthening of bargaining positions, and political participation may give some consideration to peasant interests.

The incorporative drive, accompanied as it is by an intensification of communication and exchange of goods, persons and ideas between the rural neighbourhoods and the urban centres, puts on display, as it were, a series of alternative behaviours and orientations which may be adopted by the peasants. If they are adopted, then they replace elements of the traditional, local and particular subculture by elements of a national standard, contemporary (though not necessarily 'modern') urban culture. Penetration of the rural neighbourhoods by the incorporative movement brings 'facilities' in the most ample sense.

But at the same time it establishes a new kind of dependence of rural social organization on the urban centres. The obsolescence of the local economic institutions which grow up around subsistence is accompanied by the decline of other social institutions belonging exclusively to the neighbourhood, a loss of self-containment and valorative self-sufficiency. Exogamy becomes more general, local leadership diminishes in prestige and effectiveness. The new institutions offer apparently more efficient means to the fulfilment of social goals. But the status of the peasant in these new institutions is inevitably a dependent one, since their management requires urban skills (just as entrepreneurship does), and the greater the scope of the decision to be made, the more remote and metropolitan is the locus of decision making.

The forces operating to incorporate the smallholder sector in the national economy are differential in their effects, and lead to the counterposing of two groups. The entrepreneurs and the other groups in the rural neighbourhood who have experience of the urban world and also are not dependent on their own manual labour applied to the land, seek to differentiate themselves socially from the remaining traditional peasantry. This is made possible by the increase in intensity of communications with the urban centres.

A new rural middle stratum begins to acquire identity, associating with the middle strata of the *pueblo*, and adopting behaviours and symbols taken from urban life. The values of the new rural middle strata are urban-oriented and they are sustained by urban reference-groups. Agricultural productive effort and investment are justified by urban rewards. 'Objective' justification must be found for the rejection of many traditional norms and disrespect for the traditional peasantry.

The expansion of the middle strata and the induction of the new institutions occur at the same time. It follows that the middle strata welcome the opportunity of validating their status by moving into the leading roles of the new institutions. This may mean that the use of the institution to demonstrate prestige or to exercise power may predominate over its dedication to its formal purposes. It almost certainly means the appropriation of the institution to the ends of this sector. Thus, the replacement of the traditional, peculiar and local institution-set by the modern, standardized and national institution-set is accompanied by the taking over of the new authority-roles by the emergent middle strata.

With the growing importance of the national institutions and the decline of the local ones, the local solidarity based on a tightly knit network of loyalties and obligations gives way to emancipation from local control, to the increasing isolation of the nuclear family within the neighbourhood, and at the same time, an increase in controls exercised directly over the community from the urban centres. The importance of the neighbourhood as a community declines. The characteristic unique status of the traditional rural person is replaced by the enjoyment of different levels of status in different sub-systems. There is a tendency towards differentiation and multiplication of social as well as of economic roles. Action sequences which have been valued because they fulfilled the tradition are now valued as means to economic ends.

The other group consists of the peasants who, as it were, are left behind. They may own the land and dispose of their own labour and traditional skills. Their change of status is subtle and gradual. It is likely to be initiated when pressure of the market economy renders inadequate instrumental, technological, economic and institutional means belonging to the subsistence system. Substitutes are sought for and in the new phase attempts are made to reach goals and enjoy the gratification thereof by the use of new techniques, changed productive and market relations, and the adoption of roles in the new national institutions.

The adoption of new techniques can take place without important social consequences, provided it is instrumental in reaching the desired goals. But the abandonment of the subsistence elements of the economy and of the local institutions, and full delivery to the commercial system and the national institutions, is fraught with far-reaching consequences since both exact stern conditions. To play the role of agricultural entrepreneur in the new system requires technical skill and 'bureaucrability', and access to credit on a considerable scale, assets which very few of the traditional peasantry are likely to possess individually or to dispose of jointly by collective action. The majority must be expected to suffer progressive decapitalization and to rely more and more on the sale of wage-labour, either locally or in other fields or cities. As regards the substitution of new institutional roles for old, the traditional local institutions allocated roles according to local criteria and a status system with a local apex based on local realities, such as kinship situation, control of resources essential to functioning of subsistence economy, special knowledge of lore and custom, etc. The new national institutions are profoundly and systematically hierarchical, having their apex situated in the national capital and beyond it, in Rome, Washington, Moscow, or wherever, and each one is a status sub-system in which the individual rank is derived from the measure of bureaucratic and schooled skills (which have not hitherto been available to rural peoples) and the measure of power enjoyed in the general social system, in regard to which the peasant is inevitably placed at the lowest point in the scale. Thus, the new institutions, though they may aspire formally to equity in the distribution of rights in the new society, nevertheless offer to the peasant essentially dependent roles, whose norms have not been adapted to local conditions. Their performance, therefore, is regarded as 'inadequate'.

The new dependence of the traditional peasantry on the bureaucracies of the new institutions and controllers of transport and market takes the place of the former patterns of dominance exercised by local bosses such as *caciques*, priests and big land-owners of neighbouring estates. The personal ascendence of the latter is replaced by the attachment of the peasants as clients of specific organizations.

Thus, the penetration of the rural areas by commercial relations and new institutions may be seen as a flow of action from the centre to the periphery of the society making for incorporation, but the reactions to it are varied, and result in contrasting forms of incorporation, as well as with differential speeds. It can be conceived of as the catalyst of a whole set of forces latent within the local rural structure. However, comprehending the variety of qualities of incorporation, three general dimensions of change can be conceptualized, as seen from the point of view of the destiny of the peasant and his communities:

In the economic dimension: movement from family-bound production towards productive enterprises largely dependent on industrial inputs.

In the structural dimension: movement from membership of a neighbourhood community marked by 'structural peninsularity' towards membership of a national class-society.

In the cultural dimension: movement from territorially defined cultural variety towards national cultural homogeneity modified by sub-cultural class-differentiation.

For traditional country or market-town people, change in each of these dimensions implies decisions leading to the free or forced alteration of behaviours, usages, forms of economic activity, techniques, acceptance of rules about rights and duties pertaining to new relationships and participation or deliberate abstention from participation in some of the new institutions. What generally operative principles can be adduced to explain why the traditional peasant decides to change his way of life? The answer seems to be that the alternative to changing his behaviour is a deterioration of his condition, as a result of the obsolescence of traditional technical and institutional means. At the same time, new means become available to replace them; and new goals come within the range first of his aspirations, and then of his expectations. This phase marks the passage from a static to a dynamic situation, since the new 'facilities' offering an infinitely wider range of goals than hitherto available must be competed for. Competition for the appropriation of new facilities now takes place, but their distribution is differential because the competitors are unequally equipped for the struggle. Not all facilities are scarce. Primary schooling is not a scarce facility, secondary schooling is. Land, labour and traditional agricultural skills are widely held by the peasantry, while the 'industrial inputs', credit and bargaining power, are scarce facilities. Economic differentiation is amplified in accordance with each family's potential for appropriating facilities. Those with least tend towards the provision of labour, those with most towards entrepreneurial performance. What begins as a quantitative difference becomes a qualitative one.

A third stage can be discerned in which the two differentiated groups, at odds over the price of labour, access to land and the monopolization of scarce facilities, take on the conformation of social classes, each embracing common symbols, seeking organized strength and making common cause on a national scale. The new dynamic consists of the competition and conflict between classes, and the struggle for social ascension from one class to another.

B. Analytically Marginal Groups

Section B discusses examples of what were termed in the Introduction 'analytically marginal groups' of the peasantry and their development. Feder's contribution brings *latifundia* and agricultural wage-labour into focus, viewed against the background of rural society in Latin America. Franklin considers European worker-peasants – a phenomenon occurring in situations of a high level of urbanization and industrialization, while Saul and Woods turn their attention to the other extreme, the emerging African peasantries. Saul and Woods also touch on the important issue of regional peasant groups. Galeski's analysis of structural changes affecting rural society concludes by discussing the alternative directions of development in the wide variety of rural societies. He also touches on the issue of the collective farms and in particular those typical of the Soviet Union and Eastern Europe. A number of analytically marginal groups are not represented here, in particular, members of the Chinese communes and some of the non-farming ruralities, e.g. fishermen, pastoralists and at times rural craftsmen. Again references on the reading list will have to serve as a substitute.

7 Ernest Feder

Latifundia and Agricultural Labour in Latin America

Ernest Feder, 'Tenencia de la tierra y desarrollo socio-económico del
secto agrícola: América Latina', unpublished Regional Report for the
Comité Interamericano de Desarrollo Agrícola, March 1968.
Abridged by the author.

Land tenure is sometimes defined in a relatively narrow sense as
concerned principally with rights to land and their distribution. In
reality much more is involved. In the first place, there are many
farm people – the rural 'wage' workers – who have no rights to
land whatever. These farm families are tied to the land because
they have to make a living from working for others who *have*
rights to land. In some countries, they may be the majority. In
Latin America as a whole, landless families form 40 per cent of
all farm families, no doubt a conservative estimate based on
censuses which habitually under-report the lowest strata of the
farm population.

In the second place, in predominantly agricultural societies the
ownership of land is the main source of economic, political and
social power. As a simple rule, it can be affirmed that the greater
the amount of land owned, the greater the power of its owner.
Farm people who have no land whatever have therefore no direct
economic, political and social power. They could obtain higher
incomes, political influence and greater social prestige if they
were allowed to organize into co-operatives, peasant leagues or
workers' syndicates, although even then our simple rule would
probably hold. But in an agriculture where land is highly un-
evenly distributed as in Latin America, where 1 per cent of all
farm families control, conservatively speaking, one-half of all
farm land (and probably as much as 60 per cent), the power of the
landed elite is used precisely to keep the peasantry disorganized,
poor and dependent. The curious thing is that economic wealth
derived from agriculture is today no longer crucial to the total
power of the landed elite. As will be pointed out, Latin American

economies are characterized by a high degree of integration of the various sectors. However, political power has had, and continues to have, its base in the ownership of land, and now, with their continued political influence, the landed elite has priority access to the newly developing resources of their countries. This political influence seems to be challenged in countries with a higher rate of economic development by the newly formed small groups of industrial, commercial and financial magnates. But on closer analysis, this challenge may prove to be more apparent than real, whenever the functions of land ownership, banking or marketing, for example, are fused in the same individuals, as is usually the case. In any event, even if this were to be true only partially, the interests of the Latin American financiers, industrialists or merchants are much closer to the interest of the nation's landed elite than to those of the peasantry and the same holds true for foreign holders of investments.[1] For these reasons there are now few expectations that in the foreseeable future the status of the peasantry of Latin America can be improved.

Perhaps the most significant conclusion of this brief comment on the political and social implications of Latin America's land tenure system is the evident existence of an enormous and growing *class conflict* between the landless peasants and the producers on inadequate plots of land (smallholders) on one side and the landed elite and their allies, on the other. In Latin America as a whole the landless and the smallholders now form 72 per cent of all farm families. Their number is growing in absolute and in relative terms. Access to land becomes every day more difficult, real incomes decline and unemployment is rising.

1. It might be expected that the new magnates should be more interested in developing broader markets for their products or services and welcome an improvement in the status of the peasantry. But this may only be the theorists' viewpoint, for two major reasons. A developed peasantry threatens to upset the existing social structure and the power of the landed elite and the magnates alike; for example, an organized peasantry might take over the marketing of an important export product. Equally important, however, is the fact that urban business now thrives on cheap labour, constantly replenished from rural–urban migration as the peasants seek work in urban areas.

Latifundismo, Rural Autocracy and Absenteeism

How power relations find their expression in Latin American agriculture is best described through a brief characterization of the *latifundio* system. Autocracy is a fundamental aspect of Latin America's *latifundismo* and it affects all phases of the relations between employers and workers. *Latifundismo* is a system of power. An estate is normally an autocratic enterprise, regardless of the number of people working on it or whether the owner lives on it, nearby or far away. The owner may not be directly responsible for the day-to-day operation of the farm which may be left to a tenant or an administrator (farm manager); but the final decisions on important issues such as what and how much to plant or what, when and where to sell, or even on any 'minor' issues if necessary, rest with him. Minor matters may be those regarding the life and welfare of his workers which in advanced societies have been taken over by public authorities or are resolved through co-operative and collective action. The power of the landlord extends therefore over the farming activities properly speaking as well as over the individuals who participate in these activities, including their 'private lives' and very often over people who are only indirectly involved with his farm operation.

What makes this power distinctive is the lack of check on its exercise. The organization of a *latifundio* is not unlike that of a military organization in which the top command retains the exclusive privilege of making decisions on all matters concerning the soldiers' activities and where delegation of power exists only within certain narrow limits – qualified always by the right to intervene, even arbitrarily. Decisions on minor issues made by subordinates to whom some power of decision making is granted are always subject to explicit or implicit sanctions by the top command. It is in this sense that a Brazilian sociologist could speak of estate owners as having the power of life and death over the men working for them.

It is also characteristic of estates that the *patrón* is non-resident and that he 'supervises' the management of his estate only on the occasion of visits of greater or less frequency, leaving the day-to-day management in the hands of his administrator (farm manager). Absentee management actually reinforces the autocratic nature of *latifundismo* because it increases the distance between the *patrón* and the workers.

The Economic and Social Function of Administrators (Farm Managers) and Other Agents of Authority

Absentee landlordism is too narrowly defined from a sociological viewpoint if only residence is used as a criterion. Even if an owner or producer resides on the farm, his administrator (farm manager) provides for a certain degree of absentee or indirect management because of the role played by the administrator and his functions. In fact, for the rural worker almost every estate owner is an absenteeist, as the bulk of the large estates is managed by administrators. In *Brazil*, for example, nearly 50 per cent of the *latifundios* had administrators (CIDA, Brazil, p. 132), and in *Colombia* 53 per cent of the land in the *latifundios* is managed through administrators (CIDA, Colombia, p. 168). These statistics may be conservative.[2]

With some exceptions an administrator is not a skilled and experienced person with the latest knowledge in good farming methods. In general, he is merely a worker who has been on the landlord's payroll for some years and distinguished himself by his thorough knowledge of local customs, which he respects, and his loyalty to his employer. He supervises the farm operation under orders of the landlord within a strictly limited sphere of action. He makes no major decisions with respect to the use of the land, the number and kind of livestock to be raised or fed, or what to buy or sell. His powers over operational expenditures are normally limited to small cash transactions or charge-accounts with merchants. From the point of view of the landlord, the administrator is merely another worker although he receives higher wages – usually not much higher – and certain minor privileges not accorded other workers. But the administrator is the boss's 'man of trust'.

From the point of view of the worker, the administrator

2. Owners of several estates with one administrator each, may also employ a general or business manager (*gerente*) who accounts periodically to the owner.

represents in nearly all respects the nearest authority, because his most decisive function lies in the day-to-day handling of the farm workers. He assigns the daily work, pays wages, punishes, fires a farm worker and hires a replacement – within the framework set by the landlord. This implies that decisions regarding the number or type of workers to be hired and their remuneration are exclusively with the owner. The latter may receive a request for more workers from his administrator and dispose of it as he sees fit, and he may as likely as not consult his fellow-landlords in setting the terms of their employment without resorting to his administrator's advice.

Farm workers rarely enter into direct contact with the employer and any complaints or sentiments the workers may harbour with respect to the treatment received or the 'system' as such are first directed against the administrator.[3] The administrator is then their first object of respect or (more frequently) of resentment. He also represents the worker's main contact with the outside world. He is the delegated judge and jury in most routine matters regarding the work and the life of the worker and his family. In practical terms this implies that from the point of the productive work force there is no fair mechanism which can insure that justified claims of the workers can be vented. The chances that any claims heard will be solved in favour of the workers are always slim, but the chances that they are heard at all slimmer still. Workers simply have nowhere to turn to, unless it be to a worker's syndicate or a labour court. But the latter are extremely scarce throughout Latin America.

Given his power, and although the general employment policy is laid down by the landlord, the administrator's treatment of the men can be severe and arbitrary without disapproval because the landlord needs his administrator more than he does the workers. Since he is by far the workers' most powerful superior, he usually is distinguished, like an officer in the army, by some symbol of

3. See for example CIDA, Brazil Report (p. 155). But there are exceptions. In one instance, a rich landlord listened at regular intervals to 'complaints' of his workers, seated at a large table and accompanied by his administrative assistants (staff), with the workers standing twenty feet apart so that they could not converse. The circumstances were rather intimidating for the workers (p. 153).

authority, such as a horse on which he rides around the estate to supervise, a pick-up truck, and almost always a whip or a stick, and very often a gun. One Brazilian sociologist remarked that:

The administrator, overseers, foreman are characteristic figures in the human landscape of Sape. Always robust, young, with clean, starched jackets, a long cape, elegantly mounted on their fiery horse, they are indispensable for two types of owners: the absentee owner and the physically weak who take recourse to these agents to impose their authority (CIDA, Brazil, p. 150).

The interposition of administrators as a 'sponge' absorbing the immediate reactions of farm people fulfills an important function, namely that of contributing to the stabilization and fortification of the existing power structure. The ruling class's aloofness allows its members to appear *vis-à-vis* the workers and small producers as the innocent element, in the constant role of moderators, even benefactors, as actual or potential conciliators when conflicts come to their personal attention directly or via their administrator who, in turn, absorbs the blame for any harsh treatment. Thus absentee management in the wider sense, i.e. management through administrators, is both a convenience for the landlord whose main interests normally lie outside agriculture and whose incomes from non-farm sources often exceed his farm income, and a method to maintain the existing power structure.

Administrators are also an important element in maintaining the existing production pattern, its level of efficiency or inefficiency and of technology. Absentee landlordism is a guarantee that customary methods of farming are strictly observed though they may be antiquated. Most administrators are not allowed to introduce changes in the farming pattern, and landlords hesitate to introduce them because this may require changes in the tenure status of the workers. Therefore the high rate of absenteeism is an obstacle to technological progress and improved farming. Management practices cannot improve beyond that permitted by the sparse interest and knowledge of farming of most absentee landlords, and the limited abilities and responsibilities of their administrators.

The administrators' functions to preserve the *status quo* are reinforced by the fact that on many large estates and plantations, the authority of the landlords and their agents, the administrators, is reinforced by strong-arm men, a private police force. A typical example are the *capangas* of the sugar plantations in north-eastern Brazil who make the workers 'toe the line', who intimidate or terrorize them, or give them corporal punishment. At times they kill. These 'policemen' prevent workers from joining syndicates by threatening the workers and keeping union organizers off the farms, or dismissing workers who become active union leaders. They contribute a great deal to the violent conflicts between workers and administration, and cases of great brutality arise frequently.[4]

The Impact of the Divided Interests of Landowners on Labour Relations

The traditional rural elites of Latin America commonly show indifference to, if not ignorance of, the world of the peasants. The estate owner, whether he is an absentee landlord or not, seldom participates in the rural community in which he owns property. He does not share its institutions, nor its moods and ambitions. The schools are not for his children, the homes not for his entertainment, the hospital not for his care and the roads not for his travel unless they lead to his urban residence or are useful for his pleasure. His and his children's religious, social, political and other affiliations are in the capitals of the region, the state or the nation. Not using the facilities of the countryside he has little interest in improving them, except for his convenience.

Lack of interest in the affairs of the rural communities can be explained by the owners' involvements in other activities – professional, financial, industrial or business. They endow landlord-absenteeism with its third dimension. By and large estate owners have little economic incentive to improve farm management or their relations with the rural community when they derive substantial incomes from many estates or from non-agricultural sources. Even at a low level of farm management their total earnings are sufficient for more than adequate levels of

4. A number of examples of violence can be found in CIDA, Brazil Report, chapter 4, or Ecuador Report, part 2, chapter 4.

living and large savings. The sociologist Semenzato noted of the cacao area in Brazil that:

It is invariably the same men who are in the cacao production, who are in the directorates of the banks, in the top organs of the co-operatives ... and at times in the export houses. On the other side these very firms are also owners of the cacao plantations. There are banker-cacao farmers and livestock farmers. There are members of the directorate of the co-operatives who are influential politicians, large cacao growers, livestock men and great merchants.... Besides, these are the same men who are tied, directly or indirectly, by reason of their prestige and social position, to the industry of cacao by-products. And so forth. The greatest portion of the economic sector is in the hands of the large producers (CIDA, Brazil, p. 171).

This description closely fits other Latin American countries. Relations between community and landlord are weakest when the landlord considers his properties only as a 'distraction' for spending week-ends hunting or entertaining friends (p. 175).

The implication of these facets of *latifundismo* is that estate owners cannot help solve the problems of the *campesinato*, of rural labour. If this conclusion is correct, then a policy aimed at enlisting the aid of the landlords to solve these problems lacks realism.

Besides being complex, the social structure of the estate tends to be rigid from the point of view of economic development. For farm people dependent upon estate owners this has serious consequences. An autocratic organization is well adapted to having orders from above carried out efficiently: it is efficient with respect to the use and distribution of power. However, this efficiency is highest when matters go their usual way, in a routine manner. It can be quickly diluted, in terms of the management of the farm and of its people, when emergency situations or major changes arise. But while the landed elite has no interest in the peasants' aspirations and keeps aloof from their world, it is still keenly aware of its obligations to keep the peasants in check and subservient. It can achieve this simply through inaction – as the social structure automatically ensures obedience up to a point – or actively, through coercion, sanctions and total hostility to any peasant organization.

Estate owners at times mete out physical or other punishments either directly or through their representatives or by calling on police or military forces. This makes the estate owner at times accuser, judge, jury and enforcement agent, all in one. As a result, fear and sometimes even terror have become a component of the lives of many *campesinos*. Punishments of individual workers are given for real or alleged misdeeds or for carelessness, partly to terrorize the men and 'set examples', partly to deprive them of their belongings. The severest sanctions are saved for efforts to unionize farm workers. Acts of terrorism also occur to deprive peasants of their land, both in established farming communities, as was mentioned earlier, and in the frontier areas.

The opposition of the estate owners to collective action is systematic and accompanied by drastic counter-measures which seem warranted only as an expression of the principle that to admit rightful claims in an individual case is tantamount to the landlord's surrender of the authority to determine unilaterally the working and living conditions of farm people. The *ligas camponesas* rose out of the workers' determination to fight feudal work obligations. Many of the members were small-farm owners. The history of the *ligas* is one of violence and persecution and assassination of labour leaders. In 1963, a member of one of the local organizations in the north-east said that:

The political situation here is very tense. Whoever speaks in favour of the *liga* can expect to be shot at any moment. None of us who are here in this shed are safe. A shot can come out of the dark from one of the *capangas* who must be watching us now.

Rural Wage Levels and Labour Supply

Rural workers, including smallholders and working members of their families, receive lower average wages than any other significant sector in the society.[5] Indeed, a low-cost and obedient labour force is the cornerstone of the region's *latifundio* agriculture. To the extent that estate owners who control the bulk of the physical resources in agriculture have a vested interest in

5. The term 'wages' in this context includes returns in cash or kind to sharecroppers, tenants or other workers with plots. See also Appendix 4A of the original of this Reading for more detailed discussion of income levels.

preserving such an economically and politically advantageous system, their opposition to proposed changes in land tenure institutions can be expected to continue. It is in the continuing interest of the large estate owner to have a large supply of labour on call. The existence of this pool of workers, both unemployed and partly occupied, means that wages continue low. The existing political structure in most countries offers the estate operators various means to assure that there will be no change in this situation.

In the seven countries studied by CIDA, wages remain 'naturally' at a low level because there are many more applicants for rural jobs than available work opportunities. This condition prevails because employment opportunities have not opened up in line with the natural increase in the labour force as a result of a traditional under-utilization of the land. In some cases the opportunities have been reduced by the introduction of labour-saving machinery, and secondly because the access to farm land is practically closed to farm people. Therefore there is an absolute excess of rural labour because of the growing farm population and a relative excess in comparison to the existing jobs on the land. Excess supplies of labour exert a sharply depressing influence on the wage level, and by systematically limiting employment opportunities estate owners keep this influence alive.[6]

6. Whether the large landowners limit employment opportunities as a deliberate policy is a debatable question. It is one of the characteristics of Latin American *latifundismo* that physical resources are under-employed. For example, only 4 per cent of all the land in large estates is actually in crops and there is more land held idle (fallow) than there is land in crops. It is estimated that if only the land held idle were used more intensively (without reference to any pasture land, for example, which could be cropped), the labour force on the *latifundios* could be doubled, at existing levels of farm management and technology. In recent years, some large estates have intensified their use of the land. But the use of machinery has sharply reduced the possibility of employing more labour. At best, seasonal labour is being employed on those estates. On the other hand, there has been a decided shift out of cropping in favour of extensive livestock operations, on a regionwide scale, causing widespread new unemployment.

The Trend towards Hired Cash-Wage Workers and Conflicts Associated with it

In addition to these general structural elements of a *latifundio* agriculture which affect the level of wages and employment, one must keep in mind the nature of the work contracts under which rural workers are employed by the owners of land. Payment or part-payment of remuneration in terms of some right to the use of land still has considerable advantages for rural employers in most areas of Latin America. It attaches the workers to the land and guarantees the employers an adequate – even a more than adequate – supply of labour. It reduces the employers' need for cash and allows control over their workers' activities.

In recent years the proportion of hired landless workers who work only for cash wages has increased. This has resulted both from the 'pull' of the workers who abandon rural communities to escape onerous working conditions there and seek the greater freedoms of the villages and towns, and from the 'push' of the employers who replace their workers by motorized equipment or shift to pure wage employment, both of which simplify their labour problem.[7] But the shift to cash-wage workers is in most instances only partial. In São Paulo, for example, the share-croppers and *colonos* in coffee plantations increased between 1955 and 1960 from 514,000 to 527,000, although at a slower rate than daily workers and piece workers whose number rose from 222,000 to 281,000. The former therefore still outnumbered the latter by almost two to one in 1960 although São Paulo is considered to have one of the more dynamic agricultures of Brazil (CIDA, Brazil, p. 182).

The long-run decline of traditional resident rural workers is due to a number of economic and socio-political factors. The right to

7. The type of employment – traditional or pure wage employment – is not necessarily a function of the type of land use. Livestock enterprises may employ salaried workers or sharecroppers; plantations sharecroppers, tenants or workers with or without plots of land. Employment is influenced by tradition, the owners' participation in the management of the farm, and institutional arrangements, such as labour laws, credit and banking facilities.

the use of land is becoming for the workers an increasingly un-satisfactory type of income. Cash is needed by the workers and their family to acquire necessities of life, even in the most remote rural communities of the hemisphere. On the other hand the traditional terms under which workers are hired and work their plots allow them every day less opportunity to grow enough food or provide for their own clothes and other items to satisfy their needs. As a result, many workers now seem to be paid both in kind, i.e. through the proceeds of their produce which may also bring in some cash from the sale of the produce, and in cash, usually as wage workers.

Demands for cash have accompanied many conflicts between estate owners and workers when the latter requested from the former better terms of employment and more ample access to the land resource. These demands are one of the ways in which these conflicts come out into the open. In other words, since the access to more land is practically closed, demands for better terms of employment normally imply more cash earnings and these are often opposed by the rural employers.

In Brazil, the slow shift from one type of labour use to another has been and still is exceptionally violent. In the north-east's marginal sugar-cane areas, for example, absentee landlords had rented their land to small tenants during the period of low sugar prices. They planted fruits and vegetables with which they supplied Recife and other cities and paid annual rentals, besides providing some free labour for the landlord under feudal arrangements. When prices of sugar rose after the Second World War, the owners evicted workers or forced them to destroy their permanent crops. Sometimes the owners paid compensation, but more often they did not. The conflicts which arose out of the tenants' treatment gave rise to the *ligas camponesas*. The conflicts continue as large landowners seek to reduce the number of their resident workers who live on the estates and usually are allotted a tiny garden plot. The normal method is to refuse to build new houses for the workers when the old ones become uninhabitable, or not to allow new workers to enter the houses when they become vacant, or to tear them down. All this has given rise to violent, even armed, clashes between rural workers and organized 'vigilantes' in this region.[8] The expulsion of workers is practised, however, in many parts of Brazil. It does not always have the dramatic consequences described above since open clashes occur only when workers are organized and can resist the landlords.

In Ecuador's *sierra*, numerous conflicts have arisen out of the *hacienda*-owners' attempts to reduce the number of *huasipungos* and to restrict the workers' or small owners' access to the land, and the subsequent extreme subdivisions of the *minifundios*. Demands for better wages and farm workers' aspirations toward better conditions of life are looked upon by *hacendados* as subversive (CIDA, Ecuador, p. 97). Being accustomed to request and receive free or nearly free labour services from their workers and to allow changes only when they originate under their own initiative, they see in these wage demands an attack on their status and prerogatives.

On one large typical *hacienda* of 12,000 hectares, for example, the landlord had adopted a strict policy of limiting and even decreasing the area of the *huasipungos* which caused increased deterioration and erosion of the land assigned to them. Yields became progressively smaller since the workers could not shift their cultivations to other parts of their farm, as the owner could. Furthermore, the landlord recuperated the *huasipungo* land for his own use when the head of family of the *huasipungo* died. This represented a certain break with tradition, and obliged the remaining family members to live on other *huasipungos* without obtaining new living quarters. The result was great overcrowding on the remaining *huasipungos*. Although the majority of *huasipungos* had existed on the farm for a long time, new land had been allotted to only a few and there were more families of non-*huasipungueros* (*allegados*) than there were *huasipungueros*. The conflict was of such magnitude that a solution through mutual concessions appeared to be impossible (CIDA, Ecuador, pp. 280ff.). To this – says the CIDA observer – one must add the

8. One grave clash occurred when the CIDA team was making its field studies in Paraiba. See CIDA, Brazil Report (pp. 230–33). In the same community, another fight occurred exactly a year later in which at least nineteen people were killed. This incident was reported in the Rio de Janeiro Press.

results of another process which occurs all over the area, namely that landlords are increasingly less in a position to meet the workers' growing refusal to work without remuneration and the pressure to pay cash wages in view of the low productivity of their own estates. The Indian population which for centuries was glued to particular plots of land has lost this security and is migrating in search of some means of livelihood. Human settlements are being destroyed; everywhere are abandoned huts, stables without animals, and *huasipungos* cultivated by the landlords (p. 295). The prevailing conditions oblige the workers to seek work elsewhere in order to subsist.

By and large, the shift towards cash wages is not likely to alleviate the financial hardships facing most of the workers. It does not solve the basic problem of unemployment in agriculture. This means that workers are mistaken in their expectation that remuneration through cash wages necessarily implies an improvement in their economic status.

Potential Employment Opportunities in Latin American Agricultures

It has been argued that in order to improve the level of living of farm people it is necessary to shift the excess rural population into urban-industrial jobs and to speed up the colonization of unopened frontier areas. This theory has merit if one assumes that at present rural employment cannot be expanded in existing farming areas.[9] Except for regions such as the excessively densely populated *minifundio* area bordering Lake Puno in Peru,[10] by and large the land now controlled by multi-family farms appears

9. The immediate possibilities of absorbing rural labour in urban industries are limited because of urban unemployment and the anticipated slow increase in industrial employment even with a massive industrialization programme (see Arthur Domike, 1967; Gunnar Myrdal, 1965).

10. Another example is described in CIDA, Brazil Report (pp. 377 ff.). CIDA estimated in 1966 that in the Peruvian sierra there is sufficient land available for a massive land reform and hence for a sharp increase in rural employment. If one takes into account the fact that there is considerably more land in multi-family farms than is now reported by the Census, the large-scale settlement of unopened frontier areas does not have to be considered seriously for a couple of decades.

capable of absorbing many more farm workers if it were utilized more intensively (even at prevailing levels of technology) and under improved land tenure conditions. An examination of the possibilities of providing additional employment for farm people on existing farms leads to the conclusion that there is no immediate need for a massive shift of farm families to the frontier or to the cities. In the seven countries examined by CIDA it would appear that about fifty million more workers could find rural employment on existing multi-family farms and potential new job opportunities appear to be considerably in excess of the estimated under-employment or unemployment in agriculture.

The persistent pattern of rural unemployment in Latin America is an indication that under prevailing conditions the 'expansion' of agriculture – through modest intensification of land uses and through the widening of the frontier – translated into increased rural employment takes place at best at the same, but more likely at a slower rate than the growth of the active rural labour force. In other words the creation of new rural jobs is at present inadequate to relieve unemployment. What is more, the large estates probably contribute proportionally less to new employment than the smaller units. The seriousness of the growing pattern of unemployment is exemplified by the fact that in Brazil, for example, the number of rural workers employed by the *latifundios* decreased between 35 and 52 per cent, depending on whether the statistics of the Preliminary Census (published in 1963) or the Final Census (published in 1965) are used.

References

DOMIKE, A. (1967), 'Industrial and agricultural employment prospects in Latin America', paper presented at the Conference on Urbanization and Work in Modernizing Societies, 2 November.
MYRDAL, G. (1965), 'The United Nations, agriculture and the world economic revolution', *J. Farm Econ.*, November.

The sources of the other references in this Reading are the seven CIDA reports on Land Tenure Conditions and Socio-Economic Development of the Agricultural Sectors of Argentina, Brazil, Chile, Colombia, Ecuador, Guatemala, Peru or the appendix tables 1A   12A of this Regional Report.

8 Harvey Franklin

The Worker Peasant in Europe

Excerpts from Harvey Franklin, *European Peasantry: The Final Phase*, Methuen, 1969, pp. 48–62.

Ten years ago the small peasant-farm issue dominated agrarian affairs in Germany. Numerically the small farms constituted the largest of all groups in the farm population and numerically articles on the small peasant and worker-peasant communities occupied a large part of the literature. Much of what was written at the time is now of historical interest only. But because of the very considerable effect which the evolution of these communities has had upon the nature and future of the whole rural community, and because that evolution is not yet complete, the small-farm issue deserves a particular place in any analysis of the German agrarian structure.

Four main socio-economic groups are present in the small-farm category: the war widows, the elderly, the worker-peasants and the full-time operators. The majority of the old people's farms, whether full-time farms or not, were of less than five hectares. They fulfilled the traditional role of providing security for the declining years. The farms managed by war widows are the product of a terrible phase of history. Mostly they were of less than seven-and-a-half hectares though they existed in the ten to twenty hectares group also. In time presumably they will be taken over by younger men as full or part-time enterprises, or go out of operation. Just over a half of the small farm chiefs between twenty-five and sixty years of age belonged to the worker-peasant class (they were particularly well represented in the two to five hectares as well as the half to two hectares categories); the remainder ran full-time holdings.

By its very nature the worker-peasant class fits neatly into none of the customary divisions which the social sciences have imposed upon reality. Few investigators have recognized this; in the treatment of the subject they have been confined by the limits of their own discipline. Some have stressed the historical, others the geographical aspects (Hoffman, 1935; Stockmann, 1934). A few, Linde and Hesse in particular, have dealt with the worker-peasant primarily as a feature of the evolution and the increasingly complex nature of the rural community. Agrarian economists have recognized the class as an important feature of the rural social structures (Röhm and Kuhnen), as a means of transition to an industrial form of society (Priebe), but their very orientation has led them naturally to disregard the industrial side of the activity and to stress the agrarian aspect and its significance for the evolution of agriculture. Consequently the worker-peasant family as a socio-economic type remains largely uninvestigated. Never to my knowledge has an attempt been made to analyse the phenomenon of the worker-peasant family within the context of the theory of the peasant economy.

The derivation of income, or the supplementation of income, from off-farm sources is a common feature of the peasant economy. When it is obtained by working as a temporary labourer or a domestic for other peasant families, or when it is derived from artisanal or commercial activities in the village, off-farm employment has more effect upon the social than the economic character of both the community and the family. It is an influential factor in the social stratification of the village community and a basis for the aggrandizement of certain families and the relative decline of others. However, the appearance of employment opportunities related to the penetration of capitalist, or for that matter socialist, manufacturing is of far greater significance and more permanent in effect. Not only does it introduce the technology and mores of industrial society, and enlarge the occupational opportunities of the individual, it also promotes the division of labour in an economy characterized by very little division of labour; above all, it associates the farming population with the sector in which productivity and hence earnings are more rapidly increasing. Ultimately it produces a situation in which the rationale of the peasant economy is destroyed. Though, it must be added, only in very recent times and in a relatively few areas has this situation been reached.

The peasantry have commonly entered the capitalist system of production as employees commuting to nearby small towns, or as workers in the branch factory of a large firm which has been located in their native village. In both cases a ceiling is placed upon the social promotion of all but a few. They are most unlikely to reach the level of the entrepreneurial class, and at best may only reach the level of the skilled operative and the foreman. Their status is not much different from that of the members of the working class, though their possession of land obscures this until the rise in industrial wages has reduced the contribution of the farm to negligible proportions. What is more, territorial ties, family and religious relationships tend to prevail over occupational associations. Only through individual promotion and geographic mobility are they severed. As a mass phenomenon the worker-peasant class remains part of the socio-economic life of the rural and farming community, and only slowly, through its different experiences and the divergent attitudes which result, does it become an agent of change. Only when a certain stage of economic development has been reached does the worker-peasant class become the catalyst for the abandonment of farming. Even then it is reluctant to cut all ties with the land, so that the structural predial problems remain largely unsolved.

When the worker-peasant class is given the chance to become part of the entrepreneurial class, then the impact of industrialization upon village life is far more disturbing. A new element is introduced into the matrix of the social structure: an indigenous class of capitalists and factory owners. Old kinship ties, if originally they were useful in promoting industrialization, cannot be expected to withstand the strain of increasing differentiation according to wealth and education. In the post-war period the increasing demand for labour has often led to the introduction of a second foreign element: a proletariat, composed of exogenous, landless people with no ties or associations in the village. The cumulative effect of such changes can be illustrated from the case of Gosheim, originally a small peasant, then worker-peasant community, which subsequently produced its own class of capitalists.

Automation and the diminution in wage differentials between rural and urban localities are going to have a general influence on the industrial future of the worker-peasant communities whether they are highly industrialized like Gosheim or, as is more common, they are principally *Auspendler* communities. It is too early to be precise about either the manner in which they will be affected or how successfully they will respond to the changes. But one thing ought to be clear. Any economic difficulties which may arise cannot at this late stage be overcome by a resort to or dependence upon the agricultural part of the binary economy. In earlier decades this might have been feasible, indeed it was often the intention behind the creation of the part-time holding. The contribution of the agricultural sector was then relatively much larger. The part-time holding provided security. On the basis of its residual function a family income, rather than an individual income, was accumulated from diverse sources. But the disproportion between the contribution from the industrial and agricultural parts has grown so great that a change of disposition has become impossible. The part-time holding provided also a physical base, a shelter, which alleviated the worker-peasant of the costs of rehousing as he became incorporated in the industrial system. Increasingly the farm has been retained not for the security of income it afforded but because modern means of transport have widened extensively the economic area accessible from that base.

The worker-peasant community cannot persist because of the sociological changes capitalist development produces in the community. In the 1920s, Gosheim, like near-by Bubsheim today, was a worker-peasant community. All the families owned land and the majority had members of the family working in someone else's factory or in the family concern. The entrepreneurs may have been a wealthier group, whether or not they displayed it, but the door was still open to newcomers. Now it is not. Currently it is very difficult, if not totally impossible, to set oneself up in business; not one of the immigrants has succeeded. Cheap labour no longer exists; generally there is a shortage of labour, especially of the skilled variety. Initial investment charges are high and it is doubtful if the *per capita* earnings of a one-man or two-man outfit would exceed the earning capacity of a skilled factory worker. Certainly the distinction between those who are dependent upon wages alone and those who are worker-peasants has almost disappeared. Within a very short period of time higher wage rates and shorter working hours will render the contribution of five o'clock farming to the family income of such marginal significance that its continuance will be explicable only on therapeutic grounds. The rise in the birth-rate amongst the native-born Gosheimers means that the existing properties will be subdivided further when the rising generation claims its inheritance. Many properties will be so small that their partial development as building sites will be the only sensible course. *Realteilung* and the binary economy have pulverized the holdings to the extent that individually they will soon be useless for agriculture.

Sociologically the effect of industrialization has been to diversify, differentiate and stratify an originally homogeneous population, but at the same time it has produced a larger and increasingly homogeneous class of factory workers; and by so increasing the levels of living amongst the worker-peasant class it has removed its *raison d'être*. Industrialization has put an end to the peasant economy.

References

HOFFMAN, H. (1935), *Landwirtschaft und Industrie in Württemberg*, Berlin.

STOCKMANN, G. (1934), 'Die Verbindung von Landwirtschaft und Gewerbe in Baden-Württemberg', *Schmollers Jahrbuch*, 58, Zweiter Halbband 4–6, pp. 551–68, 675–708.

9 John S. Saul and Roger Woods

African Peasantries

An original paper.

The terms 'peasant' and 'peasantry', in addition to their popular
and political usages, have been used in the social sciences for the
description and analysis of types of rural society with reference to
a wide range of geographical settings and historical periods;
unfortunately, despite considerable usage, there has been no consistent definition of the term. This conceptual inconsistency has
had the consequence that analyses of 'peasant society' are by no
means readily comparable in either their scope or their theoretical
underpinnings. There have been, it is true, some recent attempts
at a more systematic categorization in which peasants have been
differentiated from 'primitive agriculturalists' on the one hand
and from 'farmers' or 'agricultural entrepreneurs' on the other
(Wolf, 1966, p. 2). Yet what appears to be a successful way of
specifically differentiating 'peasants' from other agriculturalists
and non-agriculturalists in any particular area often presents
difficulties when applied to another. Thus the variety of peasant
types and the variety of approaches by social scientists to them
promises to provide sufficient fuel for a virtually endless debate
on the appropriate dimensions of the concept. There is a danger,
however, that the definitional exercise will obscure the real point
at issue. For the value of any concept lies in its ability to illumi-
nate and explain empirical data when used in a theoretical argument. Thus the proper questions to ask before trying to define
the 'peasant' in an African context are: what are we trying to
explain, and will a concept defined in a particular way do justice
to the empirical data and be logically appropriate to the argument?

Our interest lies in identifying and explaining the patterns of change and development in contemporary Africa, and we are therefore concerned to use terms such as 'peasantry' and 'peasant' as effective concepts within an analytical framework which does usefully structure such an explanation. A precise identification of the phases of social evolution and world economic history during which the peasant may become an important actor on the African stage and his role a crucial one in the understanding of the process of historical change thus becomes of central importance in pinpointing this category. Moreover, as we shall in fact see, the changing African social structure has thrown up, during certain periods, strata which may be usefully so identified in structural terms.

It should also be stressed, however, that any definition must not aggregate together uncritically all peasants under a monolithic category, for the peasantry may also be differentiated internally in terms of certain structurally significant variables. This becomes all the more important an emphasis in light of our focus upon the changing context within which the peasantry operates, for the category will of necessity remain fluid at the margins as various segments of society pass in and out of the relevant range of social involvements which it epitomizes and at different rates. Not surprisingly, under certain circumstances different segments of the peasantry can come to play diverse historical roles with important consequences for the pattern of historical development. In brief, there can be among the peasants *different peasantries* – differentiated according to their structural position at a specified moment of time.

This much having been said, we must still specify some criteria for differentiating peasants from other rural people. Our emphasis here is two-fold and highlights economic characteristics. Firstly, our concern with the structural position of the peasantry suggests that it must be seen as being a certain strata within some wider political and economic system. A second dimension centres on the importance to the peasantry of the family economy.[1] Thus

1. Chayanov's theory of the peasant economy (see Chayanov, 1925) with its emphasis on the dual role of the peasant *household* as both a productive and a consumptive group is a valuable conceptual tool in any study of peasants. In much of Africa the concept needs to be extended to that of a

peasants are *those whose ultimate security and subsistence lies in their having certain rights in land and in the labour of family members on the land, but who are involved, through rights and obligations, in a wider economic system which includes the participation of non-peasants.*[2] The fact that for peasants ultimate security and subsistence rests upon maintaining rights in land and rights in family labour will be seen to be an important determinant shaping and restricting their social action. It is also the characteristic which peasants share with 'primitive agriculturalists', though not with capitalist farmers. For while the capitalist farmer may *appear* to depend upon his land and even upon family labour in some cases, he is not *forced* to rely solely upon these in the last instance; he has alternative potential sources of security and investment. What the peasant does share, in general terms, with the capitalist farmer (though not with the primitive agriculturalist) is his integration into a complex social structure characterized by stratification and economic differentiation. In fact, it is precisely the characterization of the peasantry in terms of its position relative to other groups in the wider social system which has particularly important explanatory value in the analysis of development.

The work of elaborating upon such criteria can only be begun here, but it is certainly possible to carry the discussion beyond the point reached by Fallers, for example, in his article entitled 'Are African cultivators to be called peasants?' (Fallers, 1961). Confining himself to the discussion of 'traditional' social systems rather abstractly conceived and working partly in the anthropological tradition of Kroeber and Redfield, he defined

---

homestead economy as a basic unit of analysis. The homestead, which is based on the joint property rights of an extended family, frequently has rights to farm land rather than rights to a particular farm.

2. Pastoralists are an important category of the rural population in a number of African countries. Since these predominantly pastoral people are subject to the same kinds of political and economic forces as their predominantly agricultural brethren and since their productive economy (in as much as it involves rights to, and control over, the family herds) is based on a similar kind of 'homestead' principle, they would fulfil our own limited criteria for peasants. We would thus include them in any study of African peasantries, however much this might offend 'peasant purists'.

peasant society as being a society 'whose primary constituent units are semi-autonomous local communities with semi-autonomous cultures'. This semi-autonomy he broke down further into economic, political and 'cultural' dimensions. He demonstrated the involvement of many Africans in the trade and exchange of agricultural produce and even the existence, albeit more limited in scope, of political states which in some areas allowed for the emergence of many political attributes of a peasantry. But crucial to his argument was the non-existence, as he saw it, of any juxtaposition between high- and low-cultures even in those African societies which had, in effect, economic and political proto-peasantries. Fallers concludes, in fact, with the suggestion 'that one of the reasons why Christianity, Islam and their accompanying high cultures have been so readily accepted in many parts of Africa is that many African societies were structurally "ready" to receive peasant cultures'!

Yet such a conclusion graphically demonstrates the dangers of looking for cultural aspects of peasant societies within the framework of an abstract and a historical approach.[3] For the history of colonial Africa shows, on the contrary, not any structural readiness to accept, and consequent acceptance of, a 'high culture', but rather a clash between different types of social systems in which the resulting system, independent of its cultural content, was the product of the interaction of the two systems. Moreover, despite the existence of some prefigurings of a peasant class in earlier periods, it is more fruitful to view both the creation of an African peasantry, as well as the creation of the present differentiation among African peasantries, as being primarily the result of the interaction between an international capitalist economic system and traditional socio-economic systems, within the context of territorially-defined colonial political systems.

Sub-Saharan Africa viewed in continental perspective is still predominantly rural in its population, but the ubiquitous reach of colonialism has ensured that no significant numbers of the primitive agriculturalists who previously comprised the vast

3. See Frank (1967) and Harris (1964) for two very different but illuminating studies which situate Latin American peasantries in historical and structural terms.

majority of the population have remained outside the framework of a wider economic system. Under our usage most of this rural population has thus been transformed into a peasantry. Of course, in certain areas, not only have non-African immigrants established themselves as capitalist farmers but a significant number of African cultivators have moved out of the peasant category and must also be called capitalist farmers. In addition, as the logic of capitalist development has worked itself out in Africa, other peasants have lost their land rights and have been *proletarianized* either in the rural or industrial sectors of the economy. In other words the further development of capitalism has begun to phase out the very peasantry at first defined and created. Moreover in most of the continent it is a capitalist route to development that is favoured and in so far as capitalism does have the inherent strength to fully transform African societies the existence of a peasantry could be viewed all the more as a transitional phenomenon. The possibility of a realization of this kind of transformation is of course most problematic[4] and, in any event, remains a very long-term proposition. The identification of a continental bias towards the further encouragement of this possibility may therefore help to explain the fluidity at the margins of the peasant category referred to earlier; it does not relieve one of the necessity of analysing the contemporary characteristics of that peasantry itself or of suggesting its likely response to the social structures which are emerging and serving to reshape it.

The colonial situation was everywhere one in which the local populations were both exposed to new goods and services and, in many cases, subjected to specific government-enforced economic or labour demands with the result that new needs were generated which could only be met by participation in the cash-based market economy. Two ways of participating were open to them: sale of their labour or sale of their agricultural produce. Within this broad process four variables have been of particular importance in defining the nature of the 'participation' in the overall

4. See the article by Arrighi and Saul (1968, pp. 141–69) which assesses the socio-economic patterns to be found in the 'modern sector' of African countries in terms of their ability to transform the rural economy.

system by primitive agriculturalists through which they acquired, in effect, their peasant characteristics.[5] These variables are:

1. The presence, or otherwise, of centres of labour demand, such as mines, plantations, industries and the like.

2. The presence, or otherwise, of a suitable local environment for the production of agricultural crops for sale, combined with the degree of availability of marketing opportunities for these crops.

3. The presence, or otherwise, of an immigrant settler group of capitalist farmers who would be competitors with African producers.

4. And, at a later stage, the presence, or otherwise, of an indigenous elite (basing themselves upon educational attainment and, in some cases, upon political skills) which under certain circumstances (notably the absence of an immigrant settler group) could take over formal political power from the colonial regime. This new stratum might be complemented and reinforced in its exercise of authority by a newly emergent, indigenous 'national bourgeoisie', to be found in trade and in agriculture itself.

Equally important, it must be remembered that these variables have operated upon a pre-colonial Africa that was itself characterized by a large number of ethnic and political groups at different levels of political and economic organization. By taking full cognizance of such a wide variety of factors it may be easier to get a clear idea of the full range of permutations and actual consequences possible within the overall process of 'peasantization'.

It is perhaps worth extending briefly the discussion as to the importance of environmental potential, a factor which helps to define both the character of the traditional agro-economic systems as well as their subsequent responses. For the extent to which labour-exporting peasantries developed was not only a function of the labour demand/economic need dimension introduced by an absence of readily available cash-crops. It also re-

5. Our attention was drawn to the importance of seeing peasant aggregates in certain of these terms by an unpublished paper of D. L. Barnett (n.d.).

flected in some instances the degree to which adult men were under-employed in the traditional agricultural system and hence the extent to which they could be absent without threatening the security of minimal subsistence production. Similarly the extent to which a peasantry could respond to cash cropping also depended on the adaptability of the traditional agricultural system to the incorporation of new crops or the expanded production of established crops *without threatening the security of minimal subsistence production*. Of course, these complexities further contribute to the process whereby a number of 'African peasantries' are tending to be created rather than a single monolithic strata. But the reiteration of the italicized phrase is equally significant, for we are reminded of the second of the general characteristics of the peasantry mentioned earlier. In so far as particular African cultivators can continue to be identified as peasants one will observe such a calculation to be central to the defining of their existence and to the grounding of their activities.

A distinctive African peasantry exists, therefore, though it may find itself involved in broader national systems which can have a range of possible characteristics – societies in which the dominant elements will be a variable combination of international corporations, immigrant settlers and immigrant trading groups, indigenous elites and indigenous national bourgeoisies. Secondly, in each territory we can distinguish a number of peasantries who are differentiated according to locality – some localities being labour exporting, some food-crop exporting, some cash-crop exporting and some with varying proportions of each. In addition, these differentiations will often coincide with, and be reinforced by, localized cultural identifications, often of an ethnic or tribal nature. Of course the pattern will not be a static one, but rather one changing over time as the system develops. Thirdly, the dynamic of capitalist development tends to introduce a further element which cuts across the differentiation of peasants by locality with a differentiation based on the degree of involvement in the cash economy. This involves, as we have seen, the possible movements towards proletarianization of migrant labourers on the one hand and toward capitalist agriculture on the other, and these too can chip away at the peasantry, pulling it in different directions.

It will be apparent that these complexities make any attempt to identify the historical role which the African peasantry is likely to define for itself a most treacherous one. For even were 'peasants', under certain circumstances, to become conscious of their common interests and act politically on the basis of that awareness, the likely results are not readily predictable. Upon occasion, for example, one might find that the bulk of the peasantry in a given territory was available for an attempt to press its demands upon the other classes and interests in the society – where abuses by an alien authority or a highly compromised indigenous urban elite become so unbearable as to override consciousness of other fissures. More often, perhaps, localisms of various sorts (e.g. tribal consciousness) will prevail, to the point where even those aspects of the peasantry's economic and social grievances which might be generalized onto a territorial scale become obscured.[6] Similarly, where it is nascent horizontal dimensions which define a variety of peasantries these may become the overriding determinant of peasant intervention in the historical process. Thus wealthy peasantries may move merely to open their own paths to capitalist farming (thereby altering the options for other peasants, some of whose passage to the agrarian proletariat may be correspondingly accelerated).[7] Or the 'lower' peasantries may awaken to the burden of their condition and the quality of their likely fate before the latter is in fact sealed, and act on that awareness. For the latter the means of their gaining consciousness, much less power, are particularly circumscribed, and as yet this is perhaps the most speculative of the alternatives which we have thrown up.

But in any case such a discussion cannot be taken far in the abstract. Continental trends may be fruitfully discussed, of course, but cumulative insight into the peasant's role is more

6. On this point as well as for further discussion of the likely range of political roles for the peasantry in contemporary Africa see Arrighi and Saul (1969).

7. An important variable which we have not been able to explore here is the pressure of population upon the land. Taken as a whole African land resources are considerable but areas of 'population pressure' do exist and in these areas the options open to individual peasants are much more limited. There the growth of a farmer class tends to mean the proletarianization of others.

likely to be gained by bringing together an analysis of the nature of a particular national social system (situated within the context of the world economy) with a characterization of the internal dynamics of its peasantry. And this can be done satisfactorily only through case-studies of actual historical experiences. We will therefore conclude with some brief reference to three such experiences, not under any pretence of exhausting their complexity but merely in order to *begin* the task of exemplifying the various criteria which we have presented and of underscoring the range of historical possibilities which we have hinted at.

In the context of Southern Rhodesia, where the capitalist framework of colonialism was characterized by the existence of a significant settler farming community able to establish political dominance over the various forces contending for control, the ability of the local African population to develop cash-crop agriculture on a scale that would have allowed the growth of a class of non-peasant capitalist farmers was checked (Arrighi, 1966, 1967). In this specific situation only the development of tightly controlled small-scale cash farming has been permitted. The involvement of the peasantry has been forced into a pattern of subsistence agriculture with only small cash sales of agricultural produce on the one hand and periods of paid employment for most males of working age as a means of meeting cash needs on the other. An attempt to stratify the peasantry by allowing the acquisition of smallholdings with individual tenure through what was termed 'native purchase' has been on too small a scale to have significant structural effects. As population pressure on impoverished land increases and circular patterns of labour migration become more difficult to sustain, almost all African agriculturalists within Rhodesia have therefore to accept the fate of increased proletarianization for at least some among their number, as well as a declining standard of living.[8] The alternative to this situation is a growth in consciousness about their class position and a revolutionary response to it.

In Ghana where, by contrast, there was no large-scale European farming community and hence a very different economic and

8. A forthcoming study by Roger Woods on the 'Native purchase areas of Rhodesia' will elaborate upon these and related points.

political cast to the colonial situation, other patterns among the peasantry emerged. Thus in certain regions the cultivation of cocoa allowed the growth of large-scale cocoa farming by Ghanaian farmers. The peasants who developed these cocoa plantations were largely migrant farmers who quickly became capitalist farmers – to them we can hardly apply the term peasant (Hill, 1963). But their emergence profoundly affected the position of other peasants in the Ghanaian political economy. Certain areas not well endowed with agricultural resources now developed labour-exporting peasantries, these travelling not only to some mines and to the cities, but also to the cocoa farming areas. A group of tenant farmers or debt farmers also emerged and these can properly be seen as a peasantry, with a distinct class position.

Historically the capitalist cocoa farmers and wealthier peasants have been a politically conservative force, underpinning right-wing political parties as well as the post-Nkrumah military regime. In contrast, however, the lower peasantry was never fully and effectively enlisted into Nkrumah's movement, for the latter retained too many of the characteristics of a parasitic urban group to effectively mobilize their support. Market forces have therefore continued to chip away at the peasantry, albeit indecisively, for a deteriorating international market situation has sapped the power of cocoa to transform the rural economy and neither the Nkrumah regime nor its successor have developed strategies for industrialization which would provide an effective substitute. The peasantry's place has not therefore been eliminated by capitalist development, but neither have the abuses of incumbent elites proven a sufficient prod to generate its active intervention in the political arena (cf. Fitch and Oppenheimer, 1966).

By contrast, Tanzania has not seen the development of one sizeable and homogeneous group of cash-crop farmers from her peasant ranks. In many different areas (in accordance with the environmental potential that existed) annual or perennial crops have been developed as marketable cash crops, and in each such area some degree of differentiation has emerged among farmers. This differentiation is expressed not simply in terms of economic status, but by differential involvement in cooperative organizations and other modern institutions and privileged access to the advantages which they make available (Saul, 1971). Increasingly there have been for the early movers paths leading out of the peasantry into the farmer class. But once again the economic mobility of some agriculturalists changes the nature of the system in which others begin to move. Thus, the unhindered play of this process promises to result in a complex pattern of stratification, one marked by a number of strata of agriculturalists stretching all the way from capitalist farmer to landless labourer. In addition regional differences which spring in part from the realities of different agro-ecological environments and marketing opportunities may give rise, as has happened elsewhere, to 'local' peasantries (sometimes wearing the cloak of tribalism) which have different structural positions, and conflicting interests, in the total system.

The Tanzanian government has been aware of the first stirrings of these possibilities and – almost alone among governments in Sub-Saharan Africa – has chosen to confront the tasks of *pre-empting* them. So far this has involved only the tentative beginnings of that radicalization of the political structure which might enlist the support and involvement of the mass of the rural population. But the leadership does argue for the possibility of a *socialist transformation* of the peasantries and has embarked upon a search for the modern collective forms appropriate to that end (Nyerere, 1967). There has been some parallel attempt to redefine the nature of the country's relations with the international capitalist system and by so doing effect a basic change in the peasants' structural position. Whether this attempt will withstand the opposition of those non-peasants (and advanced peasants) whose positions are threatened by such a strategy remains to be seen.

It is hoped that such 'case-studies', though derisory in their brevity, will at least have indicated the importance of continuing the study of the African peasantry along some of the lines which we have indicated. It scarcely requires stating that a great deal of additional work in the spheres of conceptualization and historico-sociological investigation remains to be done.

References

ARRIGHI, G. (1966), 'The political economy of Rhodesia', *New Left Rev.*, no. 39, pp. 35–65.

ARRIGHI, G. (1967), *The Political Economy of Rhodesia*, The Hague.

ARRIGHI, G., and SAUL, J. S. (1968), 'Socialism and economic development in tropical Africa', *J. mod. Afr. Studies*, vol. 6, no. 2, pp. 141–69.

ARRIGHI, G., and SAUL, J. S. (1969), 'Nationalism and revolution in sub-Saharan Africa', in R. Miliband and J. Savile (eds.), *The Socialist Register 1969*, London.

BARNETT, D. L. (n.d.), 'Three types of African peasantry', Dar es Salaam, mim.

CHAYANOV, A. V. (1925), *Organizatsiya krest'yanskogo khozyaistva*. Translated as *The Theory of Peasant Economy*, D. Thorner, R. E. F. Smith and B. Kerkblay (eds.), Irwin, 1966.

FALLERS, L. A. (1961), 'Are African cultivators to be called "peasants"?', *Curr. Anthrop.*, vol. 2, no. 2, pp. 108–10.

FITCH, B., and OPPENHEIMER, M. (1966), *Ghana: End of an Illusion*, Monthly Review Press.

FRANK, A. G. (1967), *Capitalism and Underdevelopment in Latin America*, Monthly Review Press.

HARRIS, M. (1964), *Patterns of Race in the Americas*, Walker.

HILL, P. (1963), *Migrant Cocoa Farmers of Southern Ghana*, Cambridge University Press.

MITCHELL, J. C. (1959), 'The causes of labour migration', *Bulletin of the Inter-African Labour Institute*, vol. 6, pp. 12–47.

NYERERE, J. K. (1967), *Socialism and Rural Development*, Dar es Salaam; reprinted in J. K. Nyerere, *Freedom and Socialism: Uhuru na Ujamaa*, Oxford University Press, 1968.

SAUL, J. S. (1971), 'Marketing co-operatives in a developing country', in P. Worsley (ed.), *Two Blades of Grass*, Manchester University Press.

WOLF, E. R. (1966), *Peasants*, Prentice-Hall.

10 Boguslaw Galeski

Social Organization and Rural Social Change

Excerpts from Boguslaw Galeski, 'Social organization and rural social change', *Sociologia Ruralis*, vol. 8, 1968, nos. 3–4, pp. 258–81. Abridged by the author.

Organizational Transformation in Agricultural Production

As in the past, there are two main types of agricultural production in the contemporary epoch – two institutions or chief forms of organization of production. One is the family farm, and the other the large agricultural enterprise which today resembles the industrial enterprise based on a unit of workers who do not constitute a family.

The various kinds of farm organization existing today, constituting variants of these two basic modes of agricultural production, arose on the basis of analogical types of the past, which persist today as relics in some countries. These past types are the *latifundium*, or plantation, and the peasant family farm. Alongside organizational forms which may be regarded as transformations of the above two basic former modes of agricultural production, there also appear today distinct specific forms. These are first, reliquary forms of group economy: the tribal or consanguinity group investigated chiefly by ethnologists. These may be regarded as particular forms of family economy, in which the family organization is also of a particular kind, older than the traditional peasant or latifundial form and generally preceding the latter historically in the world's main regions. Secondly, there are forms of group agriculture based on ideological ties which are generally not composed of farmers (peasants). Their aim is to realize some religious, social, political or national mission. Among them are to be found certain agrarian communities founded by religious groups in the United States of North America, while the most complex of this type is the Israeli *kibbutz* which is of unusual interest to the sociologist as a social experiment. But the *kibbutz* cannot be regarded as a transformation of peasant or latifundial farming, although they indicate some common features with large agricultural enterprises. Both the reliquary forms of tribal economy and the agrarian community based on ideological ties lie at the periphery of the modern transformation of agricultural production, if we exclude the Chinese commune (this organizational form is not viable enough to be considered in this paper and treated as anything more than an element of the revolutionary process of extinction of previous forms).

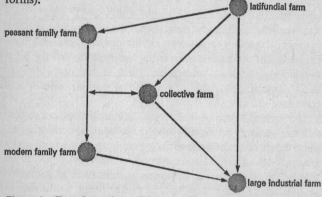

Figure 1   Transformations of the organizational units of agricultural production

If we ignore the above cited reliquary and marginal forms, the following transformations of the social organization of agricultural production may be distinguished:

1. The disintegration of a considerable part of the former *latifundia*, also plantations or manorial estates, and the emergence of peasant farming based on the family labour, as a result of agrarian reform.

2. The transformation of traditional peasant farms, and partly of the pre-peasant group farming, into multi-family collective peasant farming, the collective farms arising also on the ground of disintegrated former *latifundia*.

3. The transformation of the traditional peasant farm into the modern family farm having the character of an enterprise but based on family labour.

4. The emergence of large farms resembling industrial enterprises and based on wage labour, partially on the basis of former manorial estates, of some highly productive family farms and some multi-family collective farms.

These four types seem to exhaust the basic evolution of agriculture. One may point, of course, to numerous regions where the *latifundia* or the traditional peasant farm remain untouched by any of the transformations indicated here. But these are rather exceptional situations and their continued existence in the near future is hard to forecast. The above enumerated types of transformation cannot be regarded though as different evolutionary continua, isolated or independent of each other. A somewhat closer characterization of each of them justifies the assumption that they differ from each other with regard to the possibility of further transformation. And this leads to the conclusion that they can be conceived as a continuum of unidirectional change, and even as different forms of the same general evolutionary process.

Thus, the former *latifundia* may in favourable socio-economic situations be transformed into a large industrial-type enterprise, or undergo parcellation into small peasant farms based on family labour, sometimes also into part-time farms. The new peasant farms emerging from agrarian reform are either joined into multi-family collective farms or are modernized and changed into types of contemporary small agricultural enterprises connected with family labour. Some of them may be further transformed into industrial-type farms. This continuum hence represents the potentially greatest possibility for transformation. Other types do not possess such marked possibilities. For nowhere is the industrial-type farm converted into a *latifundia*, nor is the enterprise-type family farm changed into the traditional peasant farm. The multi-family peasant collective farm is marked by a certain elasticity. Under given conditions it may serve as a transitional form for family farms as a result of agrarian reform

(Schiller, 1966). Or it may be a germ of a large agricultural enterprise. This is therefore the only reversible form, i.e. family farms may be converted into a multi-family peasant collective farm, while the collective farm may be transformed into family farms. Although the changes are essentially of a general nature, the unidirection may take different paths and they have thus far effected the emergence of two basic forms of the present day: the modernized family farm and the industrial farm. But a one-sided relation should be noted between these two basic con-temporary farms, namely, while there are cases of the conversion of the modernized family farm into an industrial farm, change in the reverse direction is a rather exceptional phenomenon.

Terms requiring explanation have been used in reference to the character of the interrelations between different organizational types of agricultural production and their transformations – which have led to the view that they may be conceived in many aspects or as a unidirectional process of change, on a more extended historical scale, in the social organization of production. We now proceed to explain these terms while more broadly considering the mechanism of the transformations described. [. . .]

Thus the traditional peasant farm and the latifundial farm denote a continuum of intermediate forms defined according to the degree and proportions of economic and non-economic dependency of the peasant families to the owner (manager) of a large farm. The latifundial and industrial farms occupy extreme places on the scale constructed according to the degree of economic and socio-political dependence of the producers on the enterprise, and according to the structure of the manpower which rests on family groups or on workers of given professional specializations. The traditional peasant farm and the modern family farm occupy places on the scale according to the degree of separation of the domestic family economy from the agricultural enterprise, as well as to the character and intensity of the family's productive functions. The modern family farm and the industrial farm are designated on a scale according to the size of the enter-prise and the professional or family character of the labour. A separate place is occupied by the collective-type farming, which constitutes an intermediate phase between industrial farming and traditional, or modern, family farming, depending on the system of relations between the producing family and the collective farm.[. . .]

Definition of the collective farm as a multi-family peasant farm requires further elucidation. This definition is only partially true, for, as we shall see below, there are various socio-organizational forms of collective farming. Actually, the definition pertains primarily to countries of mass collectivization. The basic groups of collective farm members come from traditional peasant farms. The adoption of the organizational pattern of the Soviet *kolkhoz* essentially represents a compromise between the large agricultural enterprise conception, functioning in a non-market economic system, and the association of the small peasant family farms which are limited in area but not in respect to some production assortments. The family plot is furthermore subjected to the economic incentives of a limited, but nevertheless existing market (in the USSR – the producers' bazaar market). In this situation both tendencies are possible: (a) the intensification and even technical modernization of the small family farm, with the consequence of the collective farm being converted into an enterprise supplementing and servicing the former; and (b) the consolidation and expansion of the large collective agricultural enterprise and limitation of the role of the members' private plots to serving the family domestic economy.

But the definition of the collective farm as a multi-family peasant farm is not limited to the fact that the members' plots retain the character of petty family farms. There are also elements of family farming in the organization of a common enterprise, namely, the family constitutes the labour team and is involved in a number of acts of accounting, in money and in products, with the enterprise. The social structure of the collective farm may most often be conceived as a hierarchy of families' positions on the income, prestige and power scales. These traits naturally co-appear in the collective farm with the characteristics of an industrial enterprise, i.e. as a professional and not as a family type of organization of the labour, where the remuneration system is based on work norms and the hierarchy on the division of labour, function and decision making. The co-existence in collective farming of two organizational principles, which are in certain respects contradictory, renders a transitional character to the collective farm. It creates the alternative of its transformation either into an aggregate of small family farms or into an industrial type enterprise, although the second alternative is to be expected in the long range.

The above characterized continuum of the organizational transformation of 'the farm' has direct implications for change in the remaining two elements forming the system of rural life: the rural family and village community institutions.

The Rural Family and Village Community

Many of the characteristics differentiating the rural from the urban family are expressed quantitatively, by differences of degree. The rural family is noted, for instance, for a comparatively higher birth rate and larger number of children. It is also distinguished as a highly compact group (attested, among other things, by the lower divorce frequency), which has to a greater extent retained the patriarchal, and not the partnership relation among the consorts, as between the parents and the children. It furthermore fulfils the socialization functions on a wider range. Representing differences of degree, these characteristics may be interpreted as denoting retarded processes of modern changes in the family. The cause of these processes progressing more slowly in the rural world might be attributed to the traits of the family farm which impose a certain pattern on the rural family. However, besides the above enumerated differences in the degree and intensity of some social changes, there seems to be another trait which basically differentiates the rural from the urban family. That trait is the rural family's productive function. For the rural family is a collective producer, sometimes also a collective entrepreneur and common owner of a small plant producing the main means of existence, directly serving family consumption. This assures the family's relative autonomy to a considerable degree. It is furthermore the kind of production plant which represents a particular pattern of organization of the labour process. For it presupposes a production team composed of individuals of given age and sex, corresponding to the family demographically. Involved here, of course, is the traditional peasant farm based on the identification of the family and the production plant (Chayanov, 1925). Each of the modern organizational forms of agricultural production presumes a different type of relation to the family or a different range and intensity of the family's productive functions.

The productive functions of a peasant family connected with the *latifundium* are most often reducible to labour on the estate. Someone else directs its labour, the family members are subordinated to outsiders who stand above the internal family hierarchy. The family's relations with its neighbours are to a great extent that of equals, but this is of secondary importance, because of the basic dependence of each family on the *latifundium* owner or on the apparatus of management and supervision of labour subordinated by him. Besides the biological, other functions, such as the economic operation of the domestic economy (sometimes expanded to a larger or smaller farm under family usufruct), the educative and cultural, are dictated by the degree of intervention by the *latifundium* owner or overseer. The patriarchal pattern of relations between the family member is strengthened or weakened by the organization of the labour process in the *latifundium*. The norms and standards internalized by children in the family in the process of socialization, characterizing the ideal producer, also depends on the system of relations between it and the overseer or owner, and take either the direction desired by him or the opposite one. But these are standards characterizing either an obedient or a rebellious producer, not the entrepreneur. Of course, this schematic model does not exclude the appearance of old historical patterns among families tied to the latifundial system, or of traits characteristic of petty share tenantry – if the *latifundium* organization contains such elements.

The traditional peasant family is widely discussed in the literature and there is no need to repeat what is already known (Znaniecki, 1938, p. 1). It suffices to indicate that the productive function of the peasant family has a wider range than that of peasant families subordinated to a *latifundium* owner. For it includes management of the farm besides production. Its organizational pattern is hence shaped to the best fulfilment of family needs. The traditional peasant family's productive functions are organically linked with the totality of its economic, socializing and cultural functions. And the management pattern affects family cohesion and a patriarchal model of relations between its members which hampers individualization of attitudes. The important goal of the family's endeavours becomes not to make its vegetation as productive as possible but to increase its property, of which, in its conception, it has a temporary usufruct. The property is continuous, the generations are changing. Finally, the relations of the family as an entity with the neighbours assume a basic importance.

The modern family farm was characterized above as based on the labour of the family. But here the family's productive functions are considerably limited as compared with the traditional peasant farm. With a higher level of mechanization the farmer's wife and young children are relieved of farm work. While in the traditional peasant farm the family is first of all a production unit, in the modern family farm it is primarily a small entrepreneur's family helping with the work of mainly sharing in the management of the common property, the small agricultural enterprise. The organizational pattern of the modern family farm makes the family wide open to modern changes, weakens the patriarchal system of relation, facilitates individualized attitudes in some spheres and renders it less dependent on relations with neighbours, expanding the family's contacts beyond the local community.

In the big industrial farm there is a weakening, or even a complete severance, of identification of farm and family. The family of the owner, or owners, of the farm manager and of the producers on different levels of the professional hierarchy do not have to maintain greater contact with the farm than the family of a steel worker, of the director or stock holder in a steel corporation with the steel mill. Naturally, the proximity, the small team involved, etc. as a rule enable a more frequent and closer contact between the family and the place of work, but this contact is not imposed by the organizational form of production. Consequently, the family has no productive function in this type of enterprise and the differences between it and the urban family are reduced to lesser opportunities than are enjoyed by the urban dwellers to follow changes offered by modern civilization.

An integrated summary of the various organizational forms of agricultural production and their effects on the functions of the rural family indicates the following three types: (a) the producing family; (b) the enterprise conducting family; and (c) the producer (worker) family, detached from the production establishment, which corresponds to the general family pattern in the urban world. Naturally, the rural family pattern in most countries reflects the co-existence of two or even of all the above described types. However, they represent different and contrary organizational principles. The growth of one trait at the expense of the others indicates the processes occurring in parallel both in the farm and in rural family institutions. While the emphasis here is on the implications of the organization of production for changes in the pattern of the rural family, it is evident that the relation is two-sided. Both the farm and the family undergo transformation primarily under the influence of general economic, social and cultural processes. But if some element of this cohesive system – family farm – undergoes some change, there is a corresponding change in another element.

Connected with the 'family-farm' system is a third element of rural social organization which constitutes a specific feature of the rural world, namely, the village community. A number of characteristics of this community, such as its size and population density (Sorokin, Zimmerman and Galpin, 1965, pp. 239–40), are connected with the nature of agricultural production in which area plays a different role compared to that in non-agricultural production. This is so even if these characteristics indicate a connexion with the type of organization of production. A large agricultural establishment presumes the existence of comparatively small settlements if the type of production or the infra-structure precludes housing the producers outside the place of work in large urban type settlements. Family farming requires a relatively larger number of settlements, depending on the production type and the size structure of the farms. But the type of the organization of production determines to a greater extent such traits of the rural community as the system of stratification and social mobility, the patterns of inter-family relations and, in particular, economic relations, as well as the kind and degree of acceptance of cultural patterns, i.e. the extent to which the given community is open to the general national culture.

The local community connected with the *latifundium*-type farm expresses in its area structure a strongly polarized stratification and social barriers between the groups which are hard to surmount. The residence of the owner or overseer is as a rule isolated from the villagers, or village, from the groups of dwellings of the producers' (workers') families. The village inhabitants' basic economic and social relations are with the *latifundium* farm. Economic relations between the families of producers are weakly developed and of secondary importance, or they are connected with elements of group possession (woods, pastures). Or they may be working relations which arise if the families engage in extra farming on their account, as tenants. But the *latifundium* farming model does not in itself impose any system of relations on the families in the village besides mutual neighbourly family services or mutual aid in natural calamities. The service and power centres are also connected here with the latifundial residence. The uniform social status of the families inhabiting the villages and the relative social and cultural isolation (connected with the country's prevailing socio-economic conditions which constitute the essential context of the latifundial economy) imply homogeneous cultural patterns, distinct of course for the group of labourers and that of owners and overseers.

The village community corresponding to the traditional peasant farm gives birth to a more differentiated system of stratification and to a socio-economic system of relationships between the more well-to-do and poorer peasant families. The functions of the village community also become more varied while a division of labour takes shape within it. The service centres undergo change and rural co-operation emerges on the basis of the community's economic functions. The co-operatives become the community's economic representatives to the world outside. The political bodies connected with the various group interests and the local authority also change. However, this type of production is most often also characterized by cultural uniformity, while the community's behavioural patterns are penetrated by the system of social stratification in these villages.

Modern family farming does not imply the existence of a village community. One of the important measures for improving agricultural production is usually land consolidation which disperses the community. Of course, the regional administrative unit which embraces a certain number of single farmsteads, and creates a small rural administrative and service centre, may be conceived as a rural community. But the inhabitants of such a region do not constitute a group with cumulative social ties. In this type of production both the occupational and class stratification is more advanced and the possibilities for social mobility are greater. The system of inter-family economic, social and cultural relations is considerably weaker in such villages and gives way to relations over and beyond local bounds. This is synonymous with the community being more open to the growth of differentiated patterns and cultural standards.

Nor does industrial farming presuppose the existence of a village community. The producers and the managers, and their families, and in the conditions of private enterprise also their owners may live in an urban-type settlement of a differentiated socio-occupational structure. But even if they reside close to the place of work, such settlements differ only in respect to size, population density, and the traits which these factors imply, from those inhabited by factory workers or miners who live in the proximity of the factories or the mines.

The collective farm, having arisen on the grounds of the former village community, generally constitutes its continuation. The traits of such a community are even reinforced by the fact that the families living there are workers and co-owners of a common enterprise. Moreover, on the one hand the stratification system in these villages, primarily according to economic power and prestige, affects the informal structure of the working force in the enterprise, or, on the other hand, the stratification system, functional and occupational, changes the system of stratification in the village and creates conflicts within it.

Just as the types of organization of production may be conceived as one unidirectional continuum of transformation –

despite the polymorphism of change – so can the remaining elements of rural life, namely, the rural family and village community. There is no indication that the modern rural family was ever converted into a traditional rural family (in the meaning accepted here), nor of the village community having rejuvenated itself. On the contrary, observation reveals a currently stable tendency towards the separation of the family and the farm, and towards the withering away of the farmer's productive functions (where the consequence is not a sharp conflict between the family's productive and growing social, cultural functions) (Markowska, 1964) as well as the blurring of distinctions between the rural and the urban family. Also observable are the rising vocational and social differentiations among village inhabitants, the expansion of contacts beyond the local community, the dislodgment of local standards and cultural patterns by those common for society as a whole. Except for size and population density, the differences are diminishing between the village and the urban type settlement, while the emerging, larger rural local entities are of a polycentric character linking in one region various social groups based on various ties. [. . .]

In conceiving the farm, family and local community as one integral whole we had to make reservations here and there when distinguishing the forms of rural social organization and the types of transformation which they undergo. We had to point out that this is not an isolated, closed system, and that the source of change in each of these elements, hence of the system as a whole, lies in its relation to the general economic, social and cultural system of the given country. The limits and tempo of changes of rural social organization are furthermore determined by general conditions (technical level, demographic structure, etc.) of which the type of organization, together with the entire economic, social and cultural system, is at the same time the product and co-creator. This paper does not deal exhaustively with these dynamic correlations, but considers only some of them.

Influence of the Interactive or Directive Economic Systems on Changes in the Rural Social Organization

Interactive and directive systems (Galeski, 1967) are distinguished by the manner of linking consumption with productive activity. In the system denoted here as directive, the producers are assigned tasks by central planning bodies. The tasks are evaluated and their performance is punished or rewarded. Distribution of the goods produced is directed by a corresponding economic apparatus on the basis of the same principles. The consumer may of course purchase one or another article within the choice offered by the distribution channels, although examples of obligatory purchasing are also known. This behaviour has no direct influence on producers' or distributors' activity. The planning body is always a mediating factor here. It is not obliged to reckon with consumers' reaction in its decisions, especially since the consumer cannot refrain from buying articles which are basic necessities.

Of course, the central body functions more or less efficiently and rationally. But assuring proper incentives to economic institutions and correct criteria for evaluating their functioning are difficult and complex matters, while an inflexibility to vascillate in the operation of the co-ordinating apparatus are constant sources of social tension. However, this is not the main trait of this system. It is rather the indirect character of the links between production, distribution and consumption, which are realized by means of a system of relations between each of these spheres and the central planning and co-ordinating bodies.

In the second system, denoted here as interactive, productive activity and demand come into direct contact on the market. Consumers' behaviour is the direct source of reward or punishment for the producers. Satisfaction of demand is the condition for realizing the production process and this determines producers' opportunities. Naturally, the latter try to shape demand by introducing new goods, by advertising and price manipulation, thus modifying or creating new patterns of consumption. But the spontaneous adaptation of production to demand threatens cyclical recession, the squandering of labour and periodic economic chaos, side by side with the highly advanced specialization and rationalization of production on the enterprise level.

The above economic systems are ideal models which do not exist today in pure form. What is more, the directive system prevailing in the socialist countries is now being modified by the introduction of elements of interaction to a greater or lesser extent. The interactive type, universal in the capitalist countries, has also been modified by state intervention in the form of investment, regulating enterprise capacity, as well as the levels of prices, wages, etc. But there are still important differences between the two systems, despite these modifications, which cannot simply be defined as differences between the socialist and capitalist economic systems. Undoubtedly, the principle of private ownership of the means of production makes it very difficult to introduce a directive system, while the socialization of the means of production not only makes it easy but is directly inducive to the introduction of such a system. However, the two systems may appear under the conditions of both, the private and state ownership of the means of production (though with certain modifications). Economic control may be exercised not only by direct orders but also through steered processes of interaction.

The two economic systems bear many-sided social implications in the spheres of structure, patterns of social mobility, types of inter-personal relations (of the superior–subordinate and seller–client types), and for the sources and direction of social conflict. Their direct and indirect influence on rural social organization is therefore also many-sided.

In general, industrial farming is more frequent under the conditions of a directive system and so is collective farming (conceived as a transitional form of industrial farming), while the family farm is the basic form of the interactive system. But there are examples of collective farms in the interactive system (not to speak of industrial farms) as well as cases of the co-existence of the directive system and family farming, either traditional or modern, though with a modification of the system.

But the following question arises here. Is our frame of reference the same social mechanism and content of change when we assert analogical phenomena in these two different social systems? For instance, the appearance of collective farming, industrial farming or of continua of change, such as the transformation of the traditional peasant farm into the modern family farm.

Starting from the observation of collective forms of production in different parts of the globe and in disparate social systems (Schiller, 1966), we distinguish four varied situations in which this form appears. The first is where the principle of collective farming rests on the desire to realize given ideals (religious, political, patriotic), or to put it differently, on motivations of a religious, social, political (for example, egalitarian ideology) nature, or of a national character, i.e. serving the national aim to husband given territories. Some religious agrarian communities in the USA, the Israeli *kibbutz*, as well as some of the first communes established in the Soviet Union immediately after the revolution are of this nature. The collective farm based on these principles may be dismissed from further consideration since it is strictly speaking not a movement of farmers who desire to transform their farms and live in that manner. Even if small groups of farmers' families engage in this kind of initiative, these are marginal groups and the possibility of their attracting other farmers by example is insignificant, as is the possibility of this structure maintaining itself for an extended period either in the directive or interacting system.

The second situation is the emergence of collective farms as a result of agrarian reform, i.e. when producing families take over the lands of former *latifundia* and when landless peasant families settle on hitherto unused fallow lands. In both cases, families who thus obtain land are experienced as productive labour in agriculture, but they lack experience in independent farm operation. These families are as a rule favourably inclined to maintain the former farm *in toto*, or to take over land in larger compact groups and to farm together. But agrarian reform is not limited to distributing land. As a rule, investment is also necessary so that the land may be properly husbanded and the producers assured of a rapid improvement in living conditions. The needs are still greater in the case of new settlements on hitherto fallow land. Investment and credit, various kinds of state material aid, as well as agricultural instruction are necessary here. Under the conditions of an interactive system the situation may be regarded as transitional. As the farm becomes economically stronger, and in measure with the acquisition of experience, independent operation of a private farm becomes more attractive than collective farming with its internal conflicts and the need to adjust oneself to others. In consequence, the more efficient producers soon leave the farm. Under the directive system, the incentives to independent farming may be so weak, and the possibility of separating oneself from large-scale common farming may be so difficult to realize, that the collective farms hold on for a long time while the families involved adapt themselves to the situation.

The third situation prevails when the state, by means of the necessary socio-techniques, carries out the universal collectivization of peasant farms. From doctrinal and political considerations the most frequent motive for adopting such a decision is the industrialization of the country which requires either internal accumulation by means of tight control of the peasant population's consumption level (where industrialization requirements are as a rule drastic, with the peasantry constituting the majority of the population), or the shifting of considerable manpower from agriculture to industry. Such collectivization can be accomplished only under the conditions of a directive economic system where the idea of agricultural consolidation is in accord with the characteristics of that system.

Of course, it is possible to conceive consolidation on the industrial-type farm. But its realization may effect sharp social conflicts and burden the state with heavy investments. It would also require directing a corps of specialists to agriculture, which would not be suitable to the conditions of a country where agriculture has to bear the burden of industrialization while it simply has no specialists. Collective farming, under these circumstances, represents a compromise, and it attempts to convert itself into industrial-type farming in measure with the conditions and possibilities of a given country. The collectivized producers make use of this fact by intensifying production on the plots of which they have usufruct, with the desire to rebuild individual peasant farms and to convert the collective farms into auxiliary enterprises.

The fourth situation appears in the system of extended interaction. Here the large farm has a decided superiority over the small because of the lower costs of production. Under a market economy the smaller enterprise is as a rule impelled to enlarge. There is hence a permanent tendency for the emergence of industrial farms from family farms. This may take place by some family farmers expanding (by means of purchasing or renting additional land, increasing operating capital, hiring labour) at the expense of the bankruptcy of others. This evolution is naturally slow for it is often retarded by agrarian policy, which under farmers' pressure is calculated in many countries to support the economically weak family farm. There is also the possibility of large farming units arising not from the liquidation of family farms but by several farmers merging their land, capital and labour reserves. This leads to the potential possibility of the emergence of collective farms in economically developed countries of the interactive system. Organizational experience of this type (with the French G A E C, for instance) is still very meagre. But there is every indication that such organizations with collective traits will be very unstable for two reasons. First, because of the action of centrifugal forces, i.e. the unavoidable difficulties of adaptation of the collective's members and the constant need for re-decision whether to retain collective farming, particularly with changing generations. Secondly, because of the play of external forces, i.e. the considerable alternatives in the conditions of an interactive system to adjust to a small farm. Such an organization may partly or entirely lose its collective character: partly, when the task of directing the enterprise is left to one member while the role of the others is limited to co-ownership (of land, or capital); entirely, when they are in general eliminated from the enterprise. One way or other, collective farms in the interactive system, established by family farmers, turn into industrial farms operated by a company or a single entrepreneur (or owner).

Examination of the various situations in which collective farming arises inclines one to the view that this organizational form serves in an interactive system, either as a temporary means to husband land acquired from agrarian reform, or, on newly settled land, preceding the formation of modern family farming; or it is one of the roads (thus far a subordinated one) to the transformation of modern family farming into industrial farming. In the directive economic system this organizational form serves as an instrument of control over the agricultural producers in the interests of the economy as a whole. It is transitional in this system, regarded as a compromise by the directing centres whose objective is to transform it into industrial farming (as defined in this paper). Among the collective farm producers there is on the other hand a tendency to take advantage of the compromise by subordinating this organizational form to the family farm in the shape of the private allotment which is limited in area but is productively developing. The collective farming system, and its growing into industrial farming, are naturally strongly favoured by external factors in the directive economic system.

Although collective farming is more frequent in the directive system, this phenomenon also appears under certain conditions in the interactive economic system (though with a different content). So do modern family farming and transformation processes of these organizational forms appear in both systems, although they are proper to the interactive one.

The conversion of the traditional family farm into a family conducted enterprise takes place under the conditions of a market economy which impels specialization, increased marketable production and the lowering of costs. By undermining the autarchy of the traditional family farm, the market makes it dependent on contractors, primarily in the field of outlets for produce and of credit. In terms of the penetration of agriculture by capital seeking effective investment areas (which leads to the growth of the division of labour) the previous activity of the peasant family becomes the foundation of specialized enterprises.

The family limits itself to a phase of production: raising raw materials (fodder, for example) or to the processing of a given raw material (converting fodder into meat, for instance). Other phases of the productive cycle are undertaken by specialized enterprises. The enterprise is also an intermediary in the transfer, most often accompanied by conversion, of raw material from one family farm to another. This process has been called the vertical integration of agriculture, or more precisely, vertical integration is one of the chief elements of the process. It embraces both family farms and industrial farms, but the degree of limitation of the producer-enterpriser's area of decision is less in the second case.

With reference to the family farm this process may be defined as the emergence of 'manufacture in agriculture', if that term is understood as the organization of production based on domestic family labour (on its own or consigned material) on behalf of an enterprise engaged in marketing products, and at times also in the finishing phases of production and the preparation of articles for sale. Agricultural 'manufacture' also involves a certain number of producers, the producing families, linked with a large organizational unit by means of contracting with a processing and marketing enterprise (or enterprises). The difference consists in: (a) the fact that the family farm produces articles of basic consumption and hence has the possibility of supplying its own family; (b) the tools and often also the basic means of production, the land, are the property of the producers; and (c) the farming family conducts highly diversified activity and is connected with contractors not only of one but generally of many enterprises which specialize in processing and marketing given products and of providing certain services to the producers. These differences make it difficult to predict the rapid conversion of the agricultural manufacturing organization into an organization analogous to industry. All the more so since, as indicated, the industrial farm too is most often linked with the above characterized organization.

The existence of individual family farms in countries with a directive economic system has introduced to that system the elements of interactive relations between agriculture and other divisions of the national economy. True, these elements are weakened by the system of obligatory deliveries, the administrative distribution of production in short supply (possession of the sufficient means is not enough for their purchase, it is necessarily an administrative decision also) as well as by a number of government regulations making certain activities obligatory for farmers.

Still, as long as there are elements of interaction, the organization of agricultural manufacture based on the contracting system must ensue. One essential difference here is that the farmer actually deals with the agents of a big trust organization upon which he is furthermore dependent in extra-economic spheres, mainly in the administrative and political spheres. Rural co-operatives, autonomous local bodies and farmers' professional mutual aid associations become agencies of this organization.

It follows from the above that the organization of agriculture on a manufacturing basis possesses considerably greater possibilities under these conditions to subordinate the producers and to create advanced forms of vertical integration.

Transformation of Rural Social Organization in Perspective

The view is widespread that the industrial mode of production will dominate in the agriculture of the future. And as a consequence that: (a) agricultural articles will be produced in large organizational units by professionally differentiated working forces; (b) the rural family will lose its productive functions which have thus far determined its specific traits in relation to the urban family; and (c) the basis for the distinction between the urban and rural community will disappear and settlements will emerge which differ only in size and in the degree of intensity of one or another function. The reasoning of the present paper neither negates nor confirms the above view, though it acknowledges a common general direction of change. This most certainly flows from the fact that economic growth is proceeding everywhere on the globe, though at different rates and with interruptions caused by war and political upheavals. However, in asserting a general direction of change in rural social organization emphasis should be placed on the polymorphism of this change. This follows primarily from the level of economic and social development, chiefly expressed in the degree of industrialization, which determines the demographic and occupational structures as well as the population's cultural level. Connected with the level of economic development is the rural social organization which provides an additional foundation for further transformation. Secondly, of unusual importance here, though to a considerable degree determined by the previous factors, is the character of the economic system as a whole, the nature and direction of industrialization as well as of the links between production, distribution and consumption.

These are of course not the only, nor the only important factors in the total picture of the organizational transformation of agriculture. But they take pride of place and are mainly referred to in describing the polymorphism of change. The question arises: what of the perspective? The industrial-type (as defined here) is the most anticipated, but as a large industrial enterprise, based on wage labour in the form prevailing today, it retains in many countries considerable remnants of a feudal economy. It moreover represents a production type of relatively low skill with little chance of playing a dominant role in the future. It seems paradoxical that modern technology, by raising the productivity of the family farm at an exceptional tempo and by creating the possibility of a family operating a farm of optimum size for many branches of agricultural production, should provide the basis for the expectation that the family farm will continue to exist in the future. But these farms will be linked with the organization of production on the basis of manufacture, which will certainly acquire in time a more definitely shaped and stable structure. Other organizational forms of agricultural production, the latifundial farm and the traditional peasant family farm (not to speak of the pre-peasant relics of group economy) are passing into history in line with economic development.

As seen above, collective farming is a transitional form which appears particularly as a consequence of agrarian reform, or where there is an attempt to subordinate the agricultural producers to the needs of industrialization. Playing different roles depending on the characteristics of the system and conditions, this form leads either to modern family farming, to industrial farming or to intermediate organizational forms. However, because of the social difficulties connected with collective farming, with various conflicts, it is difficult to foresee its future. Perhaps new, autonomous forms of producers' organization will arise on its foundations connected with the industrial-type farming, which will make collective farming more attractive. Nor is there any doubt that this form will appear also in the future where it is a matter of husbanding new lands and where centralized investment is made in agriculture. Although we regard it as a transitional form it may still play a positive role.

The transformation of the organization form of agricultural production induces many mutually conditioning social changes. These are changes in the type of agricultural producer, and there is a transition here also from the working family in the direction of professionally skilled producers (of various specializations) and organizers. The type of future agricultural specialist is circumscribed by the variability of organizational forms of production, but the level of skill is undoubtedly rising. The dissimilarity of organizational forms of production also reacts on the social system, primarily on the system of vocational stratification and on the channels and intensity of social mobility, but also on the farm family's productive function (which will generally decline), on local social norms and habits, on their proximity to urban-type society.

Finally, the forms of rural social organization are connected, as mutual determinants, with global social organization. Growing links may be anticipated between agriculture and the general economic system, and hence the fuller integration of the farming population in the social system as a whole. The emergence of differential spheres of activity of industrial-agricultural enterprises, connecting the family farm with the system of industrial producers and services, is also to be expected. Such spheres will constitute bridges between agriculture and the organizational forms proper to it, and other branches of the economy.

However, the directions of change indicated here do not provide an image of a uniform, world-wide social organization of agriculture. The variegated organizational forms, conditions which render different social contents to these forms and the diverse systems with which these forms are in symbiosis, project the need for seeing the future social organization in agriculture being at least as polymorphous as it is today. Nor is it excluded that future technical development in agriculture may basically confound our prognosis. But such a change, not consistent with our anticipations, would project new fundamental organizational problems for society as a whole, of which the change in rural social organization would constitute only a small part of the question of how to set in motion new sources and directions of change.

References

CHAYANOV, A. V. (1925), *Organizatsiya krest'yanskogo khozyaistva*. Translated as *The Theory of Peasant Economy*, D. Thorner, R. E. F. Smith and B. Kerblay (eds.), Irwin, 1966.

GALESKI, B. (1967), 'Typy uprzemyslowienia', *Studia Socjologiczne*, vol. 4, no. 27, Ossolineum, Wroclaw.

MARKOWSKA, D. (1964), *Rodzina w srodowisku wiejskim*, Ossolineum, Wroclaw.

SCHILLER, O. (1966), *Gemeinschaftsformen im landwirtschaftlichen Produktionsbereich*, DLG Verlag, Frankfurt am Main.

SOROKIN, P. A., ZIMMERMAN, C. C., and GALPIN, C. J. (1965), *A Systematic Source Book in Rural Sociology*, Russell & Russell.

ZNANIECKI, F. (1938), 'Socjologiczne podstawy ekologii ludzkiej', *Ruch Prawniczy, Ekonomiczny i Socjologiczny*, vol. 18, Warsaw.

Part Two The Peasantry as an Economy

Part Two traces the processes of production, exchange and consumption typical of those social structures where the peasant family farm and the peasant village are the major units of social interaction. Dumont's contribution opens this Part by considering agriculture as the 'cornerstone' of peasant economy. Kerblay follows, discussing Chayanov's contribution to the analysis of the peasant household as a crucial economic unit. The social division of labour, in the broad sense attached to it by Adam Smith (1776), forms the key to an understanding of development and structural change in peasant economies. Aspects of it are discussed by Nash in his analysis of peasant markets, by Robinson in his description of peasant crafts and by Galeski's discussion of farming and its professionalization. (Franklin's contribution in Part One will also be relevant here.) Nash also touches on some of the mechanisms of economic equalization, which occasionally thwarts economic polarization and attempts at capitalist development of peasant economies. Thorner's article endeavours to place the peasant economy in a historical setting; both Kerblay and Thorner stress the specific character of peasant economy – for an opposite point of view, see Ortiz (p. 322) and the Further Reading list. The issue of agricultural labour and the development of modern capitalist and/or large-scale farming are at least partly covered by the contributions from Feder and Galeski respectively, in Part One. A major area unfortunately omitted here, for lack of space, is the place of money, small credit and usury in the peasant economy.

Political economy forms one of the major aspects of peasant social life and is an important, in many cases crucial, dimension of its development. It forms also a connecting link between the subject matter of this Part, its predecessor and the following one. By political economy we mean domination of man by man through the control of the means of production and distribution. The issue of land tenure in peasant societies is decisive, in this respect. Lacking a concise treatment of this subject Feder's and Pearse's contributions in Part One and Dore's discussion in Part Five partially provide a substitute. In this framework Preobrazhensky's study which completes Part Two, presents an analysis that is still valid of the alternatives open to the State and to the urban sections of the population in their relations with the peasantry in early periods of industrialization.

Reference

SMITH, A. (1776), *The Wealth of Nations*.

11 René Dumont

Agriculture as Man's Transformation of the Rural Environment

Excerpts from René Dumont, *Types of Rural Economy: Studies in World Agriculture*, Methuen, 1957, pp. 1–9. Translated by D. Magnin.

The principal aim of agriculture may be defined as follows: to supply mankind with food and with those raw materials which are of animal or vegetable origin (Dumont, 1949). Evidently some of these requirements can be provided in other ways and the earliest mode of subsistence was simply by gathering the products of untended nature. Today, fishing is still an invaluable resource, and together with hunting it still forms the mainstay of certain primitive economies. As late as 1936 there was an old peasant woman at Murols in the Auvergne, who gathered wild hazelnuts from the hedgerows, shelled them on the hearth and, after two months of spare-time work, produced three or four litres of 'wild' oil. Her only concession to progress was the use of an old mechanical press. There are few of us who have never gathered wild berries, picked dandelions from the meadows in the spring or mushrooms from the woods in the autumn. We have often, without realizing it – like Monsieur Jourdain – imitated the example of the old peasant woman.

The difference between mere collecting and agriculture is that the latter endeavours to modify the natural environment so as to secure the most favourable possible conditions for various useful species of plants and animals whose utility is further enhanced by a conscious process of selection. Agriculture tempers the extremes of the climate; with irrigation the farmer fights aridity; he houses his animals and protects his market gardens with frames and glass against wind and cold. Above all, agriculture modifies the soil. Unlike climate, this should not be regarded as part of the natural endowment of a region, the only exception being the case of certain virgin soils which have retained their original vegetation of grass or forest and which have provided the basis for pedological classification. Our own soils are highly artificial. In many cases they have been worked with plough and harrow for thousands of years, corrected for deficiencies and enriched with manure and every kind of fertilizer, natural and artificial.

Agricultural science is the practical farmer's consultant. Its domain is the whole range of organic life utilized by man. It raises the productivity of useful species by methods of selection which were once empirical but now rely increasingly on the science of genetics. It transforms the living conditions and, more particularly, the feeding of animals. Thus the stage of development of any rural economy can be estimated by noting the degree to which the natural environment has been changed and the techniques employed to this end.

In a region developed on an extensive basis, the original features are only slightly modified and are still very apparent. In the case of a pastoral economy, where the grazing animal forages – and concentrates – the natural produce of the grassland, there is no modification whatsoever and there is very little even in the permanent grasslands of Western Europe, to which the term 'natural' is often applied with good cause; indeed, as is still all too often the case in Normandy,[1] rational methods of management, with fertilizing and other forms of improvement, are on the whole unfortunately absent. So long as the soil is not actually worked, permanent grassland remains, in effect, natural grassland; in the strict sense of the term therefore it is not a form of agriculture, the symbols of which are the plough and 'ager', the ploughed field.

We must now examine the distinctions which are usually made between the two main methods of raising the level of agricultural productivity. Intensification aims primarily at high yields even if they are costly in terms of labour and the maintenance of soil capital (by means of improved seeds, fertilizers, etc., whereby biological processes are modified). This is the method which must be urgently applied in overpopulated areas where the overriding consideration is that the productivity of the scarce factor – that is, of the land – should be increased. The soil is

1. In Norway 'cultivated', i.e. fertilized, grasslands are classified separately.

cultivated repeatedly and with such minute attention that the commonest implements are often the rake and the spade; the land is heavily manured and the water resources are carefully husbanded. The net result is a greatly modified landscape, and a good example of an intensive system of this type, with high yields per unit of area, is found in a typical market garden, where the climate is completely artificial and the soil is transformed by massive additions of fertilizing substances. The same practices, though to a lesser degree, can be recognized in the Spanish *huertas*; here, however, the climate is extremely favourable.

At the other end of the scale, mechanization aims at cutting down labour and increasing its productivity. In every type of operation, cultivating and harvesting included, human energy is replaced as far as possible by the work of animals and the power of machines. The hand tool is replaced by the motorized implement. The combine-harvester does all the work which previously was performed by scythe and sickle, flail and winnowing basket. It is in sparsely populated regions such as the 'new countries' that this type of mechanization is most needed, for, contrary to the general situation elsewhere, these are sometimes afflicted by a dearth of men on the land, and the special attribute of the machine is that it increases the farm-worker's daily output.[. . .]

Whether it be farm, estate or collective, it is the individual undertaking which, by its work on the land – present and past – turns the forces of nature to advantage. For the most part, however, agriculture is still the domain of the family enterprise and is therefore carried on by a great multitude of highly dispersed units of production, some of them quite small and many of them very small indeed. The provision of machinery is thus inherently more difficult and costly than in manufacturing industry, where the trend is for ever-increasing concentration, while the discontinuous use of farm equipment heightens the contrast still further.

In some advanced types of economy, both capitalist and collectivist, the scale of agricultural enterprise is being increased, though more rapidly in some areas than in others. This is a significant trend; it is generally accompanied by the introduction of an appreciable volume of machinery and agriculture is therefore brought into line, in certain important respects, with manufacturing industry. In dealing with a particular type of farming, we shall therefore give some indication of the average size of the undertakings concerned. For instance, in the capitalist world, the family enterprise is the rule, and it gives ample proof of vitality when there is no shortage of space or of capital, as in the United States.

The farm unit operates in the context of a legal system which regulates the appropriation and disposal of the various factors of production, including the land. It also determines the farmer's relationship with the moneylender, banker or financier and, if he does not own the land himself, with his landlord. The law may either help or hinder the modernization and equipping of the countryside, but is notoriously slow in adjusting itself to technical developments and is, in consequence, rarely of much assistance. We shall indicate in outline some of the legal conditions which favour progressive farming.

Each individual farm is conditioned by its economic and social setting. Fertilizers, tractors and machines are the products of highly organized industries characterized by the efficient use of manpower and mass production methods, and commanding all the resources of modern technology. Apart from the natural environment of a region, therefore, its degree of industrialization stands out as the most important criterion in any evaluation of its agricultural future. Quite apart from the fact that it manufactures equipment for sale to the farmer, industry breaks down the barriers of self-sufficiency and precipitates the transition to a commercial economy by creating in its labour force a market for farm produce which, saving periods of depression, is well endowed with purchasing power.

Having already amassed a great fund of capital, an industrial region can the more easily continue to accrue its wealth. Moreover, increments generally accumulate more quickly in manufacturing industry and commerce than in agriculture, where the returns march in slow rhythm with the seasons. Thus, whereas the methods of former times demanded hard manual work most of all, today the farmer needs the modern tools of his craft, but almost inevitably lacks the means to buy them, and this is the most formidable obstacle which bars the way to rapid progress. The land is rarely short of hands, but very often it has neither capital nor machines.

The density of population is another important element in our analysis. When the density is high, the law of diminishing returns hinders the necessary intensification of production unless better techniques are constantly evolved and applied, but this is rarely the case in underdeveloped countries where research and education are both limited in their scope. In areas such as Spain and the Far East, where industrialization is still in a very early stage, there is the problem of finding useful outlets for the super-abundant labour of the countryside where low productivity is all too often the rule.

Where the density of population is very low, the problem of rapid development is one of finding enormous quantities of equipment as quickly as possible. But this is not always practicable, and there is always the risk that the materials will be mis-applied or used inefficiently, as may so easily happen, for example, in the administration of transport services.

A large part is also played by the educational system, and in this connexion standards of professional training are of particular significance, for successful intensive agriculture demands a very high level of competence. Whereas a large undertaking needs to fill only a small number of key posts, the proportion of highly qualified men needs to be very much greater when every farmer is the manager of his own small family enterprise.

When all these factors have been considered in turn, a clear picture will emerge of the conditions under which the farmer has to operate, and at this juncture it will be appropriate to study the broad features of his techniques of production; in a general survey such as this we cannot concern ourselves with the minutiae of his methods. We shall, however, attempt to classify various systems according to their degree of intensiveness, with particular emphasis on permanent improvements, such as schemes of drainage or irrigation, on the frequency of soil working and above all on methods of fertilization.

In some cases, no attempt whatsoever is made to fertilize the soil, and instances of this neglect are to be found in many primitive societies and even sometimes in those generally considered to be 'civilized', although here this adjective hardly seems appropriate. The next stage is when fertilization is practised sporadically; its value is hardly understood, and it exists mainly as a convenient method of waste disposal. In the final stage, soil enrichment, in one form or another, is practised consciously and for its own sake. So long as transport remains difficult and expensive, however, only the ground in the immediate vicinity of the home is affected. The first kind of fertilizer to be used is generally the residue of ashes from the hearth, and only later is the value of night soil, animal droppings, and plant remains, which are all available on the farm itself, fully appreciated. The most advanced stage of all is reached when fertilizers are brought in from outside the farm especially, when, like chemical fertilizers, they are the product of a factory process.

The degree of mechanization in an economy is indicated by the relative proportion of work done by hand, by animals, and by machines, respectively. A small proportion of manual labour obviously points to an advanced stage of development. In a primitive system, man is the beast of burden, but later he becomes a director of operations, driving the tractor which pulls or drives the machinery; furthermore, the efficiency of the latter in the performance of its highly specialized functions is constantly being improved. At the same time the need for equipment increases and fresh improvements are continually added to the work of the past.

The more he improves the physical environment, the greater is man's freedom in choosing the plants he wishes to cultivate. Having increased the volume and reliability of crop yields, he can also afford to add to his list of domestic animals. Thus, technically, he may select the precise combination he wishes to pursue[2] from a very large number of possible enterprises. In other words, he chooses a 'type' of agriculture or animal husbandry,[3] and the description of these types, together with the

2. But he is increasingly forced to produce at the lowest possible costs by economic factors.
3. Bergmann defines them in terms of: type of product (crop and animal) and factors of production employed (land, labour, capital).

varying rates at which they have been developed, is an integral part of the study of the different forms of rural economy with which they are associated.

In subsistence farming, where nothing is brought in from outside, there is generally an even greater variety of produce than in the primitive type of economy, where a wide range of necessities is supplied by collecting rather than by agriculture. Similarly, subsistence farming is more varied than modern commercial agriculture, which has grown up thanks to improvements in communications and methods of distribution – although the efficiency of the latter is more open to doubt. Commercial agriculture is free to specialize in one or several of the products best suited to the overall conditions.

Once certain crops have been selected, they will often be cultivated on the same land year after year, and the form of the rotation will be designed to make tillage and fertilizing as convenient and economical as possible. The sequence sugar-beet, wheat and barley, for instance, represented the basic rotation practised in Northern France during the latter part of the nineteenth and the early part of the twentieth centuries. Land utilization, on the other hand, is the proportion of a given area devoted to each crop: twenty-five acres of sugar-beet, twenty-five of wheat and twenty-five of barley in 1953–4, for example.

Type of farming, crop rotation system and land utilization are the appropriate criteria for the classification of modern rural economies. When properly balanced, they facilitate soil conservation and avoid extremes of seasonal labour demands. At one time, however, the same land was not cropped continuously, and even today in some backward areas periods of cultivation are separated by long intervals of fallow. Thus cultivation may be either continuous or intermittent, and the former is characteristic of all the more advanced kinds of farming, except in semi-arid regions.

In Africa and Asia especially the rearing of animals is still carried on by nomadic herdsmen who practise no form of agriculture whatsoever. They rely solely on the unimproved pastures and undertake seasonal migrations in areas where the climatic regime restricts plant growth at certain times of the year. Such an economy becomes more intensive as its interest in crop production increases; its animals then provide power for tilling the land and manure for fertilizing it.

Such a system is more productive and certain commodities plentiful at one time of the year can be stored for use when needed: hay, for example, bundles of leafy twigs and various other items culled from forest, steppe, scrub or low-lying marshland. Next, certain fields may be set aside for cattle and converted into permanent grassland. This, however, may be a retrograde step for it is often associated with a fall in productivity.

The introduction of rotation grasses, roots, kale and other fodder crops, however, always represents a very real advance, although even here, as in the case of direct food production, the intensiveness of the system will depend on how much the land is cultivated and fertilized. Later, the fodder crops may be supplemented by the purchase of feeding-stuffs – mostly industrial by-products and often rich in proteins – like cattle-cake, bran and offal. Finally comes the use of various substances, such as mineral salts and vitamins, advocated by modern science. Once this stage is reached, selective breeding can safely begin for, although pedigree animals are more delicate, the farmer is now in a position to give them the care and attention they need. It was during the eighteenth century that these techniques of selective breeding and large-scale fodder-crop cultivation began to be applied, first in England and later in the rest of Western Europe (Veyret, 1951).

Except in its very highly specialized forms – like pig-rearing and poultry-keeping, which rely almost wholly on purchases of feeding-stuffs – animal husbandry is generally an integral part of the modern type of farming system. The size of the animal population will, of course, determine the volume of fodder crops to be grown and the size of reserves needed to tide over the season of restricted plant growth. Apart from the Equatorial zone, a modern system of intensive farming should provide for a high density of animals in order to satisfy the growing demand for meat and milk derivatives from the more advanced and highly industrialized countries. The extent to which an agricultural system meets this need will enable us to evaluate its stage of development. On a number of occasions we have already pronounced most unfavourably on the position in regions which do not conform in this respect (density of cattle too low in the Paris Basin, for example).

The various ways in which different types of farming are carried on and the proportion in which the various factors of production are employed result in different levels of productivity. The effectiveness of a given type cannot be measured exactly, but estimates can be made in terms of yield per unit area or of yield per working day (productivity of labour). The number of working days required to produce a certain quantity of a specified crop can be used as a basis of comparison between the various kinds of rural economy, and the most representative unit is the hundredweight of grain.[4] But only large differences between the indices thus obtained are of any significance.

In a modern economy, agriculture can feed a large number of people while employing a relatively small labour force,[5] but although this feature is characteristic of the advanced countries the reverse is true of primitive economies. Except in countries like England which import large quantities of food, the efficiency of a nation's farming bears an inverse relationship to the proportion of the working population employed on the land. This, however, is only true if the soil is not being exploited wastefully. A further characteristic of modern farming, and of specialized farming in particular, is that the greater part of the produce is marketed. In a primitive economy, on the other hand, almost everything is consumed by the producer himself.

References

DUMONT, R. (1949), 'Observations monographiques sur quelques fermes et communes de France', *Bulletin de la Société française d'Économie Rurale*.
VEYRET, P. (1951), *La géographie de l'élevage*, Paris.

4. This is not to imply, as some have suggested without proof, that technical progress is limited to this type of product.

5. Food products make up about four-fifths of the world's agricultural output, by value. But industrial raw materials, and, foremost among them, textiles, must also be taken into account if a true picture of overall agricultural productivity is to emerge.

12 Basile Kerblay

Chayanov and the Theory of Peasantry as a
Specific Type of Economy

An original paper.

For some decades after its establishment in the 1870s the Russian
provincial administration (the *zemstva*) conducted a series of
detailed surveys of the peasantry, published in more than 4000
volumes. On the basis of this extensive literature there emerged a
flourishing school of agricultural economists who continued to
play an influential role in Russia up to the end of the NEP
in the 1920s. Their main aim was to help the peasant modernize
his farming techniques. In contrast with Populists and Marxists
both of whom saw the agrarian problem in terms of property
relations, they felt that land redistribution was an insufficient
palliative (and implied a social upheaval whose consequences
could not be predicted). They stressed the need to transform the
entire organization of peasant agriculture by a series of essentially
'Western' innovations such as co-operatives, stock selection and
the use of fertilizers etc. Hence the reason why they have been
called 'the organization and production school'. Among them
were A. Chelintsev, A. Chayanov, N. Makarov and many more.

Kossinsky (1906, p. 165)[1] and Brutskus (1913) of that group
were the first to contrast the peasant and capitalist economies
not so much on the political plane as on the plane of economic
theory.

But, it was Chayanov's genius to formulate, from *zemstva* data,

1. 'The peasant, by providing simultaneously land and labour, does not
differentiate the value created in the process of production between costs
of production and surplus value. All the value thus created returns to him
to be used as a whole and is the equivalent of wages and the capitalist's
surplus value. This is why the idea of surplus value and of interest on capital
is foreign to him. He considers his net income as the product of his own
labour.'

the theory of a specific peasant economy (i.e. peasant ownership but *without hired labour*) as an economic system *sui generis*. He tried to show that to the distinctive categories and modes of production Marx had recognized (slavery, feudalism, capitalism, socialism) there should be added another: the peasant economy.

Alexander Vasil'evich Chayanov was a man of wide interests. He wrote not only in the realm of economics and rural sociology but also in art, history and literature.[2] He became, after the Revolution, director of the Institute of Agricultural Economy. But as Soviet agricultural policy drew to an extensive collectivization he was increasingly attacked as a petit bourgeois idealizer of peasant economy and a pro-*kulak* ideologist. In 1930 Chayanov was arrested and he died in 1939.

Chayanov's main contribution was firstly to provide a theory of peasant behaviour at the level of the individual family farm, and secondly to show that at the national level peasant economy ought to be treated as an economic system in its own right, and not, as the Marxists claimed, as a form of incipient capitalism, represented by petty commodity production. In Chayanov's view peasant motivations are different from those of the capitalist; they aim at securing for the needs of the family rather than to make a profit. That is why a central role is given in Chayanov's theory to the notion of balance between subsistence needs and a subjective distaste for manual labour (dis-utility) for this determines the intensity of cultivation and the size of the net product.

Chayanov proceeds to show that the prevailing concepts of classical economics as well as the marginalist theory explaining the behaviour of a capitalist entrepreneur do not apply in a peasant family which depends solely on the work of its own family members.[3] For in this type of farm the decreasing returns of the value of marginal labour do not hinder the peasant's activity so long as the needs of his family are not satisfied; i.e. that is, when

2. Several of Chayanov's studies have been published in German, in English (Chayanov, 1925) and Japanese. Eight volumes of selected studies by Chayanov are available in Russian: *Oeuvres choisies de A. V. Chayanov* (1967).

3. For the same reason, according to Chayanov, the accounting methods used in Western Europe at the time – see for example Laur (1904) – do not apply in weakly monetized economics like those in Russia.

an equilibrium has been achieved between needs and the drudgery of his effort.

All the principles of our theory, rent, capital, price and other categories have been formed in the framework of an economy based on wage labour and seeking to maximize profits.... But we must by no means extend its application to all phenomena in our economic life. We know that most peasant farms in Russia, China, India and most non-European and even many European states are unacquainted with the categories of wage-labour and wages. The economic theory of modern capitalist society is a complicated system of economic categories inseparably connected with one another: price, capital, wages, interest, rent, which determine one another and are functionally interdependent. If one brick drops out of this system the whole building collapses.

In a natural economy human economic activity is dominated by the requirement of satisfying the needs of a single production unit, which is, at the same time a consumer unit; therefore budgeting here is to a high degree *qualitative* ... quantity here can be calculated only by considering the extent of each single need.... Therefore, the question of comparative profitability of various expenditures cannot arise – for example, whether growing hemp or grass would be more profitable or advantageous for these plant products are not interchangeable and cannot be substituted for each other.

On the family farm, the family equipped with means of production uses its labour power to cultivate the soil and receives, as the result of a year's work a certain amount of goods. A single glance at the inner structure of the labour unit is enough to realize that it is impossible, without the category of wages, to impose on its structure net profit, rent and interest on capital as real economic categories in the capitalist meaning of the word.... Thus it is impossible to apply the capitalist profit calculation (Chayanov, 1925, pp. 1–5).

Chayanov saw no validity in circumventing the absence of wages by imputing values to unpaid family labour. The annual product minus outlays is indivisible and undifferentiated. It could not be broken down into wages and other factor payments.

The family labour product (the increase in value of material goods which the family has acquired by its work during the year, or, to put it differently, their labour product) is the only possible category of income for a peasant or artisan working family unit.... The amount of labour product is mainly determined by the size and the composition of the working family, the number of its members capable of work, then by the productivity of the labour unit and – this is especially important – by the degree of labour effort, the degree of self exploitation through which the working members effect a certain quantity of labour units in the course of the year.... Thorough empirical studies on peasant farms in Russia and other countries have enabled us to substantiate the following thesis: the degree of self exploitation is determined by a peculiar equilibrium between family demand satisfaction and the drudgery of labour itself.... It is obvious that with the increase in produce obtained by hard work the subjective valuation of each newly gained rouble's significance for consumption decreases, but the drudgery of working for it which will demand an ever greater amount of self exploitation will increase.... As soon as the equilibrium point is reached continuing to work becomes pointless.... Farm size and composition and the urgency of its demands determine the consumption evaluation.... The significance of each rouble gross income for consumption is increased in a household burdened with members incapable of work. This makes for increased self exploitation of family labour power.... Thus the objective arithmetical calculation of the highest possible net profit in the given market situation does not determine the whole activity of the family unit: this is done by the internal economic confrontation of *subjective evaluations* (Chayanov, 1925, pp. 5–7).

The peasant producer would make an increased effort only if he had reason to believe it would yield a greater output which could be devoted to enlarged investment or consumption, but he does not push the drudgery beyond the point where the possible increase in output is outweighed by the irksomeness of the extra work. That is why this social mechanism has been called labour–consumer balance. Chayanov showed how, for different families, the balance between consumer satisfaction and the drudgery involved is affected by the size of the family and the ratio of working members to non-working members, and analysed effort curves and consumption–demand curves. He calculated also in what conditions the machine is preferable to manual labour for a peasant economy. He particularly emphasized the fact that calculations of the limits of possible land improvements for peasant economies must take into account the cost of the land and not the foreseeable increase in the rent, for in a peasant economy the prices agreed for the purchase of land or for land improvements are not set at the level represented by the capitalization of the rent as in a capitalist economy. That is why Chayanov concluded that the practical range of land improvements is larger for a peasant than for a capitalist economy.

In the capitalist economy land and labour are the variable factors which the entrepreneur tries to combine to obtain the maximum remuneration from his capital, considered as a fixed factor. In a typical peasant economy labour, proportionate to the size of the family, is the stable element which determines the change in the volume of capital and land.

For the capitalist entrepreneur the sum of values that serves to renew the work force is, from his private economic view-point, indistinguishable from other parts of the capital advanced to the undertaking, and is determined by the objective national economic category of wages and number of workers required for the particular volume of activity. This in its turn is determined by the total size of entrepreneur's capital (Chayanov, 1925, p. 197).

It is obvious that the family labour unit considers capital investment advantageous only if it affords the possibility of a higher level of well-being; otherwise it re-establishes the equilibrium between drudgery of labour and demand satisfaction (Chayanov, 1925, pp. 10–11).

Our analysis of the on-farm equilibrium's influence on capital circulation on the family farm enables us to formulate the following propositions:

At any particular level of technology and in a particular market situation, any working family unit able to control the amount of land for use can increase its labour productivity by increasing to a certain level optimal for this family. Any forcing up of capital intensity beyond the optimum increases labour drudgery and even reduces its payment, since, on the one hand, increased expenditure to replace exhausted capital will counteract the useful effect of further capital intensification, while on the other, the economic realization of this capital requires the farm family to intensify its labour more than is permitted by the equilibrium of on-farm factors (Chayanov, 1925, pp. 222–3).

From this thesis a distinct theory of social differentiation and mobility has been derived. Chayanov traced the natural history of the family (from the time of marriage of the young couple through the growth of the children to working age etc.) and stressed demographic differentiation in contrast to the Marxist concept of class differentiation of the peasantry.

Only by taking the family through the full extent of its development starting at birth and finishing at death, can we understand the basis laws of its composition. If we take it that a surviving child is born every third year in a young family ... we should try to explain how the relationship of the family labour force to its consumer demands changes as the family develops. (See tables.)

Table 1 Family Members' Ages in Different Years

| Year of family's existence | Husband | Wife | Age of children | | | | | | | | | | Number of persons |
			1st	2nd	3rd	4th	5th	6th	7th	8th	9th	
1	25	20										2
2	26	21	1									3
3	27	22	2									3
4	28	23	3									3
5	29	24	4	1								4
6	30	25	5	2								4
7	31	26	6	3								4
8	32	27	7	4	1							5
9	33	28	8	5	2							5
10	34	29	9	6	3							5
11	35	30	10	7	4	1						6
12	36	31	11	8	5	2						6
13	37	32	12	9	6	3						6
14	38	33	13	10	7	4	1					7
15	39	34	14	11	8	5	2					7
16	40	35	15	12	9	6	3					7
17	41	36	16	13	10	7	4	1				8
18	42	37	17	14	11	8	5	2				8
19	43	38	18	15	12	9	6	3				8
20	44	39	19	16	13	10	7	4	1			9
21	45	40	20	17	14	11	8	5	2			9
22	46	41	21	18	15	12	9	6	3			9
23	47	42	22	19	16	13	10	7	4	1		10
24	48	43	23	20	17	14	11	8	5	2		10
25	49	44	24	21	18	15	12	9	6	3		10
26	50	45	25	22	19	16	13	10	7	4	1	11

Source: Chayanov, 1925, p. 57.

Table 2 Family Members Expressed in Accounting Consumer-Worker Units

Years of family's existence	Married couple	Children 1	2	3	4	5	6	7	8	9	Total in family Consumers	Workers	Consumers/Workers
1	1·8										1·8	1·8	1·00
2	1·8	0·1									1·9	1·8	1·06
3	1·8	0·3									2·1	1·8	1·17
4	1·8	0·3									2·1	1·8	1·17
5	1·8	0·3	0·1								2·2	1·8	1·22
6	1·8	0·3	0·3								2·4	1·8	1·33
7	1·8	0·3	0·3								2·4	1·8	1·33
8	1·8	0·3	0·3	0·1							2·5	1·8	1·39
9	1·8	0·5	0·3	0·3							2·9	1·8	1·61
10	1·8	0·5	0·3	0·3							2·9	1·8	1·61
11	1·8	0·5	0·3	0·3	0·1						3·0	1·8	1·66
12	1·8	0·5	0·5	0·3	0·3						3·4	1·8	1·88
13	1·8	0·5	0·5	0·3	0·3						3·4	1·8	1·88
14	1·8	0·5	0·5	0·3	0·3	0·1					3·5	1·8	1·94
15	1·8	0·7	0·5	0·5	0·3	0·3					4·1	2·5	1·64
16	1·8	0·7	0·5	0·5	0·3	0·3					4·1	2·5	1·64
17	1·8	0·7	0·5	0·5	0·3	0·3	0·1				4·2	2·5	1·68
18	1·8	0·7	0·7	0·5	0·5	0·3	0·3				4·8	3·2	1·50
19	1·8	0·7	0·7	0·5	0·5	0·3	0·3				4·8	3·2	1·50
20	1·8	0·9	0·7	0·5	0·5	0·3	0·3	0·1			5·1	3·4	1·50
21	1·8	0·9	0·7	0·7	0·5	0·5	0·3	0·3			5·7	4·1	1·39
22	1·8	0·9	0·7	0·7	0·5	0·5	0·3	0·3			5·7	4·1	1·39
23	1·8	0·9	0·9	0·7	0·5	0·5	0·3	0·3	0·1		6·0	4·3	1·39
24	1·8	0·9	0·9	0·7	0·7	0·5	0·5	0·3	0·3		6·6	5·0	1·32
25	1·8	0·9	0·9	0·7	0·7	0·5	0·5	0·3	0·3		6·6	5·0	1·32
26	1·8	0·9	0·9	0·9	0·7	0·5	0·5	0·3	0·3	0·1	6·9	5·2	1·32

Source: Chayanov, 1925, p. 58.

We note a rapid increase in the proportion of consumers to workers. In the fourteenth year of the family's existence, this proportion reaches its highest point, 1·94. But in the fifteenth year the first child comes to the aid of the parents when he has reached semi-working age and the consumer–worker ratio immediately falls to 1·64.... In the twenty-sixth year of the family's existence, the ratio falls to 1·32.... Since the working family's basic stimulus to economic activity is the necessity to satisfy the demands of its consumers and its work hands are the chief means for this we ought first of all to expect the family's volume of economic activity quantitatively to correspond more or less to these basic elements in family composition (Chayanov, 1925, p. 60).

Taking the sown area as a measure of peasant wealth and the volume of economic activity, Chayanov shows a clearly expressed dependence between development of a peasant family and the size of area sown by it. He supports his proof with regional statistics of the evolution of peasant holdings and families from 1882 to 1911.

When we study the dynamics of these farms with the view that family size is entirely determined by its economic situation we might expect that farms sowing small areas will in the course of fifteen years continue to sow the same small areas and that farms well endowed will as before sow large areas and retain a large family. The works of Chernenkov, Khryashcheva, Vikhlyaev, Kushchenko and others, however, tell us something completely different as may be seen from the table below comparing the 1882 and 1911 censuses for Surazh uezd, Chernigov guberniya:

Table 3 Area sown in 1911 by 1882 area groups (%)

Desyatinas sown in 1882	Desyatinas sown in 1911					
	0–3	3–6	6–9	9–12	12	Total
0–3	28·2	47·0	20·0	2·4	2·4	100
3–6	21·8	47·5	24·4	8·2	2·4	100
6–9	16·2	37·0	26·8	11·3	2·4	100
9–12	9·6	35·8	26·1	12·4	16·1	100
12	3·5	30·5	28·5	15·6	21·9	100

Source: Chayanov, 1925, p. 67.

We see that a considerable part of the farms that sowed small areas gradually acquired a labour force as family age and size increased and by expanding their sown area passed into the higher groups thus also expanding the volume of their activity. Conversely, former large farms passed into lower groups corresponding to small families created after division. This shows us that demographic process of growth and family distribution by size also determine to a considerable extent the distribution of farms by size of sown area and livestock numbers (Chayanov, 1925, p. 67). In saying this of course we are not removing from our usage the concept of social differentiation; but this form of differentiation is not to be seen simply by grouping by sown areas; it has to be studied by ... direct analysis of capitalist factors in the organization of production, i.e. hired labour on farms, not brought in to help their own, but as the basis on which to obtain unearned income and oppressive rents and usurer's credit (Chayanov, 1925, p. 68).

Whereas the majority of Marxist economists believed in the advantages of concentration because such is the tendency of the capitalist mode of production, Chayanov maintained that horizontal concentration of production offered only limited advantages in agriculture. In an area of extensive cultivation where 2000–8000 hectares of grain land can be farmed with appropriate machinery, the optimal dimensions of productive units will not be the same as they are in a region of sugar beet cultivation where the more intensive use of machines makes transport costs grow disproportionately beyond an optimum of 200–250 hectares. In other words, natural conditions themselves impose certain limits on the possibilities of a horizontal concentration. These difficulties disappear however for vertical integration: small farms can benefit from all the advantages of scale by using the formula of co-operatives. That is why the competitive power of peasant farms versus capitalist farms or collective farms was much greater.

The whole point of this vertical integration was to reconcile the maintenance of peasant farms in the biological processes of intensive cultivation and livestock breeding where they were more productive than capitalist units with the requirement of technical progress, where the large enterprise had an advantage in mechanization and marketing. Chayanov had doubts about collective agriculture because the incentive problem had been solved more flexibly by co-operatives based on small family farms with their individuality intact than by the artels. Socialist society according to him had not yet found the stimuli that would impel the production units to attain their optimal organization and the economy was destined to be the victim of a gigantic bureaucracy.

The dynamic processes of agricultural proletarization and concentration of production, leading to large-scale agricultural production units based on hired labour are developing through the world and in the USSR in particular, at the rate much slower than was expected at the end of the nineteenth century[. . . .]

The sole form of horizontal concentration that at the present time may, and actually does, take place is the concentration of peasant lands into large-scale production units . . . but it is not and cannot be of such massive size that we would be able to construct on it our whole policy of agricultural concentration. Therefore, the main form for the concentration of peasant farms can be only vertical concentration and, moreover, in its co-operative forms, since only in these forms will it be organically linked with agricultural production and be able to spread to its proper extent and depth' (Chayanov, 1925, pp. 257, 267).

Many of Chayanov's views were questioned by a variety of scholars. For example, he sometimes confuses the optimal dimension of an enterprise with the optimal dimension of cultivated areas or considers the peasant economy as a static entity independent of possible capitalistic environments etc. He has also often showed more indulgence to the traditional peasant economy than to the future of industrial agriculture, yet one can hardly accuse him of singly turning his back on progress. In the chapter that Chayanov wrote in 1928 for the collection of essays on *Life and Technology in the Future*, he foresaw the prospects offered in a more or less distant future by soil-less agriculture, by factories for food products and synthetic textiles. He also predicted that man would be able to control the climate and forecast harvests.

Chayanov's theory was devised to take account of Russian conditions and, as Daniel Thorner has shown, works better for thinly populated countries than for densely populated ones where peasants could not readily buy or take in more land. Nevertheless the problem raised over forty years ago by the leader of the Russian organizational school, and the basic approach focusing analysis of peasant economies on the dynamics and structures of family farms, are just as pertinent today for developing countries where peasant economies still predominate.

References

BRUTSKUS, B. (1913), *Ocherki krest 'yanskogo khozyaistva v Zapadnoi Evrope*.

CHAYANOV, A. V. (1925), *Organizatsiya krest'yanskogo khozyaistva*. Translated as *The Theory of Peasant Economy*, D. Thorner, R. E. F. Smith and B. Kerblay (eds.), Irwin, 1966.

CHAYANOV, A. V. (1967), *Oeuvres choisies de A. V. Chayanov*, Johnson reprint, S.R. Publishers, Mouton.

KOSSINSKY, V. A. (1906), *K agrarnomu voprosu*, Odessa.

LAUR, E. (1904), *Landwirtschäftliche Buchaltung bäuerliche verhältnisse*.

13 Manning Nash

Market and Indian Peasant Economies

Manning Nash, 'Indian economies', in the Handbook of Middle American Indians series, vol. 6, *Social Anthropology*, University of Texas Press, 1967, pp. 87–101.

The economic organization of the Indians of Middle America ranges over a wide gamut.[1] It runs from the virtual isolation, little trade and almost no money of the tribal remnants of the Lacandon in the Peten to complete market interdependence of specialized communities producing for cash returns in an impersonal and competitive economic organization. There are all kinds of subtle gradients and variations between these extremes, but without doing violence to the ethnographic reality, it is feasible to sort the economic complexity of the region into three major types, each tending to be structurally, and frequently regionally, distinct. Each type carries with it some differences in the social structure and cultural pattern of which the economy is but a subsystem. The social and cultural correlates, concomitants and prerequisites of the varying economic organizations may form the basis for providing important indices to the dynamics of social change and stability among the Indians of Middle America.

The three kinds of economic organization in Middle America are:

1. *The regional marketing system.* Communities are linked into a system of rotating markets. In its most developed form the rotating markets look like a 'solar system'. A major market center is in daily operation. To it flow commodities produced throughout the region, goods from all over the nation and even items from international trade. Around the major market are a series of

1. This paper draws heavily on monographs and articles not directly cited and lists only the chief sources. I am indebted to June C. Nash for the idea of costume serving as a brand device, and to the Chiapas project of the University of Chicago for access to manuscript material.

market places which have their special days. Each of these market places tends to specialize in a given produce or commodity and to carry a reduced selection of the goods available in the central market. Goods, buyers and sellers move around the solar system in terms of the days of the week when market activity centers in a particular market place. Such solar systems of regional inter-dependence are characteristic of the western highlands of Guatemala (where they are most highly developed), the valley of Oaxaca, central Mexico, Michoacan, and eastern Guatemala among the Chorti and Pokomam. Without the marked solar qualities, regional market interdependence is found in the highlands of Chiapas among the Tzeltal and Tzotzil and in parts of the Alta Verapaz in Guatemala and a pattern of intense daily markets in the Isthmus of Tehuantepec. The regional marketing system is 'money economy organized in single households as both consumption and production units with a strongly developed market which tends to be perfectly competitive' (Tax, 1953, p. 13).

2. *The adjunct export economy*. Communities produce chiefly for home and local consumption, but tend to have one or a few commodities produced for cash and market exchange. Specialization is rare; from community to community the products, skills and economic organization are homogeneous. The economy is pecuniary, but there is much exchange of items for other items, albeit in terms of price-money equivalents. The market and the market place tend to be in the hands of non-Indians, and the Indian is more seen as seller than buyer. This sort of economy varies from the coffee growers of Sayula (Guiteras Holmes, 1952) who are mainly concerned with the export of a cash crop, or the vanilla growers of the Totonac region around the major market of Papantla (Kelly and Palerm, 1952) to the coffee, melon and citrus growers of the Sierra Popoluca (Foster, 1942). Another axis of variation is toward the paid labor role of Indians on plantations where the export economy is organized in the hands of non-Indian entrepreneurs. The paid labor, or Indian rural proletariat (Mintz, 1953), often coexists with communities growing the basic subsistence crops. In the Yucatan peninsula (Redfield, 1941) the henequen plantations approach this; in parts of the Verapaz in

Guatemala, and in the coastal regions where Indians are workers on coffee, sugar, rice or banana plantations, there occurs the extreme form of the adjunct export system.

3. *The quasi-tribal system*. Economies are concerned chiefly with meeting locally defined demands. Economic effort is directed toward subsistence needs with handicrafts for home use, and attention to the crops of the milpa. Money is part of the daily life but tends to be scant, and transactions are not a daily occurrence. The Indians with this kind of economic system tend to be in remote or not very accessible upland regions, or to be remnants of former unintensive village agriculturalists. The economic type is found among the Cora and Huichol, the Tarahumara, the Tepehuan, the Maya, and other groups of northwest Mexico, and, except for the Lacandon of the Mexico–Guatemala border, does not exist south of Mexico City, and is absent from Guatemala (except possibly for the Kekchi around Lake Izabal, Dr Nancy Solien de Gonzales reports).

The three types of economies are different in scale, in the number of Indians they include, and in the areas where they are able to function. All the economies are tied, more or less tightly, to the national and international economies; none is free from the effects of national and world fluctuations. Everywhere the Indian and his communities are enmeshed in a network of economic relationships well beyond the local ethnic unit. Even the very isolated groups like the Lacandon or the Tarahumara, or the Xcacal of Quintana Roo get involved with the passing agents of the larger economy.

The quasi-tribal system is the least complicated and hence most easily accounted for. In the southern Sierra Madre Occidental, between the states of Jalisco and Nayarit, are the Cora and the Huichol. The 2000 or 3000 Cora settled in *pueblos* of 200–300 persons, with their mixture of plow agriculture on bottom lands and digging-stick cultivation on the slopes, and the Huichol, where 4000 or 5000 Indians live in scattered *ranchos* by digging-stick agriculture (Vogt, 1955), are exemplars of the quasi-tribal system. In the first place, access to the region is difficult. The paucity of usable roads encourages few persons regularly to penetrate into the depth of Indian country. Second, the natural ecology of the area does not provide a basis for much agricultural differentiation; what is grown in one part is grown in another. Finally, what small economic opportunity exists for peddling, trade and other commercial activities tends to be in the hands of Mexicans rather than Indians. Though there are craftsmen who make artifacts of wood (stools, chairs and guitars) and of fibers (mats, bags and nets), and a few potters (who do not meet local demand), specialization in economic activity is not great, nor are whole communities dependent on trade relations (Grimes, 1961). The Huichol are chiefly growers of milpa and keepers of cattle. The maize grown is for home use; if there is a small surplus, it is used to buy cattle. Maize is supplemented by beans, squash, melons, fruits, and some orchards and vegetable gardens. The Huichol are near the Middle American extreme in self-sufficiency, meeting most of their own requirements through their own production. Cash comes to them by paid-labor service as herdsmen for Mexicans, or work on tobacco farms or through begging or performing in towns like Tepic. A market structure is absent; buyers and sellers seek each other out as transactions need to be made. Prices tend to be in terms of what things are selling for in the stores and towns of Mexicans.

In this tribal-like setting, buying and selling is a small part of daily life and reaches a market-like arrangement only during times of ceremonial festivities involving whole communities. Land and other valuable productive resources are nominally communal, and with the low level of technological development a family can exploit only a few acres, so there is no land market and no land shortage. The peak work periods in the agricultural cycle require more labor than is available to the household units, which are also the economic units. So, within a locality or settlement there is a form of exchange: unpaid, cooperative farm labor. Thus there is an economy oriented to the needs of the local community (the scattered ranchos tied together by kinship and marriage) or the compact settlement sort, with near food self-sufficiency, household units of consumption and production, no markets, primitive technology, little cash, and exchange as extraordinary rather than everyday. The chief uses of wealth are festal and ceremonial, and there is communal pressure on the wealthy, with the possibilities of envy and witchcraft directed against them, to share their goods with the needy. Hunting and gathering and fishing supplement the milpa and cattle keeping.

Like the Cora and the Huichol, the Tarahumara (Bennett and Zingg, 1935) or the remnants of the Cahita peoples (the Yaqui, Mayo and Tepehuan) exhibit the same general features of a milpa-agriculture system with supplemental products, exchange as a rarity, cooperative farm labor and general demands on wealth by the needy and through the festal cycle. These economies do not transcend a householding aspect and show little dynamism or change. Isolation, relative lack of ecological variation, a reduced political and social organization, few specialists and household attempts at self-sufficiency account for the major contours of this sort of economy.

In the western highlands of Guatemala, the solar marketing system of economic organization exists in its most highly developed form. Tax (1952, 1953, 1957) has summarized the chief features of this form, and the discussion here follows his guidelines. Lake Atitlan dominates the physical geography of the midwest highlands. Ranged around the lake are fourteen *municipios* (the *municipio* is the administrative unit of Guatemala, and is here virtually identical with ethnic units). Each *municipio* is distinct in costume, dialect, mythology, and economic specialty (Tax, 1937). In small compass lies a tremendous variety of cultural, social, and economic features. The economic variation is a condensed example of that occurring throughout western Guatemala (McBryde, 1947, especially Map 19 which shows the distribution of Indian markets in southwest Guatemala). The ecological possibilities of the *municipios* around the lake account, in part, for agricultural diversity. The variation in altitude, in possibilities of irrigation, in natural resources and in available arable land underlies crop diversity. All the communities grow some maize, but a few are maize exporters and hence may be said to specialize in growing maize, whereas others are net importers of the basic foodstuffs. The physical basis of specialization is further augmented by the juxtaposition of highland and lowland regions, with a consequent interchange of agricultural products of the temperate and cold country with those of the *boca costa* and the coastal hot lands. But specialization in the region is broader than agricultural diversity or the kinds of commodities produced; it extends to the way whole communities earn a livelihood and to trades and industries as well as agricultural products. In general the Indians of the area are nearly as dependent as modern urban dwellers on the exchange of products. Economic specialization of a community is a facet of its general cultural distinctiveness, and communities that have economic specialties likewise are individualized in other aspects of culture and society.

Around the lake, Panajacheleños grow onions and other vegetables and exploit the resources of the lake hardly at all (at least by traditional Indian canoes; with motor launches they are orienting more to the lake). In Santiago Atitlan, besides maize, canoes are produced, and the Atitecos are the leaders of the western end of the lake in navigational skills. They also provide many *comerciantes* who truck in the exchange of products between the *boca costa* and the highlands. San Pablo is a rope-making center, as is San Pedro across the lake. And as if to underline the cultural basis of specialization, San Pablo not only buys maize (from Santiago and San Pedro) but imports a good part of maguey from San Pedro, where it grows luxuriantly. San Pedro also produces a cash crop of chickpeas. Santa Catarina, only two miles from Panajachel, the municipio of *tablón* onion gardens, grows few vegetables but develops the lake resources of fishing and crabbing. The citizens there are as sensitive to the vagaries of the lake resources as the Panajacheleños are insensitive.

The communities around the lake are integrated into market exchange via the major market at Solola, and a smaller solar center at Atitlan, the only daily market on the lake itself. Not only do the communities in the region participate in the regional rotating market center and in the local markets, but they are geared into other solar systems with interchange of products, and the emergence of full-time Indian *comerciantes*, who live from the profits of product interchange between markets.

There is another solar market system center around Quezaltenango and its broad open valley, and another around Huehuetenango. The regional markets around Quezaltenango serve and draw on other groups of specialized communities. Totonicapan makes pottery on the wheel, produces lumber and weaves *huipiles*. Neighboring Chichicastenango makes no pots but uses its pine forests for lumber. Momostenango produces blankets and woolens. San Francisco mines lime, Salcaja turns out woven skirts and tie-dye materials, Cantel provides corn and cotton yard goods from electric mills. Almolonga and Zunil grow vegetables, and so on around the roster of economic specialties. Examples could be indefinitely multiplied. The points to be made are two:

1. A regional marketing system based on economic specialization moves products among communities in a solar system with a major central market (like Solola or Quezaltenango) and a subsidiary market (like Atitlan or the mushroom wholesale market of San Francisco El Alto, where every Friday thousands of Indians converge on a cold windswept town to turn it into a bustling center) and other smaller markets which have their special days. The system has grown up over time; it is not planned or regulated, but reflects the Indian response to economic opportunity.

2. The marketing system is an aspect of general cultural differentiation. It is not that individuals or families are so different from each other, but rather that whole communities have cultural traditions which vary from each other in endless small ways. Among these ways are the special crops, trades and industries that come to economic actors because they happen to be members of one rather than another local society.

The facts of ecological variation, the proximity of highland and lowland, are the physical basis for the cultural and economic diversity of the region. It is the occurrence of distinct local societies, however, with strong endogamous tendencies, which inclines to restrict handicrafts, trades and industries to a single community. The present distribution of agricultural patterns, handicrafts and special skills is the result of the operation of comparative advantage over a long time, and shifts do take place. Apparently shifts in kind of crop (other things equal, like land availability) take place more easily and rapidly than the cultural incorporation of a new handicraft or industry. This, of course, is tied to the facts of enculturation, since a handicraft or industry passes from father to son, or mother to daughter, whereas an agricultural specialty will pass from adult to adult. In addition, Indians work for each other as agricultural laborers across community lines (as they work for Ladinos) and hence are able to learn agricultural techniques more readily. But even crop shifts in a community's inventory are not easily undertaken. Indians must compete with the already established way of making a living in their own community and with the reputation of the other producing communities in the market place. For example, potatoes of Todos Santos are less valued in the Quezaltenango region than potatoes of Nahuala, or the vegetables from Zunil are thought to be the best. Indians from these communities wear their distinctive costumes, which serve as 'brand' identifications; and the customers assume that a man in the Todos Santos striped pants is selling his own potatoes, or that the blue-skirted Almolongera is selling her own vegetables, though this is often not the case. So there is some stickiness even in the transfer or diffusion of agricultural techniques and products. Specialties, of course, are subject to competition from both Indian and non-Indian producers. Many handicrafts have been lost, like the hat making of Aguacatenango which could not compete with factory-made hats, or the reduction in palm-leaf rain capes with the spread of cheap plastic tablecloths used as ponchos. Conversely, new things are stimulated through competition and contact: tourists who visit Chichicastenango favor a sort of risqué pattern on napkins; the Ladinos of Chiapas are the consumers of large pottery flowerpots. Skills and agricultural patterns change over time and in response to changing market conditions, in the context of possibilities of technique transfer and development among communities.

If the contention that ecological variation, highland–lowland proximity and distinct local societies with endogamously tied skills and economic pursuits are what underlie the degree of specialization and, with it, the width of the market is true, then where these factors are diminished, the intensity of market relations and economic specialization should in turn diminish. A brief view of the solar systems of Oaxaca and around Lake Patzcuaro adds depth to this generalization. There the posited factors are present, as well as the regional market systems, whereas in lowland Yucatan some of the factors are absent as they are among the Totonac or the Popoluca, and there the solar marketing system is also absent. The strength of the above variables changes from regional system to regional system, and thus the market patterns also shift. In the valley of Oaxaca, the city Oaxaca is the major sun around which the markets of Ocotlan, Tlacolula are secondary planets, with satellite markets at Etla, Zimatlan, Totlapa, Atzompa (where real barter does in fact take place, as is also reported from the Cuchumatanes where corn is exchanged for pots, the amount of corn depending on the size of the pot), and other communities in the valley. The market system integrates the economically specialized communities and cultural variation among speakers of Zapotec, Mixtec and Mixe (Malinowski and de la Fuente, 1957).

Around Patzcuaro (Foster, 1948), Tzintzuntzan and Santa Fe are pottery producers; Quiroga and Paracho specialize in wood and wood products, Janitzio and Ihuatzio in reed mats and fire fans, Jaracuaro in palm hats, Nahuatzen in cotton and Santa Clara in copper. The regional interdependence is organized in the periodic market system, and the market shows the same features of being free, open, competitive and hence very sensitive to fluctuations in supply and demand, with the corresponding changes in prices and price levels. The market system of Patzcuaro, like the other regional systems, is tied into the national and international markets, and its operation reflects price movement within this broader context. Around Patzcuaro, however, local societies are less distinct than in Guatemala or Oaxaca, and hence endogamy is less, and crafts pass more readily from adult to adult across community boundaries.

The distribution of specialized occupations and crops in the Chiapas region also confirms the generalization about the occurrence and intensity of market relations. Amatenango is a pottery-making community, where every woman who grows up in the community knows how to, and does, make pots. The neighboring community of Aguacatenango does not make a single pot, but keeps pigs as a supplement to its agricultural activities. The Chamulas are active traders and have a roster of handicraft specialities;

the Zinacantecos are farmers and sheepherders; Tenango makes a different sort of pottery from that of Amatenango. The ecological diversity, the highland–lowland proximity and the distinctiveness of the local societies, maintained by high rates of endogamy, give rise to economic specialization and trade. But a solar market system is not found as it is now in parts of Tehuantepec. The markets tend to be in Ladino towns (like Las Casas, Teopisca, Comitan), where Indians come to buy and sell. Local markets occur in Indian communities on special festive occasions and only a few times a year in any village. The absence of solar markets may be attributed to the difficulties of communication between Indian communities (but the great extent to which Indians in Guatemala overcome difficulties of terrain in their treks to and from the market gives little weight to this contention), or it may lie in historical factors (like the greater and more recent political and ethnic unrest in Chiapas), or it may lie in some set of social and cultural features too broad to be caught in the net of variables here proposed.

The market, as an institution, rests on the free interplay of buyers and sellers, with price established through the interaction of buyers who are not large enough to set price, and sellers who do not control enough of the supply to affect the price. There is also the feature of impersonality in an open market system. Entry (as buyer or seller) is not restricted. Anyone who pays the small tax can enter the local markets and set up a stall, though in the city markets there are some larger installations requiring more outlay than many of the vendors can muster. The interaction between buyer and seller shows indifference to person, with attention only to price. In these markets, haggling and bargaining are characteristic but they are the means of establishing the going price, and shopping is the way of getting price information where price is not posted or advertised. Vendors of similar products are usually grouped together, and from the bids of buyers and the asking of sellers a price is quickly reached. The price prevails until there is some change in the supply and demand factors. Bargaining in any single transaction reflects the state of the market place as a whole, and the market place as a whole reflects the operation of the entire regional and national markets.

Looked at closely, these markets are a series of buyer–seller transactions, an exchange of money for goods. Except for some of the food sellers, some of the medical suppliers and a few of the stores in the market or in the towns where markets are held (and to which people may be tied by credit), there does not exist a clientele for any seller, or a body of loyal customers for any purveyor of commodities. The market relationships are truly dyadic contract and fleeting (Foster, 1961). This characteristic of the market is a symptom of a prevailing fact of the economic organization of Indian communities, a fact with far-reaching structural and economic consequences. Indian buyers and sellers in the market place are members of households, and they act as members of households. These households are economic units in only one of their aspects, and they tend to see the economic sphere as only one of the areas in which maintenance needs may be met. Households are limited in the numbers and kinds of persons they can recruit, the capital and savings they can command, the sort of economic opportunity to which they can respond. Given the fact that households, not firms, are the economic organizations around which the market economy is built, the limits of planning, continuity, scale and technological complexity in economic life become readily apparent. What makes these economies different from a modern, dynamic economy with a built-in drive toward economic and technological development is thus clear. They do not lack economic rationality, the matching of means and ends for best outputs; they do not hedge economic activity with a host of traditional barriers; they do not despise wealth and hard work; and they exhibit the free market where each man follows his own economic interest. Thus they have the values, the markets, the pecuniary means of exchange, the ability to calculate, and the interest in economic activity. (In Mitla, Parsons (1936) complained that it was a 'ritual of price' that marked these Zapotec, Malinowski and de la Fuente (1957) have spoken of a 'commercial libido', and others have reported the keen interest in price and economic activity.) What is lacking is the social organization of an entity like the firm, an autonomous, corporate group dedicated to and organized for economic activity.

That such social organizations have not grown up in Indian

communities is tied to the larger social structure and cultural pattern. The specialized communities with their distinctive cultural and economic cast, maintained through endogamy and organized around a variant of the civil-religious hierarchy (Cámara, 1952; Wolf, 1955; Nash, 1958), are not conducive to a social entity based strictly on economic ends. The communities are organized to protect their corporate existence and as such have specialized controls over the free use of accumulation of resources and mechanisms to insure a democracy of poverty. In the social structure of communities like Panajachel, Cantel, Santa Eulalia or Santiago (Wagley, 1941) in Guatemala, or Amatenango, Aguacatenango, Zinacantan in Chiapas, or Mitla, Yalalag and others in Oaxaca, there operates a leveling mechanism. The leveling mechanisms (Wolf, 1955; Nash, 1961) operate to drain the accumulated resources of the community for non-economic ends, and to keep the various households, over generations, fairly equal in wealth. They are mechanisms to keep economic homogeneity within the community, so that socially important heterogeneity – age, sex, previous service to the community, control of or access to the supernatural – remains the basis of role differentiation. They militate against the rise of social classes based on wealth and economic power distinctions. The leveling mechanism rests on the following interrelated aspects:

1. Low level of technology and limited land, so that absolute wealth and accumulation are small in virtue of poor resources in relation to population and a technology which is labor intensive and not highly productive.

2. Fracture of estates by bilateral inheritance. Whatever is in fact accumulated in capital goods is scrambled among sons and daughters in nearly equal shares. Almost everywhere in the region bilateral inheritance prevails. The few places with patrilineal descent groups do not vest property rights in a corporation, but exhibit a pattern of division among the patrilineally related families.

3. Forced expenditure of time and resources in communal office. The posts in the civil and religious hierarchies require some loss

of work time, and the higher the post the more time is lost and the more direct costs in taking on the post.

4. Forced expenditure by the wealthy in ritual. Those who have been skilled or lucky and have accumulated wealth must expend it for communal ends, chiefly in feasting and drinking, so that the wealth is consumed.

The leveling mechanism keeps the fortunes of the various households nearly equal and serves to ensure the shift of family fortunes from generation to generation. The sanctions behind the operation of the leveling mechanism are generally supernatural, with witchcraft as the means to keep the economic units oriented to the communal drains and claims on their wealth. These economies, then, are market – competitive, free, open – but set into a social structure without corporate units dedicated to and able to pursue economic ends. Working with a cultural pattern forcing the accumulation of wealth into non-economic channels, and buttressed by a system of supernatural sanctions against those who do not use their wealth, they show a lack of dynamism, a technological conservatism almost equivalent to that of the most isolated communities, and an inability to seize and exploit or create economic opportunity.

This combination of features presents a startling social fact: the presence of markets, economic rationality and money form a single complex, but in addition firms, credit mechanisms, deliberate technical and economic investment are needed for economic dynamism. The latter features are part of a social structure not found in the corporate peasantry of Middle America, and their coexistence in a single society (like our own) appears a historical precipitate rather than a functionally linked set of social characteristics. Experience in other parts of the world where the market economy is set into a social structure that is not modern in the sense of organizations dedicated to purely economic ends (i.e., the bazaars of the Arab world, the regional markets of Africa or the peasant markets of Java and Haiti) leads to the expectation that such organizations do not develop from the dynamics of internal social and economic life but are a product of social change induced by pressures or privileges generated in the modern economy.

This survey of the broad type of economy in the regional marketing areas of Middle America has been taken from an aerial view, a height which may give rise to misunderstandings. The tendency toward economic homogeneity, for example, does not indicate that a given community or village is, at any one time, virtually without wealth differences. Lewis (1947) describes a three-class wealth division for Tepoztlan and relates it to the types of land and technology that different families own. Tax (1952) finds a wealth division into quarters convenient for Panajachel, and describes the functions of wealth in officeholding, marriage choice and prestige. Similarly, the emphasis on households as economic units appears to play down the role of the community as a property holder. Nowhere is land fully communal; nowhere is it fully in individual hands. Some lands (often the *monte*, scrub land, pasture land or firewood land) is owned by the community and open to use by all members. Frequently there are means to prevent the sale of land from Indians to Ladinos (as in many communities in Chiapas). But the communal control of productive resources in the form of ownership was everywhere eroded and destroyed by the middle of the 1800s, and one of the persisting problems of the corporate communities has been to hold on to their territorial base. (In some respects the *ejido* program in Mexico has strengthened Indian communities, and in others, by introducing non-Indians into the community, has weakened it.)

Such studies as these on consumption patterns in corporate communities (Tax, 1957), however, reinforce the contention that the Indian economic pattern, in terms of production, consumption and organization, tends to be discrete from the Ladino or Mexican. Even if a Mexican or a Guatemalan Ladino is poorer than an Indian, his style of life is the eroded version of a national culture, whereas the Indian continues to implement wants and tastes embedded in a local society. Some Indian societies have gone a long way toward economic Ladinoization and its attendant changes in life style and social structure; and places like Totonicapan in Guatemala, Tzintzuntzan and Tepoztlan in

Mexico, may point the way to an understanding of how Indian economies get transformed into regional examples of the national economy, whether or not the process of economic modernization is carried very far.

If the quasi-tribal economies owe their structure to isolation, relative ecological homogeneity and a reduced cultural tradition based on unintensive agriculture, and if the solar systems take their form and function from the factors outlined above, the third major type – the adjunct export economy – is more heterogeneous as are the forces underlying it. The adjunct export economy, from the viewpoint of the Indians, is an addition to the basic business of milpa agriculture. The milpa agriculture, touching self-sufficiency (as among the Popoluca and the Totonac), is not primarily a market crop and forms the chief agricultural activity of the economic unts. In addition to the growing and consuming of the milpa crops, there is, however, a cash crop, some item like coffee in Sayula, or vanilla among the Tajin Totonac, or sugar cane, or rice which is grown for the export economy. This is grown by adaptations of the basic, simple technology, with the same sorts of economic organizations, to be sold to Mexican or Ladino middlemen. The economic type is called adjunct to the export economy for obvious reasons. The cash crop is an overlay on the fundamental subsistence agricultural activities; the organization, processing, marketing and profit making lie largely in hands other than the Indian producers (in and around Papantla the Totonac face a virtual monopoly among buyers and thus do not get a 'fair' share of the proceeds of the vanilla trade, whereas in Sayula the coffee proceeds have got into the domestic economy at a much greater rate, with correspondingly greater social changes). The farmers operate in a dual economic frame, one part oriented to maintenance, the other to the export economy. In situations where crops can be rotated on the same fields (as can maize and vanilla) there are not many economic strains. Where fields can be used alternately for subsistence or for cash cropping there is often conflict among the local inhabitants. The cash cropping means stricter property rules and sometimes a full private-property emphasis, with permanent use of the fields and with permanent title, a custom sometimes in conflict with a more communal, rotating use of milpa lands based on usufruct rights.

The adjunct export economy can turn in various directions: (a) the stable dual sort as with the Totonac; (b) a movement toward a commercial peasantry, as with some of the Popoluca; (c) the development of a rural proletariat, as with the henequen workers of the Yucatan Peninsula. It is clear that the adjunct export economy is most likely to experience wide economic swings, and that movement, at least in economy, toward the rural variant of national culture is most likely here. Further voluntary organizations like the cooperative, or the labor union, and perhaps credit societies, are more likely to take root here.

Three major types fairly adequately encompass the major economic organizations of the Indians of Middle America. Each type is a distinct social form, with its own ecological, cultural and economic setting and each has its own dynamic and conditions of maintenance. The overriding presence of money, markets, economic calculations of actors, the concern with price, and the interest in and desire for expanded economic opportunities do not, however, as yet move any of the Indian economies into the category of a modern economy. It is the social and cultural context of economic operations which keeps the forms of Indian economic organization more or less distant from modernity. Perhaps the shift to modernity, the fracturing of corporate or quasi-tribal organization for the exploitation of economic opportunity, implies the loss of those mechanisms capable of sustaining the social structure in which a distinct Indian heritage is transmitted. Or, perhaps, and just as likely, people who have kept a cultural heritage alive through nearly five centuries of contact with a technologically and politically superordinate society may discover how to blend parts of their cultural heritage with those aspects of economic modernity now absent.

References

BENNETT, W. C., and ZINGG, R. M. (1935), *The Tarahumara: An Indian Tribe of Northern Mexico*, University of Chicago Press.

CÁMARA BARBACHANO, F. (1952), 'Religious and political organisation', in S. Tax *et al.* (eds.), *Heritage of Conquest: The Ethnology of Middle America*, Free Press.

Foster, G. M. (1942), 'A primitive Mexican economy', *Monogr. Amer. Ethnol. Soc.*, vol. 5, pp. 1–115.

Foster, G. M. (1948), 'The folk economy of rural Mexico with special reference to marketing', *J. Marketing*, vol. 13, pp. 153–62.

Foster, G. M. (1961), 'The dyadic contract: a model for the social structure of a Mexican peasant village', *Amer. Anthrop.*, vol. 63, pp. 1173–92.

Grimes, J. E. (1961), 'Huichol economics', *Amer. indig.*, vol. 21, pp. 280–306.

Guiteras Holmes, C. (1952), *Sayula*, Socieded Mexicana de Geografía y Estadística.

Kelly, I. T., and Palerm, A. (1952), 'The Tajin Totonac', part 1, 'History, subsistence, shelter and technology', Smithsonian Institution, pub. 13.

Lewis, O. (1947), 'Wealth differences in a Mexican village', *Sci. Monthly*, vol. 65, pp. 127–32.

McBryde, F. W. (1947), 'Cultural and historical geography of southwest Guatemala', Smithsonian Institution, pub. 4.

Malinowski, B., and de la Fuente, J. (1957), 'La economía de un sistema de mercados en México', *Acta Anthr.*, ser. 2, vol. 1, no. 2, Mexico.

Mintz, S. W. (1953), 'The folk urban continuum and the rural proletarian community', *Amer. J. Sociol.*, vol. 59, pp. 136–45.

Nash, M. (1958), 'Political relations in Guatemala', *Soc. econ. Studies*, vol. 7, pp. 65–75.

Nash, M. (1961), 'The social contect of economic choice in a small community', *Man*, vol. 61, pp. 186–91.

Parsons, E. C. (1936), *Mitla: Town of the Souls*, University of Chicago Press.

Redfield, R. (1941), *The Folk Culture of Yucatan*, University of Chicago Press.

Tax, S. (1937), 'The *municipios* of the midwestern highlands of Guatemala', *Amer. Anthrop.*, vol. 39, pp. 423–44.

Tax, S. (1952), 'Economy and technology', in S. Tax *et al.* (eds.), *Heritage of Conquest: The Ethnology of Middle America*, Free Press.

Tax, S. (1953), 'Penny capitalism: a Guatemalan Indian economy', Smithsonian Institution, pub. 16.

Tax, S. (1957), 'Changing consumption in Indian Guatemala', *Econ. Develop. cult. Change*, vol. 5, pp. 147–58.

Vogt, E. Z. (1955), 'Some aspects of Cora-Huichol acculturation', *Amer. indig.*, vol. 15, pp. 249–63.

Wagley, C. (1941), 'Economics of a Guatemalan village', *Amer. Anthr. Assoc. Mem.*, no. 58.

Wolf, E. R. (1955), 'Types of Latin American peasantry: a preliminary discussion', *Amer. Anthrop.*, vol. 57, pp. 452–71.

14 Geroid T. Robinson

Crafts and Trades among the Russian Peasantry

Excerpts from Geroid T. Robinson, *Rural Russia under the Old Regime*, Macmillan Co., 1949, pp. 104–5. First published in 1932.

Whether by choice or by necessity, the peasants were often something more than farmers – sometimes not farmers at all, for millions of them were engaged, at home or in the cities, for a part or all of their time, in self-directed non-agricultural work of some sort, or in agricultural or industrial wage-labor. Among all these activities, the handicrafts of the forest *guberniias* have held a very special interest for students of peasant life, for the reason that these craft-industries belonged in a peculiar sense to the peasantry themselves. The crafts were not free from external influence, and yet in their methods and their products they were still a rich repository of peasant science and peasant art. The workers produced an endless variety of work in wood, bark, cloth, leather, felt, clay and metal, varying in quality from the crudest articles of mass-consumption (wooden snow-shovels, brooms made of twigs, unglazed milk-pots, thick felt boots, heaped up by hundreds in the village markets), to silver ornaments and religious pictures which sometimes fully merited the name of works of art. Production was carried on sometimes quite independently in the peasant's home; sometimes at the order of an entrepreneur who distributed the raw materials to many home-workers, paid for the labor at a piece-rate, and collected and disposed of the product; sometimes, too, in a small shop set up cooperatively by an artel of-workers, or maintained by a master who hired other craftsmen to work under his direction. The entire household, men, women, and children, often worked through the short winter day and well into the night, for a beggarly return; but when the brief agricultural season did not yield a living for the peasant family, then to work for less than a subsistence through the long winter months was better than to be altogether idle – and perhaps to be buried in the spring. Strong traditions of the village, close legal restrictions upon the mobility of the peasant, favored an attempt on his part to find a source of side-earnings in the handicrafts rather than in some distant factory. The craft-industries might still live, even though they did not produce a living; they were generally supplementary to agriculture and, in effect, subsidized by agriculture, and it was this, above all, that enabled them to maintain a footing in a country where the Industrial Revolution was now well under way. Some of the craft-industries had not yet been subjected to factory competition, some survived in spite of competition, some collapsed and disappeared. Exactly what was happening, will never be known, in terms of statistical accuracy; the number of persons engaged in handicraft production, though perhaps diminishing toward the turn of the century, still very much exceeded the number employed in the factories; and yet the crafts could not be called prosperous, nor did they offer opportunities of increasing promise to a peasantry hard pressed to find help in one direction or another.

Wage-work in agriculture and other rural non-industrial occupations was also an important source of peasant income. [...] It is in the very nature of the highly specialized grain production of Russia, that for brief periods it demanded whole armies of extra plowmen and especially of harvesters, but of these short-term workers, the census took no account, nor does there exist a dependable estimate of their number. If there were more than a million and a half of long-term laborers, those hired for the harvest alone probably counted several millions more.

15 Boguslaw Galeski

Sociological Problems of the Occupation of Farmers

Boguslaw Galeski, 'Sociological problems of the occupation of farmers',
Annals of Rural Sociology, Special Issue, 1968, pp. 9–26.
Translated by Jerzy Syskind.

When can a person be said to follow the vocation of farming?
The answer seems obvious in the case of an agronomist, zoo-
technician, agricultural worker on a State farm, a cow barn overseer, a production worker or engineer in an industrial fats factory,
etc. But those engaged in big agricultural enterprises constitute such a large and differentiated community that the term
'agriculturist' is perhaps hardly suitable. As is the case with
industry, it may be more suitable to speak of agriculture as an
occupational division. The distinction between occupation, trade
or vocation, speciality or job may present certain difficulties, but
this applies to all branches of employment. And if it is accepted
that agriculture presents greater difficulties, then it is only a matter of difference in degree.

Agriculture, however, presents a particular difficulty. For involved here is a category in relation to which the term 'agriculturist' cannot be simply rejected as too general. This may aptly
apply to employees of agricultural institutions and enterprises.
But this category involves the family cultivating an individual
peasant farm. Of course, it is possible in this case too to distinguish between fruit growers, pig breeders, apiarists, tobacco
growers, etc. Yet, the majority of peasant families engage in such
differentiated production that the general term agriculturist may
be misleading here and rather apply to employees of agricultural
enterprises. The proposition that a family operating its own farm
follows the farming vocation raises many doubts, and not only
because of the general character of the term farmer. It is the fact
that the family is involved, and not a person, that raises an immediate doubt. If the term vocation is nevertheless used in refer-

ence to families operating their own farms, then this vocation must be distinguished as a particular one, essentially different from others, in relation to the traits which determine that a given kind of work is considered following a vocation. But the term vocation is then not used in relation to other traits.

Definition of the Term Vocation

The term vocation (or profession) is generally used to designate a complex of activities which:

are distinct from other activities and are continuously performed.

are rendered on behalf of, or serve other people (society),

constitute a steady source of maintenance,

require certain preparation entitling one to follow a vocation,

i.e., to work at it steadily on behalf of others, in exchange for means of subsistence.

None of these characteristics (which flow from each other) in itself suffices to define some given complex of activities as a vocation. It is possible to point to many distinct complexes of internally connected activities which – as J. Szczepanski (1963a) writes – nobody calls practising a trade or vocation (a housewife preparing meals for the family, for instance). Although, under different conditions these same activities can unhesitatingly be defined as following a vocation (cooking in a restaurant, for example). So it is possible to indicate many individuals with steady sources of maintenance who pursue no vocation whatever (persons maintained by their families or those with bank accounts). Or there may be activity one is entitled to pursue after special preparation which is not a vocation. Such is the case, for instance, with driving an automobile – unless it is done for pay and serves other people (taxi driving). Whereas many occupations, such as street cleaning, for instance, require no preparation or qualifications. Then there are people who pursue some activity without any gain in mind, which indicates that working on behalf of others is not always a sufficient vocation distinguishing criterion, although it is undoubtedly the most important one. Hence the co-appearance of a complex of characteristics constitutes the basis for distinguishing a vocation, which may be defined as a complex of activities constantly performed on behalf of other people in exchange for means of subsistence. Or more briefly – a complex of continuously performed activity which consists of exchanging individual for social labour. The term vocation is thus understood in the present paper.

It should be noted parenthetically that the term is often used to designate occupational or professional communities. One thus speaks, for example, of the doctor's vocation having in mind the totality of physicians. The term 'vocational category' will be used here in that sense, meaning a community of people pursuing the same vocation.

According to the above definition, many occupations listed in censuses cannot be regarded as vocational categories. It is difficult, for instance, to accept ownership (of land, buildings or capital, etc.) as a vocational category, if the activity is limited to profit making[1] and does not involve management of an enterprise; whereas the majority of political leaders today should be reckoned in the vocational category since their activity is the basis of their maintenance. As we saw above in reference to the housewife and automobile driver, in certain cases, given complexes of activities sometimes bear the character of vocations and the people performing them may be defined as belonging to given vocational categories, and sometimes do not. Essential here is whether or not the activity becomes a vocation, and under what conditions. It may be said in relation to some types of activity that they are undergoing a social process of professionalization. The above traits determining vocation may serve not only as criteria for regarding some complex of activity as a vocation, but also as determinants of the process of professionalization transpiring in a given field. With the above enumerated traits as a criterion, it may be accepted that the process of professionalization of some work is the more advanced and that the activity may be more basically defined as practising a vocation:

the more clearly the considered complex of activity is distinguished from others – in contradistinction to household activity;

1. They figure in the so-called North-Hatta scale – see, for instance, Kolb (1949, p. 465).

the more interlinked is the system of the social division of labour – in contradistinction to creative (or family) work for oneself;

the more it serves as a durable basis of maintenance – in contradistinction to casual occupations;

the more clearly defined are the necessary qualifications for practising it and the more specialized the institutions where the qualifications entitling one to pursue the given activity may be acquired – in contradistinction to work which anyone can do.

Because of the tendency of the family's economic function to disappear in the present epoch, it may, of course, be maintained that the work of the housewife is undergoing a process of professionalization, which as measured by the above determinants, is already evident in some countries. The same may perhaps be said about the work of a political leader (the process of professionalization is highly advanced here). This process is most evident in relation to the social changes in the characteristics of the labour of families operating individual farms.

Peculiarities of the Farmer's Vocation

As applied to the labour of a family on an individual farm the term vocation implies social characteristics which clearly distinguish it from other occupations. The following are among its most important characteristics:[2]

1. The work is done by the family. What is more, the generally accepted pattern of the organization of labour on an individual farm assumes family participation.[3] Otherwise, it is either not fully accomplished, not done properly or it meets with considerable difficulties. Contrary to the case of domestic production, which often involves the family but where it can be easily substituted by some other group, on the individual farm the range and system of activity are harmoniously linked with the family as the production crew, according to the physical capacities of the family members and their places in it.

2. For a broader treatment see Galeski (1963a).
3. Farms operated by single males or females are not considered to have full value. See, for instance, Wierzbicki (1963).

2. The farmer's (family's) place in the vocational category is designated by his class position. His vocational advance is connected with the degree of possession of means of production. This characteristic is not peculiar to the farming vocation, for class position is in general closely correlated (sometimes very closely, as in the handicrafts, for instance) with the vocational position. The director of a capitalist factory is often a co-owner, an office worker is generally a wage worker. But with the farmer there is an identification of the class and vocational position. The farmer's role as owner and as producer are inseparable. Here the class position of owner is defined as that of producer. The richer farmer, the more he is also an organizer and manager, while the small farmer works also as an executive not only for himself but also among his neighbours.

3. The farmer's labour is to a great degree autonomic. He produces objects which satisfy his own basic needs. Every other vocation may be pursued only in connexion with the practice of other vocations. Otherwise the individual producer could not work or even exist. True, the modern farmer too could not exist without the labour of people in other occupations. But it was not so long ago when the peasant family produced almost everything necessary for its existence. The relation between the farmer's vocation and other occupations is hence not of equal weight on both sides. Society could not exist without the farmer, while the life of the farmer would be immeasurably more difficult if he were not linked with a system of the social division of labour, but he would be able to keep alive.

4. The activity composing the farmer's labour covers not only a wide scope but is also the basis for separate occupations. It is not just a matter of the farmer having to know many things. There are many occupations where knowledge in many fields is useful or even necessary. Though a certain knowledge in the field of building, for example, is useful for the director of a larger enterprise so as to be able to orientate on the enterprise's building investment, he doesn't work as a carpenter or mason. The farmers, however, must often engage in labour which constitutes the basis of other occupations. He first of all carries on the farming occupation proper (breeding, gardening, production organizer, etc.),

then other trades connected with agriculture (food processing, for example), or even non-agricultural occupations (tool and implement repair, transport, minor building activity, etc.). The farmer cannot have the necessary preparation for all the jobs he does, but the most important thing is that he does them in the same manner as repairing an electric light in one's home, i.e., not professionally. But it is precisely all these tasks which compose the farmer's vocation.

Hence consideration of the peculiarity of the farmer's vocation suggests the following conclusion. The work of a family running its own farm may be defined as practising a vocation only on the grounds that, as productive labour raising means of subsistence, it occupies a definite place in the modern organization of production based on the social division of labour. In essence, however, this labour does not bear the characteristics of a vocation, and constitutes a relic of a different mode of social organization of production, one not based on the division of occupations. The range of activity composing the labour of a family farm is, however, already considerably limited and is in the process of being further restricted by the development of the social division of labour outside the farm. There is hence in effect a process of adaptation of this type of labour to the occupational pattern of the organization of production in society.

The Process of Professionalization of the Farmer's Labour

The process of professionalization of the farmer's labour may be analysed on a broad range. For it is expressed in many directions due to the character of the individual farm: the changes in the farm and the family, the farmer's manner of working, the fields of activity composing it, the farmer's mode of thinking about the farm and his attitude to his work. This process may also be conceived on the background of the general social transformations expressed in changes of the socio-occupational or class-vocational social structure.

The formulation class-vocational structure is used because of the fact that under conditions of the private ownership of the means of production there is a clear connexion between the place of the individual in the class and the vocational structure; in reference to farmers this relation has been defined as identification. The farmer (family operating an individual farm) is most often at the same time an owner of land, an entrepreneur, a producer and seller of his products. If 'owner' signifies an exclusively class, and 'producer', an occupational position – though connected with one or another class status – then the positions of entrepreneur and seller may also be of a class (if connected with ownership of means of production) as of a vocational character (production or sales manager, a worker employed at storing, shipping or processing and serving clients). Under capitalist conditions it is proper to speak of concentration of the land, primarily in the form of the mortgage debt holders. There is also the concentration and centralization of other means of production as a result of indebtedness and the activity of enterprises renting out farm equipment or providing farm services (for instance, firms conducting a number of operations for farmers with their own crews and machinery). Also in effect is the concentration of the production and marketing of agricultural produce through the operations of special food industry corporations, by contract production for private firms, complete control of the market, etc. This leads, in the words of Marx, to a situation where under capitalism 'The small holding of the peasant is now only the pretext that allows the capitalist to draw profit, interest and rent from the soil, while leaving it to the tiller of the soil himself to see how he can extract his wages' (1852, p. 178). The farmer is reduced by the development of capitalism to the class position of a worker (and not as definite as that of an industrial worker), and to the occupational role of a producer. This process of class polarization is hence simultaneously one of the professionalization of the farmer's labour. However, the basis has not been removed for the appearance of both class and occupational elements in the farmer's situation, as long as this process has not eliminated the peasant farm. One expression of this process, however, is the fact that these elements differ in individual types of farms and appear in different proportions. Although this process has thus far not abolished the individual peasant farm, its direction is clear and definite.

Under socialist conditions, both in the sphere of existence of individual farms (or in the socialist model which assumes its persistence) as with the prevalence only of multi-family farms (producers' co-operative farms) the process of professionalization, consisting of the separation of the functions of production organizer, producer and salesman, is not connected with class polarization. And though this process is far advanced in some countries, it has not been fully realized.

The process of the division of the farmer's labour into the tasks of organizer and director of production, of producer and distributor is connected both under capitalism and socialism with the emergence of large agricultural enterprises integrated vertically or horizontally. It is certain that in large agricultural enterprises there is not only a separation of the functions in question here (first of all of the organizational–managerial and productive functions). There is also a division of activities composing the farmer's labour into different occupational specialties: for instance, agricultural accounting, stock breeding, gardening, field cultivation. There emerges besides a hierarchy of occupational or professional posts: enterprise director, agrotechnician, team foreman, agricultural worker. The same applies to an enterprise based on vertical integration, except that the functions of salesman, processor and producer are clearly separated here. But there is also a differentiation of the organizational–managerial functions which are removed from the farm and concentrated in the enterprise. This is accompanied by a narrowing of the field of productive activity of the peasant family because of the production-service agencies, such as the machine station, for instance.

The emergence of large agricultural enterprises is connected with the acquisition by the individual farm of elements of an enterprise and the separation of the household economy from the production establishment. The characteristics distinguishing the farmer's vocation from other occupations hence tend to weaken. The result of the emergence of agricultural enterprises and the growth in the peasant farm of elements of an enterprise is a rise in the agricultural division of labour and the formation of differentiated vocational structures in this division of the national economy. With the formation of these structures the term farmer becomes less and less suitable, and it becomes more proper to speak of various vocational categories in agriculture in an ever broader sphere. And with the progress of the process of professionalization the term peasant class or stratum also becomes less and less applicable. These questions, however, require separate treatment.

It must be borne in mind though that the individual farm is not only an enterprise but also a household economy. The process of professionalization of the farmer's labour is effected not only by the narrowing of the scope of the family's productive activity, but also by the reduction of its tasks in the household economy. With the expansion of the general social division of labour, a number of traditional activities of the farm family (for instance, sewing clothes) are definitely transferred to industrial establishments. Other economic and upbringing tasks of the farm family are also reduced (by the school, clubroom, crèche, kindergarten) although this process is slower than in the urban areas. For it is confronted with a number of difficulties connected with the existence of the farm and the existence of family patterns subordinated to the functioning of the farm.

Finally, connected with the professionalization process is a rise in the number of small farm owners who are steadily gainfully employed in non-agricultural occupations. Here the professionalization process takes place not in connexion with the formation of agricultural labour occupational structures, and the growth of the network of productive and non-productive social services for the benefit of rural families. The process is rather effected by the changes in the very character of rural settlements which are to a great extent becoming residential centres of populations occupationally connected with the city and industry. Consideration of the family pattern of production which constitutes the foundation of the individual peasant farm and of the farmer's vocation requires noting also the above trend, for it is the cause of the family production pattern being limited, in this case by the owner going to work in non-agricultural occupations, and of the individual farm losing the characteristics of an enterprise and assuming the traits of a household economy.

It is impossible for any discussion of the professionalization process not to note that its source lies outside the farm. For it is the market and industry which create the main impulses for change. State intervention plays an important role here. Prohibition of land fragmentation, the introduction of social security and retirement pensions, the requirement of agricultural education for heirs, the dissemination of agricultural services, etc. – such are some expressions of this intervention.

On a macro-sociological scale, an analysis of the professionalization of labour, of its tempo, the difficulties it confronts and which it creates, requires investigation of the variables of the agricultural population's socio-occupational structure as well as of that of the rural inhabitants generally. This has been treated separately (Galeski, 1963b) and there is no need to develop the question here. But the process of professionalization of the farmer's labour can be analysed from another angle – that of the farmer's attitude to his labour and occupation.

The Farmer's Occupational Activity and Attitude to his Labour and the Farm

We continue to use the term 'farmer' in the sense of a family operating an individual farm or a multi-family farm. As pointed out above, this term is too general and hardly suitable in relation to other individuals employed in agriculture: on large agricultural enterprises, processing plants and establishments serving the peasant farm (and the agricultural economy in general), the agricultural administration, agricultural stations and scientific institutions as well as in the system of diffusion of agricultural knowledge. In reference to this agricultural personnel the sociological subject matter doesn't differ basically from the general theme of the sociology of labour, although there appear here certain variations connected with the small number of work establishments, the comparatively undeveloped division of labour, the relation between the place of work and residence (moreover, living in the country) as well as variations connected with the technical characteristics of agricultural production. The question of the occupational attitudes of the agricultural personnel employed off the farm is touched here only peripherally, for it is a matter of outlining primarily questions beyond the range of other branches of sociology, but are subjects of rural sociology. Only one problem of agricultural workers requires at least a few sentences here.

The conviction has been expressed in recent years in sociological literature, and first of all in journalism, that the main motive of the flight of the young people from the village is the way of life based on the individual farm, and not the conditions of life in agriculture. In other words, that it is not a flight from agriculture, but from the peasant way of life (Chalasinski, 1963). On the whole correct, this conclusion seems to be oversimplified. The rural youth undoubtedly reject this way of life which denies them the values they aspire to (first of all, a vocation or profession) which are connected with the town and industry. However, the phenomenon applies to an even greater extent to large farms, where the farming methods do not necessarily generate the characteristics of the peasantry way of life, while these characteristics certainly do not appear on a larger scale than on the peasant family farm. It therefore seems that the decisive role here is played by the difficult conditions of labour in agriculture. But then there are other factors inclining young people to leave the village which are connected with the way of life based on the individual peasant farm as well as factors which check this phenomenon. It must be said without elaborating that this question too indicates the need of a separate study of the situation of young people on individual farms. This situation is not comprehensible without considering the particular traits of the peasant family, for when they leave the farm the rural youth leave not only their place of work but also their family homes. The aversion of young people to work at agriculture in general should be regarded as a separate problem, since the matter of the peasant way of life doesn't seem to play any important role here.

We now turn to the first sociological problem in connexion with the question of the incentive to occupational activity or with the attitude on which it is based. When determining the factors which influence the level of occupational activity in some sphere, economists are usually inclined to regard as decisive the income attained as a result of the activity. This is undoubtedly an oversimplification. Work may be undertaken not only in order to obtain means of subsistence and without regard to the magnitude of the earnings it assures. Ideological incentives: the spirit of emulation, the satisfaction of a job well done, etc., may operate – besides economic incentives. Motivations for labour transcending the economic one are firmly related with certain situations (war, revolution) or with given environments (inventors, artists, scientists, writers, civic leaders), but their impact on occupational activity is undoubted. There is nevertheless a basis for the economist's simplification. Thus in both the capitalist and socialist systems income determines an individual's access to very many generally desired values. Under conditions of socialism, the influence of the material incentive is undoubtedly limited on account of the considerably reduced spread between incomes and the more limited stock of values money can acquire. Then there is the limited significance of money with respect to the values it can acquire. For instance, the acquisition of rare goods is determined under socialism not only by the amount of money one possesses (the short supply of articles doesn't always affect their price fixed by the State), but also by other factors, such as the system of distribution, for instance. Nevertheless, the principle 'to each according to his performance', adopted by socialism, finds its expression also in income differentiation, hence of access to generally desired values. This principle is the basis for the proposition that income magnitude under socialism expresses the degree of social recognition of the individual's work. It is hence obvious that the desire to obtain means of subsistence and to raise one's income is the most potent and, on a mass scale, the decisive factor of occupational activity – except for unusual situations or for particular social circles. Thus where economic policy has a decisive influence on the behaviour of incentives it to a great extent affects not only the level of occupational activity and its direction but, because of the weight of economic life, also the totality of inter-personal relations.

While recognizing the basic role of economic incentives, it would be incorrect to reduce them, in reference to the peasant family, exclusively to market incentives. For that is not their only source of income, while for some it mainly lies elsewhere.[4] What

4. For example the family of so-called part-time farmers.

is most important, it would be erroneous to think that the peasant family regards the farm only as a means of income. This is perhaps so in relation to some farms of a clearly enterprise character: capitalist farms, for instance, or some 'specialized' commercial farms in Western Europe and the USA (see Rogers, 1960). Firstly, the peasant farm is directly geared to the satisfaction of the needs of the family, hence some changes effected by the family are not connected with the market situation. Secondly, the farm is also where the peasant family lives, therefore any improvements or major investment aim directly to improve the family's living conditions. Family income may in great measure be directed to improvements (new buildings, for instance) not so much with a view to produce more, or to lower costs, but simply so the family may live more comfortably. In many cases the production and consumption aspects of investment cannot be separated. In building a new dwelling house, which is as a rule first in the order of priority of the family's investment intentions (Galeski, 1962), the family improves the farm and raises its level of living at the same time.

Thus the basis of the occupational activity of the farm family is the farm – but the farm regarded as both a source of acquiring and raising income and a goal of spending income on it as a residence and living quarters. The problem of the functioning of the incentives to occupational activity, and of economic incentives in particular, is therefore a sociological question of a specific content in relation to the farmer's vocation (to the peasant farm). It is similar with the question of the direction of this activity.

As noted above, the situation of the farm family is based on the identification of the class and vocational position. Occupational activity may perhaps therefore be examined in either aspect. The traditional desire to enlarge the farm (rarely manifested today under Polish conditions) is a type of activity which definitely leads to changes in the class as in the occupational situation. The enlargement of his holding eliminates the need (or even the possibility) of the farmer working in other occupations or for his neighbours. It often requires the employment of agricultural workers and always changes the farmer's position in his occupation, since there is a change in the proportion of his managing and executive activity with the growth of his role as entrepreneur and seller of commodities.

But remaining on the grounds of occupational activity – the established fact that the mechanism proper to capitalism of rural stratification doesn't function in Poland and other socialist countries (or has only a marginal scope), justifies the proposition that the very combination of the functions of producer, entrepreneur and seller in the farmer's vocational activity projects the necessity of regarding this activity as a factor of formation of various agricultural occupations and of the farmer's self-determination in the framework of the emerging agriculturists' occupational structure. But as long as the individual peasant farm continues to exist, that long will the farmer's vocation be an amalgam of various occupations. Consequently, when dealing with the farmer's occupational activity it is necessary to state the direction of that activity. For activity here may be measured by labour input, the result of production, the rational organization of the labour process, market orientation, introduction of technical improvements, etc. Furthermore, since the time and interest the farmer devotes to the farm cannot be separated into interest in a production establishment and in a domestic economy, all general and quantitative comparisons of the vocational activity of the farmer and non-farmer seem highly problematical (Makarczyk, 1961). It is consequently necessary to clearly define the activity under consideration: whether it is a matter of comparing different groups of the rural population (Mleczko, 1962), or of the connexion between individual and group activity (Galaj, 1961). But in any of its conceptions, the question of the farmer's occupational activity cannot be examined without taking into account the fact that involved here is a vocation which combines the activity of various occupations and which is the basis for their formation as separate occupations. Activity in the farmer's vocation is therefore always one leading to some other occupation.

The above proposition also applies to the question of the so-called good farmer. This conception, so often used in public addresses and in journalism, as an investigation shows (Marek, 1964), is by no means a uniform one in the countryside. First of all, in some regions of a traditional peasant culture a 'good farmer' is as a rule one who has much land.[5] Secondly, even where occupational traits possess an independent value, this conception contains different contents – a 'good farmer' is a good organizer of the labour processes, a diligent person, one who knows what is profitable to produce, an innovator in some agricultural speciality, a person of much experience, the director of an agricultural school or a popularizer of agrarian science. The accepted 'good farmer' stereotype may differ in individual communities and be the basis for the characterization of the more general changes they are undergoing as well as for grasping the difficulties confronted by activity which aims to convince the farmers of one or another measure advantageous to them. For example, the activity of an agronomist in convincing farmers than it is irrational to own horses may be in vain if in the given community a farmer's prestige is based on possession and not on the economic effects of his labour (Mendras, 1958). This is why it is necessary to recognize distinctions between different types of 'good farmers' in practical determinations and in research; while in propagating the ideal 'good farmer' image one must be clear on which 'good farmer' he has in mind.

This leads to the problem of the paths to advancement in the farmer's vocation. It follows from the character of the peasant farm that the hierarchy of positions in the vocation is connected with that held in the family. Becoming head of the family is synonymous with attaining vocational independence. Advancement in the vocation is consequently connected with changes in the family and not with qualification. Reaching maturity means acquisition of experience. The farmer's vocation begins with apprenticeship and proceeds from tending geese, pasturing the cows and serving as farm hand to the status of farmer.

As shown above, advancement in the farmer's vocation takes place also on the class plane by passage from the position of owner of small means of production to that of operator of a larger farm. The place of the individual in the family and the position of the family in the class hierarchy thus determine the main paths of

5. Research conducted in 1960 by the Workshop of Rural Sociology at the Institute of Agricultural Economy shows that 70 per cent of respondents consider that one with little land cannot be a good farmer.

advancement in this vocation. Undoubtedly, here too acquiring a speciality in some of the above mentioned fields of activity is essential for attaining generally desired values, and recognition by the community of neighbours, in particular. Research on the farmer's occupational ambitions would enable one to establish the exact importance of this factor. So far, though, this factor has not designated the main paths of advancement in the vocation. The relatively lesser significance of preparatory schooling, of acquiring qualifications (here primarily the qualification of landownership) to vocational advancement is the consequence of particular variables of this occupation which alienate many young people from tying their future to the farm.

The process of professionalization of farm labour and the emergence of large agricultural enterprises with a differentiated occupational structure open new paths of advancement in the vocation. But as long as the individual peasant farm persists, a considerable part of the population will continue to be excluded from that mechanism.

A young adult generally acquires enough experience on a peasant farm to be able to manage it. Activities which the boy or girl perform on the family farm are connected with their age and prepare them for the role of farmer (Chalasinski, 1937, vol. 1). The transmission of knowledge consists in the gradual initiation of the apprentices in all the rites of the occupation (Dobrowolski, 1937), which goes hand in hand with the inculcation of given standards and moral values, beliefs and customs. But the nature of the knowledge which consists of the accumulated experience of their forefathers and the mechanism of its transmission bear the heavy weight of tradition and constitute the foundation of conservatism in the farmer's mode of labour. The school in this system of knowledge transmission is a foreign element, coming from the outside. It limits the family's rearing influence, tears the child from the harmonious system of work and life and introduces into its consciousness patterns which are dissonant with, and values foreign to or impossible of realization within that system (Chalasinski, 1937, vol. 4): hence the resistance confronted by the school in rural areas. But the constantly growing orbit of conflicts between the farmer and society outside the village impels recognition of the need for this institution and is the basis for its acceptance. Still, while the general academic school has been fully accepted in many countries, the agricultural vocational school still meets with considerable reluctance to recognize its value in preparing a young person to run a farm,[6] and even more to accept its actual utilization for that purpose (Galeski and Wyderko, 1959). As in the case of the general school, the agricultural school becomes an indispensable element of vocational preparation mainly as a result of government regulations, hence of pressure from the outside.[7] Nevertheless most countries have taken steps to diffuse agricultural services.

In the majority of countries the press, radio and television conduct chats with farmers, along the same lines as the practical advice programmes for women. This is due to the specific characteristics of farm labour which is only formally and not actually regarded – and cannot be regarded – as a vocation. No other vocation is surrounded with such all-sided activity calculated to diffuse scientific knowledge. Sociological themes in relation to this activity are most often of a practical character and the aim of research in this field is usually to work out effective principles guiding the activity. Thus sociologists investigate how agricultural knowledge reaches the farmer, the effectiveness of the advice by agronomists or suppliers of agricultural means of production (feed, machinery, fertilizers). They also investigate the penetration mechanisms of new technological information originating with agronomists or farmer-innovators and disseminated by leading farmers to the rest, as well as the mechanisms of the anchoring of some technology as an obligatory standard in a given community (Rogers, 1960, p. 419), etc. But the process of diffusion of agrotechnical knowledge has a broader sociological scope. We have in mind first of all the nature of resistance to technical innovations in the countryside. Often this resistance has an economic content. It is not easy for a small

6. In a poll conducted by the Public Opinion Poll Centre 20 per cent of farmers considered the agricultural school unnecessary for the farmer. See Galeski (1961).

7. The Polish Seym (parliament) adopted an ordinance in 1963 on the obligatory agricultural education of inheritors of a peasant farm.

farmer to purchase the necessary equipment, the risk of introducing some branch of production is great and the labour input is high. Most often though the economic motive is not the only one for the farmer's reluctance to introduce improvements. As indicated earlier, economic arguments may not convince the farmer if he is activated by other considerations, such as prestige based on ownership and not on productivity, for instance.

Technical improvement changes the manner of working fixed as the standard by family upbringing and, as already pointed out, meets with opposition from rural conservatism. Changes in the mode of labour also alter the division of obligations in the family or cause their unequal distribution. They furthermore alter the prevailing family way of life, its customs and order of tasks fixed for generations. Questions connected with improvement are therefore inseparable from the whole system of rural life on which the farm is based.

Moreover, the penetration of technical innovations originates first of all in the system of neighbourly contacts, which are elements of the rural social structure. Outside influences which ignore this structure may effect some change or another but will be of little effect. The initiation of any measure by a family low in the rural prestige hierarchy, for instance, is rarely successful. The opinion of neighbours and self-evaluated social position may consequently exert an essential influence on whether the farmer under takes some initiative or not. Also of importance in this respect is the kind of contact with the farmers by those who conduct vocational educational work among them, i.e., whether the positions of imparters and receivers of information are those of equals or not, and what their personal relations are. An agronomist enlightening a farmer head of the family in the presence of his wife and children how he is to manage his farm is an example of an ineffective way of diffusing agricultural science. Hence this question cannot be treated in separation from the rural family and the village community.

The diffusion of agrotechnical knowledge is carried on by the State and farmers' professional organizations. This question, like the problem of the farmer's place in the occupational structure as well as the related question of the position occupied by prestige in the farmer's vocation, require separate treatment. But it is worth nothing here that farmers' professional organizations generally bear particular traits in comparison with other professional organizations. These are traits connected with the peculiarities characterizing the farmer's vocation. They are generally of a more or less clear class character, though that is not their specific trait. They are organizations of representatives of small enterprises and household economies. Their function is therefore to organize the combined activity of producers and consumers, who are at the same time sellers and entrepreneurs in fields profitable to them. Hence the priority of economic questions. Simultaneously the farmers' professional organizations must deal with matters concerning the families living in given territorial communities. They must hence acquire a communal character. This type of professional organization thus combines the characteristics of a political party, a co-operative (producers, consumers), and of a territorial self-government. Under socialist conditions, with the lack of a foundation for rural stratification (as a result of the socialization of the means of production) or of conditions for its deepening, the class role of the farmers' professional organizations either vanishes or is limited. There may thus ensue an identification of professional, co-operative and farmers' self-government organizations. However, the formation of the vocational structure of agricultural labour prepares the ground for vocational organizations in other occupations too. Organizations of this type do not embrace the peasant farm even where they are of a multi-family character, i.e., producers' co-operatives.

The questions connected with the farmer's vocation treated above constitute at least a preliminary basis for explaining the farmer's place in the occupational structure of society. Omitting the connexion between occupational and class structure, which appears with special sharpness here, it must be asserted that because of the objective characteristics of the farmer's vocation it is necessary rather to separate it from the system of occupations, as that part of the social division of labour which has so far not been fully mastered by the occupational model, but which is subjected to and adopted by that model. This accounts for the fact that the relatively high social evaluation of the farmer's occupation (Wesolowski and Sarapata, 1961) doesn't correspond to its objective attractiveness, i.e. attractiveness measured by the influx of people into agriculture. In considerations of the decline of the farmer's vocation there is usually a lack of perception of the contradictions between the declared recognition and that expressed in behaviour. Nor is it adequately perceived that this situation cannot be basically altered as long as agriculture remains the domain of the family production model.

The sociological problems of the farmer's vocation outlined here pertain, as indicated, to the peasant family farm. The question of agricultural workers may be successfully treated (despite its undoubtedly distinct features) by the sociology of labour (of occupations). For rural sociology is interested specifically in the occupations pursued by the peasant family, so basically different from others and so inseparably connected with reliquary elements of rural life: the peasant farm, the family, rural society.

The thematology of this vocation embraces:

the determination of its general uniqueness,

disclosure of the paths followed by the process of professionalization of the farmer's vocation.

Expressions of the professionalization process and the distinctness of the farmer's vocation may be observed in sociological problems involved in the investigation of occupation, consequently in the problems of:

the foundation for occupational activity and its incentives,

the direction of that activity,

authority and roads to occupational advancement,

manner of acquiring knowledge and the necessary qualification to pursue that vocation,

the paths to the penetration and diffusion of occupational know-how.

The subject of the farmer's vocation is related to the specific character of farmers' professional organizations and the place of the vocation in the social occupational structure. But this question is more closely connected with the sociological problems of rural society and peasant strata and requires separate treatment.

References

CHALASINSKI, J. (1937), *Mlode pokolenie chlopow* [*The Young Generation of Farmers*], Warsaw.

CHALASINSKI, J. (1963), 'Referat na zebraniu plenarnym I Wydzialu P.A.N.' ['Report at plenary session of Department I of the Polish Academy of Sciences'].

DOBROWOLSKI, K. (1937), 'Chlopska kultura tradycyjna' ['Traditional peasant culture'], *Etnografia Polska*, vol. 1.

GALAJ, D. (1961), *Aktywnosc spoleczno-gospodarcza chlopow* [*Socio-Economic Activity of Farmers*], Warsaw.

GALESKI, B. (1961), 'Tresci zawodowe w opiniach rolnikow' ['The essence of their occupation in farmers' opinions'], *Wies Wspolczesna*, no. 7.

GALESKI, B. (1962), 'Badania nad aktywnoscia zawodowa rolnikow' ['Research on farmers' occupational activity'], *Studia Socjologiczne*, no. 1.

GALESKI, B. (1963a), *Chlopi i zawod rolnika* [*Peasants and the Farmers' Occupation*], Warsaw.

GALESKI, B. (1963b), 'Zawod jako kategoria socjologiczna: Formowanie sie zawodu rolnika' ['Occupation as sociological category: Formation of the farmers' vocation'], *Studia Socjologiczne*, no. 3, (10).

GALESKI, B., and WYDERKO, A. (1959), 'Poglady chlopow na przyszlosc wsi' ['Peasants views on the future of the village'], *Wies Wspolczesna*, no. 4.

KOLB, L. (1949), *Sociological Analysis*, New York.

MAKARCZYK, W. (1961), 'Czynniki stabilnosci i aktywnosci zawodowej rolinkow w gospodarstwach indywidualnych' ['Factors of the stability and occupational activity of individual farmers'], *Studia Socjologiczne*, no. 2.

MAREK, J. (1964), 'Z badan nad autorytetem w zawodzie rolnika' ['Research on authority in the farmers occupation'], *Roczniki Socjologii Wsi*, vol. 1.

MARX, K. (1852), 'The Eighteenth Brumaire of Louis Bonaparte', in Karl Marx and Frederick Engels, *Selected Works*, vol. 1, Lawrence & Wishart, 1950.

MENDRAS, W. (1958), *Les paysans et la modernization de l'agriculture*, Paris.

MLECZKO, F. (1962), 'Konceptualizacja badan nad aktywnoscia spoleczno-zawodowa rolnikow' ['The conceptualization of research on the socio-occupational activities of farmers'], *Studia Socjologiczno-Polityczne*, no. 13.

ROGERS, E. M. (1960), *Social Change in Rural Society*, Appleton-Century-Crofts.

SZCZEPANSKI, J. (1963a), 'Czynniki ksztaltujace zawod i strukture zawodowa' ['Factors shaping occupation and the occupational structure'], *Studia Socjologiczne*, no. 3 (10).

SZCZEPANSKI, J. (1963b), *Elementarne pojecia socjologii* [*Elementary Sociological Concepts*], Warsaw.

WESOLOWSKI, W., and SARAPATA, A. (1961), 'Hierarchia zawodow i stanowisk' ['The hierarchy of occupations and positions'], *Studia Socjologiczne*, no. 2.

WIERZBICKI, Z. T. (1963), *Zmiaca w pol wieku pozniej* [*Zmiaca after Fifty Years*], Warsaw.

16 Daniel Thorner

Peasant Economy as a Category in Economic History

Daniel Thorner, 'Peasant economy as a category in economic history',
*Deuxième Conférence Internationale d'Histoire Économique,
Aix-en-Provence*, 1962, vol. 2, Mouton, pp. 287–300.

Peasant economies, we suggest, have been and still are a wide-spread form of organization of human society.[1] Because of their historical persistence, peasant economies would appear to be well worthy of study in their own right and in their own terms. When we search the literature of agrarian history for discussions of peasant economies we find them scattered among such diverse categories as 'subsistence', 'feudal' or 'oriental'. In discussions of the so-called 'under-developed' areas, peasant economies are frequently dealt with as conglomerations of 'small-scale' units or 'minifundia'. Or they may be relegated to an intermediate or transition stage between 'primitive' and 'modern' (or 'developed') economies. By contrast, we believe there is hope of rich analytical yield if we can find a way of treating 'peasant economies' as a distinctive group.

For this purpose, it is essential to define peasant economy as a system of production and to distinguish it from other historical systems such as slavery, capitalism and socialism. We shall accordingly set out a tentative definition of peasant economy, and then illustrate it by several examples. These will show some of the varied forms which peasant economies have assumed in different continents in modern times. Beneath the apparent variety we shall find in each case a common core.

Before we specify the determining characteristics of peasant economy, we should make our level of analysis absolutely plain.

1. Many writers have utilized the term peasant economy to describe the functioning of *individual* household units. We prefer to reserve the term for entire economies having certain characteristics which we shall specify in the course of this paper.

We are dealing here with the features of the whole economy of sizeable countries. Our units will be at the scale of kingdoms or empires (Japan, Tsarist Russia, China), nations (Mexico) and grand imperial possessions (India, Indonesia).

We exclude from our coverage little possessions, tiny states, and sub-regions of larger states. Nor do we deal with peasant sectors of economies which, taken as a whole, are not peasant economies. We do *not* exclude small nations. Quite a number of them, eg., Ceylon, Paraguay, Syria, Sardinia, Ireland and Scotland before the Union, have had peasant economies, and a few still do today. But in the present paper we have thought it would be clearer if we presented as our examples only countries of a substantial size.

We use five criteria for determining whether the total economy of a given country, nation or large colonial area is to be taken as a peasant economy. All five of these must be satisfied before an entire economy of a given country can be termed peasant. Our first two criteria relate to production and working population. They are intended to help distinguish peasant economies from industrialized economies, whether capitalist or socialist. In a peasant economy, roughly half of the total population must be agricultural; and more than half of the working population must be engaged in agriculture. In a word, we are saying that, to be termed 'peasant', an economy must be primarily agricultural. In a capitalist or a socialist state which has been industrialized, there may remain thousands or even millions of peasants, but we would no longer apply the term 'peasant' to such an economy, *taken as a whole*. The question would rather become one of the 'peasant' sector in a non-peasant economy; the setting would then be different, and a different level of analysis would be required.

Our third criterion[2] requires the existence of a State power and a ruling hierarchy of a particular kind: one in which the 'kinship' or 'clan' order has weakened sufficiently to give way to a 'territorial State'. I am not saying that kinship or kin ties have

2. Re criterion of existence of a State: the administrative structure of the State must comprise a total of at least five thousand officers, minor officials, flunkeys and underlings.

disappeared, for that would be absurd. Rather I require the passage, in the sense of Moret on Egypt (1926), or, in the sense of ancient Greece, the formation of the territorial State.[3] The question of peasant economies in 'feudal' regimes is delicate. So are practically all questions involving that ticklish word 'feudalism'! If I were to be forced to specify now what I have in mind, I would say that I am concerned with the economies of the feudal monarchical States of Western Europe in the late twelfth and thirteenth centuries, rather than with those of the disintegrated and practically non-urban regimes in the ninth and tenth centuries. Here, however, our fourth criterion also comes into play, the rural–urban separation.

We presuppose, for peasant economies, the presence of towns, and a division or break between these towns and the countryside that is simultaneously political, economic, social and cultural. In practice or belief, or both, the peasants are held to be a lesser or 'subject' order, existing to be exploited by all concerned. In social terms, this is considered to be the 'natural order'. We do not consider an economy to be 'peasant' unless it contains a significant number of towns with a definite pattern of urban life, quite different from that of the countryside.[4] Simply as a rough quantitative indication, we can say that the total urban population should amount to at least half a million persons; or, alternatively, that at least 5 per cent of the entire population of a given country should be resident in towns. By insisting that a peasant economy must have towns, we wish to do more than establish the mere fact that the economy is not purely agricultural. We posit a fairly marked degree of division of labour in society, and a dis-

3. The area of the ancient Greek states, however, was so small that most of them would have to be excluded from our consideration because of failure to meet our initial precondition of sufficient size.

4. There is much literature on the separation between city and country. For the eighteenth century see Sir James Steuart (1767). Marx considered that the entire economic history of human society could be summed up in the movement of the antithesis between town and country (see Marx, 1867, p. 345). Robert Redfield was one of the twentieth-century writers much interested in this theme, particularly in cultural terms, see his study (1956). In an interesting article Lloyd A. Fallers (1961) has carried forward Redfield's line of work.

tinct urban concentration of artisans, or other industrial and intellectual workers of various skills. By the same token we presume that agriculture is sufficiently developed to feed not only the peasants and the governing hierarchies, but also the townspeople.

Our fifth and final criterion, the most fundamental, is that of the unit of production. In our concept of peasant economy the typical and most representative units of production are the peasant family households. We define a peasant family household as a socio-economic unit which grows crops primarily by the physical efforts of the members of the family. The principal activity of the peasant households is the cultivation of their own lands, strips or allotments. The households may also engage in other activities: for example, in handicrafts, processing, or even petty trade. Some members of the family may work, perhaps be forced to work, outside the household from time to time. The household may include one or more slaves, domestic servants or hired hands. But the total contribution of these non-family members to actual crop production will be much less than that of the family members.

In a peasant economy half or more of all crops grown will be produced by such peasant households, relying mainly on their own family labour. Alongside of the peasant producers there may exist larger units: the landlord's demesne or home farm tilled by labour exacted from the peasants, the *hacienda* or estate on which the peasants may be employed for part of the year, the capitalist farm in which the bulk of the work is done by free hired labourers. But if any of these is the characteristic economic unit dominating the countryside, and accounting for the greater share of the crop output, then we are not dealing with a peasant economy. We also exclude specifically all economies in which the most representative agricultural unit is the Roman-style slave estate or the sugar- or cotton-growing slave plantation of modern times.

We may state categorically that in a peasant economy the peasant family members are not slaves. But we shall not try to specify whether the peasants are serfs, semi-free or free. There are, it hardly needs saying, other contexts in which this question is of the highest importance. For the definition of peasant economy, however, the distinction is unnecessary, and the effort to make it likely to prove analytically sterile. We have already indicated that in peasant economies the peasantry as a group is subject and exists to be exploited by others. The peasant may very well have to work one or more days of the week for the baron or the lord of the manor. He may also be obliged to make payments or presents to landlords, functionaries, aristocrats or other important persons. At the same time, from the point of view of production, the peasant households constitute definite – one is almost tempted to say 'independent' – entities. Because of this duality in their position, these peasantries inevitably straddle the line between free and unfree. In a sense the peasant in such economies is simultaneously subject and master.

Within a particular country at a particular time, many varieties or blends of freedom and unfreedom may co-exist. It is usually difficult to say with any precision what proportion of the peasantry are serfs and what proportion are not serfs. With the passage of time, the proportions may change. In some areas, the working populations have oscillated over the centuries through most of the range from freedom to serfdom and back again.

In a peasant economy the first concern of the productive units is to grow food crops to feed themselves. But this cannot be their sole concern. By definition, they live in a State and are linked with urban areas. They must willy-nilly sustain the State, the towns, the local lords. Hence, in one way or another, they must hand over, surrender or sell to others part of their food crops. Although the conditions of exchange are such that the peasants usually give more than they get, they may obtain in return a bit of iron, some salt, spices, perhaps fancy cloth for a marriage.

We should be careful not to slip into the trap of imagining a 'pure' type of peasant household which consumes practically everything it produces and practically nothing else, as distinct from an 'impure' type which produces for a market as well as for its own immediate needs. The latter is historically more common and more characteristic. In point of fact, the household units in peasant economies frequently dramatize their dual focus by growing two crops. The first is the cereal essential to their own sustenance and that of society as a whole; the second is much more likely to be a non-foodgrain (perhaps a fruit, fibre or oilseed) produced precisely with an eye to barter, sale or exchange of some sort. It is as habitual with peasants in many areas to grow two crops as to walk on two feet.

We are sure to go astray if we try to conceive of peasant economies as exclusively 'subsistence' oriented and to suspect capitalism wherever the peasants show evidence of being 'market' oriented. It is much sounder to take it for granted, as a starting point, that for ages peasant economies have had a double orientation towards both. In this way, much fruitless discussion about the nature of so-called 'subsistence' economies can be avoided.

We might say that in a peasant economy roughly half or more of all agricultural production is consumed by the peasant households themselves, rather than being 'marketed'. We do not, however, include as 'marketed' produce those foodgrains handed over around harvest time by indebted or dependent peasant families to the local landlords, merchants, or moneylenders, and subsequently doled back before the next harvest, generally on unfavourable terms, to the same peasant families. Such foodgrains, in our view, have not passed through an organized market process. They have not moved on, via genuine commerce, for consumption by parties other than the original producers. Instead, they have remained in the village where they were grown and have returned to source, to the original producers. In effect, the productive unit is the household, and the consumption unit is the same peasant family household. This is certainly not the indirect process, mediated by a market, which is characteristic of capitalist agriculture. Instead, in a peasant economy, the movement of foodgrains inside the village away from the producing family and back again to that same family is tied in with long-established modes of economic domination and exploitation. When such relationships are typical at the village level, we have an almost sure sign, in an agricultural economy, that we are dealing with a peasant rather than capitalistic structure.

To summarize, we have defined peasant economies in terms of the predominance of agriculture, both in total product and in the working population. We have required the existence of a territorial State, and a separation between town and country. We have indicated that the characteristic unit of production must be the peasant family household with a double orientation, that is, both to its own sustenance and to the greater world beyond the village. We must emphasize that no single one of these elements will suffice to determine whether or not a given economy is indeed a peasant economy. All these features must be found together and must relate to the economy of a whole country.

When we look for examples of peasant economy, in terms of the set of criteria just listed, we find many different kinds scattered throughout recorded history and in all continents except Australia. We shall discuss, in the present paper, only six examples, all within the two hundred years since 1750. There are several reasons for limiting ourselves to the period of the Industrial Revolution and its aftermath. It is, in the first place, the period with which I am most familiar. The modern age is the one for which we have the best documentation, particularly in terms of quantitative materials. More important, under the impact of the expanding industrial system, the two-hundred-odd years since 1750 have witnessed the most fundamental transformations in peasant economy known in history. We ourselves are living witnesses of this process of transformation, which is still continuing; in fact, it is accelerating before our eyes. We are in a position to study at first hand both the nature of peasant economies and the ways in which they resist or yield to change.

As illustrations of cases of peasant economy in this era of change, I propose to characterize in a few words the salient features of the economic structure of six different countries. Any such characterization in so limited space must necessarily appear incomplete and somewhat impressionistic. For this I apologize in advance. My purpose is solely to draw your attention to a few of the chief aspects of each case. My examples are Tsarist Russia, Indonesia, Mexico, India, Japan and China.

Tsarist Russia

Among the peasant economies of the nineteenth century that of Tsarist Russia had the richest and most complicated history, and has left us with the largest literature. As a group, Russian scholars carried the analysis of peasant economies further than anyone else, and were perhaps the first to formulate a theory of peasant economy.[5]

In the century and a half before 1917, the imperial structure of Tsarist Russia was expanding outwardly into Siberia, while inwardly it was decaying at home. In terms of peasant economy, the most distinctive feature of the countryside in the late Tsarist era was the close interdependence of landlord estates, *mir* (village community) lands and rights, and small peasant holdings. In the centuries before the emancipation of the serfs in 1861, the bondage of the peasantry guaranteed the landlords the labour supply needed for their estates. The emancipation enabled cultivating peasant families to get more land of their own, provided they could raise oppressive redemption payments. The size and importance of the old landlord estates was much reduced. By the late nineteenth century individual peasant tenures were gradually increasing in importance.

In the decades before the First World War, a growing proportion of the peasantry devoted themselves to producing for the market with the aid of regularly hired agricultural labourers. In the same period there was a rapid expansion of railways, cities, commerce and factory production on capitalistic lines. The significance of the growth of capitalism in city and country became a hotly debated national issue. Criteria were advanced for distinguishing peasant production from capitalistic agriculture. Many of the questions taken up in the present paper were posed at that time, in one form or another, in the works of Chernyshevsky, Danielson (Nicolai-on), Hourwich, Plekhanov, Kossinsky, Lenin, Chayanov and others.

In the decades after the Revolution of 1917, Russia ceased to be a peasant economy, emerging instead under socialism as both urbanized and industrialized.

5. The leading scholar appears to have been A. V. Chayanov, a number of whose studies were translated into German in the 1920s. Of these, one of the most fundamental was *Die Lehre von der bäuerlichen Wirtschaft*, translated by F. Schlömer and published in Berlin in 1923. A revised, enlarged edition of Chayanov's work appeared in Moscow in 1925 under the title, *Organizatsiya krest'yanskogo khozyaistva*. (Chayanov's book has just been translated into English; this translation [was] published in 1966.)

Indonesia

Under the Dutch, Indonesia constituted one of the oldest and most striking examples of colonial rule in both of its major forms, 'direct' and 'indirect'. For some decades in the middle of the nineteenth century, the peasants were compelled, under the so-called 'culture system', to grow certain crops which the Dutch wanted to export. After that policy was given up in 1870, the Dutch energetically developed large plantations for the growth of export crops. For their labour supply for these plantations, the Dutch drew on the peasants from the bordering villages. There emerged, particularly in Java and Sumatra, a pattern of large plantations, village communities with group rights in land, and small peasants among whom, in the course of time, the sentiment for individual family holdings deepened.

Although the parallel must not be pressed unduly, the pattern of large estates and their labour supply, village community rights in land, and ascendant feeling for family land, bears some resemblance to late Tsarist Russia. The missing element was *indigenous* capitalism which, in a colonial setting, was practically negligible, both in city and country. As of 1949, when the Dutch relinquished control, Indonesia had very little modern industry and a quite limited urban population – barely, enough in fact, to qualify under our criteria as a peasant economy.

Mexico

Striking similarities between the peasant economies of Java and Mexico have already been observed and discussed in an important article by Eric Wolf (1957; see also, 1956). In Mexico, during the century after the end of Spanish rule in 1823, we find a pattern of large estates (*haciendas*), unfree labour supply (peonage), weakening village community rights in land and a very slow growth of individual family holdings.

A great part of Mexican history in the twentieth century turns on the savage struggle of the peasants for land and for resources with which to cultivate it. The revolutionaries, especially those led by Zapata, at first demanded and obtained, in principle, the restoration of village commons which had been seized by the great landholders. In practice, however, very little land was handed back to the villages under restoration proceedings. By 1915 the revolutionary programme called for taking from the great estates land which had not previously been held by the villages, and endowing the peasantry with it. This endowment policy was implemented so vigorously under President Cardenas in the 1930s, that eventually more than 30 per cent of the villagers in Mexico received grants of land. Tens of millions of hectares were transferred either to individual small-holders or to communities (*ejidos*).

Once set up, however, the *ejidos* failed to fulfil the high hopes placed in them. Much of the land turned over to the peasantry was poor in quality and in water supply. The amount of agricultural credit supplied by the Government through the Ejido Bank has been grossly inadequate. Moreover, the funds tended to be directed towards the good risks among the peasants, that is, the peasants with the most fertile land, preferably irrigated. Among the less fortunate peasantry some have leased their lands to the better-off and gone to work for them as hired agricultural labourers. Meanwhile, there has arisen, with the aid of private credit, a new large-scale agriculture utilizing modern techniques to produce profitable export crops.

During the present century, industry has expanded rapidly in certain parts of the country, thanks in large part to substantial foreign investment. Hundreds of thousands of peasants have left their villages to find work in the rapidly growing cities. In recent decades well more than half of the national product has been non-agricultural; and now half of the country's population is urban. Mexico has left her phase of peasant economy (as herein defined) well behind.

India

Up to 1947, India, like Indonesia, was a colonial empire in which both 'direct' and 'indirect' rule prevailed. In India, as compared with Indonesia, the plantations and other large units of cultivation occupied a very minor position in the economy as a whole. There were great landlords in India, some holding hundreds of villages. But cultivation almost everywhere was by peasant families, most of them working very small amounts of land.

Caste and untouchability are distinctive characteristics of India. One of the principal economic functions of caste in the countryside has been to emphasize the inferiority of the lower castes who have for ages served their superiors as a cheap, dependent supply of agricultural labour. Few observers would be so rash as to say that caste has stopped serving that function in the villages of contemporary India.

During their regime, the British developed in India one of the half-dozen largest railways systems in the world. Along with this appeared many other elements of what, in economists' jargon, is called the 'infra-structure' of development. Around Calcutta, Scottish houses developed a jute manufacturing industry, while in Bombay and Ahmedabad Indian entrepreneurs built up several hundred cotton textile mills. Since India attained independence in 1947, the government has thrown its weight behind the rapid development of a comprehensive range of heavy industries. In the 1950s, agriculture, principally carried on by small peasant families still accounted for roughly half of the total national product. India is today still a peasant economy.

Japan

Less than fifty years after the Meiji Restoration of 1868, Japan had ceased to be a peasant economy. There is by now a vast literature assessing this apparently abrupt and dramatic revolution. The leading authorities today agree that the foundations for this genuine and rapid economic transformation antedate the 1868 restoration and go back, particularly in agriculture, far into the preceding period, the Tokugawa era (see Dore, 1959, ch. 1; Smith, 1959).

It was in the Tokugawa period, roughly from the seventeenth to nineteenth centuries, that the Japanese countryside took on the pattern of cultivation in small units by individual peasant families which has persisted to the present. Taxes were collected in kind from the villages for the great feudal overlords and amounted at times to as much as 60 per cent of the crop. The warrior class, for the most part, had been gathered up into the castle towns where they lived on rice stipends. In the relatively few large holdings which remained, cultivation by serfs (*nago*) and servants, gradually gave way to tenancy. The 1720 reform, which permitted the mortgaging of land, was followed by the emergence of a group of moneylender-landlords (rich peasants, town merchants, petty rural capitalists, village headmen) whose tenants were often the original cultivating owners.

After the Meiji Restoration of 1868, the peasant proprietors were freed from their feudal obligations and confirmed in the ownership of the land they cultivated. The old rice levies were supplanted by a fixed annual tax in money, payable to the State. At first a heavy burden, these taxes declined progressively in real terms with the long-run rise in the prices of agricultural products.

On the other hand, the need to raise cash to pay the taxes placed the small peasant – always at the margin of his resources – in the position of having to sell his crop at the most unfavourable moment, immediately after the harvest. The same situation worked to the advantage of the richer peasants who sometimes acted as rice brokers.

For tenants, the Meiji reforms brought no benefits. They still had to pay rents in kind and at the rate of about half of an average crop. The rise in the price of rice did not help them, since they marketed so little. In the early 1880s, about one-third of all arable land was worked under tenancy; by the time of the First World War, the fraction had increased to nearly one-half.

The average area worked by Japanese peasants (i.e. the total of the several scattered strips cultivated by the household) was about one hectare (2·47 acres) around 1868, and remained, for most households, roughly the same right up to 1918. In the fifty years after 1868, the total output of rice in Japan nearly doubled, partly because more land was brought under cultivation, but mostly because of an increase in output per acre of the order of 50 per cent. During this period, population increased by roughly 60 per cent. None the less, the standard of living went up.

The story of the fostering of modern industry by the Meiji regime is too well-known to need summary here. One of its important results for the countryside was that the natural increase of rural population was siphoned off by the towns and cities. Thus the size of the agricultural population of Japan remained roughly the same (around five and a half million households) from 1868 to 1918. We must also note that the agricultural households themselves engaged increasingly in non-agricultural side activities, such as handicrafts and other rural industries. Whereas less than one-quarter of the peasant households had such activities in 1884, more than one-third were so recorded by 1919.

The decline in the relative position of agriculture in modern Japan can be indicated in three ways. First, the proportion of the population living in villages, usually defined for Japan as places with less than 10,000 inhabitants: this percentage was put at 87 per cent in 1888, then at 68 per cent in 1918, and fell to 50 per cent in 1940. Our second indicator is the proportion of the total working force returned as in agriculture. According to Professor Ohkawa, one of Japan's foremost authorities, this proportion stood at 76 around 1880, at 59 around 1915, and at 44 around 1940. Lastly, the percentage contribution of agriculture to total national income; again following Professor Ohkawa, this stood at 64 per cent around 1880, dropped sharply to 36 per cent around 1915, and fell to only 17 per cent around 1940. In terms of our first criterion of peasant economy, contribution of agriculture to total national production, Japan, by the eve of the First World War, had unmistakably stopped being a peasant economy.[6]

China

As in India and Japan, the agriculture of China for several centuries before 1950 had been the *petite culture*. Nearly all crops were grown by families holding roughly on the average about one hectare (somewhat more in the wheat areas of the north, somewhat less in the rice areas of the south). These holdings were generally made up of tiny, uneven, scattered patches. Family members themselves did the farm labour; only a very small percentage of the cultivators, the best-off ones with the most land, used much hired labour.

6. The data of Professor Ohkawa are taken from the comprehensive summary article which he and Henry Rosovsky prepared under the title, 'The role of agriculture in modern Japanese economic development'. This appeared in a special number of *Economic Development and Cultural Change* devoted to the topic, 'City and Village in Japan'; and contains many other relevant contributions.

Before the Revolution of 1911 there was much tenancy in China; and, as the century advanced, more peasants had to give up the ownership of part or all of their land. By the 1930s, half, or more than half, of the Chinese peasants were tenants or petty owners-cum-tenants. Rents generally were paid in kind and amounted to 50 or 60 per cent of the crop. Paying such heavy rents on their tiny holdings, the Chinese peasantry could not make do from the land alone. For most of them, unfortunately, there was insufficient alternative work.

The peasant handicrafts, which had traditionally offered supplementary employment, weakened before the competition of machine-made goods from Japan and the West. The development of modern cities was very limited and entirely inadequate to drain off (as in Japan) population from the countryside. Instead, about 70 per cent of the population continued to work in agriculture.

The difficulties of the peasantry were compounded by multiple exactions from landlords, warlords, usurers and petty government officials. They suffered further in the course of wars, invasions, famines, civil war and revolution.

In the years since 1950 the Peking regime has exerted tremendous efforts to transform this peasant economy. In the cities there has been an immense development of modern industry. In the countryside the vast programme of land reform began by taking away the properties of the landlords and redistributing the land in small bits to the peasants. This has been followed by a series of efforts to encourage or to impose large-scale cultivation: mutual aid in the form of work teams, village co-operatives, collective farming and the establishment of very large rural communes.

We are not in a position to assess the extent to which these programmes have reduced the importance of peasant family cultivation in Chinese agriculture. Nor do we know whether agriculture contributes half or more of the total national product. It is hard to say with any assurance whether or not China is still a peasant economy.

Since our six examples of peasant economy have been drawn from the modern world, we have been more explicit with regard to those criteria separating them from industrial economies than to those separating them from slave or 'tribal' systems. We have, in effect, dealt only with peasant economies in their 'high' or 'late' phase. None the less, we have seen that conditions differed in several important respects, which may be worth listing:

1. Indigenous or colonial rule.

2. Small-scale cultivation only; or small-scale juxtaposed with large-scale cultivation and, if the latter, the arrangements for labour supply on the large-scale units.

3. Individual family holdings of land only; or individual family holdings in the context of larger group holdings or village community rights in land.

4. Hierarchy of peasantry at the village level; existence and social role of a class of agricultural labourers.

5. Urbanization and industrialization as factors in reducing the relative importance of the peasantry in the economy taken as a whole, and in leading to the transformation of peasant production.

We might say we have sketched in a preliminary way cases of countries at the exit, or seeking the exit, from peasant economy. It would, of course, be possible and desirable to take up cases of entrance into peasant economy. In the largest sense, the study of peasant economies should encompass the whole process of their appearance, the changes they undergo through time, and the ways in which they become – or fail to become! – transformed into modern industrial economies.

It may be of interest to situate peasant economy, as we have defined it, in relation to Karl Marx's well-known modes of production. Our peasant economies include societies falling under both Marx's feudal mode of production and his 'Asiatic Societies'. In addition, they take in those periods of history which he characterized as marked by small peasant agriculture and which he treated as transitions from one main mode of production to another.

We believe that our broader grouping, peasant economy, is justified analytically in terms of the common characteristics which we have just discussed and illustrated. It would, of course, be possible to extend the term 'feudal' (with or without the prefixes 'semi-', 'proto-' and 'pseudo-') to cover this whole range, but that would be unfortunate. The term feudalism originated in Western Europe and carries with it a set of specific connotations. We cannot help but be reminded of the feudal lord, the vassal, the fief, the feudal contract, the manor and the serf. This full complex of phenomena, however, occurs only in a small number of centuries in quite confined areas of extreme Western Europe and Japan. Peasant economies, by contrast, existed long before feudalism, alongside of feudalism, and long after it. They persist in our contemporary world. No matter how the content of the term is thinned out, feudalism cannot serve to cover a historical canvas stretching eastward from the Caribbean to the China Seas.

From our perspective, European feudalism of the high Middle Ages may be seen as embodying a particular form of peasant economy. Nothing is gained by trying to view *all* peasant economies as variations of that one rather special form. The time has arrived to treat European experience in categories derived from world history, rather than to squeeze world history into western European categories.

References

DORE, R. P. (1959), *Land Reform in Japan*, Oxford University Press.
FALLERS, L. A. (1961), 'Are African cultivators to be considered "peasants"?', *Curr. Anthrop.*, vol. 2, pp. 108–10.
OHKAWA, M., and ROSOVSKY, H. (1960), 'The role of agriculture in modern Japanese economic development', *Econ. Devel. cult. Change*, vol. 9, no. 1, part 3, pp. 43–67.
MARX, K. (1867), *The Capital*, D. Torr (ed.), London, 1939.
MORET, A. (1926), *From Tribe to Empire*, London.
REDFIELD, R. (1956), *Peasant Society and Culture*, Chicago University Press.
SMITH, T. C. (1959), *The Agrarian Origins of Modern Japan*, Stanford University Press.
STEUART, J. (1767), *An Inquiry in the Principles of Political Economy*, vol. 1; reprinted by Oliver & Boyd, 1967.

WOLF, E. R. (1956), 'Aspects of group relations in a complex society: Mexico', *Amer. Anthrop.*, vol. 58, no. 6, pp. 1065–78.

WOLF, E. R. (1957), 'Closed corporate peasant communities in Meso-American and central Java', *Southwest. J. Anthrop.*, vol. 13, pp. 1–18.

17 Evgenii Preobrazhensky

Peasantry and the Political Economy of the
Early Stages of Industrialization

Excerpts from Evgenii Preobrazhensky, *The New Economics*, translated
by B. Pearce, Clarendon Press, 1965, pp. 80–124. First published in 1924.

For capitalist accumulation to begin, the following prerequisites
were needed:

1. A preliminary accumulation of capital in particular hands to an
extent sufficient for the application of a higher technique or of a
higher degree of division of labour with the same technique.

2. The presence of a body of wage-workers.

3. A sufficient development of the system of commodity economy
in general to serve as the base for capitalist commodity production and accumulation. [. . .]

By *socialist* accumulation we mean the addition to the functioning means of production of a surplus product which has been
created within the constituted socialist economy and which does
not find its way into supplementary distribution among the agents
of socialist production and the socialist State, but serves for expanded reproduction. *Primitive socialist* accumulation, on the
other hand, means accumulation in the hands of the State of
material resources mainly or partly from sources lying outside
the complex of state economy. This accumulation must play an
extremely important part in a backward peasant country, hastening
to a very great extent the arrival of the moment when the technical and scientific reconstruction of the State economy begins and
when this economy at last achieves purely economic superiority
over capitalism. It is true that in this period accumulation takes
place also on the production-base of State economy. In the first
place, however, this accumulation also has the character of preliminary accumulation of the means for a really socialist economy

and is subordinated to this purpose. Secondly, accumulation of the former kind, that is, at the expense of the non-State milieu, greatly predominates in this period. For this reason we should call this entire stage the period of primitive or preliminary socialist accumulation. This period has its special features and its special laws. [...]

Let us now examine systematically the main methods of primitive capitalist accumulation and compare them, so far as possible, with the analogous or closely related methods and processes of primitive socialist accumulation. We shall take for purposes of comparison not only the period preceding capitalist production but also the epoch of the first steps of capitalist production, because this primitive accumulation, as accumulation from outside the range of capitalist production, was also carried on, under very varied forms, after the appearance of capitalist enterprises.

Let us begin with the plundering of non-capitalist forms of economy. In essence the whole period of the existence of merchant capital, from the moment when the craftsman's work for the customer and the local market gave place to work for distant markets and when the buyer-up [putter-out] became a necessary agent of production, can be regarded as a period of primitive accumulation, as a period of systematic plundering of petty production.

Another form of plundering which was of very great importance was the colonial policy of the world-trading countries. We have in mind here not the plundering which is connected with the exchange of a small quantity of labour for a larger quantity on the base of 'normal' trade, but plundering in the form of taxes on the natives, seizure of their property, their cattle and land, their stores of precious metals, the conversion of conquered people into slaves, the infinitely varied system of crude cheating, and so on. To this category also belong all methods of compulsion and plundering in relation to the peasant population of the metropolitan countries. The robbery of small peasant production in the interests of primitive accumulation assumed many different forms. The celebrated 'enclosure movement', to which Marx devoted such brilliant pages of the first volume of *The Capital*, was not the typical method of primitive accumulation for all countries. The most typical methods were, first, plundering of the serf peasants by their lords and sharing of the plunder with merchant capital, and, second, crushing taxation of the peasantry by the State and transformation of part of the means so obtained into capital.

When the landlord's estate began to be transformed from a purely natural economy into a money or semi-money economy, when the landlords thereby promoted trade on a large scale, and when the growth in their demands stimulated an increase in extortion from the peasantry, they entered into a certain kind of unconscious co-operation with merchant capital. Everything that was plundered in the countryside, except what was consumed on the spot, was sold to merchants. In return the merchants supplied the landlords with the products of urban or foreign industry which served to satisfy their growing and increasingly refined demands. Merchant capital sold these products at a profit of 100 per cent and more. Then it lent money to the ruined gentlefolk at usurious rates of interest. As a result, the feudal lords were in this period in a certain sense agents for merchant capital, transmission pumps for the plundering of small-scale rural production in the interests of primitive capitalist accumulation. Being 'higher class' in comparison with the third estate, legally speaking, they co-operated economically with the merchants, who took not the greater but the smaller share in the matter of extortion from the peasantry.

The other form in which petty production was plundered was State taxes. Out of their receipts from taxation the absolute States encouraged the development of manufacture, giving subsidies to merchants who had become industrialists or to nobles who had transformed themselves into manufacturers. This support was rendered especially to manufactories which in one way or another served to supply the army: textile mills, arms works, metallurgical enterprises, and so on. This kind of transfer of resources from the channels of petty production through the State machine to large-scale production, especially to heavy industry, takes place also in a much later period.

On the role of the state, and in particular on the role of state pressure in the period of primitive accumulation, Marx wrote: 'These methods depend in part on brute force, e.g., the colonial system. But they all employ the power of the state, the concentrated and organized force of society, to hasten, hothouse fashion, the process of transformation of the feudal mode of production into the capitalist mode, and to shorten the transition. Force is the midwife of every old society pregnant with a new one. It is itself an economic power' (1867, p. 776).

This force played a very big role also in the formation of national states as arenas for the activity of merchant capital. The profound class analysis, full of concrete historical truth, to which M. N. Pokrovsky subjected the policy of the Muscovite Tsars, evokes a clear picture of this aspect of the period under consideration. The conquest of the necessary territory, trade routes and so on, is also nothing else but a link in the chain of primitive capitalist accumulation, because without accumulation of the necessary territorial prerequisites the development of merchant capital and its transition to industrial capital could not be carried through successfully. From this standpoint the peasant paid tribute to the Moloch of primitive accumulation not only when part of the rent he paid passed through the hands of the lord into those of the merchant, not only when part of the taxes he paid passed via the State to the manufacturer, but also when he gave the blood of his sons for the winning of new trade routes and the conquest of new lands.

An important role in the process of primitive accumulation is played by the system of state loans, under which there takes place the transfer of part of the annual income of the small producers, in the form of interest payments, into the hands of the capitalist creditors of the state which has contracted the loan. In this connexion Marx says:

The public debt becomes one of the most powerful levers of primitive accumulation. As with the stroke of an enchanter's wand, it endows barren money with the power of breeding and thus turns it into capital, without the necessity of its exposing itself to the troubles and risks inseparable from its employment in industry or even in usury. The State creditors actually give nothing away, for the sum lent is transformed into public bonds, easily negotiable, which go on functioning in their hands just as so much hard cash would. But further, apart from the class of lazy annuitants thus created, and from the improvised wealth of the financiers, middlemen between the government and the nation – as also apart from the tax-farmers, merchants and private manufacturers, to whom a good part of every national loan renders the service of a capital fallen from heaven – the national debt has given rise to joint-stock companies, to dealings in negotiable effects of all kinds, and to agiotage, in a word to stock-exchange gambling and the modern bankocracy (1867, pp. 779–80).

Let us now dwell upon the methods of primitive accumulation which we have enumerated, based mainly on plundering of small-scale production and non-economic pressure upon it, and let us see how matters stand in this connexion in the period of primitive socialist accumulation.

As regards colonial plundering, a socialist State, carrying out a policy of equality between nationalities and voluntary entry by them into one kind or another of union of nations, repudiates on principle all the forcible methods of capital in this sphere. This source of primitive accumulation is closed to it from the very start and for ever.

It is quite different in the case of the alienation in favour of socialism of part of the surplus product of all the pre-socialist economic forms. Taxation of the non-socialist forms not only must inevitably take place in the period of primitive socialist accumulation, it must inevitably play a very great, a directly decisive role in peasant countries such as the Soviet Union. We must consider this point in some detail.

From the foregoing we have seen that capitalist production was able to begin to function and develop further only by relying on the resources obtained from petty production. The transition of society from the petty-bourgeois system of production to the capitalist could not have been accomplished without preliminary accumulation at the expense of petty production, and would thereafter have proceeded at a snail's space if additional accumulation at the expense of petty production had not continued alongside capitalist accumulation at the expense of the exploited labour-power of the proletariat. The very transition presumes, as a system, an exchange of values between large-scale and petty production under which the latter gives more to the former than it receives. In the period of primitive socialist accumulation the State economy cannot get by without alienating part of the surplus product of the peasantry and the handicraftsmen, without making deductions from capitalist accumulation for the benefit of socialist accumulation. We do not know in how great a condition of ruin other countries in which the dictatorship of the proletariat is going to triumph will emerge from civil war. But a country like the USSR, with its ruined and in general rather backward economy, must pass through a period of primitive accumulation in which the sources provided by pre-socialist forms of economy are drawn upon very freely. It must not be forgotten that the period of primitive socialist accumulation is the most critical period in the life of the socialist State after the end of the civil war. In this period the socialist system is not yet in a condition to develop all its organic advantages, but it inevitably abolishes at the same time a number of the economic advantages characteristic of a developed capitalist system. How to pass as quickly as possible through this period, how to reach as quickly as possible the moment when the socialist system will develop all its natural advantages over capitalism, is a question of life and death for the socialist State. At any rate, that is the problem before the USSR today, and that will perhaps be the problem for a certain time for a number of European countries in which the proletariat will come to power. Under such conditions, to count only upon accumulation within the socialist field would mean jeopardizing the very existence of the socialist economy, or prolonging endlessly the period of preliminary accumulation, the length which, however, does not depend on the free will of the proletariat. In the concrete part of this work, which will be devoted to the industry and agriculture of the USSR, we shall cite numerical calculations as to how long we should expect the restoration of our industry even to its pre-war levels to take if we were to rely only on the surplus product of industry itself. In any case the idea that socialist economy can develop on its own, without touching the resources of petit-bourgeois (including peasant) economy is undoubtedly a reactionary petit-bourgeois Utopia. The task of the socialist State consists here not in taking from the petit-bourgeois producers less than capitalism took, but in taking more *from the still larger* incomes which will be secured to the petty producer by the rationalization of the whole economy, including petty production, on the basis of industrializing the country and intensifying agriculture. [. . .]

We can formulate a law, or at least that part of it which relates to the redistribution of the material resources of production, in this way:

The more backward economically, petit-bourgeois, peasant, a particular country is which has gone over to the socialist organization of production, and the smaller the inheritance received by the socialist accumulation fund of the proletariat of this country when the social revolution takes place, by so much the more, in proportion, will socialist accumulation be obliged to rely on alienating part of the surplus product of pre-socialist forms of economy and the smaller will be the relative weight of accumulation on its own production basis, that is, the less will it be nourished by the surplus product of the workers in socialist industry. Conversely, the more developed economically and industrially a country is, in which the social revolution triumphs, and the greater the material inheritance, in the form of highly developed industry and capitalistically organized agriculture, which the proletariat of this country receives from the bourgeoisie on nationalization, by so much the smaller will be the relative weight of pre-capitalist forms in the particular country; and the greater the need for the proletariat of this country to reduce non-equivalent exchange of its products for the products of the former colonies, by so much the more will the centre of gravity of socialist accumulation shift to the production basis of the socialist forms, that is, the more will it rely on the surplus product of its own industry, and its own agriculture.[1]

1. This law must of course, undergo certain modifications when there is a transfer of means of production from an advanced socialist country to a backward one.

Reference

MARX, K. (1867), *The Capital*, F. Engels (ed.), trans. S. Moore and E. Marx Aveling, Allen & Unwin, 1946.

Part Three **The Peasantry as a Class**

Part Three treats the peasantry as a class, i.e. as a social entity based on a community of economic interests, shaped by conflict with other classes, expressed in typical patterns of cognition and political consciousness and capable of united political action on a national level. Attention is focused upon the specific character of peasant political action and in particular on the peasant revolt, very much in the centre of contemporary scholarly attention. The section opens with Marx, the founder of contemporary class theory, whose contribution remains illuminating despite its age. Shanin provides comment on the patterns of political action typical of peasantry, and Wolf concludes with an analysis of the place of peasant rebellions in the shaping of the contemporary world. Feder's study in Part One as well as Fanon's contributions in Part Five are also relevent here. So too is an important analysis of peasantry in history by Barrington Moore Jr, details of which can be found in the Further Reading list.

The major issue not covered is the specific discussion of autonomous peasant political movements operating in legal or semi-legal conditions, though Feder's and Huizer's contributions in Parts One and Five respectively touch on the issue. (For more systematic discussions see the Further Reading list.) The discussion in this Part relates mainly to the national level. The political life at village level is partly considered in Part One.

18 Karl Marx

Peasantry as a Class

Excerpts from Karl Marx, 'The Class Struggles in France 1848–1850' and 'The Eighteenth Brumaire of Louis Bonaparte', in Karl Marx and Frederick Engels, *Selected Works*, vol. 1, Foreign Languages Publishing House, 1950; Lawrence & Wishart, 1950, pp. 159, 302–8. First published in 1850–52.

10 December 1848, was the day of the *peasant insurrection*. Only from this day does the February of the French peasants date. The symbol that expressed their entry into the revolutionary movement, clumsily cunning, knavishly naïve, doltishly sublime, a calculated superstition, a pathetic burlesque, a cleverly stupid anachronism, a world-historic piece of buffoonery and an undecipherable hieroglyphic for the understanding of the civilized – this symbol bore the unmistakable physiognomy of the class that represents barbarism within civilization. The republic had announced itself to this class with the *tax collector*; it announced itself to the republic with the *emperor*. Napoleon was the only man who had exhaustively represented the interests and the imagination of the peasant class, newly created in 1789. By writing his name on the frontispiece of the republic, it declared war abroad and the enforcing of its class interests at home. Napoleon was to the peasants not a person but a program. With banners, with beat of drums, and blare of trumpets, they marched to the polling booths shouting: *plus d'impots, à bas les riches, à bas la république, vive l'Empereur!* No more taxes, down with the rich, down with the republic, long live the emperor! Behind the emperor was hidden the peasant war. The republic that they voted down was the *republic of the rich*.

10 December was the *coup d'état* of the peasants, which overthrew the existing government. [. . .]

Bonaparte represents a class, and the most numerous class of French society at that, the *small-holding [Parzellen] peasants*.

Just as the Bourbons were the dynasty of big landed property and just as the Orleans were the dynasty of money, so the Bonapartes are the dynasty of the peasants, that is, the mass of the French people. Not the Bonaparte who submitted to the bourgeois parliament, but the Bonaparte who dispersed the bourgeois parliament is the chosen of the peasantry. For three years the towns had succeeded in falsifying the meaning of the election of 10 December and in cheating the peasants out of the restoration of the empire. The election of 10 December 1848, has been consummated only by the *coup d'état* of 2 December 1851.

The small-holding peasants form a vast mass, the members of which live in similar conditions but without entering into manifold relations with one another. Their mode of production isolates them from one another instead of bringing them into mutual intercourse. The isolation is increased by France's bad means of communication and by the poverty of the peasants. Their field of production, the small-holding, admits of no division of labour in its cultivation, no application of science and, therefore, no diversity of development, no variety of talent, no wealth of social relationships. Each individual peasant family is almost self-sufficient; it itself directly produces the major part of its consumption and thus acquires its means of life more through exchange with nature than in intercourse with society. A small-holding, a peasant and his family; alongside them another small-holding, another peasant and another family. A few score of these make up a village, and a few score of villages make up a Department. In this way, the great mass of the French nation is formed by simple addition of homologous magnitudes, much as potatoes in a sack form a sack of potatoes. In so far as millions of families live under economic conditions of existence that separate their mode of life, their interests and their culture from those of the other classes, and put them in hostile opposition to the latter, they form a class. In so far as there is merely a local interconnexion among these small-holding peasants, and the identity of their interests begets no community, no national bond and no political organization among them, they do not form a class. They are consequently incapable of enforcing their class interest in their own name, whether through a parliament or through a convention. They cannot represent themselves, they must be represented. Their representative must at the same time appear as their master, as an authority over them, as an unlimited governmental power that protects them against the other classes and sends them rain and sunshine from above. The political influence of the small-holding peasants, therefore, finds its final expression in the executive power subordinating society to itself.

Historical tradition gave rise to the belief of the French peasants in the miracle that a man named Napoleon would bring all the glory back to them. And an individual turned up who gives himself out as the man because he bears the name of Napoleon, in consequence of the *Code Napoléon*, which lays down that *la recherche de la paternité est interdit*.[1] After a vagabondage of twenty years and after a series of grotesque adventures, the legend finds fulfilment and the man becomes Emperor of the French. The fixed idea of the Nephew was realized, because it coincided with the fixed idea of the most numerous class of the French people.

But, it may be objected, what about the peasant rising in half of France, the raids on the peasants by the army, the mass incarceration and transportation of peasants?

Since Louis XIV, France has experienced no similar persecution of the peasants 'on account of demagogic practices'.

But let there be no misunderstanding. The Bonaparte dynasty represents not the revolutionary, but the conservative peasant; not the peasant that strikes out beyond the condition of his social existence, the small-holding, but rather the peasant who wants to consolidate this holding, not the country folk who, linked up with the towns, want to overthrow the old order through their own energies, but on the contrary those who, in stupefied seclusion within this old order, want to see themselves and their small-holdings saved and favoured by the ghost of the empire. It represents not the enlightenment, but the superstition of the peasant; not his judgement, but his prejudice; not his future, but his past; not his modern Cevennes, but his modern Vendée.[2]

1. Inquiry into paternity is forbidden – *Ed.* of *Selected Works*.
2. In *Cevennes*, a mountainous region of France, a large uprising of Protestant peasants (the so-called Camisards) took place in the beginning

The three years' rigorous rule of the parliamentary republic had freed a part of the French peasants from the Napoleonic illusion and had revolutionized them, even if only superficially; but the bourgeoisie violently repressed them, as often as they set themselves in motion. Under the parliamentary republic the modern and the traditional consciousness of the French peasant contended for mastery. This progress took the form of an incessant struggle between the schoolmasters and the priests. The bourgeoisie struck down the schoolmasters. For the first time the peasants made efforts to behave independently in the face of the activity of the government. This was shown in the continual conflict between the *maires* and the prefects. The bourgeoisie deposed the *maires*. Finally, during the period of the parliamentary republic, the peasants of different localities rose against their own offspring, the army. The bourgeoisie punished them with states of siege and punitive expeditions. And this same bourgeoisie now cries out about the stupidity of the masses, the vile multitude, that has betrayed it to Bonaparte. It has itself forcibly strengthened the empire sentiments [*Imperialismus*] of the peasant class, it conserved the conditions that form the birthplace of this peasant religion. The bourgeoisie, to be sure, is bound to fear the stupidity of the masses as long as they remain conservative, and the insight of the masses as soon as they become revolutionary.

In the risings after the *coup d'état*, a part of the French peasants protested, arms in hand, against their own vote of 10 December 1848. The school they had gone through since 1848 had sharpened their wits. But they had made themselves over to the underworld of history; history held them to their word, and the majority was still so prejudiced that in precisely the reddest Departments the peasant population voted openly for Bonaparte. In its view, the National Assembly had hindered his progress. He had now merely

---

of the eighteenth century. Their watchwords were, 'No Taxes!', 'Freedom of Conscience!' The insurgents seized feudal castles, hid in mountains, engaged in guerrilla warfare. The struggle lasted almost three years.

Vendée: The region in France which was a seat of counter-revolution during the French Bourgeois Revolution of the end of the eighteenth century – *Ed.* of *Selected Works*.

broken the fetters that the towns had imposed on the will of the countryside. In some parts the peasants even entertained the grotesque notion of the Convention side by side with Napoleon.

After the first revolution had transformed the peasants from semi-villeins into freeholders, Napoleon confirmed and regulated the conditions on which they could exploit undisturbed the soil of France which had only just fallen to their lot, and slake their youthful passion for property. But what is now causing the ruin of the French peasant is his small-holding itself, the division of the land, the form of property which Napoleon consolidated in France. It is precisely the material conditions which made the feudal peasant into a small-holding peasant and Napoleon into an emperor. Two generations have sufficed to produce the inevitable result: progressive deterioration of agriculture, progressive indebtedness of the agriculturist. The 'Napoleonic' form of property, which at the beginning of the nineteenth century was the condition for the liberation and enrichment of the French country folk, has developed in the course of this century into the law of their enslavement and pauperization. And precisely this law is the first of the '*idées napéoloniennes*' which the second Bonaparte has to uphold. If he still shares with the peasants the illusion that the cause of their ruin is to be sought, not in this small-holding property itself, but outside it, in the influence of secondary circumstances, his experiments will burst like soap bubbles when they come in contact with the relations of production.

The economic development of small-holding property has radically changed the relation of the peasants to the other classes of society. Under Napoleon, the fragmentation of the land in the countryside supplemented free competition and the beginning of big industry in the towns. The peasant class was the ubiquitous protest against the landed aristocracy which had just been overthrown. The roots that small-holding property struck in French soil deprived feudalism of all nutriment. Its landmarks formed the natural fortifications of the bourgeoisie against any surprise attack on the part of its old overlords. But in the course of the nineteenth century the feudal lords were replaced by urban usurers; the feudal obligation that went with the land was replaced by the mortgage; aristocratic landed property was replaced by bourgeois capital. The small-holding of the peasant is now only the pretext that allows the capitalist to draw profits, interest and rent from the soil, while leaving it to the tiller of the soil himself to see how he can extract his wages. The mortgage debt burdening the soil of France imposes on the French peasantry payment of an amount of interest equal to the annual interest on the entire British national debt. Small-holding property, in this enslavement by capital to which its development inevitably pushes forward, has transformed the mass of the French nation into troglodytes. Sixteen million peasants (including women and children) dwell in hovels, a large number of which have but one opening, others only two and the most favoured only three. And windows are to a house what the five senses are to the head. The bourgeois order, which at the beginning of the century set the State to stand guard over the newly arisen small-holding and manured it with laurels, has become a vampire that sucks out its blood and marrow and throws them into the alchemistic cauldron of capital. The *Code Napoléon* is now nothing but a *codex* of distraints, forced sales and compulsory auctions. To the four million (including children, etc.) officially recognized paupers, vagabonds, criminals and prostitutes in France must be added five million who hover on the margin of existence and either have their haunts in the countryside itself or, with their rags and their children, continually desert the countryside for the towns and the towns for the countryside. The interests of the peasants, therefore, are no longer, as under Napoleon, in accord with, but in opposition to the interests of the bourgeoisie, to capital. Hence the peasants find their natural ally and leader in the *urban proletariat*, whose task is the overthrow of the bourgeois order. But *strong and unlimited government* – and this is the second '*idée napoléonienne*', which the second Napoleon has to carry out – is called upon to defend this 'material' order by force. This '*ordre matériel*' also serves as the catchword in all of Bonaparte's proclamations against the rebellious peasants.

Besides the mortgage which capital imposes on it, the small-holding is burdened by *taxes*. Taxes are the source of life for the bureaucracy, the army, the priests and the court, in short, for the whole apparatus of the executive power. Strong government and heavy taxes are identical. By its very nature, small-holding property forms a suitable basis for an all-powerful and innumerable bureaucracy. It creates a uniform level of relationships and persons over the whole surface of the land. Hence it also permits of uniform action from a supreme centre on all points of this uniform mass. It annihilates the aristocratic intermediate grades between the mass of the people and the State power. On all sides, therefore, it calls forth the direct interference of this State power and the interposition of its immediate organs. Finally, it produces an unemployed surplus population for which there is no place either on the land or in the towns, and which accordingly reaches out for state offices as a sort of respectable alms, and provokes the creation of state posts. By the new markets which he opened at the point of the bayonet, by the plundering of the Continent, Napoleon repaid the compulsory taxes with interest. These taxes were a spur to the industry of the peasant, whereas now they rob his industry of its last resources and complete his inability to resist pauperism. And an enormous bureaucracy, well-gallooned and well-fed, is the '*idée napoléonienne*' which is most congenial of all to the second Bonaparte. How could it be otherwise, seeing that alongside the actual classes of society he is forced to create an artificial caste, for which the maintenance of his regime becomes a bread-and-butter question? Accordingly, one of his first financial operations was the raising of officials' salaries to their old level and the creation of new sinecures.

Another '*idée napoléonienne*' is the domination of the *priests* as an instrumentality of government. But while in its accord with society, in its dependence on natural forces and its submission to the authority which protected it from above, the small-holding that had newly come into being was naturally religious, the small-holding that is ruined by debts, at odds with society and authority, and driven beyond its own limitations naturally becomes irreligious. Heaven was quite a pleasing accession to the narrow strip of land just won, more particularly as it makes the weather; it becomes an insult as soon as it is thrust forward as substitute for the small-holding. The priest then appears as only the anointed bloodhound of the earthly police – another '*idée napoléonienne*'. On the next occasion, the expedition against Rome will take place in France itself, but in a sense opposite to that of M. de Montalembert.

Lastly, the culminating point of the '*idées napoléoniennes*' is the preponderance of the *army*. The army was the *point d'honneur* of the small-holding peasants, it was they themselves transformed into heroes, defending their new possessions against the outer world, glorifying their recently won nationality, plundering and revolutionizing the world. The uniform was their own state dress; war was their poetry; the small-holding, extended and rounded off in imagination, was their fatherland, and patriotism the ideal form of the sense of property. But the enemies against whom the French peasant has now to defend his property are not the Cossacks; they are the bailiffs and the tax collectors. The small-holding lies no longer in the so-called fatherland, but in the register of mortgages. The army itself is no longer the flower of the peasant youth; it is the swamp-flower of the peasant *lumpenproletariat*. It consists in large measure of *remplaçants*, of substitutes, just as the second Bonaparte is himself only a *remplaçant*, the substitute for Napoleon. It now performs its deeds of valour by hounding the peasants in passes like chamois, by doing *gendarme* duty, and if the internal contradictions of his system chase the chief of the Society of 10 December over the French border, his army, after some acts of brigandage, will reap, not laurels, but thrashings.

One sees: *all* 'idées napoléoniennes' *are ideas of the undeveloped small-holding in the freshness of its youth*; for the small-holding that has outlived its day they are an absurdity. They are only the hallucinations of its death struggle, words that are transformed into phrases, spirits transformed into ghosts. But the parody of the empire [*des Imperialismus*] was necessary to free the mass of the French nation from the weight of tradition and to work out in pure form the opposition between the State power and society. With the progressive undermining of small-holding property, the State structure erected upon it collapses. The centralization of the State that modern society requires arises only on the ruins of the military-bureaucratic governmental machinery which was forged in opposition to feudalism.[3]

3. In the 1852 edition this paragraph ended with the following lines, which Marx omitted in the 1869 edition: 'The demolition of the State machine will not endanger centralization. Bureaucracy is only the low and brutal form of a centralization that is still afflicted with its opposite, with feudalism. When he is disappointed in the Napoleonic Restoration, the French peasant will part with his belief in his small-holding, the entire State edifice erected on this small holding will fall to the ground and *the proletarian revolution* will obtain *that chorus without which its solo song becomes a swan song in all peasant countries*' – *Ed.* of *Selected Works*.

19 Teodor Shanin

Peasantry as a Political Factor[1]

Teodor Shanin, 'The peasantry as a political factor', *Sociological Review*, vol. 14, 1966, no. 1, pp. 5–27.

Peasants are the majority of mankind. For all but comparatively few countries, 'the people' (as opposed to 'the nation') still denotes 'the peasants'; the specific 'national culture' closely corresponds to peasant culture; 'the army' means young peasants in uniform, armed and officered by men different from themselves. And yet one has to be reminded of this.

'It is a commonplace to say that agrarian history, as such, is neglected – the fact is too obvious to be denied' (Davring, 1956, p. 5): this holds true for many branches of social science as far as the countryside is concerned. The dozen years which have elapsed since this passage was written have not much improved the situation, apart from several notable exceptions in the fields of anthropology and history in the last few years. Indeed, in the growing flood of social science publications, the few existing rural studies have almost been submerged. But reality seems to confute this solipsism of the 'civilized' mind. Day by day, the peasants make the economists sigh, the politicians sweat and the strategists swear, defeating their plans and prophecies all over the world – Moscow and Washington, Peking and Delhi, Cuba and Algeria, the Congo and Vietnam.

Even more striking that the neglect of its study are the emotional undertones and diversities of opinion which shroud this subject. Mitrany's[2] 400 pages bring together but a fraction of the

---

1. This article is a revised and somewhat extended version of a paper that was originally prepared for the first Annual Conference on the Peasantry, held by the Centre for Russian and East European Studies, University of Birmingham in 1965.
2. Mitrany (1961), dealing with Marxist as well as populist ideologies.

views expressed. Writers, scientists and politicians have all contributed to the discussion – in which the image of the peasant has swung from that of an angelic rustic humanist to a greedy, pig-headed brute. For example, in Russia, in one and the same period, the peasantry was held to be 'the real autocrat of Russia'[3] and 'non-existent, historically speaking'.[4] This kind of verbal contest did not make reality much clearer. The peasantry went its own way, quite oblivious of being an intellectual nuisance.

The emotional tension underpinning ambiguous contempt or utopian praise, the replacement of definition by allegory, as well as acute shortcomings in the conceptual grasp of the peasantry, were only too strongly felt in the Western intellectual tradition. The neglect of the subject is but a symptom of this. It calls for a serious study, in the field of the sociology of knowledge, of the *eidos* of intellectual image-makers when dealing with a 'class that represents the barbarism within civilization' (Marx and Engels, 1950, vol. 1, p. 159). The treatment of peasant action as an 'undecipherable hieroglyphic to the understanding of the civilized' (Marx and Engels, 1950, vol. 1, p. 159) seemed to be determined by a conglomeration of factors, of which one stands out as crucial. The peasantry does not fit well into any of our concepts of contemporary society. This 'maddening' peasant quality seems to lie at the roots of the problems of research in this field.

In this paper, we shall start by an attempt to define the *differencia specifica*, of the peasantry – the uniqueness by which the peasantry may be defined and selected. This analytical definition[5] will then be used as a reference-point in historical context. From here we shall proceed to the problem of the peasantry as a part of society, and then to the patterns of political action of this entity. In dealing with this subject, other approaches are feasible – and, indeed, needed. The translation of rich complex reality into a verbal form of fewer dimensions makes many approaches possible and valid, subject to recognition of the limitations involved.

3. V. Chernov, as quoted by Maynard (1962, p. 97).

4. G. Plekhanov on the Russian peasantry.

5. This definition would appear as general type based on comparison of concepts evolved in studies by a number of scholars, but the limited number of societies utilized for comparison makes for a certain tentativeness in the character of this generalization.

The Peasantry: An Analytical Definition

'Peasant society and culture has something generic about it. It is a kind of arrangement of humanity with some similarities all over the world' (Redfield, 1956, p. 25). In this way, Redfield summarizes a wide comparison made of peasants in different period and countries. The peasantry appears to be a 'type without localization – not a typical anthropologist's community' (p. 23).

The peasantry consists of small agricultural producers who, with the help of simple equipment and the labour of their families, produce mainly for their own consumption and for the fulfilment of obligations to the holders of political and economic power. Such a definition implies a specific relation to land, the peasant family farm and the peasant village community as the basic units of social interaction, a specific occupational structure and particular influences of past history and specific patterns of development. Such characteristics lead furthermore to some peculiarities of the position in society and of the typical political action.

1. The *relationship to land* and the specific character of agricultural production lies at the root of some of the specific features of the peasant economy. The produce from the farm meets the basic consumption needs of the peasant family and gives the peasant relative independence from other producers and from the market. This makes for relative stability in peasant households which, in crises, are able to maintain their existence by increasing their efforts, lowering their own consumption and partially withdrawing from any market relations they may have.

The mainly agricultural nature of production puts limits on the density and concentration of population and determines patterns of social intercourse, notably the characteristic annual and other cycles of peasant labour and household life. Nature introduces an element of chance-factors beyond human control – with which all the peasant community is faced.

The holding of land, by being 'a necessary and generally sufficient condition to enter the occupation' (Galeski, 1963, p. 48), acts (along with some other factors) as an entrance ticket into the peasantry. Moreover, position in the hierarchy of peasant subgroups is, to a large extent, defined by the amount of land held.[6]

We shall define property in land as a socially accepted exclusive right to hold and utilize the land concerned, right which is separate from rights acquired by the investment of labour and capital. This right finds expression in the holder's competence to transfer it, at least temporarily. Property in land, in a wide sense, may have the form of, on the one hand, the peasant family holding defined by custom, on the other hand, of politically formalized, legal ownership. In peasant households, land appears as the object of traditionally defined and stable holdings and does not necessarily constitute the object of legal ownership. In actual fact, the legal ownership of peasant land, as seen by a townsman, may lie with the peasant himself, the commune, the landlord or the State; the land being correspondingly a private plot, commune property or a customary lease-holding. 'Landlords are not needed to establish the fact of a peasantry' (Redfield, 1956, p. 28). Their appropriation of part of the peasants' produce, and even their political and administrative domination has generally failed to break the basic features of the peasant/land relationship.

2. The *family farm* is the basic unit of peasant ownership, production, consumption and social life. The individual, the family and the farm, appear as an indivisible whole. 'The identification of interest of family and farm-holding seems to be a typical characteristic of the traditional peasant family' (Galeski, 1963, p. 140). The farm takes the dual form of a production–consumption unit. The balance of consumption-needs, available family labour and the farm's potential, strongly influences a peasant's activities. The profit and accumulation motives rarely appear in their pure and simple form, which makes the neat conceptual models of maximization of income, normal in a market economy, of most doubtful applicability to a peasant economy.[7] The new, rapidly

6. 'A rise within the professional group of farmers is traditionally achieved by enlargement of the land holding, by a rise from the position of owner of a small farm to the position of an owner of a bigger one, and the description "good farmer" is generally attached in the view of the village to all owners of the biggest farms without exception and is not linked to the real professional skill or effectiveness of their work' (Galeski, 1963, p. 47).

7. Proof of this statement cannot be summarized; the reader is referred to the studies by Znaniecki, Galeski or Chayanov and his group.

developing, patterns of industrializing society are to be 'found outside agriculture, which still remains the domain of the family-based model' (Galeski, 1963, p. 57).

Peasant property is, at least *de facto*, family property. The head of the family appears as 'the manager rather than proprietor of family land' (Thomas and Znaniecki, 1918, p. 92), and his function 'has rather the character of management of common family property' (Mukhin, 1888, p. 62). These two descriptions, given by different scholars about the peasantries of two different countries, show striking similarities. Whatever the imposed national legal structure, peasants seem to act within this social frame of reference.

The family's social structure determines the division of labour, the locus of status and social prestige. Moreover, 'the family is the production-team of the farm and position in the family determines duties on the farm, functions and rights attached. The rhythm of the farm defines the rhythm of family life' (Galeski, 1963, p. 140).

The prestige and position of an individual in peasant society is basically determined by two ascribed factors, as is his own evaluation and image of himself. These factors are, firstly, the status of the family he belongs to and, secondly, his position within his family. His position within the family depends primarily on his progression through certain basic ascribed positions – i.e. childhood, partial maturity before marriage, the period after marriage but before full independence, independence (which may be gained either by leaving the family farm and establishing his own, or by becoming head of the family farm on his parents' death or retirement) and, finally, the period of retirement (Thomas and Znaniecki, 1918, p. 93; for a very similar analysis, see Vasil'chakov, 1876, vol. 2, p. 21). Family labour is an essential requirement for conducting a farm adequately. Therefore marriage is 'an absolute postulate' (Thomas and Znaniecki, 1918, p. 107). Family interest directs the choice – and an unmarried man (even a farm-owner) 'arouses unfavourable astonishment' and 'does not count' (Thomas and Znaniecki, 1918, p. 107), since he cannot fully conform to the norms of the way of life of his fellow villagers.

The main defining feature of family membership lies in full participation in the life of the farm unit, the hard core of which consists of a married couple or polygamous group and their offspring. The family to the Russian peasant at the beginning of the twentieth century was generally 'the people who eat from the same pot' and, to the French peasant of the same period, 'the people who are locked behind the same lock' (Chayanov, 1925, p. 21). Family solidarity provides the basic framework for mutual aid, control and socialization. The individualistic element of personal feelings is markedly subordinated to the formalized restraints of accepted family role behaviour. Forming the basic nucleus of peasant society, the life of a family farm determines the pattern of peasants' everyday actions, interrelationships and values. Together with the mainly natural economy, it makes for the segmentation of peasant society into small units with a remarkable degree of self-sufficiency and ability to withstand economic crises and market pressures.

3. The fundamental importance of *occupation* in defining men's social position, role and personality is well known, if little studied. Galeski, however, in his book, which we have already quoted from, concerns himself with this problem both analytically and empirically (Galeski, 1963, ch. 2). The ambiguity residing in the definition of the trade of farmer seems to stem from its unique character. Apart from its family base, its necessary connexion with land-holding and its relatively high degree of independence of the market, its uniqueness lies in its consisting of a peculiarly wide set of interrelated functions carried out at a rather un-specialized level. Although many of the jobs done by the peasant are also done by other occupational groups, the specificity of the peasant's work lies in their unique combination. This leads to the many special features characterizing everyday peasant life, as well as its power of resistance to industrialization. Growing specialization in the countryside, leads to the development of a rural non-farming population. Simultaneously, the farming function is progressively narrowed and more professionalized as peripheral jobs and jobs requiring very high specialist skills are unloaded onto specialists. The farm begins to develop into an

enterprise. The peasant becomes a farmer. However, the tasks which cannot easily be broken down into a few repetitive actions and mechanized (for example livestock management) still remain largely his special province.

These features of farming determine the form of the process of socialization and occupational training of the young as one which gives rise to relationships which are highly diffused, personal, informal and lying mainly within the framework of the family.

4. The *village structure*, to a much greater extent than that of the family farm, presents us with features unique to a specific country and period.[8] In the setting of the village community or peasant commune, the peasant reaches a level of nearly total social self-sufficiency. The appropriation and division of land, marriage, social and religious needs are generally taken care of at the village level. A common interest in commune rights as well as in providing for productive activity requiring the participation of more than one family generates co-operation, generally coupled with some type of grass-roots democracy. The characteristics of the peasant village – its members being born into a single community, undergoing similar life-experiences and necessarily involved in close, personal interaction – with a consequent absence of anonymity – make for the highly traditional and conformist culture peculiar to a rural community. All this makes the word *mir* (meaning 'the world' or 'peace') used by the Russian peasants to refer to their village commune, a significant description of its function. The village is the peasant's world. A society of small producers consists of innumerable village segments generally, dominated and exploited by alien, political hierarchies.

5. The peasantry is a *pre-industrial social entity* which carries over into contemporary society specific elements of a different, older, social structure, economy and culture. This point will be elaborated in the following section but, at this stage, it should be stressed that we are referring not only to the 'relics of the way

8. For a relevant tabulation, see Eisenstadt (1963, pp. 34–5 and the supplementary tables).

of production which already belongs to the past' (Marx and Engels, 1950, vol. 2, p. 303), not only to delayed development, but also to specific features of development.

A major part of the existing definitions of the peasantry have been taken into account above. One definition, not so far considered, stands apart from the others – that formulated by Kroeber and adopted by Redfield – which approaches the peasantry as 'a part society, with part culture' (Kroeber, 1923, p. 284; Redfield, 1953). In accordance with the adopted line of reasoning it will be taken into account on pp. 251–5 on the inter-relationships of the peasantry with society as a whole.[9]

No concept of a social stratum can be made exactly to coincide with any empirically defined group. Yet the importance and validity of attempting a conceptual definition of the peasantry for research seems to us beyond question.

The Peasantry: The Historical Context

The peasantry manifests itself not only as a distinctive social group, but as a general pattern of social life which delimits a stage in the development of human society. 'The peasantry . . . is a way of living', says Fei[10] in his classical description of Chinese society. This general pattern of social life makes its appearance as a sector in earlier tribal (mainly nomadic) society, becomes decisive and typifies a historically distinct period (that of a society of small producers) and then gradually sinks to being a sector within industrial society. The appearance of the small-producer pattern of life is marked by that major change which has been referred to as the 'agricultural revolution' (Childe, 1963). The coming of this stage of development created the basis for stable settlement, land-division and the revolutionary rise in productivity which brought with it the possibility of a comparatively stable surplus. Production came to be determined, to an

9. The article was written before the publication of Wolf (1966), which came to stress the 'underdog' position of the peasant as the crux of its specifity. Our attitude was made clear on pp. 251–5 below.

10. See Bendix and Lipset (1953, p. 32). 'The peasantry, the key towards understanding of China, is a way of living, a complex of formal organization, individual behavior and social attitudes, closely knit together for the purpose of husbanding land with simple tools and human labor'.

increasing extent, by labour utilized (Mandel, 1964, pp. 33–6, 41).

Property-relations and nuclear units of social interaction may be treated as the major indicators of development of economic and social life, to be used to delineate the society of small producers.

The concept of property-relations barely exists in tribal-nomadic society.[11] They appear, in the wide sense discussed above, in a small producers' society, and become fully legally formalized in a capitalist, industrial society. The kinship group is the basis of social relationships in tribal-nomadic society, and remains so in the more narrowly defined familialism of a small producers' society. The individual in his own right 'doesn't count': he is but a part of the family as a whole. The town- and market-centred industrializing society, however, breaks down this system of relationships. The individual becomes the basic nuclear unit of society, free to interact with any others in the huge new complex of social hierarchies and structures. The prevalence of *family property* may well, therefore, serve to identify societies of small producers and the historical periods characterized by their predominance.

Furthermore, a society of small producers shows a distinctive cultural pattern,[12] features of which persist at least partly among the peasantry of industrializing societies.[13] The basically social, rather than economic way of reasoning, the lack of calculation (i.e. of seeking to maximize income in money terms) have been widely documented already by Thomas and Znaniecki and stressed by every keen student of peasant life.[14] A great deal has been said about the 'irrational' behaviour of peasants as far as land (Thomas and Znaniecki, 1918, p. 173), loans (p. 161), prices

11. Except for that of tribal hunting territories, defended from strangers.

12. A cultural pattern being seen for this purpose, as 'the lens of mankind through which men see; the medium by which they interpret and report what they see' (C. Wright Mills, *Power, Politics and People*, Ballantine Books, 1962, p. 406).

13. For a discussion of this, see Redfield (1956, chs. 2 and 3).

14. Even Marx referred to rural societies in which the operation of 'law of value' never emerged and to which, therefore, the 'general economic laws of society' did not apply (Marx and Engels, 1962, vol. 25, part 2, pp. 184–7).

(p. 169) and income (p. 166) are concerned. Peasant thinking often seems to the outsider to be capricious and subjective,[15] containing large elements of what may be called pre-Socratic thought, in which two contradictory opinions may be held simultaneously. What sometimes remains overlooked is the fact that the 'stupidity' exposed by peasants is not necessarily evidence of an absence of thought, but rather of a frame of reference and patterns of thought peculiar to the group, and actually serving their needs well.[16]

This point is borne out increasingly in recent studies. R. E. F. Smith has pointed out the cyclical – rather than linear – concept of time held by Russian peasants, which is clearly linked to their productive life (1964, p. 11). Pitt-Rivers notes the main features of a closed community to be habitual personal contact, widespread endogamy, homogeneity of values, emphasis on strict conformity, intense group solidarity and marked egalitarianism;[17] this may serve as a generalization of the results of much recent anthropological research into specific peasant cultures. The clash of this particular culture and its gradual giving way to the new, foreign, *Weltanschauung* of the industrializing 'civilized' world is an important part of modern social history.

Small producers' society falls historically in the intermediate period between tribal-nomadic and industrializing societies. The word 'intermediate' often tends to be used interchangeably with 'transitional', 'unstable' and even 'not important to look at'. However, the small-producer pattern of society proved as lasting as and no less stable than most other historical types of social structure; society based on a biological, cyclical, non-structural

15. See, for example, Mukhin (1888, p. 311) who states that the peasants' court or meeting tends to decide about property disagreements 'according to men' – i.e. according to the personalities of the people involved rather than general principles or formal precedences.

16. See, for example, the Polish sociologists' studies of the prestige determinants of peasant economic action or Chayanov's demonstrations of the 'economically irrational' renting of land when the cost of letting is higher than the additional income gained, and yet which is a sensible thing in conditions of an otherwise unemployable labour surplus.

17. See Pitt-Rivers (1957). For a summary of anthropological research into peasant communities, see *Biennial Review of Anthropology*, 1961, 1963 and 1965.

dynamism, with the family farm as its nuclear unit, has demonstrated exceptional stability all over the world. Indeed, one does not need Witfogel's hydraulic Eastern Despotism to explain the striking examples of arrested structural change collected in his book (1963). The basic social nuclei of family subsistence farm and peasant village community and their cyclical stability seem to constitute much more of a common element than do their 'hydraulic' features, for the 'stagnant societies' considered by Witfogel. Furthermore, it is the surplus-appropriating highly-centralized State which bears there the potentialities for structural change – by the introduction of powerful external pressures into this world of natural economy and cyclical stability.

The peasant back-bone in the small producers' society dissolves under the influence of the rise of a market- and town-centred money economy and consequent industrialization. An analysis of the appearance and development of an economic surplus and of capital-formation is needed to understand this process (Mandel, 1963, 1964). The development of agriculture provided a basis for industrialization but the farms themselves remained, to a great extent, apart from the new social framework which emerged.[18]

The producing and trading town introduces social patterns alien to the old world of small producers. In it, impersonal, warfare-like, profit-centred market relations underlie human relations. A man freed from the bonds and the protection of his family, here becomes an individual participant in a mass society, structured by huge bureaucratic hierarchies. Accumulation of anonymous capital determines economic growth. The pursuit of profit, efficiency and achievement provide the core of the social value system.

By its advantages of capital-concentration, population growth, high productivity, widespread education and political weight, the urban society rapidly overtakes the rural and becomes the main determinant of social and economic change. The small producers' world of the peasant becomes a mere segment of a

18. Mandel (1964, p. 173). According to Mandel's evidence, even in the present day in the USA there are 1,250,000 small farms exhibiting the features of a mainly natural economy.

world very differently structured. Moreover, whilst still preserving elements of uniqueness, the countryside develops a special relationship with the town – one which becomes increasingly decisive for its own development. The town's lead is felt through the increasing influence of market relations, the draining-off of surplus labour and capital, the professionalization of agriculture, the spread of mass products and mass culture and by anomie and 'social disorganization' (Thomas and Znaniecki, 1918, p. 1122).

The view that the development of the peasant sector of a town-centred society is simply a lagging one, not different in kind, has proved wrong but persistent. In fact, three *parallel patterns* of spontaneous development for the countryside can clearly be distinguished.

1. Competition from *large-scale, capital-intensive, mechanized agriculture* gradually destroys the small farms. Concentration of land-ownership is followed by concentration of production. Agriculture, fully taken over by industrial methods of production, becomes 'merely a branch of industry' (Lenin, 5th edn., vol. 3, p. 58). The development is apparent in the large farms of the United States, North Italy and Central France, as well as in some of the Soviet *sovkhozy*. Yet the special features in the techniques of farming occupation create obstacles to breaking them down into simple, repetitive actions – i.e. to its full automation. This, together with the resilience of the family-farm unit and the fact that synthetic foods still remain relatively unimportant, has prevented 'food factories' becoming the main form of food-production.

2. A town-centred society makes for the development of the peasants into a *professional stratum of farmers*. The poorer villagers are increasingly sucked in from the countryside by the expanding urban areas. The same happens to peasant entrepreneurs – and to part of the economic surplus in agriculture. At the same time the middle peasants, relying on the advantages of the family production-unit and an increasing co-operative movement, fight successfully for a place in market society. These unique features of the development of the farmer stratum were

pointed out as early as Marx[19] and seen as the only way for the peasantry to be able to develop by Bauer (1926, p. 203) and others. The latest studies of Polish and German sociologists have shown, furthermore, the growth of a new stratum of worker-peasants, who supplement their agricultural, mainly subsistence, production by hiring out their labour.

This pattern-transformation of the peasantry into a cohesive, increasingly narrow and professionalized occupation group of farmers is clearly seen in most parts of North-Western Europe. Although becoming ever more tied to industrial society, farming still retains some of its peculiar elements. The socialist States which permit the activity of small producers in the countryside and provide them with necessary aid, though curbing capitalist development (Russia in the NEP period, contemporary Poland and Yugoslavia), bring this pattern to its clearest expression.

3. The third pattern of development appears mainly in the so-called under-developed societies and is characterized by *cumulative pauperization* of the peasantry (Myrdal, 1957, chs. 2, 3, 10). A population explosion, developing market relations and the industrial competition with traditional peasant handicrafts break up the cyclical equilibrium of society. A relatively slow industrialization is neither able to drain the countryside of its excess labour nor to provide sufficient capital-accumulation. The potential surplus is swept away by growing consumption needs. In the small-producer world, this is not expressed by increasing unemployment, but by 'hidden' under-employment, 'agrarian over population', falling *per capita* income and increasing misery.[20]

19. 'The moral of this story, which may also be deduced from other observations in agriculture, is that the capitalist system works against a rational agriculture, or that a rational agriculture is irreconcilable with the capitalist systems – even though technical improvements in agriculture are promoted by capitalism. But under this system, agriculture needs either the hands of the self-employed small farmer, or the control of associated producers' (Marx and Engels, 1962, vol. 25, pt 1, p. 135).

20. See for example, *Pourquoi les travailleurs abandonnent la terre* (United Nations, 1960, pp. 138, 144), which reports, on India, that during the years 1941–51 the natural growth of the labour-force in the countryside was absorbed as follows:

4. As distinct from these three spontaneous trends of development, the increasing strength of the modern state and the wish of the revolutionary elites to tackle the problem of development within the framework of socialist, collectivistic thinking make for the appearance of *State-organized collectivization* of agriculture. This pattern is qualitatively different from the spontaneous trends by being a conscious plan put into operation by a political hierarchy. Long-period evaluation of its success, in any of the different forms it has taken, would seem premature; in the Soviet Union, where the earliest attempts were made, the capacity of the elements of specifically peasant life, especially the strong base of the peasant farm plot and the unique ability of farming to defeat town-designed plans was demonstrated to quite a remarkable extent.

The Peasantry and Society

The difficulties involved in obtaining an overall conceptual grasp of the nature of a peasantry have been clearly felt in debates about the place of the peasantry in society. Even people starting from similar theoretical assumptions have reached opposite conclusions. Among the Russian Marxists peasantry was 'a class' to Stalin (1945, p. 510), a 'petit bourgeois mass' to Kritsman (Gaister, 1928, p. xiii), and 'not a class but a notion' to Plekhanov.

This has been partly due to differences in definition. For example, Ossowski has distinguished at least three different ways in which the concept of social class was used by Marx (Ossowski, 1963); many more conceptual sub-divisions of society have been used by other writers. The different definitions have, in fact, reflected different analytical aims and different concepts of society.

---

into agriculture ... 70·3 per cent
into services   ... 28·3 per cent
into industry   ... 1·4 per cent

During the years 1931–51, the share of workers engaged in agriculture rose from 71 per cent to 74 per cent of the working population; in 1952, 74 per cent of peasant families held less than 2 hectares of land and one-third was reported as landless. For an elaboration of the mechanism of such social processes, see Boeke (1953).

The main European sociological tradition[21] of conceptual sub-division of modern society, stems from Marxist class analysis. Social class is here approached as a unity of interest, expressed in group sub-cultures, group consciousness and group action, shaped in turn by the conflict-relationships with other classes. Society is structured by class domination and the working out of the dialectics of inter-class conflict and unity.

If we take the criteria for defining class as being relationships to the means of production (Lenin, 5th edn., vol. 39, p. 15; Marx and Engels, 1950, p. 33), or locuses of power (Dahrendorf, 1959) or capacity to organize production,[22] the peasantry in an industrializing society will fall either into a huge amorphous group of 'the ruled', or into an even more amorphous group of 'middle classes'. The peasantry, as a qualitatively distinct entity, disappears. This led the majority of Marxist social scientists to approach the peasantry as a fading remnant of pre-capitalist society – as 'non-existent, historically speaking'. Yet, when a major part of the population remains outside the concept of society as a whole, the definition in use does seem to be sadly inadequate, even if the consolation of a glimpse into the future is offered in exchange. Unfulfilled predictions would seem to be the inevitable result of working to such a model.

Max Weber's modification of the Marxist concept of class puts market relationships at the heart of the definition with the issue of class domination retreating into the background.[23] 'Class situation is, in this sense, ultimately market situation' (Gerth and Wright Mills, 1961, p. 182). 'Class situations are further differentiated, on the one hand, according to the kind of property that is usable for returns, and, on the other hand, according to the kind of services which can be offered in the market' (Bendix and Lipset, 1953, p. 64). For Weber, therefore, 'owners of warehouses' and 'owners of shares', for example, constitute social classes, as much as do industrial workers and peasants. The shortcomings

21. We shall not touch upon the hierarchial status groups, concentrated upon in the American studies of social stratification, as they are irrelevant to the present work.

22. See works by Bogdanov, Makhaiski, etc. – and back to Saint Simon.

23. For a discussion of this, see Rex (1961).

of an unlimited analytical division of society into small subgroups, when approaching social reality were pointed out already by Marx in his unfinished manuscript on social class (Marx, 1867, pp. 1031–2).

In history, the peasantry many times has acted politically as a class-like social entity. Moreover, the peasantry in industrial societies has shown an ability for cohesive political action – and not only when facing traditional land-owners in belated battles of a pre-capitalist type; their common interests have driven peasants into political conflicts also with large capitalist land-owners, with various groups of townsmen and with the modern State.

The polarization of the countryside in an industrializing society – into capitalist owners and a rural proletariat (as predicted by Marxists) – was checked by the draining-off of capital and labour into the towns, as well as by the specific features of a peasant family-farm economy. The widely accepted picture of the countryside as being rapidly sundered by an inevitable economic polarization proved oversimplified. Economic counter-trends seem to have acted in the opposite direction and greatly influenced the final result. Furthermore the significance of specific culture, consciousness and 'the meaning attached' (Rex, 1961, p. 138) to the class position proved to be most important. All this made peasant cohesiveness as a potential basis for political class formation much stronger than the predictions of the Russian Marxists or of the American strategists would have led us to believe.

On the other hand, inescapable fragmentation of a peasantry into small local segments and the diversity and vagueness of their political aims considerably undermine their potential political impact. Hence, how far a peasantry may be regarded as a class is not a clear-cut problem, but should be seen rather as a question of degree and historical period. If we posit an imaginary scale or continuum, we could say that the peasantry would appear as a social entity of comparatively low 'classness', which rises in crisis situations.

But the peasantry's specific features as a socio-political group are not just to be seen as merely quantitative. Marx's classical description of the duality in the social character of the peasantry (on the one hand, it is a class; on the other, it is not)[24] leaves the riddle unsolved. In so far as the peasantry is not a class, what is it – granting its qualitative existence?

A class position is basically a social interrelationship – a conflict interrelationship with other classes and groups. Outside these interrelations, a class ceases to exist. Yet 'because the farmer's produce is essential and, at the lowest level, sufficient for human existence, the labour of the farmer is necessary for the existence of society; but the existence of society as a whole is not to the same extent necessary for the existence of the farmer' (Galeski, 1963, p. 49). Peasants prove this by withdrawing from the market in crisis situations and indeed, sometimes consciously use this ability as a means of exercising political pressure.

The main duality in the peasants' position in society consists in their being, on the one hand, a social class (one of low 'classness' and on the whole dominated by other classes) and, on the other, 'a different world' – a highly self-sufficient 'society in itself', bearing the elements of a separate distinctive and closed pattern of social relations. The peasantry is the social phenomenon in which the Marxist approach to class analysis meets the main conceptual dichotomies of non-Marxist sociological thinking; Maine's brotherhood versus economic competition; de Coulangue's familistic versus individualistic; Tönnies's *Gemeinschaft* versus *Gesellschaft* or Durkheim's mechanic (segmentary) versus organic societies (Redfield, 1955, pp. 139–43). This unique duality ('class' and 'society') leads to conceptual difficulties, yet may well serve as a qualitative definition of the peasantry – especially when differentiating this entity from wider, more amorphous groupings such as 'middle classes', 'exploited masses' or 'remnants of feudalism'.

As has already been mentioned, A. L. Kroeber advanced a definition of peasants as those who 'constituting part societies

24. Marx and Engels (1950, vol. 1, p. 303), 'In so far as millions of families live under economic conditions of existence that separate their mode of life, their interests and their culture from those of other classes, and put them in hostile opposition to the latter, they form a class. In so far as there is merely a local interconnexion among these small-holding peasants, and the identity of their interests begets no community, no national bond and no political organization among them, they do not form a class.'

with part cultures, definitely rural, yet live in a relation to a market town ... [those who] lack the isolation, political autonomy and self-sufficiency of a tribal population, yet their local units maintain much of their old identity, integration and attachment to the soil' (Kroeber, 1923, p. 284). Redfield elaborates Kroeber's point and concludes 'there is no peasantry before the first city' (Redfield, 1953, p. 31).

The anthropological approach, under which the extent of cultural self-sufficiency is used as an index of social development, is no doubt valid. Moreover, research centering round the problem of development from tribal to small-producer society will, necessarily, stress different factors to research centering round the problem of development from small-producer to industrial society. However, Redfield's definition of the peasantry seems to be too narrow and his definition of tribal society too wide. Groups of settlers in many parts of the world, cut off from towns, far from noblemen and out of reach of the State and its tax-collectors, can hardly *ipso facto* be labelled tribal. These groups share the main features of a peasantry. They seem to demonstrate peasantry's self-sufficiency, its ability to exist out of the thrall of noblemen and town. It was the socio-political significance of these features which gave rise to the characteristic structure of power-relations found in pre-capitalist society – it was this very self-sufficiency which made *political* control a necessity for the rulers.

The Peasantry in Political Action

The political impact of the peasantry has been generally marked by its basic socio-political weaknesses. The vertical segmentation of peasants into local communities, class and groups and the differentiation of interest within these communities themselves has made for difficulties in crystallizing nationwide aims and symbols and developing national leadership and organization which, in turn, has made for what we have called low 'classness'. Technological backwardness, especially in the fields of communications and of weaponry and tactical expertise, has brought to naught many attempts at political action. Yet the peasantry does have its socio-political points of strength – being the main food-producer, being dispersed in rural areas and being numerically preponderant. Its monopoly of food production has often proved of crucial importance in times of crises. The vastnesses of the countryside can become a stronghold. Numerical strength can tip the balance.

Yet in the long run it is the basic weaknesses of the peasantry which have tended to stand out. The peasantry has proved no match for smaller, closely knit, better organized and technically superior groups, and has, time and time again, been 'double-crossed' or suppressed politically and by force of arms. However, granting all this, the peasantry cannot be ignored as politically impotent and its actions dismissed, therefore, as without significance. For it is not only victors and rulers who determine political reality.

The spread of industrialization and mass culture gives the peasantry new possibilities of communication and cultural and political cohesion. Yet, at the same time, it lowers the importance of the countryside in the national production, curbs its 'food-monopoly' by developing international trade, stimulates village-level polarization and improves the government forces' relative advantage in terms of mobility, weaponry and other forms of repressive power. Once again, the course of historical development seems to weaken peasants' political influence.

However, the peasants' chances of influencing the political sphere increase sharply in times of national crises. When non-peasant social forces clash, when rulers are divided or foreign powers attack, the peasantry's attitude and action may well prove decisive. Whether this potential is realized is mainly dependent upon the peasants' ability to act in unison, with or without formal organization. This, in turn, is dependent upon the cohesion of the peasantry, its economic, social and cultural homogeneity as well as interaction and, on the reflection of these in the ideological sphere.

A comparison of a peasantry's political and armed action in pre-industrial society with that in contemporary society has still to be made. In a modern society the patterns of peasant political action and influence are determined by its character as a social entity. We may discern three main types of it:

1. *Independent class action*, as described by Marxist class theory. In this pattern of action, a social class crystallizes in the course of conflict, creates its own nationwide organization, works out its ideology, aims, and symbols, and produces leaders from within. This form of political action seems to be fairly typical of the main social classes. However, for today's peasantries, this pattern of political action is the least frequent. Some of the 'green' movements in Eastern Europe, the peasant unions in Russia in 1905 and China of 1926, the Zapata movement in Mexico and their counterparts in the rest of the world need to be studied comparatively to understand the mechanics of this pattern of peasant action.[25]

2. *Guided political action*, in which the social group concerned is moved by an external uniting power-elite. This pattern of action may become especially important as far as the peasantry is concerned. The conservative cyclical stability of both the farm and the village and the political implications of this can generally be overcome only by a severe crisis, accompanied by the existence of some exogenous organizing factor of sweeping political and emotional power. This external organizer of the peasantry may be found in millennial movements, secret societies, the Russian cossacks, French Bonapartism or Mao's people's army; it provides the peasantry with the missing factor of unity on a wide scale. The common element found in all these very different movements is the existence of a closely-knit group of activists, having its own impetus, specific organizational structure, aims and leadership – a group for which the peasantry is an object of leadership or manipulation. The peasantry, in this case, may be 'used' (i.e. deliberately tricked into some action alien to its own interests) or 'led to achieve its own aims': yet, the very definition of 'aims' is in the hands of qualitatively distinct leaders. The peasants' interests and attitudes are only one of the factors to be taken into account by them. As Marx said, referring to the French peasantry in the mid-nineteenth century: 'they are ... incapable of enforcing their class interest in their own name,

25. For an important insight into the influence of the stratification of the peasantry on political action, see Alavi (1965).

whether through a parliament or through a convention. They cannot represent themselves, they must be represented. Their representative must at the same time appear as their master ...' (cf. Marx and Engels, 1950, vol. 1, p. 303). The only thing to be objected to in this statement is the absoluteness of its terms which has been refuted by later events.

The low 'classness' of the peasantry makes the study of peasant movements especially illuminating for the sociological analysis of the external elites which lead them. The peasantry's weak influence on such leaders seems to make the elite group's dynamics appear in a 'purer' form. Moreover, it leads us to look into the problem of class-like masses (i.e. of social groups such as Russian soldiers in 1917–18 which are acting temporarily as class entities though not bearing all the features of a class) and their place in political processes.

3. *Fully spontaneous, amorphous political action.* This pattern seems to be highly typical of peasants' impact on politics, and may take one of two forms:

a. *Local riots* which 'suddenly' appear as short outbursts of accumulated frustration and rebellious feeling. Generally easily repressed by the central authorities, these riots may act as a check on central policy and stimulate change. When related to crisis in other areas and spheres, they may develop into nationwide movements capable of determining major political development.

b. *Peasant passivity.* The conceptual grasp of passivity as a factor of the dynamics poses some complex questions. Yet the spontaneous restriction of production by the Russian peasantry in 1920 proved strong enough to frustrate the will of a government victorious in a war against powerful enemies. Enormous numbers of government decrees and orders have, all over the world, been voided of effect by the peasantry's spontaneous, stubborn and silent non-fulfilment. The influence of conservative peasant 'apathy' has also many times proved decisive for the victory of the establishment over the revolutionaries. That passive resistance is actually a specifically peasant contribution to politics with a long history, no more than elaborated and sophisticated by Tolstoy and Gandhi, has been already suggested by R. E. F.

Smith. The existence of a relationship between the basic features of peasant society and passive resistance seems evident.

In the study of the political life of societies, especially those which include numerous peasants, armed action has a place of special importance. Clausewitz's remark that 'war is an extension of politics by other means' holds true not only for the relations between states. This leads us to the need specially to consider the army and guerrilla warfare as frameworks of peasant political action.

The modern conscript army is one of the few nationwide organizations in which the peasantry actively participates. The segmentation of the peasantry is thereby broken. The cultural intercourse involved, even if there is no indoctrination, teaches the peasant-soldier to think in national and not just village-limited terms. He is taught organization, complex co-operative action, co-ordination, modern techniques and military skills. The army provides him with a hierarchial institution through which he may rise as a leader and be trained for this position. Even where other national bodies have organizations represented in the rural level, it is generally the army which has provided the peasant with the framework for the most active participation.

This increase in the peasant's ability to act politically is, while he is in the army, on the whole successfully curbed by rigid discipline and by control exercised by non-peasant officers. Yet, in a time of crisis, this repression may disappear and the attitudes, action or refusal to act of a peasant army may become decisive. Moreover, the experience gained in army service acts as an important influence later in the villages. The ex-serviceman, because of his new experiences, tends to become a leader and a channel through which outside influences reach other villagers. In attempting to organize politically, peasants frequently refer back to their army experience. The Russian *Tamanskaya armiya* and 'Green Army of the Black Sea', the F L N, the Chinese 'People's Militia', the Zapata and Villa armies in Mexico served not only as the military organizations but also as the main political organizations – a kind of party in arms.[26]

26. One such force is described by Marx in the *Communist Manifesto* when speaking of the early stage of bourgeois class organization as 'an

The army, as this kind of organization, may bear the marks of both the first and second patterns of political action we have described – i.e. the peasantry as 'a class for itself' and as a 'guided' socio-political entity.

During the last decade, *guerrilla warfare*, by its success, moved into the centre of public attention. American strategists approach guerrilla warfare as a specific military technique to be taught by smart sergeants along with saluting and target practice. Their failures in both guerrilla and anti-guerrilla warfare in Vietnam is the best comment on this approach.

Guerrilla warfare is the most suitable form for the expression of armed peasant action. The record of it seems to be as old as the peasantry itself. Innumerable rebels, brigands and outlaws appear in the myth, the folk-memory of every people, as well as in its real history. The ability of the amorphous guerrilla 'army' to dissolve itself in times of need into the sympathetic peasant mass and vanish into the expanses of the countryside, its ability to utilize various degrees of peasant militancy and friendly passivity, its ability to survive without outside supplies and the adequacy for this type of warfare of primitive weapons may make guerrillas unbeatable by modern military methods.

Yet the essentially peasant character of guerrilla warfare provides not only its strength but also its weaknesses: segmentation, lack of crystallized ideology and aims, lack of stable membership. These essential weaknesses may be overcome by the injection of a hard core of professional rebels, making the revolt into guided political action. The professional rebels' nationwide ideological and organizational cohesion, their stability and zeal and their ability to work out a long-term strategy may enable them to unite the peasantry, sometimes transforming its revolt into a successful revolution. Yet the main key to the understanding of guerrilla warfare has to be sought not in the marvels of the rebels' organization, but in their relationship with the peasantry; not only in the military techniques of the few, but in the sociology of the masses.[27]

---

armed and self-governing association in the medieval commune' (Marx and Engels, 1950, vol. 1, p. 34).

27. Inroads into research on this subject have been made by Hobsbawm

There are *subjective determinants of military action – generally labelled 'morale'* – whose resistance to quantification does not negate their importance in the shaping of reality. Peasant revolts all over the world display common cultural features which, in all their complexity, seem to have been better caught in the synthetic expressions of the arts than dissected by the analytical tools of the social sciences. The leader-hero, the legends which surround him, his personal charisma – these to a large extent take the place of ideology and organization as unifying factors. The picturesque image of the young peasant rebel challenges the mundane nature of everyday peasant life. The childish display of exhibitionism, described by Znaniecki, as typical of the peasant's attempts to establish his own personality when breaking out of rigid family ties (Thomas and Znaniecki, 1918, p. 103), explains much of the spirit of peasant fighters. All these features influence the general character of peasant units as a fighting force, together with the specific values and self-images of the leading elites.

The main stream of contemporary sociology has by-passed the traditional peasantry. Rural sociology has been localized in and financed by rich industrial societies and has consequently been centred upon the problem of how to promote members of farming minorities into fully productive and prosperous members of 'civilized society'. Few sociologists have so far elevated the peasantry from the footnote to the page. Yet, were historical and social significance the criteria for the choice of objects of study, we should be almost overwhelmed by the flood of publications on the peasantry. Innumerable problems of our world's political and economic development lead us back to the subject of the peasantry, to the understanding and misunderstanding of it by policy makers. To take but one example, the history of the Soviet Union has time and time again (in 1918, 1920, 1927–9, etc. – up to the 1960s) largely been shaped by unexpected responses to the ruling party's policies, based on such evaluation and prediction. Countless other examples could be cited from Africa, Asia, Latin America, etc.

in *Primitive Rebels* (1959, p. 19). See also *Monthly Review*, vol. 17, on guerrilla activities in Latin America.

Only a cross-disciplinary combination of both conceptual and factual studies may overcome the astonishing short-comings in our knowledge of the peasantry, in spite of the methodological difficulties involved. Limping along main roads achieves more than strolling along side roads.

References

ALAVI, H. (1965), 'Peasantry and revolution', *The Socialist Register 1965*, Merlin Press.

BAUER, O. (1926), *Bor'ba za zemlyu*, Moscow.

BENDIX, R., and LIPSET, S. M. (eds.) (1953), *Class, Status and Power: A Reader in Social Stratification*, rev. edn. 1966, Free Press.

BOEKE, I. H. (1953), *Economies and Economic Policy in Dual Societies*, New York.

CHAYANOV, A. (1925), *Organizatsiya krest'yanskogo khozyaistva*, Moscow. Translated as *The Theory of Peasant Economy*, D. Thorner, R. E. F. Smith and B. Kerbley (eds.), Irwin, 1966.

CHILDE, V. G. (1963), *Social Evolution*, C. A. Watts.

DAHRENDORF, R. (1959), *Class and Class Conflict in Industrial Society*, London.

DAVRING, F. (1956), *Land and Labour in Europe, 1900–1950*, The Hague.

EISENSTADT, S. N. (1963), *The Political System of Empires*, New York.

GAISTER, A. (1928), *Rassloenie sovetskoi derevni*, Moscow.

GALESKI, B. (1963), *Chlopi i zawod rolnika*, Warsaw.

GERTH, G. H., and WRIGHT MILLS, C. (1961), *From Max Weber*, Routledge & Kegan Paul.

HOBSBAWM, E. (1959), *Primitive Rebels*, Manchester University Press.

HOBSBAWM, E. (1965), 'Vietnam and the dynamics of guerrilla warfare', *Monthly Review*, vol. 17.

KROEBER, A. (1923), *Anthropology*, Harrap.

LENIN, V. I. (5th edn), *Collected Works*, London.

MANDEL, E. (1963), *The Tradition from Feudalism to Capitalism: A Symposium*.

MANDEL, E. (1964), *Traité d'économie marxiste*, Jerusalem.

MARX, K. (1867), *The Capital*.

MARX, K., and ENGELS, F. (1950), *Selected Works*, Lawrence & Wishart.

MARX, K. and ENGELS, F. (1962), *Sochineniya*, 2nd Russian edn.

MAYNARD, J. (1962), *Russian Peasant and Other Studies*, Collier.

MITRANY, D. (1961), *Marx against the Peasant*, Collier.

MUKHIN, V. (1888), *Obychnyi poryadok nasledovaniya krest'yan*, St Petersburg.

MYRDAL, G. (1957), *Economic Theory and Underdeveloped Regions*, Duckworth.

OSSOWSKI, S. (1963), *Class Structure in the Social Consciousness*, Routledge & Kegan Paul.

PITT-RIVERS, J. (1957), 'The closed community and its friends', *Kroeber Anthropological Society Papers*, no. 16.

REDFIELD, R. (1953), *The Primitive World and its Transformation*, Cornell University Press.

REDFIELD, R. (1955), *The Little Community*, University of Chicago Press.

REDFIELD, R. (1956), *Peasant Society and Culture*, University of Chicago Press.

REX, J. (1961), *Key Problems of Sociological Theory*, Routledge & Kegan Paul.

SMITH, R. E. F. (1964), 'A model of production and consumption on the Russian farm', *Discussion Papers*, University of Birmingham, CREES, RC/D, no. 1.

STALIN, J. (1945), *Problems of Leninism*, Moscow.

THOMAS, W. I. and ZNANIECKI, F. (1918), *The Polish Peasant in Europe and America*, Dover Publications, 1958.

UNITED NATIONS (1960), *Pourquoi les travailleurs abandonnent la terre*, Geneva.

VASIL'CHAKOV, A. (1876), *Zemledel'e i zemlevladenie*.

WITFOGEL, K. (1963), *Oriental Despotism*.

WOLF, E. R. (1966), *Peasants*, Prentice-Hall.

Teodor Shanin   263

20 Eric R. Wolf

On Peasant Rebellions

Eric R. Wolf, 'On peasant rebellions', *International Social Science Journal*, vol. 21, 1969.

Six major social and political upheavals, fought with peasant support, have shaken the world of the twentieth century: the Mexican revolution of 1910, the Russian revolutions of 1905 and 1917, the Chinese revolution which metamorphosed through various phases from 1921 on, the Vietnamese revolution which has its roots in the Second World War, the Algerian rebellion of 1954 and the Cuban revolution of 1958. All of these were to some extent based on the participation of rural populations. It is to the analysis of this participation that the present paper directs its attention.

Romantics to the contrary, it is not easy for a peasantry to engage in sustained rebellion. Peasants are especially handicapped in passing from passive recognition of wrongs to political participation as a means for setting them right. First, a peasant's work is more often done alone, on his own land, than in conjunction with his fellows. Moreover, all peasants are to some extent competitors, for available resources within the community and for sources of credit from without. Second, the tyranny of work weighs heavily upon peasants: their life is geared to an annual routine and to planning for the year to come. Momentary alterations of routine threaten their ability to take up the routine later. Third, control of land enables him, more often than not, to retreat into subsistence production should adverse conditions affect his market crop. Fourth, ties of extended kinship and mutual aid within the community may cushion the shocks of dislocation. Fifth, peasants' interests – especially among poor peasants – often cross-cut class alignments. Rich and poor peasant may be kinfolk, or a peasant may be at one and the same time owner, renter, sharecropper, laborer for his neighbors and seasonal hand on a nearby plantation. Each different involvement aligns him differently with his fellows and with the outside world. Finally, past exclusion of the peasant from participation in decision making beyond the bamboo hedge of his village deprives him all too often of the knowledge needed to articulate his interests with appropriate forms of action. Hence peasants are often merely passive spectators of political struggles or long for the sudden advent of a millennium, without specifying for themselves and their neighbors the many rungs on the staircase to heaven.

If it is true that peasants are slow to rise, then peasant participation in the great rebellions of the twentieth century must obey some special factors which exacerbated the peasant condition. We will not understand that condition unless we keep in mind constantly that it has suffered greatly under the impact of three great crises: the demographic crisis, the ecological crisis and the crisis in power and authority. The demographic crisis is most easily depicted in bare figures, though its root causes remain ill-understood. It may well be that its ultimate causes lie less in the reduction of mortality through spreading medical care, than in the world-wide diffusion of American food crops throughout the world which provided an existential minimum for numerous agricultural populations. Yet the bare numbers suffice to indicate the seriousness of the demographic problem. Mexico had a population of 5·8 million at the beginning of the nineteenth century; in 1910 – at the outbreak of the revolution – it had 16·5 million. European Russia had a population of 20 million in 1725; at the turn of the twentieth century it had 87 million. China numbered 265 million in 1775, 430 million in 1850, and close to 600 million at the time of the revolution. Vietnam is estimated to have sustained a population between 6 and 14 million in 1820; it had 30·5 million inhabitants in 1962. Algeria had an indigenous population of 10·5 million in 1963, representing a fourfold increase since the beginning of French occupation in the first part of the nineteenth century. Cuba had 550,000 inhabitants in 1800; by 1953 she had 5·8 million. Population increases alone and by themselves would have placed a serious strain on inherited cultural arrangements.

The ecological crisis is in part related to the sheer increase in numbers; yet it is also in an important measure independent of it. Population increases of the magnitude just mentioned coincided with a period in history in which land and other resources were increasingly converted into commodities – in the capitalist sense of that word. As commodities they were subjected to the demands of a market which bore only a very indirect relation to the needs of the rural populations subjected to it. Where, in the past, market behavior had been largely subsidiary to the existential problems of subsistence, now existence and its problems became subsidiary to the market. The alienation of peasant resources proceeded directly through outright seizure or through coercive purchase, as in Mexico, Algeria and Cuba; or it took the form – especially in China and Vietnam – of stepped-up capitalization of rent which resulted in the transfer of resources from those unable to keep up to those able to pay. In addition, capitalist mobilization of resources was reinforced through the pressure of taxation, of demands for redemption payments, and through the increased needs for industrially produced commodities on the part of the peasantry itself. All together, however, these various pressures disrupted the precarious ecological balance of peasant society. Where the peasant had required a certain combination of resources to effect an adequate living, the separate and differential mobilization of these resources broke that ecological nexus. This is perhaps best seen in Russia where successive land reforms threatened continued peasant access to pasture, forest and plowland. Yet it is equally evident in cases where commercialization threatened peasant access to communal lands (Mexico, Algeria, Vietnam), to unclaimed land (Mexico, Cuba), to public granaries (Algeria, China), or where it threatened the balance between pastoral and settled populations (Algeria). At the same time as commercialization disrupted rural life, moreover, it also created new and unsettled ecological niches in industry. Disruptive change in the rural area went hand in hand with the opening up of incipient but uncertain opportunities for numerous ex-industrial peasants. Many of these retained formal ties with their home villages (Russia, China, Algeria); others migrated between country and industry in continuous turnover (especially Vietnam). Increased instability in the rural area was thus accompanied by a still unstable commitment to industrial work.

Finally, both the demographic and the ecological crisis converged in the crisis of authority. The development of the market produced a rapid circulation of the elite, in which the manipulators of the new 'freefloating resources' – labor bosses, merchants, industrial entrepreneurs – challenged the inherited power of the controllers of fixed social resources, the tribal chief, the mandarin, the landed nobleman (see Eisenstadt, 1966). Undisputed and stable claims thus yielded to unstable and disputed claims. This rivalry between primarily political and primarily economic powerholders contained its own dialectic. The imposition of the market mechanism entailed a diminution of social responsibilities for the affected population: the economic entrepreneur did not concern himself with the social cost of his activities; the traditional powerholder was often too limited in his power to offer assistance or subject to cooptation by his successful rivals. The advent of the market thus not merely produced a crisis in peasant ecology; it deranged the numerous middle-level ties between center and hinterland, between the urban and the rural sectors. Commercialization disrupted the hinterland; at the very same time it also lessened the ability of powerholders to perceive and predict changes in the rural area. The result was an ever-widening gap between the rulers and the ruled. That such a course is not inevitable is perhaps demonstrated by Barrington Moore (1966) who showed how traditional feudal forms were utilized in both Germany and Japan to prevent the formation of such a gap in power and communication during the crucial period of transition to a commercial and industrial order. Where this was not accomplished – precisely where an administrative militarized feudalism was absent – the continued widening of the power gap invited the formation of a counter-elite which could challenge both a disruptive leadership based on the operation of the market and the impotent heirs of traditional power, while forging a new consensus through communication with the peasantry. Such a counter-elite is most frequently made up of members of provincial elites, relegated to the margins of commercial mobilization and political office; of officials or professionals who stand mid-way between the rural area and the center and are caught in the contradictions between the two; and of intellectuals who have access to a system of symbols which can guide the interaction between leadership and rural area.

Sustained mobilization of the peasantry is, however, no easy task. Such an effort will not find its allies in a rural mass which is completely subject to the imperious demands of necessity. Peasants cannot rebel successfully in a situation of complete impotence; the powerless are easy victims. Therefore only a peasantry in possession of some tactical control over its own resources can provide a secure basis for on-going political leverage. Power, as Richard Adams has said (1966, pp. 3–4), refers ultimately

to an actual physical control that one party may have with respect to another. The reason that most relationships are not reduced to physical struggles is that parties to them can make rational decisions based on their estimates of tactical power and other factors. Power is usually exercised, therefore, through the common recognition by two parties of the tactical control each has, and through rational decision by one to do what the other wants. Each estimates his own tactical control, compares it to the other, and decides he may or may not be superior.

The poor peasant or the landless laborer who depends on a landlord for the largest part of his livelihood, or the totality of it, has no tactical power: he is completely within the power domain of his employer, without sufficient resources of his own to serve him as resources in the power struggle. Poor peasants, and landless laborers, therefore, are unlikely to pursue the course of rebellion, *unless* they are able to rely on some external power to challenge the power which constrains them. Such external power is represented in the Mexican case by the action of the Constitutionalist army in Yucatan which liberated the peons from debt bondage 'from above'; by the collapse of the Russian army in 1917 and the reflux of the peasant soldiery, arms in hand, into the villages; by the creation of the Chinese Red Army as an instrument designed to break up landlord power in the villages. Where such external power is present the poor peasant and landless laborer have latitude of movement; where it is absent, they are under near-complete constraint. The rich peasant, in turn, is unlikely to embark on the course of rebellion. As employer of the labor of others, as money-lender, as notable coopted by the State machine, he exercises local power in alliance with external powerholders. His power domain with the village is derivative; it depends on the maintenance of their domains outside the village. Only when an external force, such as the Chinese Red Army, proves capable of destroying these other superior power domains, will the rich peasant lend his support to an uprising.

There are only two components of the peasantry which possess sufficient internal leverage to enter into sustained rebellion. These are (a) a land-owning 'middle peasantry' or (b) a peasantry located in a peripheral area outside the domains of landlord control. Middle peasantry refers to a peasant population which has secure access to land of its own and cultivates it with family labor. Where these middle peasant holdings lie within the power domain of a superior, possession of their own resources provide their holders with the minimal tactical freedom required to challenge their overlord. The same, however, holds for a peasantry poor or 'middle', whose settlements are only under marginal control from the outside. Here land holdings may be insufficient for the support of the peasant household; but subsidiary activities such as casual labor, smuggling, livestock raising – not under the direct constraint of an external power domain – supplement land in sufficient quantity to grant the peasantry some latitude of movement. We mark the existence of such a tactically mobile peasantry in the villages of Morelos in Mexico; in the communes of the central agricultural regions of Russia; in the northern bastion established by the Chinese Communists after the Long March; as a basis for rebellion in Vietnam; among the *fellahin* of Algeria; and among the squatters of Oriente province in Cuba.

Yet this recruitment of a 'tactically mobile peasantry' among the middle peasants and the 'free' peasants of peripheral areas poses a curious paradox. This is also the peasantry in whom anthropologists and rural sociologists have tended to see the main bearers of peasant tradition. If our account is correct, then – strange to say – it is precisely this culturally conservative stratum which is the most instrumental in dynamiting the peasant social order. This paradox dissolves, however, when we consider that it is also the middle peasant who is relatively the most vulnerable to economic changes wrought by commercialism, while his social relations remain encased within the traditional design. His is a balancing act in which his balance is continuously threatened by population growth; by the encroachment of rival landlords; by the loss of rights to grazing, forest and water: by falling prices and unfavorable conditions of the market: by interest payments and foreclosures. Moreover, it is precisely this stratum which most depends on traditional social relations of kin and mutual aid between neighbors; middle peasants suffer most when these are abrogated, just as they are least able to withstand the depradations of tax collectors or landlords.

Finally – and this is again paradoxical – middle peasants are also the most exposed to influences from the developing proletariat. The poor peasant or landless laborer, in going to the city or the factory, also usually cuts his tie with the land. The middle peasant, however, stays on the land and sends his children to work in town; he is caught in a situation in which one part of the family retains a footing in agriculture, while the other undergoes 'the training of the cities' (Tillion, 1961, pp. 120–21). This makes the middle peasant a transmitter also of urban unrest and political ideas. The point bears elaboration. It is probably not so much the growth of an industrial proletariat as such which produces revolutionary activity, as the development of an industrial work force still closely geared to life in the villages.

Thus it is the very attempt of the middle and free peasant to remain traditional which makes him revolutionary.

If we now follow out the hypothesis that it is middle peasants and poor but 'free' peasants, not constrained by any power domain, which constitute the pivotal groupings for peasant uprisings, then it follows that any factor which serves to increase the latitude granted by that tactical mobility reinforces their revolutionary potential. One of these factors is peripheral location with regard to the center of State control. In fact, frontier areas quite often show a tendency to rebel against the central authorities, regardless of whether they are inhabited by peasants or not.

South China has constituted a hearth of rebellion within the Chinese State, partly because it was first a frontier area in the southward march of the Han people, and later because it provided the main zone of contact between Western and Chinese civilization. The Mexican north has similarly been a zone of dissidence from the center in Mexico City, partly because its economy was based on mining and cattle raising rather than maize agriculture, partly because it was open to influences from the United States to the north. In the Chinese south it was dissident gentry with a peasant following which frequently made trouble for the center; in the Mexican north it was provincial businessmen, ranchers and cowboys. Yet where you have a poor peasantry located in such a peripheral area beyond the normal control of the central power, the tactical mobility of such a peasantry is 'doubled' by its location. This has been the case with Morelos, in Mexico; Nghe An province in Vietnam; Kabylia in Algeria; and Oriente in Cuba. The tactical effectiveness of such areas is 'tripled' if they contain also defensible mountainous redoubts: this has been true of Morelos, Kabylia and Oriente. The effect is 'quadrupled' where the population of these redoubts differs ethnically or linguistically from the surrounding population. Thus we find that the villagers of Morelos were Nahuatl-speakers, the inhabitants of Kabylia Berber-speakers. Oriente province showed no linguistic differences from the Spanish spoken in Cuba, but it did contain a significant Afro-Cuban element. Ethnic distinctions enhance the solidarity of the rebels; possession of a special linguistic code provides for an autonomous system of communication.

It is important, however, to recognize that separation from the State or the surrounding populace need not be only physical or cultural. The Russian and the Mexican cases both demonstrate that it is possible to develop a solid enclave population of peasantry through State reliance on a combination of communal autonomy with the provision of community services to the State. The organization of the peasantry into self-administering communes with stipulated responsibilities to State and landlords created in both cases veritable fortresses of peasant tradition within the body of the country itself. Held fast by the surrounding structure, they acted as sizzling pressure-cookers of unrest which, at the moment of explosion, vented their force outward to secure more living-space for their customary corporate way of life. Thus we can add a further multiplier effect to the others just cited. The presence of any one of these will raise the peasant potential for rebellion.

But what of the transition from peasant rebellion to revolution, from a movement aimed at the redress of wrongs, to the attempted overthrow of society itself? Marxists in general have long argued that peasants without outside leadership cannot make a revolution; and our case material would bear them out. Where the peasantry had successfully rebelled against the established order – under its own banner and with its own leaders – it was sometimes able to reshape the social structure of the countryside closer to its heart's desires; but it did not lay hold of the state, of the cities which house the centers of control, of the strategic non-agricultural resources of the society. Zapata stayed in his Morelos; the 'folk migration' of Pancho Villa simply receded after the defeat at Torreon; the Ukranian rebel Nestor Makhno stopped short of the cities; and the Russian peasants of the central agricultural region simply burrowed more deeply into their local communes. Thus a peasant rebellion which takes place in a complex society already caught up in commercialization and industrialization tends to be self-limiting and, hence, anachronistic.

The peasant Utopia is the free village, untrammelled by tax collectors, labor recruiters, large landowners, officials. Ruled over, but never ruling, they also lack any acquaintance with the operation of the state as a complex machinery, experiencing it only as a 'cold monster'. Against this hostile force, they had learned, even their traditional powerholders provided but a weak shield, even though they were on occasion willing to defend them if it proved to their own interest. Thus, for the peasant, the state is a negative quantity, an evil, to be replaced in short shrift by their own 'home-made' social order. That order, they believe, can run without the state; hence peasants in rebellion are natural anarchists.

Often this political perspective is reinforced still further by a wider ideological vision. The peasant experience tends to be dualistic, in that he is caught between his understanding of how the world ought to be properly ordered and the realities of a mundane existence, beset by disorder. Against this disorder, the peasant has always set his dreams of deliverance, the vision of a *mahdi* who would deliver the world from tyranny, of a Son of Heaven who would truly embody the mandate of Heaven, of a 'white' Tsar as against the 'black' Tsar of the disordered present (Sarkisyanz, 1955). Under conditions of modern dislocation, the disordered present is all too frequently experienced as world order reversed, and hence evil. The dualism of the past easily fuses with the dualism of the present. The true order is yet to come, whether through miraculous intervention, through rebellion, or both. Peasant anarchism and an apocalyptic vision of the world, together, provide the ideological fuel that drives the rebellious peasantry.

The peasant rebellions of the twentieth century are no longer simple responses to local problems, if indeed they ever were. They are but the parochial reactions to major social dislocations, set in motion by overwhelming societal change. The spread of the market has torn men up by their roots, and shaken them loose from the social relationships into which they were born. Industrialization and expanded communication have given rise to new social clusters, as yet unsure of their own social positions and interests, but forced by the very imbalance of their lives to seek a new adjustment. Traditional political authority has eroded or collapsed; new contenders for power are seeking new constituencies for entry into the vacant political arena. Thus when the peasant protagonist lights the torch of rebellion, the edifice of society is already smoldering and ready to take fire. When the battle is over, the structure will not be the same.

No cultural system – no complex of economy, society, polity and ideology – is ever static; all of its component parts are in constant change. Yet as long as these changes remain within tolerable limits, the overall system persists. If they begin to exceed these limits, however, or if other components are suddenly introduced from outside, the system will be thrown out of kilter. The parts of the system are rendered inconsistent with each other;

the system grows incoherent. Men in such a situation are caught painfully between various old solutions to problems which have suddenly shifted shape and meaning, and new solutions to problems they often cannot comprehend. Since incoherence rarely appears all at once, in all parts of the system, they may for some time follow now one alternative, now another and contradictory one; but in the end a breach, a major disjuncture will make its appearance somewhere in the system (Wilson and Wilson, 1945, pp. 125–9). A peasant uprising under such circumstances, for any of the reasons we have sketched, can – without conscious intent – bring the entire society to the state of collapse.

References

ADAMS, R. N. (1966), 'Power and power domains', *América Latina*, year 9, pp. 3–21.

EISENSTADT, S. N. (1966), *Modernization: Protest and Change*, Prentice-Hall.

MOORE, B., Jr (1966), *Social Origins of Dictatorship and Democracy*, Beacon Press; Penguin Books, 1969.

SARKISYANZ, E. (1955), *Russland und der Messianismus des Oriens: Sendungsbewusstsein und politischer Chiliasmus des Ostens*, J. C. B. Mohr, Tübingen.

TILLION, G. (1961), *France and Algeria: Complementary Enemies*, Knopf.

WILSON, G., and WILSON, M. (1945), *The Analysis of Social Change*, Cambridge University Press.

Part Four The Peasantry as a Culture

Part Four contains papers relating to the issue of peasant culture. The focus here is not on the concept of culture in its broadest anthropological sense (i.e. as essentially everything created in the world by humans), but in the sense of cognitions and values typical of peasant society.[1] At least, to an extent, peasant culture is intertwined with, and inseparable from, the cultural pattern specific to the life of small rural communities. The section opens with Dobrowolski's description and analysis of the broad scope of peasant customs, views, etc. It is followed by a description of some typical peasant cognitions of reality by Bailey. Ortiz's article challenges the tendencies to approach peasant views and choices as either irrational or self-explanatory and points to the general rationale behind them. On a more general level, this analysis questions the applicability of generalizations about peasantry, stressing the specific character of every peasant group. Finally, Redfield's and Singer's contribution sets peasant culture in relation to urban society in terms of Kroeber's definition of the peasantry as 'part-societies with part-cultures' – segments of a larger urban-centred society (see the Introduction). The main relevant issues not covered in this Part are those dealing specifically with socialization in peasant society, the acculturalization and the disintegration of specifically peasant culture under external influences and the typical networks of

1. For discussion of the 'cultural apparatus' see Wright Mills (1962, pp. 407–22). For a systematic discussion see also Berger and Luckmann (1967). The issues of the sociology of knowledge are still extremely underdeveloped which accounts for the descriptive rather than analytical character of the majority of the contributions in the field.

communication in peasant societies. These are however partly covered by the contributions of Znaniecki, Shanin and Pearse (in Part One) and Galeski (in Part Two).

References

BERGER, P., and LUCKMANN, T. (1967), *The Social Construction of Reality*, Allen Lane The Penguin Press.

WRIGHT MILLS, C. (1962), *Power, Politics and People*, Ballantine Books.

21 Kazimierz Dobrowolski

Peasant Traditional Culture

Kazimierz Dobrowolski, 'Peasant traditional culture', *Ethnografia Polska*, vol. 1, 1958, pp. 19–56. Abridged by the author and translated by A. Waligorski.

Introduction

The present essay is an attempt at a theory of traditional peasant culture as it existed in the area of Southern Poland (Southern Malopolska) in the nineteenth and twentieth centuries. It is based in the first place on field material which was collected by the author in the interwar period and partly after the Second World War. It is not an exhaustive view of the subject; merely an attempt to extract from a great many individual facts a pattern of typical, recurring processes which reflect the cultural dynamics of definite phases of historical development. These generalizations aim at grasping: (a) the main forces shaping and maintaining traditional culture, (b) the basic characteristic features of that culture and (c) the dynamics of its disintegration. Together these may reveal the real mechanism behind the functioning of a given traditional culture. The present essay does not give all the generalizations which could be extracted from the source of material, nor does it claim to offer wider generalizations reaching beyond the said territory of Southern Poland.

The Concept of Traditional Culture

Generally speaking, 'tradition', covers the total cultural heritage handed down from one generation to the next. Two basic media of transmitting social heritage are known. The first comprises transmission by means of speech and other sound stimuli, (e.g. musical sounds) which are received by the sense of hearing, as well as demonstration of actions and objects which are perceived by visual organs. This mode of transmission always involves direct human contact. Secondly, there exist transmission media which possess a mechanical character. These include, print, musical scores, various iconographic techniques and phonographic apparatus. Such media relieve the producers and receivers of the cultural content from direct human contact, and they establish indirect, impersonal human relationships.

It has become customary for ethnographers and culture historians to speak about 'traditional culture', meaning all those cultural contents and values *which are transmitted orally*. We have accepted this linguistic convention, and in that sense the term 'peasant traditional culture' has been used in this paper.

In all domains of social life, in all efforts of human co-operation, in the production and accumulation of cultural gains and achievements, we can always observe two fundamental, though contrasting tendencies which manifest themselves with varying intensity in different phases of historical development. Firstly, there is a tendency which is essentially conservative and stabilizing, which is expressed in a propensity for the preservation and maintenance of the existing social order. It is always based on the acknowledgement of previous experience and is essentially focused on the past. The past, here, supplies a pattern for living and provides a model for human action. Conversely, there exists a tendency which has grown out of doubt and dissatisfaction and which is invariably conducive to social change. This tendency is often destructive and revolutionary *vis-à-vis* the existing social order, and has often been expressed in terms of a more or less violent opposition to, and negation of, the surrounding reality. This tendency is usually born out of the deep human craving for new and better forms of social life, new moral truths and more adequate technical innovations. Such a vision of new life, forward looking, yet generated by concrete conditions of human existence, can become a powerful, driving force for human action.

These tendencies reflect two fundamental needs of human existence: (a) that of the regulation and ordering of human relationships founded on a set of established values, skills and capabilities, truths and experiences; and (b) that of the improvement of human existence by the securing of greater mastery over the natural environment, by extending knowledge of the surrounding reality, by obtaining a greater security and protection against hostile forces, by the reduction of human effort and by making human co-operation rest on a more balanced foundation.

Now, the first tendency is known to manifest itself with greatest strength in all those cultures which rely exclusively on oral transmission and direct demonstration in handing down their cultural contents and experience. The second, on the other hand, is apt to come to the fore, in the crucial periods of social upheaval and revolution which are known to have opened up new eras in human history.

The glorification of the past, which finds its expression in so-called traditionalism, occurs also in literate civilizations, i.e. in those cultures which, for some length of time, have employed writing as a principal means of social transmission. What is more, cases are on record where writing itself has become a factor strengthening the importance of tradition. This has been often the case with sacred texts which for many centuries acted as canons regulating and controlling human behaviour. In the majority of cases, however, the written word has been a positive, if not altogether decisive factor of change. For literacy invariably carries with it unlimited possibilities for the quantitative transmission of cultural contents, between generations. By its very nature, writing implies the possibility of a more intensive cultural accumulation in all spheres of human activity. Writing makes possible a more adequate and precise transmission of those contents, values and achievements which form the essence of a given culture. In literate societies the processes of transmission and diffusion of cultural contents are always much more widespread, rapid and effective than in oral cultures. Finally, writing, by the very fact of accumulation of texts implies an infinitely greater scope for comparison and for critical examination, including a critical appraisal of the achievements of past generations and of their handed down knowledge – technical, natural, historical, etc. – than was ever possible with an orally transmitted heritage.

Hence when discussing the dynamics of a conservative, traditionalist culture, we inevitably turn our attention to such communities which hand down their cultural contents by oral transmission. Here it will be seen that the process is both diachronic and synchronic. It is diachronic in the sense that the passing generation hands over its cultural experiences to its successors. But it is also synchronic, in so far as the achievements of individuals or groups of individuals are directly spread by actual human contacts.

The basic transmission process in traditional culture consists of education, which introduces the novice into a definite world of both material and immaterial values. This takes place by means of intentional teaching and demonstration as well as by a corresponding reception of the above instruction through auditory and visual perception. These processes may have a conscious character which is the case when the transmission takes place in a deliberate, purposeful and institutionalized manner; but they must also be natural or spontaneous when they result from mere contact and imitation.

The classical domain of traditional cultures are, of course, the so-called primitive, preliterate communities which can still be found in more remote parts of the globe. But their numbers are rapidly dwindling, and, only a few such pure, uncontaminated communities un-affected by the impact of higher civilizations and relying essentially on mechanical means of transmission, exist.

Of a different character are peasant traditional cultures which originated out of class divisions prevailing in feudal Europe. They developed under the influence of the ruling class and the educated minority, though that influence took quite a different form in various phases of historical development. In the early medieval period, for instance, the cultural distance between the peasants and the feudal knights resolved itself chiefly into the differences in wealth and material endowment, but there were no marked differences in education and mentality. The situation changed during the Renaissance when education became increasingly based upon institutionalized schooling, embracing much wider groups of lay classes, who succeeded in partially emancipating themselves from the influence of the Church and who in the course of time obtained a dominant cultural role within society. Ruling class influence was and is different again in particular phases of the Capitalist and Socialist systems.

The Basic Conditions of the Existence of Traditional Culture

Traditional culture is a reality *sui generis* with its own specific dynamics. A low level of agricultural technology and stability of peasant settlement represents, perhaps, its most important foundations. In the Beskid villages, studied by the writer, agricultural tools and implements were simple, made chiefly of wood, and as late as the 1880s iron was only used on a small scale. Equally simple was the organization of work, which combined with a tendency towards economic self-sufficiency and with mystical and magical patterns of thought, reflected a rather simple state of economic and social development. When to the above is added a more or less permanent peasant occupation of the land, inherited together with the farmstead from fathers and involving very little spacial mobility, we shall have in a nutshell a picture of peasant traditional culture as well as the condition in which such cultures are apt to thrive.

Another important factor of peasant conservatism, was the patriarchal family and kinship system which was expressed in the father's authority and power over children, in the children's economic and intellectual dependence upon parents, and the young people's submissive attitude. In a peasant family close co-operation between the generations (usually three and sometimes even four) was a rule, extending over family affairs, work and recreation in the household and on land attached to it. This too was conducive to the maintenance of traditional culture.

In this connexion, the social situation of the peasantry has to be briefly reviewed. Legal and economic oppression of peasants in the feudal system greatly hampered their economic development and debarred them from a wider participation in national culture. Legal barriers, too, blocked any possible social advancement. In these circumstances, a strong feeling of social degradation and inferiority often arose in peasant minds, animated by the depravating experience of many centuries of oppression. This did not preclude a simultaneous attitude of hatred, and more active opposition raged from time to time against the dominant class. Thus the steadily deepening social distance between the upper classes and the peasantry up to the emancipation, produced a stagnant peasant living standard reflected in their material culture, in their dress, and in their food and household equipment, and which by association, came to typify, in all outward aspects, a distinct peasant social class. Despite the breakdown of the feudal system in Galicia in 1848, this state of affairs survived tenaciously for a long time afterwards.

Oral Transmission and its Social Functions

Relying mainly on the field data, the consequences of transmission of culture orally are now examined.

We have already seen that one of the most important effects of this was the limited possibility of cultural transfer from generation to generation. This limitation affected not only the number of the elements transferred, but also their quality, i.e. their exactness and lasting character. Thus, quantitative limitations were particularly pronounced in cases where new technological inventions and new literary and philosophical contributions were concerned. This type of intellectual achievement, coming mainly from anonymous members of the highland community, never had an enduring character. Usually expressed in agricultural practice, in natural science and medical observations, in literary and musical production or ideological conceptions, it was never written down, and in the great majority of cases it perished with the death of the original creator.

Thus, an important consequence of the oral transmission of culture was a gradual decline in the public memory for older usages and artefacts. New technological advances, new terms, customs and songs began to oust the old ones, and ultimately, despite long co-existence, in some cases completely replaced them. This usually happened when the old form did not find a material embodiment or iconographic representation or was not preserved in a written shape. Then it fell into the limbo of social oblivion and was irrevocably lost.

Selection in Cultural Transmission

The process of selection in cultural transmission acquired a characteristic pattern. When analysing what was likely to become preserved in a given society, and what was likely to perish, the writer was able to establish a set of rules and general principles, which were valid for the type of culture under investigation, but which even there could show deviations and modifications according to phase of historical development.

In the first place it would appear that all that had an individual character, all that resulted from the capability and skills of individuals, that did not become objectified during the lifetime of its originators, at least in a small community, tended to disappear. In other words, all that failed to enter into a concrete scheme of action, that did not become a pattern for behaviour, or a set of mental attitudes, or a stereotype of a given culture, can safely be regarded as potentially lost. Many examples are on record; they include such non-material products as songs, tunes, folk tales, popular artistic productions, ideas and concepts connected with a ' *Weltanschauung* ' of the members of a given community. This type of cultural production met with a much better chance of survival when it encountered men with similar interests, capabilities and dispositions to the original creator. In material production and technology the position was similar; when a new technological invention or improvement in production became a part of the routine of a working team connected with the original creator, there was much greater chance of its being permanently established.

Passing to the factors which helped to maintain a product, its practical utility must be stressed above all else. As long as it was important in the life of the community, and satisfied, effectively, the needs of its members – economic, technological, social and emotional – and did not compete with new, but relayed, or rival products, it had a chance of long survival. In this connexion prominence must be given to various objects of material culture which would have been particularly difficult to change, as this would have required an enormous output of labour. A classic example is the field system, which, in certain villages of Podhale has retained its original medieval arrangement of fields and strips. If certain products well tested during several centuries' experience, despite their outward simplicity, met productive needs, e.g. certain items of farming equipment, they also had a chance of survival. The same is true of numerous techniques of work connected with soil cultivation, harvesting, flax processing, wood working and pottery.

Specific instruments of social transmission in traditional culture

Apart from direct oral transmission and practical demonstration, the peasant community developed other means which allowed knowledge to be transmitted with greater precision. These include, above all, the compact and highly expressive linguistic formulae, often put into rhyme, which contained meteorological statements, facts about climate, information relating to agriculture and animal farming, religious and moral instruction as well as a whole realm of experiences, forming what is popularly known as 'wise sayings'. Many of these formulae belonged to the category of proverbs. They are common in current speech, adding much to its vigour and expressiveness.

The verse form was also used to an extent in magical formulae, which improved the chances of faithful repetition of the formula during the magical performance. Some versification was also applied with gusto, in various folk-tales with a dramatic plot. These stirred popular imagination and were for the most part sung, by wandering musicians and beggars. Such a form was more suitable for chanting reproduction by the audience.

Connected with this was the application of traditional schemes and models which served as guiding principles in practical action. For example, the old village carpenters in Podhale did not make use of any drawn plans of blueprints, or resort to written-down calculations. Their entire technological knowledge was based exclusively on memory and was reduced to the repetition, in practical action, of a few basic models. Thus, there existed a model of a larger, two-roomed house and a smaller one having one room only, with certain variants which consisted of adding summer-rooms and stores (*komora*). Similar basic schemes existed in the work of rural tailors and other craftsmen.

Sociability in Traditional Life

Institutionalized social gatherings were very important media for the preservation of traditional culture. They consisted either of meetings at home, in the inn, in the summer often outside the building in the open, or else contacts made during the journey to church, to the market, or to the annual Church Fête on patron saint day. With each type of social intercourse were connected certain definite groupings of people, as well as traditionally prescribed subjects of conversation. Thus men walked separately to the local parish church, while women formed another group, young and old people still another. Groups based on neighbourhood walked together to the local fair. The Church Fête was mainly attended by the young, the journey providing many opportunities for making new acquaintances.

Of special importance however, were the neighbours' meetings, which gathered for certain ceremonial occasions like spinning or tearing feather, as well as for more informal events like regular evening gatherings, especially in the winter months. These gatherings, common in Southern Poland by the end of the nineteenth century and early twentieth century were the forerunners of the modern book or newspaper.

The subject matter of these evening talks embraced gossip about local events and household and community affairs, as well as 'news from the wide world'. There were also numerous tales often legendary, mystical and magico-religious in character. The tales carried a great power of attraction, and the narrator became the centre of popular interest and general social recognition. Their subjects centred around various figures belonging to the world of popular demonology – spirits of the dead, ghosts and devils, but also various types of fairies and gnomes, on the whole rather malignant, but some of them at least propitious. To this, various saints must be added, as well as the figure of Jesus wandering over the earth.

Passing to the social function of these tales, it should first be observed that they probably grew out of age-old human ideas and discoveries, by means of which early mankind sought to explain the forces which govern the world of nature and human destiny. Their contents acted, both for the narrators and the recipients, as a living truth, a concrete reality. In these circumstances these tales constituted an important instrument of the strengthening of the old, mystico-magical outlook. They contained many practical hints on how to protect oneself from evil forces, or how to placate them. Some of the tales, especially those which contained religious motifs, had often additional ethical and moral objectives, stressing the reward for good deeds, and punishment for wrongdoers. In this way various moral precepts were enhanced, which from Church lore made their way into traditional culture, usually with characteristic local adaptations. A special category of tales referred to hidden treasures and benevolent robbers, who aided the poor in acts of revenge over the cruel nobles. The unusual popularity of these legends probably reflected the deep peasant desire to improve their lot, to compensate for their grief and humiliations suffered in real life.

Anonymity of Products

One of the most characteristic features of traditional culture is the anonymous character of its original producers and contributors. The introduction of new and better tools and techniques, the invention of new ornamental patterns, new tunes or harmonic discoveries were often connected with the process of objectivization which meant that a given community adopted and incorporated an individual product. At first, the identity of the original contributor or innovator was common knowledge. In the course of time, however, this person was forgotten, the product became separated from its original creator, lost its individual character and became indistinguishable from other techniques. It is but seldom that the name of the original creator penetrated and survived in the collective consciousness of the community, although such cases are on record.

The Power of the Village Authorities

A very slow rhythm and tempo of development is a characteristic feature of every traditional culture. Many technological arrangements and economic habits have shown unusual tenacity throughout centuries of feudalism, and even after the nineteenth century emancipation the position was not radically altered. As late as the inter-war period one could find in the remote villages of the Beskid mountains as well as in the older forest settlements in the Central Polish plain an astonishing number of traditional relics of material culture (farm tools and implements, agricultural techniques, land tenure systems, interiors of peasant cottages), to a lesser extent, of social organization (e.g. certain forms of patriarchal family and even some relics of the old clan system), as well as of certain interesting manifestations of the traditional peasant mentality. In result, the permanent unchanging character of social institutions developed, implying belief in their intrinsic value. 'Thus our fathers and grandfathers have always done, thus we shall do', is a statement which can be accepted as typical and which is often heard from peasants from the old traditional culture. In these circumstances any conscious rational motivation for economic activity or manner of conduct was of little relevance. Similarly, of little importance was the rationalization of the character and peculiarities of any social institution, or economic and legal norm, or rule of conduct. What was of great importance was any action undertaken without a deeper intellectual reflection; one which consisted of a passive reception of the existing cultural system on the one hand, and a strong emotional attachment to it, on the other. In this way, cultural contents and institutions acquired an unusual importance, becoming a working authority which exerted a binding influence upon human beings. The essence of this authority consisted in the acknowledgement of a definite cultural product, which as a rule was devoid of any cultural judgement, but which was further enhanced by a strong belief in its intrinsic value, and sometimes even developing into certain manifestations of religious reverence or a cult. Closely connected with this attitude was the consequent high authority vested in the main carriers and transmitters of traditional culture. Clearly, the most influential were the old people, whose long life and numerous contacts with people permitted them not only to accumulate the greatest amount of traditional knowledge, but also to gain the richest experiences through economic and social practice. Owing to the lack of written knowledge, they inevitably constituted the main source of information on work and production, on the world and on life from which younger generation could amply draw.

In order to understand properly how this authority worked, it is necessary to stress another important aspect of traditional knowledge. It is explained by the fact that many of its elements were esoteric and jealously guarded from general circulation. These secret contents could only be passed to a small number of chosen people. Even in agricultural pursuits, before the introduction of official farming knowledge and agricultural instructors, not every son was fortunate to be entrusted by the father with full knowledge of traditional farming methods. This idea of the secrecy in production can also be found in various economic pursuits other than agriculture as well as in the craftsmen guilds. It was naturally most pronounced in folk-medicine and veterinary knowledge as well as in various magical practices. In these circumstances the intellectual as well as the economic superiority of the elderly was enhanced. The economic dominance resulted in the children's submission to parents and found expression in the division and the allotment of work. Food and living quarters were provided in return but no cash. Paternal authority also controlled endowment at marriage, the disposal of property at death, and generally made the leaving of the parental home and migration in search of alternative work extremely difficult.

The Role of Magic and Religion in Traditional Culture

One of the salient features of traditional culture was the unusually great role allotted to magical beliefs and practices compared with activities based on empirical and rational foundations. Among Polish highlanders, dairy farming was most permeated with magical beliefs and practices. Nearly every activity connected with sheep rearing, grazing, milking as well as the milk processing was associated with certain practices which aimed either at securing success or averting pending danger or misfortune. They formed a body of secret lore which was passed on by the senior shepherd (*baca*), often after reaching an advanced age or even sometimes at his deathbed, to his successors. The latter, before they could be entrusted with the magical power they entailed, had to undergo a kind of initiation ceremony.

A strict observance of the traditionally prescribed order and sequence of rites and formulae played a very important part in highlanders' magical practices, as, in fact, in any magic. To reverse the order, to change a formula could be very dangerous, for it might turn success into misfortune, and even bring about magical retaliation, of which the frail and dependent human being has been always afraid. It is interesting to note that this important magical attitude in traditional highland culture was often extended to the domain of rational and empirical action. Thus, any rejection of the usual and traditionally sanctioned technological activity, any change of the old tools and techniques, any abandonment or breaking of traditional custom would be commonly dreaded and regarded as a dangerous act, which might invite misfortune, or produce disaster. For that reason matches were never used for making fire in the old mountain dairy huts, but the traditional method of flint and steel was employed. This was also the reason why the introduction of new equipment in the mountain chalets, like tin vessels in the inter-war period, met with resistance, for this, it was feared, might reduce the proceeds from sheep. When by the end of the nineteenth century iron ploughs became common in the Galician villages, the peasants, especially of the older generation, often expressed fear that the soil cut with iron might retaliate and refuse to yield crops. Similar forebodings were expressed with regard to farm machinery, like chaff-cutters or threshing-machines, which, it was feared, might adversely affect the crops.

Such a magic ridden frame of mind was therefore a serious obstacle to progress in all branches of culture, and at the same time became an important factor in the preservation of the old regime. In this mental climate, permeated with belief in ancestral authority and deeply saturated in the magical *Weltanschauung*, any attempt at change, in material culture, as well as in customs and social relations, met with apprehension and fear of retaliation by the mystical powers who acted as guardians of the old established order. It should be added that magical thinking confirmed the authority and social position of a certain category of people, like the *bacas* (sheepmasters), medicine-men and blacksmiths. The village commoners believed in their secret lore and their ability to control hidden forces, which could bring about success or misfortune. For that reason they often acted as intermediaries between the world of the super-natural and peasant rank and file, who, feeling helpless, looked for support to these highly influential people.

A few words must now be said about those religious beliefs which played an important part in the preservation of traditional values. Underlying them was a deep rooted belief in 'divine omnipotence' which created and controls everything, in the 'will of God' regulating equally the social order and the destiny of individuals as well as controlling the laws of nature. Against this there developed a system of transcendental sanctions, including religious commands and prohibitions, exerted over the peasantry by the clergy and the ruling class. These acted as powerful safeguards of the feudal system, and afterward of capitalism. Such commands and prohibitions extended to the sphere of family life, and also to the wider network of human relations. Those who broke them would meet with 'God's punishments', those who accepted them and acted in accordance with the 'will of God', could reckon on His support, since the ultimate mastery of things and people lay with Him.

Tendency towards Cultural Uniformity

We have already said that in every human community, irrespective of time and space, we can find a collective tendency towards the maintenance and conservation of the existing state, and, conversely, an individualistic, emancipating tendency towards the introduction of new elements into culture.

The old peasant culture in Southern Poland at the close of the feudal era and, also to a certain extent under Capitalism, had a predominantly traditional character. But it is important to realize that it never constituted a uniform equalitarian cultural monolith with regard to the consumption and share in the production of cultural goods. It was a highly differentiated culture, both socially and economically; its social contrasts were often considerable, especially those which existed between rich peasants and the village poor. Thus there were great differences in the sizes of farms and the number of cattle, in the interior of peasant cottages, furniture, implements, food, dress etc. In social and ceremonial life, there was much splendour and pomp among rich peasants, best seen at such occasions as weddings, christening feasts and funerals. This sometimes developed into a consciousness that certain material objects accompany a certain social status, such as the gate in front of the house, one or even two chimneys on the roof of the cottage, chests for personal belongings, certain type of furniture and dress. The consumption of certain types of food, was regarded as a duty associated with social rank. On the other hand, the scale of consumption of social goods by the village proletariat was much smaller. In addition, there was a strong pressure exerted by the rich peasants on the poorer section of the community (the landless and village labourers) which aimed at debarring them from using such elements of culture which the rich claimed as their sole prerogative. Yet it was the poor who played a very conspicuous part in the creation of cultural values. They were the main carriers of technological knowledge in various branches of production, like wood and metal working, pottery, weaving, tailoring and so on. They possessed wide knowledge of wild fruit, roots, herbs and the like collected in forests and fields to supplement their diet. It was they who provided the great majority of craftsmen-carpenters, coopers, wheelrights, weavers, blacksmiths, potters, The village proletariat produced a large number of folk-artists, sculptors, painters, ornament makers, tailors, singers and players, saga-tellers and folk-writers.

Despite this differentiation, traditional culture manifested a tendency towards uniformity. It was expressed in the social pressure towards a common, unchanging pattern of social institutions and ideological contents within particular classes or village groups. The individuals who deviated from the commonly accepted pattern of behaviour obtaining within their respective classes or groups, met with such repressive measures as ridicule, reproach, moral censure, ostracism or even the application of official legal sanctions.

It is a significant feature of the type of peasant culture we are analysing that there is a relative paucity of material examples in contrast to the highly developed system of behavioural patterns. Thus, on the one hand, we have a limited number of such material arrangements as types of houses, plans of the interior, furniture, dress, ornaments, etc., and on the other, a great number of highly differentiated social situations, each demanding a special, customarily prescribed form of conduct. These extended both over the sphere of family life, as well as over neighbourly relations, village affairs and inter-village relationships. Connected with these regulated forms of conduct were numerous attitudes, evaluations, moral and legal norms. However despite these strong tendencies towards uniformity, the village community was never a levelled, well-adjusted social reality. Different starts in life, personal abilities and unequal opportunities played a very important role in a peasant community. An inquiring individual often led to the discarding of mechanical lines of thought. In my many years of field study I came across several village philosophers whose thoughts upon life were independent and bold. Thus, among a variety of peasant thinkers I found sceptics who doubted the reality of heaven and hell, and even the existence of the human soul.

The Poverty of Historical Perspective

The peasant population which in the feudal period was divided up into small and isolated village and parish communities and into somewhat larger sections within the so-called patrimonial estates (*latifundia*) lived under conditions which did not favour the development of a broader historical perspective.

It is clear that in a community which relied mainly on oral tradition, the memory of the past must have had a limited, local character. Apart from topographical facts (village and field boundaries), it was mainly concerned with the events, which, owing to their unusual character and their far reaching effects, left deep traces in the mind of the people. Thus, events associated with vital aspects of human existence, such as famines, epidemics, wars, class struggles with landlords were remembered above all. These form the destructive nature of peasant history. In a later period, they consisted of memories of the conditions of living under serfdom, of constant and sometimes angry disputes with the squire, of his economic oppression of the villagers, of his robbing of their land to enlarge his own estates; they also included tales of great highland robbers, some of them becoming figures of legendary fame. It should be stressed that such traditions of serfdom retained their strength even in modern times, becoming, one of the factors mobilizing the peasant masses in their struggle for social and political emancipation. Here, however, they concern us above all as an important factor in the awakening of peasant interest in their past and of the deepening of their general historical perspective.

The poverty of historical perspective was also the result of a short collective memory, caused simply by the continual process of death of one generation and succession by a new one. This may seem obvious enough, yet the stressing of this simple process leads to the discovery of another interesting aspect of the peasant historical sense, namely, that historical events were assigned no clear cut chronology. Often events remote from each other merged, in the peasant memory, into one picture without a definite sequence; sometimes even passing into synchronic vision.

The Village Community in Traditional Culture

A very significant feature of the peasant traditional culture was a strong bond of social cohesion which, despite the existing class differentiation, joined the population of individual settlements into well-defined territorial groupings, the village communities. The Beskid villagers of that time had relatively little contact, economic, administrative, religious and educational, with the town and other villages. This, combined with the almost complete absence of a wider peasant organization, resulted in a situation where village communities of that time lived their own lives, being practically self-sufficient. Somewhat closer relations existed only between those villages which formed a common parish. The village bond was above all manifested in a strong community of interest, which operated within the village.

Although sharp social contrast existed among the village population which was divided into several landowning classes as well as into different types of landless peasantry,[1] there existed a well-developed sense of internal solidarity.

1. Thus among the landed peasantry there were owners of full fields (*kmiecie*), half-fields (*pokmiecie*), half a *rola* (another type of field) (*oorolnicy*), quarter-*rola* (*ewiererolnicy*), owners of forest recovered fields (*zarebnicy*) and finally the owners of quite small plots (*zagrodnicy, hortulani*). The landless population were differentiated into craftsmen (*rzemieslnicy*),

Outwardly it was expressed in a common name, like 'we the Porebianie', 'we the Bubkowinianie' etc., i.e. we, the people of Poreba, Bukowina etc. The common ownership of pasture-land, bogs and forest, in which even the smallest owners of land had their share, provided an additional link. The institution of mutual neighbourly assistance, as well as an elaborate system of exchange of gifts, was practised on a large scale. Another manifestation of the solidarity was the practice of common migration in groups for seasonal work and the formation of work parties on the basis of a common village or parish origin. The same principle of grouping obtained in common pilgrimages to the acknowledged shrines or places of religious worship. There was also a tendency towards settling down together in towns and industrial settlements, as well as towards seeking employment in the same factories. This principle was maintained in the Polish emigration settlements abroad, in the United States for example.

A village community with a strong sense of internal solidarity had also a well-defined sense of distinctness in relation to the outside world. Thus, the inhabitants of neighbouring villages were always treated as strangers. They were treated differently, though with varying degree of antipathy. The following statement by one of my informants will best illustrate this ethical relativism: 'It is not permissible to beat the people from our own village (*swojacy*, dialect) but the people from other villages can (and should) be beaten.'

Such an attitude often led to conflicts with the inhabitants of other communities, which sometimes developed into prolonged and acute antagonism. These often passed into open brawls, in which groups mainly of youngsters took part. There were many locations in which such a fight could take place, the usual ones being the boundary between the two villages, the inn, or fêtes and parties, mainly in connexion with the courting of local girls by the *niepilce* (dialect for strangers).

Attitudes towards strangers were thus, on the whole, antagonistic. They found expression in depreciatory and sometimes

---

village labourers (*wyronicy*) who either had a household of their own, or a room (*komora*) and food provided by a rich peasant for whom they had to work (*komornicy*).

even abusive nicknames for people of other villages. Their evaluations, descriptions and stories of them were usually totally distorted. Numerous examples are on record, though it would be difficult, if at all possible, to reproduce in English the atmosphere and the expressiveness of the local dialect.

It should also be added that an important function of the above mentioned village antagonism was to provide a barrier to the access of strangers into the village. For they, by marriage or by other means, it was thought, would get hold of the land, of which there was always a great shortage in Southern Poland.

The Dynamics of Disintegration of Traditional Cultures

Before we branch into a discussion of the process of disintegration of traditional peasant culture under the impact of capitalism, a few words must be said about its historical antecedents. We have already seen that any traditional culture, based exclusively on oral transmission, could maintain its pure form only in those situations where the community that carried it was not subject to the influence of more advanced, literate civilizations. But such a situation never existed in Europe, where the peasant cultures since the earliest times had developed as dependent products, in a state of symbiosis with the cultures of the ruling classes. The latter, since feudal times and then throughout the period of capitalism, have always applied writing and later on printing as a means of accumulation and perfecting of cultural achievements. The position was similar in Poland, where the development of peasant culture was not independent, but contained within a framework of a political and social system imposed by the ruling classes. In the feudal system there were two principal ways of transferring the elements of ruling class culture to that of the peasantry: (a) by a conscious pressure and coercion on the part of the ruling class, (b) by imitation on the part of the peasantry.

The peasantry in the feudal system constituted – as is generally known – the most numerous, and at the same time the most exploited and oppressed class, on whose labour the well-being of the nobles, gentry, and clergy depended. Hence the tendency for the ruling class to control the social and economic life of the peasants, as well as other aspects of their culture. The result was that various cultural elements of the upper classes were inevitably introduced in the life of the villagers. To illustrate this process, which was, of course, gradual and extended over a long time, it is enough to mention the role of the ruling class in the regulation of the land system and rural housing, and in numerous rules and instructions issued (most of them in writing and some even in a printed form) to the peasantry regulating various aspects of their material well-being (e.g. peasant dress and costumes). Or, one may mention the role of the clergy and the products of Church culture, for centuries transmitted by written and printed media, which extended over vital systems of peasant life and mentality such as religious concepts and practices, family life, views on life and the world and literary motifs which from the sermons passed to folktales. It should be added that the institution of parish schools, although in feudal times they trained a relatively small number of children, had existed for several centuries and its teachers, the rectors, were often of peasant stock.

Of considerable importance was the fact that in numerous villages the actual organizers of settlement, the so-called 'locators', were often townsmen, while the legal foundations of these settlements consisted of written civil and penal codes brought from Western Europe. Shortly afterwards, during the fifteenth century, a large number of the village scribes were of village origin. For that period saw a powerful drive for social advancement among the villages, who on an increasing scale began to send their sons to schools. The latter afterwards took up lower administrative posts in the Church and municipalities. It is therefore no accident that already at that time the countryside was producing a number of eminent men, scholars, writers and poets. However the great majority of peasants who became literate, took minor posts in the villages as the rectors of parish schools, vicars, church organists, scribes in village courts, and accountants in large estates. It was from this group that the leaders of peasant movements and jacqueries were recruited as well as the originators of a rebel peasant ideology, searching in the gospels for a justification for peasant rights. In this respect, attention should be drawn to a very real connexion which existed between peasant culture and the peasants' prolonged struggle for emancipation which often led to violence. For it was in that struggle that many peasant songs originated with a strong anti-nobility bias, condemning the manor and life in it.

Apart from the social coercion exerted by the ruling class, another process was simultaneously in operation, that of imitating certain cultural forms and practices belonging to the privileged classes. Although this process was much more voluntary in character, it was not quite spontaneous. For it should not be forgotten that for the exasperated peasantry various culture elements pertaining to the dominant classes must have looked attractive, be it custom, etiquette, music or literary production.

In this way non-peasant cultural elements penetrated – by enforcement or imitation – into folk-culture. At the same time they often perished in the culture of the ruling classes, e.g. in literature, official science or other branches of artistic production. Having been retained in the peasant culture, they often underwent changes, both in quality and in quantity, acquiring after some time a folk-character. This important process which had already taken place with varying intensity in the feudal period remained, so far as the mechanism of development was concerned, little altered in the nineteenth and twentieth centuries.

Generally it may be said that the peasant culture of Southern Poland showed a preponderance of the traditional elements until the emancipation of the peasants in 1848, and even beyond that to about 1870. The disintegration of traditional peasant culture was a long process. The dissolution of traditional elements after 1848 was due to a strengthened forward-looking perspective among the peasantry. Among the factors which heralded this tendency were: (a) the growing infiltration into the villages of products demanding higher technical skill and knowledge about how to use them, improved agricultural tools and machinery for example; (b) a more intensive exchange of goods between town and country and the breaking up of the spacial isolation of the countryside; (c) the development of rural education; (d) the wider connexion of village populations with social, political and cultural movements on a national scale. The tide of displacement of elements of traditional culture among the villages was not an even one; slow at the end of the feudal epoch, it speeded up at the turn of the nineteenth and early twentieth century, and became rapid in the new Poland.

22 F. G. Bailey

The Peasant View of the Bad Life

F. G. Bailey, 'The peasant view of the bad life', *Advancement of Science*,
December 1966, pp. 399–409. A presidential address delivered to
Section N (Sociology) on 2 September 1966 at the Nottingham meeting
of the British Association for the Advancement of Science.

I will speak here about the way in which some poor peasants,
living in the hills and jungles of one of the less advanced states of
the Indian Union – Orissa – think about themselves, about
leaders, about the politicians and officials who govern them, and
how they conceptualize time and the future.

I have chosen this restricted subject for several reasons. Firstly
– and negatively – a presidential address need not always be a
speech by the President on the state of the nation. The importance
of sociology and the direction in which it should develop are
subjects at once too easy and too difficult for this occasion. In
any case, that, broadly, is one topic for our meetings here in
Nottingham. Of course, in so far as sociology is an under-
developed subject, it may be that my discourse will not be wholly
without interest for those concerned with the politics of the social
sciences in this country, since it concerns closed minds and in-
flexible attitudes.

Secondly, although one cannot fail to be impressed with the
Niagara of writing by sociologists and political scientists on
problems of development and modernization,[1] their work is
heavily biased towards the elite. There are many reasons why
this should be. Top people, we assume, are the people who shape

---

1. There are many ways of defining 'modernization': my training inclines me towards a definition based upon role pattern – diffuse as against
specific roles – and I make use of one such definition later. But I do not
consider it necessary to discuss the question at length here since my argument applies to any kind of innovation into the peasant world whether or
not we would want to class this innovation as modern.

history. Top people, too, behave in ways that the alien social scientist can understand: for example, many of them speak – and write books in – English or French. But the alien social scientist cannot so easily understand what the human majority of the developing nations – the mass, the non-elite – are thinking, or why they are thinking it: they are strange, remote, annoyingly diverse, unpredictable, a mystery even to their own elite, apathetic, afraid to take risks, improvident, parochial in their outlook, superstitious – and so on through a string of adjectives which range from the patronizing to the contemptuous. These attitudes no doubt reinforce the morale of the modernizing elite and convince them that they are right to fight for the good of the peasants against peasant ignorance and prejudice. But a conviction of one's own effortless superiority is no adequate substitute for knowledge, for intelligence, in the military sense of that word.

There is, in fact, an inverse relationship between the force which a modernizer must use, in his war against traditional values and behaviour, and the knowledge which he must have of the enemy's dispositions. If he has overwhelming force – and this is not the case in any of the developing nations – then he can wipe the board clean and in one generation write upon it a new set of modern roles and values. But short of this hypothetical extreme, the modernizer cannot compel but must persuade: to do this he must know what values the people already hold; how they see the world and society around them; in short, he must know their cognitive maps.[2] In this situation knowledge is a substitute for – one might say a kind of – power; with an adequate map – an adequate understanding of the traditional way of life – the modernizer can most economically and most effectively deploy his limited resources.

Here I shall talk about those peasants in India whom I happen to know, about certain concepts which they hold and which a modernizer should take into account. I shall also outline a very

2. There are many near synonyms for 'cognitive map', some more and some less inclusive: ethos, world view, collective representations, beliefs and values, ideology and – most inclusive – culture. The metaphor of a map is appropriate because it suggests a guide for action. Cognitive maps consist of a set of value directives and existential propositions which together help to guide social interaction.

broad strategy for those who wish to promote economic, social and political development. On another occasion I hope to make similar analyses of the cognitive maps of the elite themselves: of politicians, administrators, merchants, entrepreneurs, students and (one might add) city mobs.

For a number of reasons tracing the cognitive map of a culture not one's own is difficult. In recent years linguistic anthropologists have developed a technique which may provide the scientific exactness so far lacking, but as yet these tools have been used to elicit the categories through which people perceive their kinsmen, or the types of food they eat or the way they think about the consumption of alcohol, or about disease, or about the land on which they grow their food. The more general moral categories with which I am here concerned – good and bad, success and failure, and the difficult idea of the moral community – remain beyond the reach of these techniques. My account, there, will be impressionistic and difficult to verify.[3]

Anthropologists begin by selecting native concepts and teasing out their meanings. A one-word translation is always inadequate. Often the concepts are presented in the native language: *mana*, *taboo*, *totem* are well-known examples, and they can be described only by specifying the contexts in which they may be correctly used. Sometimes the people themselves have no general term. For example the concept of an 'outsider' is my summary of a range of terms which peasants have for particular outsiders: *Sircar* (government); *Marwari* (a trader); *Gujerati* (another kind of trader); *Kataki* (a man from the coastal plain); and so forth. In short, there are quite considerable problems of translation.

Thirdly, it is not easy to decide at what level of generality to make the translation. Perceptions of the world vary according to sex, to age, to caste status and so forth. In the context of modernization in peasant India it is usually appropriate to look at the cognitive maps of adult males, but this does not get round variations in caste and ethnic allegiances. I shall be talking of the hill peasants of Orissa who, in the area in which I lived, are

3. I am not competent to discuss psychological techniques for ascertaining peasant attitudes.

either Oriyas or Konds.[4] The cognitive maps of both these peoples contain the same element of xenophobia, but they differ radically in their perceptions of human inequality. To average out these differences makes nonsense; there is nothing to do but make two cognitive maps, for ideas of rank are clearly relevant in the modernization process. In what follows I shall be talking mainly about the Oriyas, who, being a caste society, see the social world in categories of rank. The other themes which I shall discuss are found to a greater or lesser degree in many peasant societies: but I could not claim that they are universal.

Every society discriminates between different categories of persons, giving to the highest full status as members of the community, able to bear social responsibilities and commanding the corresponding social rights, and relegating the lowest into a category which is scarcely human at all. Those who are so marginal as to be considered outsiders can be used as if they were objects or instruments, providing the user has the power to do so: this is not regarded as a moral relationship, but as one of exploitation. Standards of honesty, respect and consideration in so far as they are moral imperatives are diminished as the status of the person at the other end of the relationship becomes more marginal. Moreover, one expects him to reciprocate. One justifies cheating government agencies by saying that the officials concerned are cheating you. This perception is often so firm that even behaviour which is patently not exploitative, but benevolent, is interpreted as a hypocritical cover for some as yet undisclosed interest: by definition all horses are Trojan.

The steps by which categories of people are charted as marginal are not evenly spaced. For the villagers whom I knew the moral community[5] comprises their own family, the members of their

4. For a detailed account of Konds and Oriyas see Bailey (1960, pp. 121–93).

5. The concept of a moral community is complex and difficult. In everyday language this is the distinction between 'we' (the moral community) and 'they' (the outsiders). For those who follow Durkheim the adjective 'moral' is perhaps redundant, since the society (or community) is co-extensive with moral action. Nevertheless, I retain the adjective to emphasize the continuous judgement of right and wrong which characterizes interactions

own caste in the same village, their fellow villagers (markedly graded according to their distance from ego in the caste system), their kinsmen in other villages and their caste fellows in other villages, and getting near to the limit, people of other castes in those same villages. Then, after a gap, come people who are villagers like oneself, with the same style of life and speaking the same dialect, but with whom, as yet, no connexion can be traced: if they desire to be admitted to the moral community, the villagers use elaborate and rigorous techniques to test their cultural credentials.

Beyond this category are people whose culture – the way they speak, the way they dress, their deportment, the things they speak about as valuable and important – places them unambiguously beyond the moral community of the peasant; revenue inspectors, policemen, development officers, health inspectors, veterinary officials and so on; men in bush shirts and trousers, men who are either arrogant and distant or who exhibit a camaraderie which, if the villager reciprocates, is immediately switched off; men who come on bicycles and in jeeps, but never on their feet. These are the people to be outwitted: these are the people whose apparent gifts are by definition the bait for some hidden trap.

The significance of this for political modernization and for development is obvious. Suggestions or commands to assume modern political or economic roles come from outside the moral community: they are therefore automatically categorized as dangerous and sinful, and those villagers who adopt the new roles run the risk of being marked as deviants and punished. Equally if any innovation does in fact turn out to be harmful (for example, the improved seed that fails) the villager does not feel

---

within the community. Beyond the community such judgements do not apply: to cheat an outsider is neither right nor wrong: it is merely expedient or inexpedient.

It is also difficult to draw a boundary around a particular moral community, for each one varies according to the ego who is chosen as the point of reference. The Brahmin and the Sweeper do not have the same moral community even within the one village. Nevertheless, for both of them, there are some common – and large – discontinuities, so that *vis-à-vis* for instant outsiders, it is possible to regard both Brahmin and Sweeper as members of the one moral community.

obliged to search for what he would regard as a rational scientific cause; he finds a perfectly satisfactory explanation in the fact that it came from outside; and he also finds confirmation of his perception that external things are evil and dangerous (cf. Bailey, 1959, pp. 252–4).

It is, therefore, something of a paradox that the way a peasant tries to exploit a politician or an official, or to avoid being exploited by him, is by transforming the modern specialized relationship which he has with that man into a multiplex relationship, a type which is characteristic of his own peasant world. The peasant dealing with a clerk finds a broker to help him establish a personal relationship which will soften the rigorous unpleasantness of the official relationship. The politician seeking votes or the development official seeking peasant co-operation will call them 'brothers and sisters'. When the peasants want something out of the official they will address him as if he were a king and therefore has the obligation to be generous, or perhaps by that opening to many Indian petitions 'You are my mother and my father....' The implication in all these cases is that the official relationship, which is single-interest and specialized, is not enough: it must be reinforced with other relationships.

Relationships within a peasant or tribal community are for the most part multiplex: that is to say, they are not specialized to deal with a single activity. There is, of course, some division of labour, as, for example, between the landowners and the landless: but even then this relationship, which I have described through its economic strand, will also carry political and ritual and possibly familial strands. This, indeed, is the characteristic pattern of the caste system as it works inside an Indian village.

It is to be noticed that whether the initiative comes from the official and politician or from the peasant, it is the supplicant who seeks to make the relationship diffuse: to make it a moral relationship. The dominant partner will usually play hard-to-get; if the official or politician is dominant he will try to retain the transactional character of the relationship and not have the sharp edge of the bargain blunted by moral considerations; if the peasant is dominant, he is likely to reject the proferred relationship, because it comes from an outsider, or to accept it simply as a transaction and get what he can out of it. I have ample evidence that this was overwhelmingly the attitude of villagers towards campaigning politicians in India.

When, as a supplicant, the peasant tries to bribe a clerk, or to establish a dependent relationship with an official in the idiom of family relationship or of a courtier at the king's palace, he is in fact trying to coerce the clerk or the official by including him within his own moral community. He is trying to transform the transaction, which he knows is one of exploitation, into a moral relationship, *because it is in his interest to do so*. In just the same way, when the campaigning politician addresses him as 'brother', the peasant sees this as an act of hypocrisy, and looks behind the façade of symbolic friendliness for the hidden interest.

The watershed between traditional and modern society is exactly this distinction between single-interest and multiplex relationships. The hallmark of a modern society is the specialized role and the whole apparatus of its productive prosperity rests upon the division of labour between specialized roles. Of course we have diffuse institutions like the family, but the public official who finds jobs for his relatives or the fact that a large part of Macmillan's cabinets could be shown on a chart of kinship and affinity, is something which our modern culture condemns: or at least we feel uncomfortable about it.

This feeling of ethical disquiet may be the reason why planners in India resolutely close their eyes to the fact that the society they are attempting to modernize is founded upon multiplex relationships. No doubt there is bribery and nepotism; but it is loudly condemned. Even in situations which could be met without bruising the modernist conscience, the official gaze is resolutely averted: for example, when the zemindari holdings in Orissa were abolished, the zemindar's place was taken by an official specialized in the collection of revenue; but the zemindar's other functions – money-lending, dispute settling, and so forth – were not systematically provided for.

The attitude of the peasant towards single-interest relationships is not, I think, marked by ethical displeasure. Such relationships, being with outsiders are not *im*moral so much as *a*moral: when one is dealing with an instrument, standards of what is just and unjust do not apply: one wants only to use the instrument most effectively.

A second important theme in the peasants' cognitive map is what we would call leadership. Villagers recognize two kinds of big men: a secular leader whom we will call 'chief' and a man of religious eminence whom the villagers call a 'yogi' or a 'guru' (teacher) but whom we will call a 'saint'. I will argue that the idea of disinterested service to the community is only a minor element in one of these categories and is absent altogether from the other.

A chief is a man who is able to take care of his honour (*mohoto*), and who regards honour as the supreme value in social life. Honour entails the notion of competition and conflict, for a man gets honour by demonstrating, in various stylized ways, that his rivals have less honour: that is to say, by shaming them. Heads of families, especially wealthy men of high caste, are all chiefs, and they treat one another, when not in combat, with a dignified formality and restraint.

In so far as a man is a chief he is expected to protect the interests *not* of the community at large, but the interests of his own followers against rival chiefs and their followers. Moreover, even within this relationship between chief and follower the notion of disinterested service is weakly developed: loyalty, except for the innermost circle of followers, is bought by the protection which the chief gives and by the largesse which he hands out to his own followers. If the chief cannot provide these things, then the follower is not expected to go through an agony of heart searching but to use his head and find a stronger and richer chief. There is an element here of the amorality found in the 'outsider' relationship. Notice also that although the chief is expected to provide a service for others, the notion of this service is the very antithesis of what we mean by '*public* service': as their equivalent in our civilization might say, 'chiefs are not in business just for their health'. Notice also that the idea of service from a posture of humility is entirely absent.

Some of these chiefs, when they become old men, turn into 'philanthropoids'. They build temples, or rest-houses for pilgrims, or plant trees to give shade, or excavate bathing pools where the devout may take purifying baths. Peasants certainly mark with approval wells and bathing ghats and shade trees: but the act of giving is considered cynically as a kind of conscience money. A man in a village close to where I lived had cheated and bullied his way to great eminence, but in middle age was still without a son. He then invested in a number of spectacular public works and in a new young wife: in due time she presented him with a son. This son lived to manhood, but, as the man who told me noted with satisfaction, the old man outlived him and there were no grandchildren.

Villagers look more kindly on a man of religious eminence than upon a chief. But, like the chief, the saint too is looking after himself and his own soul, as we would say: his life is not spent in the service of others. Even if he is a *guru* (a teacher), he is a consultant helping individuals with their particular difficulties, rather than a man active in the public service. The saint is respected – even loved in a special numinous sense of that word – not for what he does for the community, but simply for what he is – a holy man.

Some traditional ideas about secular leadership are relevant to political modernization and economic development. Notice that the appropriate relationship between a leader and a follower is not inconsistent with the attitude which one has towards an outsider. Leader–follower relationships within a moral community have a degree of hardness and calculation of self-interest: when the relationship crosses the boundary of the moral community, wariness hardens into suspicion and double-dealing. Within the moral community the peasant understands the range of possible action; within limits, he knows what his opponent will do, because he and his opponent (whether leader or follower) share certain basic values; furthermore the relationship is seen to be regulated by councils or panchayats or superior leaders. But outside the moral community none of these controls apply: official action is unpredictable; values are not shared; and adjudicative institutions like courts of law, are not part of the peasant moral community but are regarded as instruments or weapons to be used in the contest. Within the moral community, one looks carefully to see if the leader is fulfilling his side of the bargain: outside the moral community, one knows that a bargain will not be fulfilled, and one must therefore insure oneself by anticipatory cheating.

Secondly, the language of co-operation is almost completely absent from the traditional leader–follower relationship. The language of co-operation is, of course, found in the village but it is a language used between equals and within the moral community. It is found in the formalized equality symbolized in the procedures of the village council or in the ceremonial meeting of the senior kin of a bride and groom; it is also found, with less formality, in co-operative work parties or in hunting when the men, after a rest, urge one another to resume the chase with those strange staccato cries of mutual encouragement that one hears coming out of a pack of rugby forwards. Everyone gives the orders to no one in particular. But leaders do not appeal to their followers to pull together as a matter of moral obligation: rather they offer them inducements (rewards or punishments) to do so.

Traditional leaders do not ask for co-operation. Outsiders *cannot* effectively ask for co-operation from the peasants. But they do so continually, and to the villagers this seems either a joke or something to be very worried about, as a football player would be if he heard himself being urged on and urged to co-operate by the captain of the opposing team.

The peasant looks upon outsiders (including officials) as his enemies. But there are also, within his conceptual world, a number of persons whom we might see as peacemaking or mediating. How does the peasant see these persons? The men could be traitors; they could be enemy agents; or they could be accepted and given moral status as true mediators, thus widening the boundaries of the peasant moral community.

At first sight some chiefly roles – in India rajas or non-absentee zemindars – could span the gap between officials and the peasant world. These statuses combine in the one person general administrator, tax collector, justice of the peace, welfare officer and money-lender, custodian of sacred symbols and organizer of collective rituals at harvest or sowing time or on other religious occasions.[6] All these people have now been legally – but not always effectively – dethroned in India. They were to some extent a part of the moral community of their peasants. We anthropologists have made much of a relationship of this kind: emphasizing that the king, as the custodian of sacred objects and the performer of sacred rituals, symbolized the unity of his people and their values. I am sure we were right to do so, and not a few difficulties in enforced modernization arise from ignoring non-political components of traditional leadership roles and neglecting to make provision in modern institutions for these components.

But, for several reasons, it is hard to see rajas or landlords as mediators in the modernizing situation. Firstly, they were not allowed to do so because the cognitive map of the modernizing elite marked them as enemies identifying them correctly as an important part of the political system created by the British authoritarian administration. Secondly, since they are the very apogee of the chiefly role, their status as members of the peasant moral community was somewhat precarious. One Orissa ex-raja, who had been elected – almost unanimously – to the Legislative Assembly, told me that he did not bother to campaign and that if he had chosen to nominate his elephant his people would have returned it to the Assembly. But, in the next election, he was defeated. His State had been abolished for ten years and the many roles that he had combined in his person were either not being performed or were being done by a scatter of administrators. I think he underestimated the transactional nature of his tie with his former subjects. The love, of which he boasted, turned out to be cupboard love (the contents of the cupboard being, of course, culturally defined). Thirdly – and the fate of the raja will serve to illustrate this too – once such men begin to behave like outsiders, then inevitably they take on the role of outsiders and lose their place in the moral community of the peasants. A few exceptional

6. Dr B. D. Graham has suggested to me that the political 'bosses' of State Congress parties and their subordinates succeed partly because they play the same kind of multiplex role as did landowners and rajas. In Orissa party politicians used to complain about the diversity of demands made by their own constituents ('He wanted me to find a bride for his son') and mock their rivals by saying they held *durbars* for their constituents. Peasants find it hard to accept the idea of functional specialization in authority roles.

men – there were two striking examples in Orissa – built up a transactional following in the modern role of politician: no doubt they were helped by their royal status to make a start, but this status alone would not carry them for very long. Incidentally, the modernizing elite was very reluctant to admit that these two men were in fact playing modern roles.

The second kind of potential mediator is the man who has recently made the jump into the elite, and who still has close kinsmen who have remained peasants. In most parts of tropical Africa the indigenous elite are new boys: so too, in India, are many politicians at the State and even at the national level; but this is less true of the civil services. This happens because the children of the elite acquire education and the children of the poor do not. This has been the case for many generations in India. I suppose it will also become true of Africa, and one already hears reports from West Africa that the elite is hardening into a class (see Lloyd, 1966, intro.).

How do peasants regard a kinsman who has become part of the elite? He is still part of their moral community and is expected to take the responsibilities and obligations of a kinsman. That these obligations may conflict with his modern roles is not countenanced. Such a man must take care what role-signs he displays: when he goes on leave, he discards the bush shirt and trousers for a *dhoti* before he enters his village. Indeed those actions which the modern world stigmatizes as nepotism and corruption, are in fact often the fulfilling of a man's obligations in the traditional world. The conclusion must be – and it is something of a paradox – that the newly joined member of the elite can act neither as a mediator between the two worlds nor as a modernizing agent among his own people: he can in fact only retain the tie with his own people so long as he acts in accordance with their values.

The third category of brokers are those who use religious symbols which are valued by the peasants, in order to seek membership of the peasant moral community: or (which perhaps more accurately describes the motives of the most famous of them), in order to disclaim membership of the modernizing elite. How do the villagers look upon such men and women?

The saintly figure is part of their known world. He stands for something – however vague – which they value: one might call it personal salvation. They do not bargain with or try to exploit a saint. For most people the relationship is distant and impersonal, one of respect and reverence symbolized by giving alms and receiving what we call blessing. Those who form a closer relationship as pupils or disciples choose to do so for ideological or moral reasons: the saint does not drum up a following in the way that a chief does.

But the politician who presents himself in the saintly style, clad in a *dhoti* and sandals and arriving on his feet, does not always behave in the manner which the villagers associate with his appearance. The visitor does not sit silently under the tree or give his advice only to those who ask for it; he makes speeches. Moreover, what he advocates must seem to the villagers very surprising, like sacred music sung to rock-and-roll. He talks about hygiene, or basic education, or why the poor should be given land – all topics which suggest to the villagers *Sircar*, the Government. Vinoba Bhave's men came to the village where I lived and were rejected as completely as if they had been Government agents – indeed, more completely, for it was known that they had no force to back up their requests. We talk easily of charismatic leaders since Weber gave us the word, but I think we are often taken in by the propaganda of those who have ambitions to be charismatic leaders.

The remaining mediating role has probably been the most effective in spanning the gap between peasants and elite. This is the village broker: the man who makes a profession of helping officials or politicians and peasants to communicate with one another, and is paid either directly or indirectly for doing so. He knows how to get licences and remission of tax, he knows where to place bribes, he can get real medicine from the hospital dispensary: for the other side he recruits voters or agents or people to make a good showing when some superior visitor is coming down; he can do privately and discreetly all those jobs which the rulers of modern institutions forbid, but which modern people find must be done (see Bailey, 1963, pp. 55–67).

Although his stock in trade is the favours he has done for

people, such a man is not honoured or even trusted by the villagers. He is a renegade, a half-outsider, albeit necessary to temper the cold winds of bureaucracy. But no such man could possibly achieve moral status as a mediator between traditionalists and modernizers. Both sides place him in the category of outsider. In fact he does positive harm: for his makeshift activities perpetuate the gap in communication between peasants and elite.

From the point of view of those who wish to modernize, the picture which I draw is not encouraging. There are a few exceptional people who can become, so to speak, honorary members of the peasants' moral community and yet urge peasants to take on new and modern roles. But they can do this only to a very limited extent, for the peasants have a very low threshold of tolerance for those of their own members who connect too closely with the outside world.

The root of my argument is that building a modern society is not a routine process in which all the steps are known and all contingencies anticipated. On the contrary: it is a world of mistakes, frustrations, disappointments, anxiety and conflict. On the quite rare occasions when peasants enter this world voluntarily, they do so because they think they are going to get something out of it: they are out to exploit. If their expectations are disappointed, they withdraw, as they would withdraw their allegiance from an unsuccessful leader. Only people who have a moral commitment to a modern society will persist in the face of disappointment and failure. I have been discussing a number of roles which, at first sight, might seem to provide this moral commitment by holding the trust of the peasants. But in virtually all cases this trust is withdrawn if the broker is seen to be a missionary for modernization.[7]

7. There is an extensive literature on 'hinge men': those who mediate between different cultures or between different levels in the same culture. A good example is Wolf (1956). The range of such roles extends from simple transactions (for example, the petition-writer at an Indian administrative headquarters) to highly developed patron roles which come near to attaining moral status, see Boissevain (1961). The roles considered in this essay are not those of '*cultural* brokers' in the sense of providing a communication of ideas and a meeting of minds: on the contrary the village broker at least is a device which enables the peasants and the elite to avoid a meeting of

I have talked about the peasants' categories of outsiders, leaders and brokers: that is, about persons. Now, at a more abstract level I shall ask what peasants think, not about politicians, but about policies. Much has been written about what particular peasants or tribesmen think about particular policies; but not so much about the idea of policy-making.

In this idea, there are two main components, neither of which forms part of peasant culture. The first is that man has a good chance of controlling his own destiny and his environment: no one would continue to formulate policies if he thought that he could never implement them. Indeed the essence of policy making is that it is a plan for manipulating variables which we know we can control, in order to adapt ourselves to those variables which we know we cannot control: and so, in a paradoxical way, to achieve some kind of control over the uncontrollable.

One of the components of our romantic view of rural life is its certainty and dependability. The four seasons follow one another: year after year life renews itself in the same way. This cycle of eternity, recorded and edited and abridged for us in poetry or at the cinema, gives us a sense of security. We do not doubt, when we go to sleep, but that the same world will be there when we wake up in the morning.

I do not know whether the peasants with whom I lived have this mystical sense of life's continuance: I doubt it, since, unlike us, they know rural life in the raw, unexpurgated, unabridged and uncleaned for dramatic presentation. Certainly, whatever the stability of nature's grand design, they see little security in their own life. No one can be sure whether the harvest will be good or bad: no one can be sure who will be alive this time next year, or even next week. In two or three years a rich man can become poor or a poor man rich. Women die in childbirth: there were women in Bisipara (a village where I lived) who had had five or eight or, in one case, ten children and raised not one beyond its second year. In circumstances like this, no one can feel that man is the master of his environment: nature may have a grand continuing design, but a man's life is filled with discontinuities. No peasant thinks in

minds. By providing pragmatic contracts they render unnecessary normative communion.

terms of five-year plans, and I would argue that the idea of planning can exist only in those cognitive maps which include the idea of man in control of predictable and controllable *impersonal* forces.

Even in our cognitive maps, persons seem less predictable and controllable than things. Sometimes we attribute our failures to other people's malevolent actions; we do this particularly when the undertaking is difficult and a gamble – if the five-year plan fails, that is because of the wicked internal opposition, the stupid peasants and the intrigues of the neo-colonialists: witch-hunting is found in everyone's culture. But we also stress and widely employ the idea that failures can be the result of our miscalculation of variables which are purely impersonal, which have no will of their own, and which cannot be held to be morally responsible. In such cases the idea of punishment or revenge or deterrence makes nonsense: it is the mistake that must be corrected, not the person. To the extent that a cognitive map does not include the idea of impersonal non-moral forces, it also cannot include the idea of planning. To a much greater extent than we do, peasants blame failure upon the malevolence of human agents.[8] It is true that in India and in some other cultures, fate is used as an explanation: but fate, although predictable, cannot be controlled. Success, too – spectacular success – is attributed to human wickedness. The man who, as we say, makes a killing, is not reaping the rewards of hard work and correct calculation, but made his way through sorcery or magic or at least in some way which was harmful to his fellows. Judging from the stories I was told of how men in Bisipara first became wealthy the peasant mythology contains no category of honest riches. Notice the significance of this for innovation and modernization: any peasant who adopts new ways and becomes rich, must have cheated, must have exploited his fellows, and to that extent should be punished or put outside the moral community.

In brief, both the uncertainty of peasant life and the fact that they explain failure by blaming people rather than by supporting a miscalculation or impersonal forces means that policy making

8. The best-known exposition of this outlook on life is in Evans-Pritchard (1937).

and planning are not part of their cognitive map of the world and human society. They do not reject the idea of planning as wicked: they simply do not have the category.

At first sight such a statement seems wrong, for no peasant could survive unless he planned the use of his resources. They breed cattle; they save for marriages; nowadays they make wills; they plan with Machiavellian subtlety ways of doing one another down; and, to name the simplest and most fundamental act of planning, they keep seed for next year's sowing. But, I would argue, such activities are not to be considered planning in the way in which that word is used in, for example, the phrase 'five-year plan'. This brings me to the second component in the idea of policy-making.

The second component in policy-making is innovation. The policy-maker sees a future which is different from the present not just because it is separated from the present by a week or a year, but because life then will be of a different kind from what it is now. Let us separate these two kinds of thought about the future by calling the first 'the round of time' and the second 'time's arrow' (Bourdieu, 1963).

The peasant plans for the round of time. He allocates resources as if he held the assumptions that with minor variations and barring accidents next year will be this year over again. Each resource is seen against a round of time: so many years before the ox must be replaced; so many years before the son replaces the father; thatching every third or second year. In this world, too, people are not so ready to look for the witch behind every failure. A man whose crop is poor when all around have good crops cannot blame witches if he is known to be a slovenly cultivator: it is recognized that with luck (i.e. the absence of human malevolence and adverse fate) good crops are the result of hard work and skilled cultivation. But, as is perhaps true also in our society, few people think hard work and skill a means of changing a poor man into a rich man in twenty years' time: if changes like that happen, they come overnight by mystical means, by magic or fate or luck; by finding a crock of gold; in our culture by devious and anti-social property deals or by winning on the football pools.

Those who make five-year plans are thinking of time as an

arrow. The work has a beginning and an end: there is a target to be reached. The end is a state of affairs quite different from the beginning, and itself is a starting point for further ventures. We have no difficulties with this notion. To plan a future state of affairs which is radically different from the present is to us quite rational. But those who think in terms of the round of time see such changes as coming from mystical forces like fate, or luck, or witchcraft or acts of God, and to plan for such events makes nonsense. The politician who promises a good life in store for everyone, if they help to implement the plan, is heard by the peasants as we would hear a man promising everyone a first dividend on the pools every week.[9]

These are cultural categories and, as with statistical norms, they allow that individuals can be found holding different ideas. Some peasants have learned to see time as an arrow: and most peasants, at least in countries like India, are from time to time compelled to behave as if they saw time that way. But when there is a failure, where accidents occur and the arrow misses the target, then they look for explanations and they take initiatives in the idiom of the round of time – in terms of human wickedness rather than of scientific error. Even those who make the plans, in whom the idea of time as an arrow is internalized, may react to failure by looking for the scapegoat rather than the cause.

This concludes my examination of a few basic cultural themes in the cognitive map of the Indian peasant. These themes hang together: the relationship with a leader is instrumental and exploitative: still more so is that with an outsider. Spectacular success is evil because your success means my failure: my failure is caused by your malevolence. Outsiders talk about spectacular change and spectacular success, but we peasants can only be instruments in their schemes: in any case, if their fantasies were realized, this could only be by anti-social means.

How shall I conclude this discourse, which for a modernizer is certainly a jeremiad? I would insist that to look upon the bright side and simply deny what I have said, is to pretend that the

9. For peasants social life is a zero-sum game. One man's gain is, of necessity, another's loss. See Foster (1965).

enemy's bullets will turn to water and his tanks are made of cardboard.

Furthermore, it makes little sense to ask why people hold these values, in the hope that, discovering the causes, we can bring about change. At this level values and categories of thought are ultimate and given; they have no causes and they cannot be further reduced. Indeed it is as pointless as to ask *why* peasants think in the round of time, as it is to ask why the Oriya numeral for unity is 'eko' while we say 'one'. We can explain values by relating them to one another, as one analyses the structure of a painting or a poem: but we cannot ask what is the cause of a set of values.

What we can do, however, is to show how a particular set of ideas, such as those I have been discussing, and the experience of the people validate one another. The connexion is a functional one and the line of causation between ideas and experience points in both directions. Belief and action are connected with one another. My argument is that fundamental categories of thought (like those of time) and fundamental values (like those attached to leadership and authority) are impervious to direct ideological attack – at least in the short run and given the resources at the disposal of modernizing elites in most of the new nations. The sensible tactic, therefore, is to change the 'action' element (which is another word for 'experience'), in those sectors of action that are least connected with ideological convictions.[10]

The operational prospects are not in fact so bad. I have been talking about collective representations – about thought: and thought is not the same as action. People can be pressured by carrots or sticks into doing things, which they consider are evil or foolish; and a long enough experience may convince them that in

10. Peasants are generally distinguished from tribesmen by their contact with towns, markets and high cultures. Routine experiences in traditional towns are unlikely to modify the broad features of the map of peasant cognition sketched here, since these experiences are part of this same map. But the traumatic experience of migrant labour and factory work in 'modern' towns is likely to bring change in peasant values and beliefs: so also is production largely for a market, which turns the peasant into a farmer. I cannot here discuss urban contacts, except to say that my argument applies to peasants and not to farmers or to industrial workers.

fact these things are neither evil nor foolish. Vaccination and DDT spraying and some agricultural innovations (especially some cash crops) have this kind of success. But parliamentary democracy or other kinds of political modernization and many economic innovations and social reforms do not and could not show such immediate and tangible returns; they may in fact seem to produce immediate and tangible disasters. The conclusion must be that, given peasant resistance, a radical policy of political and economic modernization can only be achieved by pressure and by continued success in material terms.

Short of this – but consistently – those resources which are available for modernization are wasted if they are used directly for propaganda about duty, service, self-sacrifice and so forth. Modernization is an end too vague and too complex to be readily symbolized and understood: even 'swaraj' (independence) was a non-message so far as Indian peasants were concerned: they listened when Congress began to exploit agrarian discontents. 'Democratic decentralization' is a non-message: remission of rent or the removal of a greedy landlord will be understood and accepted (with due suspicion). Any plan for modernization which is based on the assumption that peasants will feel an immediate moral commitment to modernity as such and will persist voluntarily in the face of failure and frustrations because they are so committed, must be ineffective.

Let me repeat that my discourse is about collective representations – about the way peasants think. This is but one – indeed, the last – of the variables with which the modernizer must operate. If his plans fail, clearly his first question should be about physical and technical matters. Leaving aside human wishes, is it possible for anyone to carry out that particular plan? Perhaps there is something special about the soil of the demonstration farm, absent from most peasant farms? Perhaps the price of fertilizer is too high, so that even if the peasants want it, they cannot buy it? There are many factors of this kind, and their control is usually far easier than attempts to influence and control peasant values and categories of thought.

Secondly, there is a set of variables which belong to peasant social structure rather than to peasant values. The line between social structure and values is a difficult one to draw, but I have in mind a great variety of particular role constraints which affect the peasant's life. For a simple example, given a certain level of poverty, the contribution which children make to transplanting paddy can be crucial: where I lived in India the village schools were closed at planting time and this seemed to me a sensible recognition of the productive role of children in the peasant family. Again – an all too familiar example in many Indian villages – to give the vote to untouchables in elections for village panchayats, without the additional protections of a secret ballot, is to invite failure. In other words, innovations may have social costs, which are unknown to or have been ignored by the modernizer.

Both the technical and the structural factors can only be discussed against the background of particular cases. What prospect there is of successful modernization in India and other developing nations, rests upon the willingness of the planning elite to improve continuously their manipulation of technical and structural variables – to make sure that the price of water from the canal is reasonable and is seen by the peasants to be reasonable, that improved seed developed on the demonstration farm will in fact grow on peasant plots, and to remember that the headman will come under great pressure from his kinsmen, and so forth. I suspect that there is a temptation to evade the drudgery of seeking technical – and I suppose we might say 'structural' – efficacy by saying that the peasants need a change of heart and rushing out to make a speech. If all the technical and structural variables have been correctly handled and the project still fails, one might argue that there is no recourse but to bring about a voluntary change of heart in the peasants. To argue this is to argue that the task is impossible.

From this there emerges one broad strategic directive. Resources for modernization, if they are limited, are most effectively spent if they bring about a change in the physical environment, which the peasant must accept willy-nilly and which force him to adapt himself to the new conditions. When change has come about, at least in village India, it is generally because new methods of irrigation have been introduced, or a road has been built to the market, and so forth. Such measures, of course, do not always succeed; but I suspect that they succeed more often than does a direct onset upon peasant social structure, and still more often than an attack upon those generalized and internalized values and perceptions about which I have been talking here.

Cognitive maps do change: but for the most part they do so slowly as the result of experience. As the flow of water can change the course of a river, so experience can erode received ideas and allow others to settle in their place. With this most modernizers must be content. Occasionally force of circumstances or a massive expenditure of resources can produce a flood of new experiences that change the map overnight: but this is rare. For the most part modernizers must think small: and the least effective use of their resources is to plan directly that the peasants shall have a change of heart. The cultural themes which I have been discussing here are like swamps and rocky mountains: the modernizers should plan to make a detour.

Beyond that, one can make few recommendations. The gnarled oak of peasant alienation (as the modernizers would see it) is only one tree in the forest. It is a tree which takes many different forms, even in India, even within the one village from which I have drawn my material. One needs a much wider sample. One should also look at some of the other trees, at the many divisions within the elite. What view do they have of themselves, of each other, and of the peasants? Armed with all these maps and with a systematic knowledge of technical factors and of social structure, one might begin to understand some of the diverse changes which have occurred – or failed to occur – in the new nations.

References

BAILEY, F. G. (1959), *Caste and Economic Frontier: Village in Highland Orissa*, Manchester University Press.
BAILEY, F. G. (1960), *Tribe, Caste and Nation*, Manchester University Press.
BAILEY, F. G. (1963), *Politics and Social Change*, Oxford University Press.
BOISSEVAIN, J. (1961), 'Patronage in Sicily', *Man*, n.s., vol. 1, pp. 18–33.

BOURDIEU, P. (1963), 'The attitude of the Algerian peasant towards time', in J. Pitt-Rivers (ed.), *Mediterranean Countrymen*, Mouton.

EVANS-PRITCHARD, E. E. (1937), *Witchcraft, Oracles and Magic among the Azande*, Clarendon Press.

FOSTER, G. (1965), 'Peasant society and the image of limited good', *Amer. Anthrop.*, vol. 67, no. 2, pp. 293–315.

LLOYD, P. C. (ed.) (1966), *The New Elite of Tropical Africa*, Oxford University Press.

WOLF, E. R. (1956), 'Aspects of group relations in a complex society', *Amer. Anthrop.*, vol. 58, no. 6, pp. 1065–78.

23 Sutti Ortiz

Reflections on the Concept of 'Peasant Culture' and
'Peasant Cognitive Systems'

An original paper.

The word peasant is full of emotive associations. Yet there is no
other word that will describe the rural dwellers who, lacking a
strong tribal identity, remain marginal to the world of the cities
and yet dependent upon them. It is worth considering, however,
whether we should use the word peasant as a meaningful analytical concept. Who are they? Can we define the word instead of
simply describing the people whom we call peasants? We must
answer this question before considering whether or not peasants
share a culture and social organization which is distinct from the
culture of commercial farmers, shopkeepers, urban dwellers,
etc.

According to Eric Wolf (1966), peasants are farmers who grow
crops and raise livestock in rural areas, but who unlike commercial American farmers are more concerned with satisfying the
needs of the household than with obtaining a profit. Peasants do
produce for exchange; surpluses are transferred to a dominant
group of rulers who use them in part to underwrite their own standard of living and in part to distribute food to urban dwellers
and specialists. Among primitives, exchanges are instead equivalent and direct.

Raymond Firth defines peasants using essentially economic
criteria. By peasant he means: 'A system of small producers, with
a simple technology and equipment, often relying primarily for
their subsistence on what they themselves produce' (1951a,
p. 84). While the primary means of livelihood of peasants is
usually seen as the cultivation of the soil, Firth also makes a case
for the inclusion of other rural folks, for example fishermen
(1951b).

Daniel Thorner (1963) prefers to talk about peasant economies rather than peasants. In his view a peasant economy is an agricultural economy where producers are able to feed not only themselves but also contribute towards the subsistence of specialists and urban dwellers; peasants thus produce for exchange. This characteristic distinguishes peasants from primitive producers. The family is the main unit of production; in some cases, however, the household may not just consist of members of a family but of hired hands, slaves and domestic servants. Peasants may also engage in other activities like handicraft or occasional wage labour.

Redfield adds another condition for the use of the term peasant: 'that the system of values ... be consistent, in the main, with those of the city people who constitute, so to speak, its other dimension of existence' (1953, p. 40). This definition is in accord with Kroeber's use of the term peasant to indicate part-societies with part-cultures (1948, p. 284) and with Marriott (1955) who describes peasant culture as a 're-interpretation' and 're-integration' of the elements of the higher culture. In this view, social, political and cultural criteria are necessary to define peasants.

Foster (1967a) argues that if the conclusions to be drawn from his study of Tzintzuntzan are to have any general validity it is essential to place the community in the context of a societal type. He suggests that people of Tzintzuntzan belong to that category of people we call peasants. According to Foster, peasants are communities which, historically speaking, 'have grown up in a symbiotic, spatial-temporal relationship with the more complex components of their greater society, i.e. the pre-industrial market and administrative city' (1967a, p. 7). As cities become modern manufacturing centres the dependent peasant clusters begin to disappear, but slowly, since their potential for change is low. It is irrelevant to Foster whether the producer is a fisherman, craftsman or a farmer. It is not the internal economic organization but the external economic dependency that matters to him. This subordinate relationship produces political, cultural and often religious dependence as well.

Can we use the term peasant to describe most of the small

producers in Latin America? Are the same societies encompassed by the term as used by Firth, or Wolf, or Redfield or Foster?

As Firth defines it we would include under the term peasant a vast population of small producers, all of whom have limited capital assets and restricted access to cash. Indians, *mestizos*, small farmers of European descent, freehold farmers, sharecroppers in feudal *haciendas*, sharecroppers in efficiently run commercial *estancias*, etc. All of these individuals share some of the same economic problems, but are different from each other with respect to type of subjugation to the political and economic elite, and bargaining position in economic transactions.

Wolf's use of the term peasant implies a political relation where one party holds greater power over the other. This imbalance is not a consequence of the wealth of assets held by each party, but a consequence of the rights and obligations assigned to each. Small farmers of European descent and some freehold farmers are not included in his definition.

Daniel Thorner is not so much interested in the behaviour of individuals we may call peasants as in the performance of economies which he defines as peasant. Only when at least half or more of the national product comes from small peasant farms can the economy be called a peasant economy. Most Latin-American societies are no longer peasant in character according to this definition.

By introducing cultural criteria of very general nature Redfield restricts further the use of the term peasant. The difficulty is that it is not often easy to decide who should be classed as a peasant and who should not. As an example let us take two neighbouring communities in the Department of Cauca, Colombia. In the locality of San Andrés there is a Páez Indian reservation. These Indians have joint rights to land, elect their own authorities, speak their own language and consider themselves quite different from the rest of the Colombian population. Páez farmers grow their own food, plant coffee for sale and purchase their own tools, clothing and other items with the money they earn from coffee growing or working as peons. Neighbouring the reservation live a number of Colombian families who migrated into the area about 1930. Most of them own less land than some of the Indian families, but they also plant their own food crops whenever possible, using the same techniques as the Indians. Shortage of land and personal relation with townspeople have encouraged these newcomers to become part-time traders and storekeepers. Some are quite poor, others are wealthier than most Indians. The difference is that they spend greater amounts of time in cash earning activities and that they have to purchase a larger amount of food to feed their families. With reference to economic activities, the Páez are more clearly peasant than their Colombian neighbours. However, the value system of the Indian community is less consistent with the values of Colombian cities. They are Catholics but only nominally so. Ritual situations are used to differentiate themselves from the neighbouring Colombian community. There are in fact a number of features, like dress, housing, forms of expression which serve as signs which people look for and exhibit in order to show their identity with one or the other group. In this sense, the Páez, eager to maintain their distinctiveness from local Colombian immigrants, look away from urban centres and have reinterpreted little from national culture. Thus, culturally speaking, the Colombian farmers here described are more peasant than the Páez. More important still is to note that the cultural orientation of each group is a consequence of the economic competition between them, a point I discuss later.

Most small farmers in Latin America can be described as peasants according to Foster's definition as they are in a subordinate economic position to urban clusters. Yet many of the other attributes he describes for Tzintzuntzanos do not apply to other communities, a fact he clearly acknowledges (Foster, 1967a, p. 298).

While we cannot then hope to encompass all peasants in any definition, we can and must at least rid the term peasant of any vagueness and ambiguity. Serious blunders in analytical thinking occur because the meaning of the term is changed imperceptibly in the course of use; there is less chance of this happening if writers clearly define what they mean by the term peasant.

Clarification of the term must relate to the intent of the analyst.

In some cases the intent may be to cluster similar societies or relationships in order to gain some insight on the subject, as Firth has attempted. In other cases the intent of the definition is to expose the principal features or structure in order to allow for a *systematic* exploration of the subject (see Wolf, 1966). If a definition of peasant could focus on the fundamental features of this sector then one may be able to deduce other features. In the last instance the knowledge derived from the defined universe can only be true in reference to it; this same knowledge or hypothesis cannot necessarily be extended to other populations which share some but not all of the characteristics.

The confusion over definitions as well as their vagueness stands at the core of my objection to the generalizations about peasant social organization and peasant culture. In the first place not all authors use the term in the same way and all exclude some sectors of the population. Secondly, unless cultural criteria are used to define who is and who is not a peasant, social units with disparate 'world views' may be grouped together. The cultural differences between Páez and neighbouring Colombian peasants illustrate this point (see Foster, 1967a and b, for other contrasting examples).

Thirdly, the factors which shape behaviour and ideologies are so numerous that it is unthinkable to imagine that individuals who are grouped together because some of them share *certain* economic arrangements and perhaps face a *particular kind* of political domination, will hold the same cultural values, cognitive systems, and very similar social organization. At most one can foresee probable social consequences of particular structural arrangements. For example, modes of production may indeed affect authority within the family; wage labour opportunities and land shortage has undermined the traditional authority of the Páez father. Yet paternal authority does also depend on the existence of lineages, the political importance of lineages (as illustrated by the Mapuche peasants of Southern Chile; see Faron, 1961), the relative political independence of peasant communities from more important centres, etc. Thus paternal authority may not be seriously undermined by economic events if political institutions uphold the father's authority. As a general argument it can be said that while it is possible to deduce probable social arrangements from the criteria used to define peasants, other factors of equal relevance may cancel out the predicted social effect. The caution does not deny the validity of the deductive approach. Unwarranted, however, are the generalizations about peasant attitudes and cultures which cannot be deduced logically from the defining characteristics.

There are further objections to the proposition that peasants both share a culture and that this culture is distinctive from the culture of other social types. Kaplan and Sadler (1966) object to the empirical validity of the peasant culture construct; they suspect that it is derived *a priori* and that non-congruent behaviour is excluded.

A more serious contention is that usually *a priori* models emerge from a set of values which stand out in the mind of students of the topic as being distinctly peasant because they are opposed to our stereotyped image of Western economic man. Peasants are often described as irrational, lacking in motivation, unable to delay gratification, in pursuit primarily of social goals, and pessimistic about opportunities available to them. Although economic theory is based on the assumption that Western businessmen and Western farmers act eminently rationally when planning their economic activities, economists are well aware that reality is quite different. There is a considerable body of literature on economic behaviour which illustrates how moral values, social goals, institutional settings, tastes and temperament affect behaviour and define what satisfies the producer (see Edwards, 1967; Katona, 1963; Simon, 1959). In fact producers are well known for maximizing satisfaction instead of profit.

Some attitudes which are described as characteristic of peasants, as for example withdrawal and unwillingness to make use of opportunities (see Hagen, 1962; Redfield, 1953), may be a coalition response to existing local conditions which are not shared by all individuals whom the author defines as peasants. The Páez Indians mentioned earlier have been described as traditional in their orientation and unwilling to exploit the opportunity to sell food to the highest bidder. When questioned they explain that frequent sales are considered as *morally improper* behaviour. Those residents who need some plantains or cassava to feed their families have to visit the Indians and literally beg them to sell them some. Páez prefer to save their harvest and either consume it themselves or lend it or sell it at a much lower price to an Indian kinsmen or friend. The uncertainty of their income and harvest accounts for their attitude with regard to food crops: they are to be used to feed those with whom one shares strong reciprocal obligations. The social tension and economic competition between Indian peasant and non-Indian peasant in this region of Colombia precludes strong social ties of co-operation between them. The moral rule condemning the sale of food is not a traditional value but an appropriate solution to existing economic conditions. At the same time Páez sell their coffee harvest or their services to the highest bidder, calculating of course at the same time the cost in time and transport of the sale or other economic benefits that he may derive from the transaction (Ortiz, 1967).

In the department of Chiapas in Southern Mexico, Oxchuc Indians who invest in new equipment or explore new techniques to increase yield, or show in any other way their ambition to become wealthy, are distrusted by their community members and often accused of practising witchcraft (Siverts, 1969). Foster (1967a, p. 140) interprets these accusations as a sanction by the community against those who attempt to gain wealth at the expense of others; peasants, he explains, view the world as a fixed set of opportunities which ought to be equally distributed amongst all: if an Indian becomes rich it must be because he is taking a larger share than is his due. It may well be that people of Oxchuc, like the people of Tzintzuntzan hold this perception of the world and that witchcraft accusation is a sanction used to enforce conformity to an ideology of equality. It is however not clear from Tzintzuntzan and certainly not from Oxchuc that equality is the overriding cultural value. In the first place individuals are ranked within the community according to prestige, and traditionally those who had assumed greater numbers of religious obligations and who shouldered the cost of celebrating a larger number of *fiestas* were given greater political power. In the second place we have learned from studies of witchcraft and sorcery in Africa, that accusations are not just branded against those who transgress moral rules but also against personal enemies, competitors and individuals with whom relations are difficult and tense. In any Indian community where land is corporately owned according to laws which originated in colonial time and where population pressures make it impossible to find a just and equitable distribution, relations amongst neighbours are bound to be competitive and tense. Heads of families can ask the community for land to cultivate according to need and ability; hence the adoption of more efficient methods which may allow for expansion of holdings can be interpreted as a threat by the less efficient farmer. The accusation of witchcraft is not a community decision but an individual act. Although the accusation of witchcraft implies that beliefs of witches exist, the act of accusing and the frequency of accusations rests probably on shortage of resources and tense competitions amongst neighbours. But why does the accused oblige and refrain from innovating? The answer for Oxchuc is neatly summarized by Siverts (1969). For an Indian of this region to disown his origin, to disregard the opinion of his neighbours is an expensive proposition. As long as he remains a member in good standing he can be assured some land, some co-operation in labour exchanges and a basic though minimal life insurance. The opportunities open to him given his limited wealth, knowledge of Spanish, occupation and Indian characteristics are minimal. If he wants to buy land he has to compete with a better capitalized Mexican farmer; if he wants to work for wages in order to accumulate cash he will be offered small jobs or coffee-picking labour at lower wages; when he sells his harvest his dress and language will make him easy prey to dishonourable transactions; he has no influence on local authorities and his plight has no official representation; he cannot convert his assets to other enterprises as the land belongs to the community. His only alternative is to migrate to the city and join the ranks of the very poor where uncertainty is greater than in Oxchuc. Thus most Indians prefer to maintain existing bonds and to resolve tense relations with neighbours which may threaten their sense of security. Thus if one Indian accuses another it is not necessarily because he is trying to protect the values of the community and enforce adherence to an ideology of equality, but because he is trying to cope with a difficult relation ridden with competition and conflict. The accusation converts him from a personal enemy to a social enemy; the accused must deal with it because he needs the co-operation of the community. It is also important to note that not all individuals who excel themselves are accused of being witches. Siverts (1969) tells us that an Indian from Chiapas became a very wealthy trader who maintained the respect of his community because by not cheating in commercial transactions he performed a useful function.

Peasants are described as traditionally oriented and slow to change their patterns of behaviour. The Páez and Oxchuc examples illustrate that this behaviour may not be the result of tradition but a withdrawal or coalition in response to unrewarding competitive relations. The patterns of behaviour, language, etc. are used as symbols of distance. The degree to which Indians, peasants or minority groups make use of such a device depends on their evaluation of their success in the competitive game. This success in turn depends on opportunities available to the Indians, to the non-Indians, the political power of each group, knowledge and ability to manipulate circumstances. Not all communities face the same situations and hence not all are 'traditionally oriented'.

Peasants are described as individuals resigned to their fate (Banfield, 1958) and passive when faced with prospects. A good harvest is said to be the result of supernatural intervention and misfortunes are blamed on fate. Such an attitude of mind, according to some writers, discourages efforts of self-help, a point I discuss later. First let us examine why peasants are ready to explain events as the result of fate. Oscar Lewis (1960, p. 77) feels that fatalism is due to upbringing in an authoritarian family structure. A more direct explanation is possible if we examine the degree of uncertainty which pervades the agricultural activities of peasants. Crops suffer from drastic climatic changes, attacks by pests, rodents, damage by animals, etc. Variability of yields to an individual farmer may be 400 per cent. A farmer can formulate an expectation about his harvest only if he can have a mental picture of the outcome and if he has any confidence about the likelihood of his prognosis. With such a high degree of uncertainty few individuals could formulate an expectation; it should not surprise us that as uncertainty decreases farmers are less likely to express prospects in terms of fate or supernatural events. This is illustrated in a study quoted by Myren (n.d.). Farmers with non-irrigated land answered questions about future plans with 'what God wishes'. Neighbouring farmers who had access to irrigated land where yields are less variable answered the same question with concrete plans; they could think ahead because they could estimate future outcomes.

Peasants are believed to be fearful of the world at large, hostile in inter-personal relations and resigned to the will of God. Holmberg (1967) indicates that these attitudes are objective evaluations of their own experiences and not distorted by cultural preconceptions. Accidents and illness took their toll amongst the serfs in *haciendas* of highland Peru, others died executed by the police at the instigation of *hacienda* owners. Throughout his life the Indian serf has also become accustomed to endure corporal punishment. Every highland *hacienda* used to jail Indians without trial, either in punishment for insubordination to the *hacendero*, or for transgression of his property, or unwillingness to co-operate in regional projects. Serfs have limited opportunities to better their levels of living and almost no political protection against the excesses of administrators and *hacenderos*. It is not surprising that they are fearful of authority, fearful of loosing their animals or land and fearful of hunger. In order to minimize conflict with authority they behave meekly and are always ready to verbally comply; furthermore they teach their children to avoid contact with strangers. In order to alleviate hunger they steal from the *hacendero* and from each other. Holmberg suggests that behavioural patterns similar to the ones he describes are exhibited by any population suffering the same degree of deprivation and domination. The 'culture of repression' as he describes such a behaviour, discourages social change. Poverty is accepted as inevitable and innovation is regarded as pathological behaviour. Thus Holmberg argues very much like Foster. The 'culture of repression', like the 'image of the limited good', are objective perceptions of the peasant world. Their perceptions become internalized and institutionalized and constitute the lens through which they view the real world, even when that real world changes and offers them more rewarding opportunities. Both writers suggest that peasant communities will not develop unless their 'culture' or 'cognitive systems' are first changed.

The sequel to the argument that peasants share a culture, regardless of whether it is considered distinct or not, is that their economic behaviour can be explained in terms of their attitudes, value and cognitive systems. Some scholars like Foster are careful to indicate that peasant-like attitudes are also shared by other agriculturalists (Foster, 1965). But more often than not it is assumed that Western farmers allocate resources rationally in such a way as to maximize profit. I have indicated that this is not exactly correct; Western farmers are just as much influenced by values, social rewards and desire for satisfaction of their own personal needs and family needs as a peasant farmer. Social factors are always relevant and their understanding helps to elucidate the outcome of decisions made by producers. But although sociological analysis helps elucidate economic behaviour, it does not fully explain it. Peasants after all produce for a market and buy in a market; some of their decisions or inactions may just as easily be explained in terms of the state of the market. Furthermore, in order to attain a goal – regardless whether the goal is profit or satisfaction of social obligations – all producers have to develop economic strategies. When a peasant decides how much maize to plant – the amount varies from year to year – he has to consider the cash to buy seeds, the labour he will need, his ability to attract labourers, as well as the implication of this choice on all other economic activities. He will very likely evaluate likelihood of a yield and the certainty of the same. There is thus an economic context to productive actions; the outcome of these actions has also to be explained in terms of limitation of resources as well as in terms of goal gratification, cultural values and culturally determined perceptions.

Another objection to a purely sociological explanation of economic performance is that behaviour is not a simple function of cultural values. Ideologies may guide behaviour, but may be used also to justify past acts which are motivated by other factors. There is a considerable argument in the literature (see Edwards, 1967) as to whether individuals rank prospects and rewards always in the same order or whether the ranking depends on particular conditions and the set of opportunities which are evaluated at the moment.

Furthermore, there is no reason to assume that in any society there is a consistent system of values. Certainly this is less likely to be the case in peasant societies as according to most definitions peasants are part and parcel of larger national systems. An ideology provides the individual with one view of his own immediate world. Another view is derived from his own experiences and the realities of his social environment. A peasant in Tzintzuntzan or in Southern Mexico may be imbued with ideas of equality and moderation, but he also perceives internal social differentiations as for example the ranking of religious offices already described. Community members also compete for wealth and prestige by virtue of their membership in the wider society. They are aware of and share as well values which pertain to national culture; the example of the Indian trader in Chiapas is a clear illustration of the acceptance by all concerned of a double set of value systems.

Some of the purely sociological explanations of economic behaviour or resistance to innovation illustrate a naïveté on the part of the analyst as to some of the economic problems faced by peasants. Much would be gained if the field-worker interested in these problems would not only gather information on attitudes but also test his interpretations against the hard economic realities.

When any individual, whether peasant, Western businessman or farmer becomes aware that a particular action entails a risk, he evaluates it and decides how to act. The number of elements are numerous and relate to his income, cost of the enterprise, the pay-offs, the type of assets he holds, whether his livelihood may be threatened, the alternative opportunities he forgoes, means of insuring the well being of his family, his social status, etc. If on occasion a peasant hesitates to take a risk this does not imply that he always shies away from a gamble. There is a considerable amount of literature on gambling behaviour and investment tendencies which shows that individuals gamble and buy insurance at the same time (see Friedman and Savage, 1948). Peasant behaviour does not seem so different from Western producers and it is best analysed in the context of the more general scheme than as a special case; the Páez example illustrates how they insured their subsistence and gambled with a cash crop.

Many so-called traditional techniques are no more than well-tested ways of minimizing the chance of total loss and starvation. Without government price supports, peasants have to devise other means of insuring themselves. I mentioned earlier that the Páez condemn as morally wrong the sale of large quantities of food by other Indians in the market place. It was not a rigid rule imposed on any one who sold food. In fact few Indians produced food for sale to traders and they remained as good members of the community. Their behaviour was not judged simply in terms of the rule but was evaluated in terms of the economic significance of the rule, that is, whether or not it threatened the security of those who did depend on him.

New agricultural techniques imply usually a cash cost which may be out of proportion with the increase in yield promised by experts. They often also entail long-range cost, e.g. in upkeep of equipment, and hidden indirect costs often perceived only by the peasant farmer. For example a new seed may require a higher labour in-put which may affect the time the farmer has for other *safer* farming activities. Social consequences have also to be considered. Furthermore new techniques suggested by extension workers are not properly tested and adjusted to the highly variable local conditions. Rogers (1962), while holding to the idea that peasants' attitudes explain reluctance to accept changes, remarks that the higher the income of the farmer the more likely he is to accept new techniques. It has been estimated that the cost of fertilizer can absorb most of the benefits that a low income farmer can gain from the innovation, hence commercial farms are more likely to try new techniques. Only a high degree of confidence in a new method can induce a poorer farmer to accept it. Farmers accept a new technique only as long as the annual risk does not endanger the subsistence level.

When making a decision an individual selects, from innumerable opportunities offered by the environment, a set small enough to be able to evaluate the probable outcomes of each and to compare them against each other. The opportunities included are those which are obvious to him. Cultural condition does indeed affect perception but does not define it. Past experiences by the individual have also a bearing. The opportunity also has to have immediate relevance to the individual in question. Furthermore the individual has to be able to estimate the chances of an outcome with sufficient conviction to allow him to choose. If he is terribly uncertain about all outcomes and if all the opportunities are equally desirable, the farmer delays actions and searches for more opportunities (see Edwards, 1967; Johnson, 1961; Shackle, 1952). If a search does not lead to the discovery of a more suitable set of opportunities from which selection can be made, then either aspirations are lowered (see Simon, 1959) or passivity ensues until the event forces the farmer to act. The passivity and distrust of the Indians described by Holmberg can be understood in the context of the uncertainty of their social and economic environment and not simply as determined by the culture of oppression.

References

BANFIELD, E. C. (1958), *The Moral Basis of a Backward Society*, The Free Press.

BENNETT, J. W. (1966), 'Further remarks on Foster's "image of the limited good"', *Amer. Anthrop.*, vol. 68, pp. 206–10.

EDWARDS, W. (1967) 'The theory of decision making', in W. Edwards and A. Tversky (eds.), *Decision Making*, Penguin Books.

FARON, L. C. (1961), *Mapuche Social Structure: Institutional Reintegration in a Patrilineal Society of Central Chile*, University of Illinois Press.

FIRTH, R. (1951a), *Elements of Social Organization*, C. A. Watts.

FIRTH, R. (1951b), *Malayan Fisherman: Their Peasant Economy*, Routledge & Kegan Paul.

FOSTER, G. M. (1965), 'Peasant society and the image of limited good', *Amer. Anthrop.*, vol. 2, pp. 293–315.

FOSTER, G. M. (1967a), *Tzintzuntzan: Mexican Peasants in a Changing World*, Little, Brown.

FOSTER, G. M. (1967b), 'Peasant character and personality', in J. M. Potter, M. N. Diaz and G. M. Foster (eds.), *Peasant Society: A Reader*, Little, Brown.

FRIEDMAN, M., and SAVAGE, L. J. (1948), 'The utility analysis of choices involving risk', *J. polit. Econ.*, vol. 56, pp. 279–304.

HAGEN, E. E. (1962), *On the Theory of Social Change: How Economic Growth Begins*, Dorsey Press.

HOLMBERG, A. R. (1967), 'Algunas relaciones entre la privación psicobiológica y el cambio cultural en los Andes', *Amer. Indig.*, vol. 27.

JOHNSON, G. L. (ed.) (1961), *Study of Managerial Processes of Midwestern Farmers*, Iowa State University Press.

KAPLAN, D., and SADLER, B. (1966), 'Foster's image of the limited good: an example of anthropological explanation', *Amer. Anthrop.*, vol. 68, pp. 202–6.

KATONA, G. (1963), *Psychological Analysis of Economic Behavior*, McGraw-Hill.

KROEBER, A. (1948), *Anthropology*, Harcourt, Brace & World.

LEWIS, O. (1960), *Life in a Mexican Village; Tepotzlán Re-Studied*, University of Illinois Press.

MARRIOTT, M. (1955), 'Little communities in an indigenous civilization', in M. Marriott, *Village India*, Amer. Anthrop. Assoc. Memoir 83.

MYREN, D. T. (n.d.), 'The role of information in farm decisions under conditions of high risk and uncertainty', First Interamerican Research Symposium on the Role of Communications in Agricultural Development.

ORTIZ, S. (1967), 'The structure of decision-making', in R. Firth (ed.), *Themes in Economic Anthropology*, Tavistock Publications.

REDFIELD, R. (1953), *The Primitive World and Its Transformation*, Cornell University Press.

ROGERS, E. (1962), *Diffusion of Innovations*, Free Press.

SHACKLE, G. L. S. (1952), *Expectations in Economics*, Cambridge University Press.

SIMON, H. A. (1959), 'Theories of decision-making in economics', *Amer. econ. Rev.*, vol. 49, pp. 253–83.

SIVERTS, H. (1969), 'Ethnic stability and boundary dynamics in southern Mexico', in F. Barth (ed.), *Ethnic Groups and Boundaries*, Little, Brown.

THORNER, D. (1963), 'Peasant economy as a category in economic history', *Economic Weekly*, special number, Bombay.

WOLF, E. R. (1951), 'Closed corporate communities in Meso-America and Java', *Southwest. J. Anthrop.*, vol. 13, pp. 1–18.

WOLF, E. R. (1955), 'Types of Latin-American peasantry: a preliminary discussion', *Amer. Anthrop.*, vol. 57, pp. 452–71.

WOLF, E. R. (1966), *Peasants*, Prentice-Hall.

24 Robert Redfield and Milton B. Singer

The Cultural Role of Cities

Excerpts from Robert Redfield and Milton B. Singer, 'The cultural role of cities', *Economic Development and Social Change*, vol. 3, 1954, pp. 53–73.

This paper has as its purpose to set forth a framework of ideas that may prove useful in research on the part played by cities in the development, decline or transformation of culture. 'Culture' is used as in anthropology. The paper contains no report of research done. It offers a scheme of constructs; it does not describe observed conditions or processes; references to particular cities or civilizations are illustrative and tentative.

Time Perspectives

The cultural role of cities may be considered from at least three different time perspectives. In the long-run perspective of human history as a single career (Brown *et al.*, 1939; Redfield, 1953b, pp. ix–xiii), the first appearance of cities marks a revolutionary change: the beginnings of civilization. Within this perspective cities remain the symbols and carriers of civilization wherever they appear. In fact the story of civilization may then be told as the story of cities – from those of the Ancient Near East through those of Ancient Greece and Rome, medieval and modern Europe; and from Europe overseas to North and South America, Australia, the Far East, and back again to the modern Near East. In the short-run perspective we may study the cultural role of particular cities in relation to their local hinterlands of towns and villages (Mandelbaum, 1949).[1] The time span here is the several-year period of the field research or, at most, the lifespan of the particular cities that are studied. Between the long- and short-run perspectives, there is a middle-run perspective delimited by the

1. cf. Redfield (1941). This study, short-run in description, also aims to test some general ideas.

life-history of the different civilizations within which cities have developed.[2] This is the perspective adopted when we consider the cultural bearings of urbanization within Mexican civilization,[3] or Chinese civilization or Indian civilization or Western civilization. It is a perspective usually of several thousand years and embraces within its orbit not just a particular city and its hinterland, but the whole pattern and sequence of urban development characteristic of a particular civilization and its cultural epochs.[...]

In the many useful studies of cities by urban geographers, sociologists and ecologists we find frequent reference to 'cultural functions' and 'cultural centers' (Dickinson, 1951, pp. 253–4; Harris, 1943; Kneedler, 1951). Under these rubrics they generally include the religious, educational, artistic centers and activities, and distinguish them from administrative, military, economic centers and functions. This usage of 'cultural' is too narrow for the purpose of a comparative analysis of the role cities play in the transformations of the more or less integrated traditional life of a community. Economic and political centers and activities may obviously play as great a role in these processes as the narrowly 'cultural' ones. Moreover, these different kinds of centers and activities are variously combined and separated and it is these varying patterns that are significant. In ancient civilizations the urban centers were usually political–religious or political–

2. Kroeber has recently discussed the problems of delimiting civilizations in his article, 'The delimitation of civilizations' (1953). See also Jefferson (1931).

3. Kirchhoff (1952, p. 254): 'It seems to me that the fundamental characteristic of Mesoamerica was that it was a stratified society, one like ours or that of China, based on the axis of city and countryside. There was a native ruling class, with a class ideology and organization, which disappeared entirely; there were great cultural centers which, just as in our life, are so essential, if you described the US without New York, Chicago, etc., it would be absurd. The same thing happens when you describe these centers in ancient Mexico.... It's not only the arts, crafts and sciences which constitute the great changes, but the basic form of the culture changing from a city structure to the most isolated form, which is, in my opinion, the most total and radical change anywhere in history.... When the city is cut off what is left over is attached as a subordinate to the new city-centered culture....'

intellectual; in the modern world they are economic (Fei Hsiao-Tung, 1953, pp. 91–117; Gadgil, 1944, pp. 6–12; George, 1952; Rowland, 1953, p. xvii; Spate and Ahmad, 1950). The mosque, the temple, the cathedral, the royal palace, the fortress are the symbolic 'centers' of the pre-industrial cities. The 'central business district' has become symbolic of the modern urban center. In fact a cross-cultural history of cities might be written from the changing meanings of the words for city. 'Civitas' in the Roman Empire meant an administrative or ecclesiastical district. Later, 'city' was applied to the ecclesiastical center of a town – usually the cathedral. This usage still survives in names like 'Île de la Cité' for one of the first centers of Paris. With the development of the 'free cities', 'city' came to mean the independent commercial towns with their own laws (Dickinson, 1951, pp. 251–2; Pirenne, 1956). Today, 'the city' of London is a financial center, and when Americans speak of 'going to town' or 'going downtown' they mean they are going to the 'central business district'. They usually think of any large city as a business and manufacturing center, whereas a Frenchman is more likely to regard his cities – certainly Paris – as 'cultural centers'.[4]

This symbolism is not of course a completely accurate designation of what goes on in the city for which it stands. The ecclesiastical centers were also in many cases centers of trade and of craftsmen, and the modern 'central business district' is very apt to contain libraries, schools, art museums, government offices and churches, in addition to merchandising establishments and business offices. But allowing for this factual distortion, this symbolism does help us to separate two quite distinct cultural roles of cities, and provides a basis for classifying cities that is relevant to their cultural role. As a 'central business district', the city is obviously a market-place, a place to buy and sell, 'to do business' – to truck, barter and exchange with people who may be complete strangers and of different races, religions and creeds. The city here functions to work out largely impersonal relations among diverse cultural groups. As a religious or in-

4. See article on 'Urbanization' by W. M. Stewart in the fourteenth edition of *Encyclopaedia Brittanica* for some cultural variables in the definition of 'city'.

tellectual center, on the other hand, the city is a beacon for the faithful, a center for the learning, authority and perhaps doctrine that transforms the implicit 'little traditions' of the local non-urban cultures into an explicit and systematic 'great tradition'. The varying cultural roles of cities, so separated and grouped into two contrasting kinds of roles with reference to the local traditions of the non-urban peoples, point to a distinction to which we shall soon return and to which we shall then give names.

Types of Cities

[. . .] The distinction that is basic to consideration of the cultural role of cities is the distinction between the *carrying forward into systematic and reflective dimensions an old culture* and the *creating of original modes of thought that have authority beyond or in conflict with old cultures and civilizations*. We might speak of the orthogenetic cultural role of cities as contrasted with the hetero-genetic cultural role.

In both these roles the city is a place in which cultural change takes place. The roles differ as to the character of the change. In so far as the city has an orthogenetic role, it is not to maintain culture as it was; the orthogenetic city is not static; it is the place where religious, philosophical and literary specialists reflect, synthesize and create out of the traditional material new arrangements and developments that are felt by the people to be outgrowths of the old. What is changed is a further statement of what was there before. In so far as the city has a heterogenetic role, it is a place of conflict of differing traditions, a center of heresy, heterodoxy and dissent, of interruption and destruction of ancient tradition, of rootlessness and anomie. Cities are both these things, and the same events may appear to particular people or groups to be representative of what we here call orthogenesis or representative of heterogenesis. The predominating trend may be in one of the two directions, and so allow us to characterize the city, or that phase of the history of the city, as the one or the other. The lists just given suggest that the differences in the degree to which in the city orthogenesis or heterogenesis prevails are in cases strongly marked.

The presence of the market is not of itself a fact of heterogenetic change. Regulated by tradition, maintained by such customs and routines as develop over long periods of time, the market may flourish without heterogenetic change. In the medieval Muslim town we see an orthogenetic city; the market and the keeper of the market submitted economic activities to explicit cultural and religious definition of the norms. In Western Guatemala the people who come to market hardly communicate except with regard to buying and selling, and the market has little heterogenetic role. On the other hand the market in many instances provides occasions when men of diverse traditions may come to communicate and to differ; and also in the market occurs that exchange on the basis of universal standards of utility which is neutral to particular moral orders and in some sense hostile to all of them. The cities of group 2, therefore, are cities unfavorable to orthogenetic change but not necessarily productive of heterogenetic change.

The City and the Folk Society[5]

The folk society may be conceived as that imagined combination of societal elements which would characterize a long-established, homogeneous, isolated and non-literate integral (self-contained) community; the folk culture is that society seen as a system of common understandings. Such a society can be approximately realized in a tribal band or village; it cannot be approximately realized in a city. What are characteristics of the city that may be conceived as a contrast to those of the folk society?

The city may be imagined as that community in which orthogenetic and heterogenetic transformations of the folk society have most fully occurred. The former has brought about the Great Tradition and its special intellectual class, administrative officers and rules closely derived from the moral and religious life of the local culture, and advanced economic institutions, also obedient to these local cultural controls. The heterogenetic transformations have accomplished the freeing of the intellectual, esthetic, economic and political life from the local moral norms, and have developed on the one hand an individuated expediential motivation, and on the other a revolutionary, nativistic,

5. See Redfield (1953a).

humanistic or ecumenical viewpoint, now directed toward reform, progress and designed change.

As these two aspects of the effects of the city on culture may be in part incongruent with each other, and as in fact we know them to occur in different degrees and arrangements in particular cities, we may now review the classification of cities offered above so as to recognize at least two types of cities conceived from this point of view:

1. *The city of orthogenetic transformation: the city of the moral order:* the city of culture carried forward. In the early civilizations the first cities were of this kind and usually combined this developmental cultural function with political power and administrative control. But it is to be emphasized that this combination occurred because the local moral and religious norms prevailed and found intellectual development in the literati and exercise of control of the community in the ruler and the laws. Some of these early cities combined these two 'functions' with commerce and economic production; others had little of these. It is as cities of predominating orthogenetic civilization that we are to view Peiping, Lhasa, Uaxactun, fourteenth-century Liège.

2. *The city of heterogenetic transformation: the city of the technical order:* the city where local cultures are disintegrated and new integrations of mind and society are developed of the kinds described above ('The heterogenetic role of cities'). In cities of this kind men are concerned with the market, with 'rational' organization of production of goods, with expediential relations between buyer and seller, ruler and ruled, and native and foreigner. In this kind of city the predominant social types are businessmen, administrators alien to those they administer, and rebels, reformers, planners and plotters of many varieties. It is in cities of this kind that priority comes to be given to economic growth and the expansion of power among the goods of life. The modern metropolis exhibits very much of this aspect of the city; the town built in the tropics by the United Fruit Company and the city built around the Russian uranium mine must have much that represents it; the towns of the colonial administration

in Africa must show many of its features. Indeed, in one way or another, all the cities of groups 2, 3 and 4 are cities of the technical order, and are cities favorable to heterogenetic transformation of the moral order.[6]

This type of city may be subdivided into the administrative city, city of the bureaucracy (Washington, D. C., Canberra), and the city of the entrepreneur (Hamburg, Shanghai). Of course many cities exhibit both characteristics.

'In every tribal settlement there is civilization; in every city is the folk society.' We may look at any city and see within it the folk society in so far as ethnic communities that make it up preserve folk-like characteristics, and we may see in a town in ancient Mesopotamia or in aboriginal West Africa a half-way station between folk society and orthogenetic civilization. We may also see in every city its double urban characteristics: we may identify the institutions and mental habits there prevailing with the one or the other of the two lines of transformation of folk life which the city brings about. The heterogenetic trans-formations have grown with the course of history, and the development of modern industrial world-wide economy, together with the great movements of peoples and especially those incident to the expansion of the West, have increased and accelerated this aspect of urbanization. The later cities are predominantly cities of the technical order. We see almost side by side persisting cities of the moral order and those of the technical order: Peiping and Shanghai, Cuzco and Guayaquil, a native town in Nigeria and an administrative post and railway center hard by.

The ancient city, predominantly orthogenetic, was not (as remarked by Eberhard) in particular cases the simple outgrowth of a single pre-civilized culture, but was rather (as in the case of Loyang) a city in which conquered and conqueror lived together, the conqueror extending his tradition over the conquered, or accepting the latter's culture. What makes the orthogenetic aspect

6. In the heterogenetic transformation the city and its hinterland be-come mutually involved: the conservative or reactionary prophet in the country inveighs against the innovations or backslidings of the city; and the reformer with the radically progressive message moves back from Medina against Mecca, or enters Jerusalem.

of a city is the integration and uniform interpretation of preceding culture, whether its origins be one or several. Salt Lake City and early Philadelphia, cities with much orthogenetic character, were established by purposive acts of founders. Salt Lake City created its own hinterland on the frontier (as pointed out by Harris). Other variations on the simple pattern of origin and development of a city from an established folk people can no doubt be adduced.

Transformation of Folk Societies: Primary and Secondary Urbanization

The preceding account of different types of cities is perhaps satisfactory as a preliminary, but their cultural roles in the civilizations which they represent cannot be fully understood except in relation to the entire pattern of urbanization within that civilization, i.e. the number, size, composition, distribution, duration, sequence, morphology, function, rates of growth and decline, and the relation to the countryside and to each other of the cities within a civilization. Such information is rare for any civilization. In the present state of our knowledge it may be useful to guide further inquiry by assuming two hypothetical patterns of urbanization: primary and secondary.[7] In the primary phase a pre-civilized folk society is transformed by urbanization into a peasant society and correlated urban center. It is primary in the sense that the peoples making up the pre-civilized folk more or less share a common culture which remains the matrix too for the peasant and urban cultures which develop from it in the course of urbanization. Such a development, occurring slowly in communities not radically disturbed, tends to produce a 'sacred culture' which is gradually transmuted by the literati of the cities into a 'Great Tradition'. Primary urbanization thus takes place almost entirely within the framework of a core culture that develops, as the local cultures become urbanized and transformed, into an indigenous civilization. This core culture dominates the civilization despite occasional intrusions of foreign peoples and cultures. When the encounter with other peoples and

7. This distinction is an extension of the distinction between the primary and secondary phases of folk transformations in Redfield (1953b, p. 41).

civilizations is too rapid and intense an indigenous civilization may be destroyed by de-urbanization or be variously mixed with other civilizations (Kirchhoff, 1952).

This leads to the secondary pattern of urbanization: the case in which a folk society, pre-civilized, peasant or partly urbanized, is further urbanized by contact with peoples of widely different cultures from that of its own members. This comes about through expansion of a local culture, now partly urbanized, to regions inhabited by peoples of different cultures, or by the invasion of a culture-civilization by alien colonists or conquerors. This secondary pattern produces not only a new form of urban life in some part in conflict with local folk cultures but also new social types in both city and country. In the city appear 'marginal' and 'cosmopolitan' men and an 'intelligentsia'; in the country various types of marginal folk: enclaved-, minority-, imperialized-, transplanted-, remade-, quai-folk, etc., depending on the kind of relation to the urban center.

This discussion takes up a story of the contact of peoples at the appearance of cities. But, here parenthetically, it is necessary to note that even before the appearance of cities the relations between small and primitive communities may be seen as on the one hand characterized by common culture and on the other by mutual usefulness with awareness of cultural difference. The 'primary phase of urbanization' is a continuation of the extension of common culture from a small primitive settlement to a town and its hinterland, as no doubt could be shown for parts of West Africa. The 'secondary phase of urbanization' is begun before cities, in the institutions of travel and trade among local communities with different cultures. In Western Guatemala today simple Indian villagers live also in a wider trade-community of pluralistic cultures (Redfield, 1939); we do not know to what extent either the pre-Columbian semi-urban centers or the cities of the Spanish-modern conquerors and rulers, have shaped this social system; it may be that these people were already on the way to secondary urbanization before any native religious and political center rose to prominence.

While we do not know universal sequences within primary or secondary urbanization, it is likely that the degree to which any civilization is characterized by patterns of primary or secondary urbanization depends on the rate of technical development and the scope and intensity of contact with other cultures. If technical development is slow and the civilization is relatively isolated, we may expect to find a pattern of primary urbanization prevailing. If, on the other hand, technical development is rapid and contacts multiple and intense, secondary urbanization will prevail.

It may be that in the history of every civilization there is, of necessity, secondary urbanization. In modern Western civilization conditions are such as to make secondary urbanization the rule. But even in older civilizations it is not easy to find clear-cut examples of primary urbanization – because of multiple interactions, violent fluctuations in economic and military fortunes, conflicts and competition among cities and dynasties, and the raids of nomads. The Maya before the Spanish Conquest are perhaps a good example of primary urbanization (Redfield, 1953b, pp. 58–73; see also Gann and Thompson, 1931; Morley, 1946). The cases of the Roman, Greek, Hindu, Egyptian and Mesopotamian civilizations, although characterized by distinctive indigenous civilizations, are nevertheless complex because little is known about the degree of cultural homogeneity of the peoples who formed the core cultures and because as these civilizations became imperial they sought to assimilate more and more diverse peoples. Alternatively the irritant 'seed' of a city may have been sown in some of them by the conquering raid of an outside empire, the desire to copy another empire in having a capital, or simple theft from another people – with the *subsequent* development around this seed of the 'pearl' of a relatively indigenous, primary urban growth, sending out its own imperial secondary strands in due time. Thus while Rome, Athens, Chang-An and Loyang in early China and Peiping in later, Pataliputra and Benares, Memphis and Thebes, Nippur and Ur may have been for a time at least symbolic vehicles for loyalty to the respective empires and indigenous civilizations, it was not these relatively 'orthogenetic' cities but the mixed cities on the periphery of an empire – the 'colonial cities' which carried the core culture to other peoples. And in such cities, usually quite mixed in character, the imperial great tradition was not only bound to be very dilute but would also have to meet the challenge of conflicting local traditions. At the imperial peripheries, primary urbanization turns into secondary urbanization.[8]

Similar trends can be perceived in modern times: Russian cities in Southern Europe and Asia appear to be very mixed (Harris, 1945), non-Arabic Muslim cities have developed in Africa and South Asia, and the colonial cities of the European powers admit native employees daily at the doors of their skyscraper banks. Possibly the nuclear cultures are homogeneous and create indigenous civilizations but as they expand into new areas far afield from the home cultures they have no choice but to build 'heterogenetic' cities.

Modern 'colonial' cities (e.g., Jakarta, Manila, Saigon, Bangkok, Singapore, Calcutta) raise the interesting question whether they can reverse from the 'heterogenetic' to the 'orthogenetic' role. For the last one hundred or more years they have developed as the outposts of imperial civilizations, but as the countries in which they are located achieve political independence, will the cities change their cultural roles and contribute more to the formation of a civilization indigenous to their areas? Many obstacles lie in the path of such a course. These cities have large, culturally diverse populations, not necessarily European, for example, the Chinese in South-East Asia, Muslims and Hindu refugees from faraway provinces, in India; they often have segregated ethnic quarters, and their established administrative, military and economic functions are not easily changed. Many new problems have been created by a sudden influx of postwar refugee populations, and the cities' changing positions in national and global political and economic systems. While many of these colonial cities have been centers of nationalism and of movements for revival of the local cultures, they are not likely to live down their 'heterogenetic' past.[9]

8. The case of China is particularly striking, since the evidence for a dominant core culture is unmistakable but its relation to local cultures which may have been its basis is unknown. See Chi Li (1928) and Eberhard (1937).

For a good study of imperial 'spread' and 'dilution', see Jones (1940).

9. See Fryer (1953) and Spencer (1951), the latter is a summary of an article by Jean Chesneaux. See also *Record of the XXVIIth Meeting of the*

The Cultural Consequences of Primary and Secondary Urbanization

The discussion of primary and secondary urbanization above has been a bare outline. It may be filled in by reference to some postulated consequences of each type of process. The most important cultural consequence of primary urbanization is the transformation of the Little Tradition into a Great Tradition. Embodied in 'sacred books' or 'classics', sanctified by a cult, expressed in monuments, sculpture, painting and architecture, served by the other arts and sciences, the Great Tradition becomes the core culture of an indigenous civilization and a source, consciously examined, for defining its moral, legal, esthetic and other cultural norms. A Great Tradition describes a way of life and as such is a vehicle and standard for those who share it to identify with one another as members of a common civilization. In terms of social structure, a significant event is the appearance of literati, those who represent the Great Tradition. The new forms of thought that now appear and extend themselves include reflective and systematic thought; the definition of fixed idea-systems (theologies, legal codes); the development of esoteric or otherwise generally inaccessible intellectual products carried forward, now in part separate from the tradition of the folk; and the creation of intellectual and esthetic forms that are both traditional and original (cities of the Italian Renaissance; development of 'rococo' Maya sculpture in the later cities).

In government and administration the orthogenesis of urban civilization is represented by chiefs, rulers and laws that express and are closely controlled by the norms of the local culture. The chief of the Crow Indians, in a pre-civilized society, and the early kings of Egypt, were of this type. The Chinese emperor was in part orthogenetically controlled by the Confucian teaching and ethic; in some part here presented a heterogenetic development. The Roman pro-consul and the Indian Service of the United States, especially in certain phases, were more heterogenetic political developments.

International Institute of Differing Civilizations (1952), especially the papers by R. W. Steel and K. Neys.

Economic institutions of local cultures and civilizations may be seen to be orthogenetic in so far as the allocation of resources to production and distribution for consumption are determined by the traditional system of status and by the traditional specific local moral norms. The chief's yam house in the Trobriands is an accumulation of capital determined by these cultural factors. In old China the distribution of earnings and 'squeeze' were distributed according to familial obligations: these are orthogenetic economic institutions and practices. The market, freed from controls of tradition, status and moral rule, becomes the world-wide heterogenetic economic institution.

In short, the trend of primary urbanization is to coordinate political, economic, educational, intellectual and esthetic activity to the norms provided by the Great Traditions.

The general consequence of secondary urbanization is the weakening or supersession of the local and traditional cultures by states of mind that are incongruent with those local cultures. Among these are to be recognized:

1. The rise of a consensus appropriate to the technical order: i.e. based on self-interest and pecuniary calculation, or on recognition of obedience to common impersonal controls, characteristically supported by sanctions of force. (This in contrast to a consensus based on common religious and non-expediential moral norms.) There is also an autonomous development of norms and standards for the arts, crafts and sciences.

2. The appearance of new sentiments of common cause attached to groups drawn from culturally heterogeneous backgrounds. In the city proletariats are formed and class or ethnic consciousness is developed, and also new professional and territorial groups. The city is the place where ecumenical religious reform is preached (though it is not originated there). It is the place where nationalism flourishes. On the side of social structure, the city is the place where new and larger groups are formed that are bound by few and powerful common interests and sentiments in place of the complexly interrelated roles and statuses that characterize the groups of local, long-established culture. Among social types that appear in this aspect of the cultural

process in the city are the reformer, the agitator, the nativistic or nationalistic leader, the tyrant and his assassin, the missionary and the imported school teacher.

3. The instability of viewpoint as to the future, and emphasis on prospective rather than retrospective view of man in the universe. In cities of predominantly orthogenetic influence, people look to a future that will repeat the past (either by continuing it or by bringing it around again to its place in the cycle). In cities of predominantly heterogenetic cultural influence there is a disposition to see the future as different from the past. It is this aspect of the city that gives rise to reform movements, forward-looking myths, and planning, revolutionary or melioristic. The forward-looking may be optimistic and radically reformistic; it may be pessimistic, escapist, defeatist or apocalyptic. In the city there are Utopias and counter-Utopias. In so far as these new states of mind are secular, worldly, they stimulate new political and social aspirations and give rise to policy.

Consequences for World View, Ethos and Typical Personality

The difference in the general cultural consequences of primary and secondary urbanization patterns may be summarily characterized by saying that in primary urbanization, all phases of the technical order (material technology, economy, government, arts, crafts and sciences) are referred, in theory at least, to the standards and purposes of a moral order delineated in the Great Tradition, whereas in secondary urbanization different phases of the technical order are freed from this reference and undergo accelerated autonomous developments. With respect to this development, the moral order, or rather orders, for there are now many competing ones, appears to lag (Redfield, 1953b, pp. 72–83).

There is another way of describing these differences: in terms of the consequences of the two kinds of urbanization for changes in world view, ethos and typical personality.[10] To describe the consequences in these terms is to describe them in their bearings and meanings for the majority of individual selves constituting

10. For a further discussion of these concepts, see Redfield (1953b, ch. 4) and (1955, chs. 5 and 6) on personality and mental outlook.

the society undergoing urbanization. We now ask, how do primary and secondary urbanization affect mental outlook, values and attitudes, and personality traits? These are in part psychological questions, for they direct our attention to the psychological aspects of broad cultural processes.

There are many accounts of the psychological consequences of urbanization. These have described the urban outlook, ethos and personality as depersonalized, individualized, emotionally shallow and atomized, unstable, secularized, blasé, rationalistic, cosmopolitan, highly differentiated, self-critical, time-coordinated subject to sudden shifts in mood and fashion, 'other-directed', etc.[11] The consensus in these descriptions and their general acceptance by social scientists seem great enough to indicate that there probably is a general psychological consequence of urbanization, although it cannot be precisely described and proven. We should, however, like to suggest that the 'urban way of life' that is described in the characterizations to which we refer is primarily a consequence of secondary urbanization and of that in a particular critical stage when personal and cultural disorganization are greatest. To see these consequences in perspective, it is necessary to relate them on the one hand to the consequences of primary urbanization and on the other to those situations of secondary urbanization that produce new forms of personal and cultural integration. Most of all it is necessary to trace the continuities as well as the discontinuities in outlook, values and personality, as we trace the transformation of folk societies into their civilized dimension. The 'peasant' is a type that represents an adjustment between the values of the pre-civilized tribe and those of the urbanite. The 'literati' who fashion a Great Tradition do not repudiate the values and outlook of their rural hinterland but systematize and elaborate them under technical specialization. The cosmopolitan 'intelligentsia' and 'sophists' of the metropolitan centers have a prototype in the 'heretic' of the indigenous civilization. And even the most

11. See Fromm (1941); Kroeber (1948, sec. 121); Riesman *et al*. (1950); Simmel (1950) and Wirth (1938). For the effects of urban life on time-coordination see Hallowell (1937) and H. A. Hawley (1950, ch. 15).

sophisticated urban centers are not without spiritualists, astrologers and other practitioners with links to a folk-like past (Masson-Oursel, 1916; Park, 1952a; Redfield, 1941).[12]

The connexions between the folk culture, the Great Tradition and the sophisticated culture of the heterogenetic urban centers can be traced not only in the continuities of the historical sequence of a particular group of local cultures becoming urbanized and de-urbanized, but they also can be traced in the development of two distinct forms of cultural consciousness which appear in these transformations.

Cultural Integration between City and Country

From what has been said about primary and secondary urbanization it follows that city and country are more closely integrated, culturally, in the primary phase of urbanization than in the secondary phase. Where the city has grown out of a local culture, the country people see its ways as in some important part a form of their own, and they feel friendlier toward the city than do country people ruled by a pro-consul from afar. The stereotype of 'the wicked city' will be stronger in the hinterlands of the heterogenetic cities than in those of the orthogenetic cities. Many of these are sacred centers of faith, learning, justice and law.

Nevertheless, even in primary urbanization a cultural gap tends to grow between city and country. The very formation of the Great Tradition introduces such a gap. The literati of the city develop the values and world view of the local culture to a degree of generalization, abstraction and complexity incomprehensible to the ordinary villager, and in doing so leave out much of the concrete local detail of geography and village activity. The Maya Indian who lived in some rural settlement near Uaxactun could not have understood the calendrical intricacies worked out in that shrine-city by the priests; and the rituals performed at the city-shrine had one high level of meaning for the priest and another lower meaning, connecting with village life at some points only, for the ordinary Indian.

12. Chaudhuri (1951, pp. 361–2) gives some interesting observations on the survival of 'folk' beliefs and practices among the people of Calcutta.

On the other hand, primary urbanization involves the development of characteristic institutions and societal features that hold together, in a certain important measure of common understanding, the Little Tradition and the Great Tradition. We may refer to the development of these institutions and societal features as the universalization of cultural consciousness – meaning by 'universalization', the preservation and extension of common understanding as to the meaning and purpose of life, and sense of belonging together, to all the people, rural or urban, of the larger community. Some of the ways in which this universalization takes place are suggested in the following paragraphs. The examples are taken chiefly from India; they probably have considerable cross-cultural validity.

1. The embodiment of the Great Tradition in 'sacred books' and secondarily in sacred monuments, art, icons, etc. Such 'sacred scriptures' may be in a language not widely read or understood; nevertheless they may become a fixed point for the worship and ritual of ordinary people. The place of the 'Torah' in the lives of Orthodox Jews, the Vedas among orthodox Hindus, the 'Three Baskets' for Buddhists, the thirteen classics for Confucianists, the Koran for Muslims, the stelac and temples of the ancient Maya, are all examples of such sacred scriptures, although they may vary in degree of sacredness and in canonical status.

2. The development of a special class of 'literati' (priests, rabbis, Imams, Brahmins) who have the authority to read, interpret and comment on the sacred scriptures. Thus the village Brahmin who reads the *Gita* for villagers at ceremonies mediates a part of the Great Tradition of Hinduism for them.

The mediation of a great tradition is not always this direct. At the village level it may be carried in a multitude of ways – by the stories parents and grandparents tell children, by professional reciters and storytellers, by dramatic performances and dances. in songs and proverbs, etc.

In India the epics and *puranas* have been translated into the major regional languages and have been assimilated to the local cultures. This interaction of a 'great tradition' and the 'little tradition' of local and regional cultures needs further study, especially in terms of the professional and semi-professional 'mediators' of the process.

3. The role of leading personalities who because they themselves embody or know some aspects of a Great Tradition succeed through their personal position as leaders in mediating a Great Tradition to the masses of people. There is a vivid account of this process in Jawarhalal Nehru's *Discovery of India*, in which he describes first how he 'discovered' the Great Tradition of India in the ruins of Mohenjo-Daro and other archeological monuments, her sacred rivers and holy cities, her literature, philosophy and history. And then he describes how he discovered the 'little traditions' of the people and the villages, and how through his speeches he conveyed to them a vision of *Bharat Mata* – Mother India – that transcended the little patches of village land, people, and customs (Nehru, 1946, pp. 37–40, 45–51).

4. Nehru's account suggests that actual physical places, buildings and monuments – especially as they become places of sacred or patriotic pilgrimage – are important means to a more universalized cultural consciousness and the spread of a Great Tradition. In India this has been and still is an especially important universalizing force. The sanctity of rivers and the purifying powers of water go all the way back to the Rig Veda. The Buddhists – who may have started the practice of holy pilgrimages – believed that there were four places that the believing man should visit with awe and reverence: Buddha's birth place, the site where he attained illumination or perfect insight, the place where the mad elephant attacked him, and the place where Buddha died. In the *Mahabharata*, there is a whole book on the subject of holy places (Arareyaka Book). Even a sinner who is purified by holy water will go to heaven. And the soul ready for *moksha* will surely achieve it if the pilgrim dies on a pilgrimage (Patil, 1946, Appendix B). Today the millions of pilgrims who flock to such pre-eminent holy spots as Allahabad or Banaras create problems of public safety and urban over-crowding, but they, like Nehru, are also discovering the *Bharat Mata* beyond their villages.

In India 'sacred geography' has also played an important part in determining the location and layout of villages and cities and in this way has created a cultural continuity between countryside and urban centers. In ancient India, at least, every village and every city had a 'sacred center' with temple, tank, and garden. And the trees and plants associated with the sacred shrine were also planted in private gardens, for the households too had their sacred center; the house is the 'body' of a spirit (Varta Purusha) just as the human body is the 'house' of the soul (Ayyer, n.d.; Geddes, 1947; Kramrisch, 1946; Linton Bogle, 1929; Mudgett *et al.*, n.d.; Ramanayya, 1930; Rao, n.d.).

At each of these levels – of household, village and city – the 'sacred center' provides the forum, the vehicle and the content for the formation of distinct cultural identities – of families, village and city. But as individuals pass outward, although their contacts with others become less intimate and less frequent, they nevertheless are carried along by the continuity of the 'sacred centers', feeling a consciousness of a single cultural universe where people hold the same things sacred, and where the similarities of civic obligations in village and city to maintain tanks, build public squares, plant fruit trees, erect platforms and shrines, is concrete testimony to common standards of virtue and responsibility.

Surely such things as these – a 'sacred scripture', and a sacred class to interpret it, leading personalities, 'sacred geography' and the associated rites and ceremonies – must in any civilization be important vehicles for the formation of that common cultural consciousness from which a Great Tradition is fashioned and to which it must appeal if it is to stay alive. It is in this sense that the universalization of cultural consciousness is a necessary ingredient in its formation and maintenance. Moreover, as the discussion of the role of 'sacred geography' in the formation of Hinduism has intimated, this process does not begin only at the point where the villager and the urbanite merge their distinct cultural identities in a higher identity, but is already at work at the simpler levels of family, caste and village, and must play an important part in the formation and maintenance of the Little Tradition at these levels.[13]

13. See Robert Redfield (1955, ch. 8) on the little community 'as a community within communities'.

In addition to the above factors, it has been usual to single out special

The integration of city and country in the secondary phase of urbanization cannot rest on a basic common cultural consciousness or a common culture, for there is none. Rural–urban integration in this phase of urbanization rests primarily on the mutuality of interests and on the 'symbiotic' relations that have often been described (Park, 1952c). The city is a 'service station' and amusement center for the country, and the country is a 'food basket' for the city. But while the diversity of cultural groups and the absence of a common culture makes the basis of the integration primarily technical, even this kind of integration requires a kind of cultural consciousness to keep it going. We refer to the consciousness of cultural differences and the feeling that certain forms of intercultural association are of great enough benefit to override the repugnance of dealing with 'foreigners'. We may call this an 'enlargement of cultural horizons sufficient to become aware of other cultures and of the

---

items of content of the world view and values of a Great Tradition as explanations of the 'universalization' of Great Traditions. It has been frequently argued, e.g., that religions which are monotheistic and sanction an 'open class' social system will appeal more to ordinary people and spread faster than those which are 'polytheistic and which sanction 'caste' systems. (See for example Kissling, 1955). F. S. C. Northrop and Arnold Toynbee both attach great importance to the ideological content of cultures as factors in their spread, though they come out with different results. It may be that such special features of content are important in the formation and spread of some particular religions at some particular time, but it is doubtful that they would have the same role in different civilizations under all circumstances. In his recent study of the Coorgs of South India, Srinivas argues with considerable plausibility that the spread of Hinduism on an all-India basis has depended on its polytheism, which has made it easy to incorporate all sorts of alien deities, and on a caste system which assimilates every new cultural or ethnic group as a special caste.

Another difficulty about using special features of content of some particular tradition as a general explanation of the formation and maintenance of any Great Tradition is that one inevitably selects features that have been crystallized only after a long period of historical development and struggle. These are more relevant as factors in explaining *further* development and spread than they are in explaining the cultural-psychological processes that have accompanied primary urbanization. The 'universalization' of universal faiths takes us into the realm of secondary urbanization where diverse and conflicting cultures must be accommodated.

possibility that one's own society may in some ways require their presence. To paraphrase Adam Smith, it is not to the interest of the (Jewish) baker, the (Turkish) carpet-dealer, the (French) hand laundry, that the American Christian customer looks when he patronizes them, but to his own.

This is the practical psychological basis for admission of the stranger and tolerance of foreign minorities, even at the level of the folk society.[14] In a quotation from the *Institutions of Athens*, which Toynbee has, perhaps ironically, titled 'Liberté-Egalité-Fraternité', we are told that the reason why Athens has 'extended the benefits of Democracy to the relations between slaves and freemen and between aliens and citizens' is that 'the country requires permanent residence of aliens in her midst on account both of the multiplicity of trades and of her maritime activities' (Toynbee, 1950, pp. 48–9; see also Mandelbaum, 1939).

When all or many classes of a population are culturally strange to each other and where some of the city populations are culturally alien to the country populations, the necessity for an enlarged cultural consciousness is obvious. In societies where social change is slow, and there has developed an adjustment of mutual usefulness and peaceful residence side by side of groups culturally different but not too different, the culturally complex society may be relatively stable (Redfield, 1939). But where urban development is great, such conditions are apt to be unstable. Each group may be perpetually affronted by the beliefs and practices of the other groups. Double standards of morality will prevail, since each cultural group will have one code for its 'own kind' and another for the 'outsiders'. This simultaneous facing both inward and outward puts a strain on both codes. There may then be present the drives to proseletize, to withdraw and dig in, to persecute and to make scapegoats; there may even be fear of riot and massacre. In such circumstances the intellectuals become the chief exponents of a 'cosmopolitan' enlarged cultural consciousness, inventing formulas of universal toleration and the benefits of mutual understanding, and extolling the freedom to experiment in different ways of life. But they do not always

14. See Redfield (1953b, pp. 33–4), for the institutionalization of hospitality to strangers in peasant societies.

prevail against the more violent and unconvinced crusaders for some brand of cultural purity.

In primary urbanization when technical development was quite backward, a common cultural consciousness did get formed. The travelling student, teacher, saint, pilgrim or even humble villager who goes to the next town may be startled by strange and wonderful sights, but throughout his journey he is protected by the compass of the common culture from cultural shock and disorientation. In ancient times students and teachers came from all over India and even from distant countries to study at Taxila, just as they came from all over Greece to Athens. In secondary urbanization, especially under modern conditions, technical developments in transportation, travel and communication enormously facilitate and accelerate cultural contacts. The effects of this on common cultural consciousness are not easy briefly to characterize. They make the more traditional cultural differences less important. They provide a wide basis of common understanding with regard to the instruments and practical means of living. It is at least clear that the integration of country and city that results is not the same kind of sense of common purpose in life that was provided to rural–urban peoples through the institutions mediating Little and Great Traditions referred to above. At this point the inquiry approaches the questions currently asked about the 'mass culture' of modern great societies.

Cities as Centers of Cultural Innovation, Diffusion and Progress

It is a commonly stated view that the city rather than the country is the source of cultural innovations, that such innovations diffuse outward from city to country, and that the 'spread' is more or less inverse to distance from the urban center (Chabot, 1931, pp. 432–7; Hiller, 1941; Jefferson, 1939; Park, 1952b; Park, 1952d; Sorokin and Zimmerman, 1929, ch. 17; Spate, 1942). The objection to this view is not that it is wrong – for there is much evidence that would seem to support it – but that the limits and conditions of its validity need to be specified. It seems to assume for example that in the processes of cultural change, innovation and diffusion, 'city' and 'country' are fixed points of reference which do not have histories, or interact, and are not essentially related to larger contexts of cultural change. Yet such assumptions – if ever true – would hold only under the most exceptional and short-run conditions. It is one thing to say that a large metropolitan city is a 'center' of cultural innovation and diffusion for its immediate hinterland at a particular time; it is another to ask how that center itself was formed, over how long a period and from what stimuli. In other words, as we enlarge the time span, include the rise and fall of complex distributions of cities, allow for the mutual interactions between them and their hinterlands, and also take account of interactions with other civilizations and *their* rural–urban patterns, we find that the processes of cultural innovation and 'flow' are far too complex to be handled by simple mechanical laws concerning the direction, rate and 'flow' of cultural diffusion between 'city' and 'country'. The cities themselves are creatures as well as creators of this process, and it takes a broad cross-cultural perspective to begin to see what its nature is. While this perspective may not yield simple generalizations about direction and rates of cultural diffusion, to widen the viewpoint as here suggested may throw some light on the processes of cultural change, including the formation and cultural 'influence' of cities.

In a primary phase of urbanization, when cities are developing from folk societies, it seems meaningless to assert, e.g., that the direction of cultural flow is from city to country. Under these conditions a folk culture is transformed into an urban culture which is a specialization of it, and if we wish to speak of 'direction of flow' it would make more sense to see the process as one of a series of concentrations and nucleations within a common field. And as these concentrations occur, the common 'Little Tradition' has not become inert; in fact, it may retain a greater vitality and disposition to change than the systematized Great Tradition that gets 'located' in special classes and in urban centers. From this point of view the spatial and mechanical concepts of 'direction' and 'rate' of flow, etc., are just metaphors of the processes involved in the formation of a Great Tradition. The cultural relations between city and country have to be traced in other terms, in terms of sociocultural history and of cultural-psychological processes. Physical space and time may be important obstacles and facilitators to these processes but they are not the fundamental determinants of cultural 'motion' as they are of physical motion.

Under conditions of secondary urbanization, the spatial and mechanical concepts seem more appropriate because people and goods are more mobile and the technical development of the channels of transportation and communication is such as to permit highly precise measurement of their distributions and of 'flows.' But here too we may be measuring only some physical facts whose cultural significance remains indeterminate, or, at most, we may be documenting only a particularly recent cultural tendency to analyse intercultural relations in quantitative, abstract and non-cultural terms. The assumption of a continuous and quantitatively divisible 'diffusion' from a fixed urban center is unrealistic.

We may see Canton or Calcutta as a center for the diffusion of Western culture into the 'East'. We may also see these cities as relatively recent metropolitan growths, beginning as minor outliers of Oriental civilizations and then attracting both foreign and also uprooted native peoples, varying in fortune with worldwide events, and becoming at last not so much a center for the introduction of Western ways as a center for nativistic and independence movements to get rid of Western control and dominance. 'Everything new happens at Canton,' is said in China. We have in such a case not simple diffusion, or spread of urban influence from a city, but rather a cultural interaction which takes place against a background of ancient civilization with its own complex and changing pattern of urbanization now coming into contact with a newer and different civilization and giving rise to results that conform to neither.

The city may be regarded, but only very incompletely, as a center from which spreads outward the idea of progress. It is true that progress, like the ideologies of nationalism, socialism, communism, capitalism and democracy, tends to form in cities and it is in cities that the prophets and leaders of these doctrines are formed. Yet the states of mind of Oriental and African peoples are not copies of the minds of Western exponents of progress or of one or another political or economic doctrine. There is something like a revolution of mood and aspiration in the non-European peoples today.[15] The Easterner revolts against the West. He does not just take what can be borrowed from a city; he does sometimes the opposite: the Dutch language is set aside in Indonesia. There, anthropology, because associated with Dutch rule, does not spread from any city but is looked on with suspicion as associated with Dutch rule. Moreover, the influence of the West does not simply move outward from cities; it leap-frogs into country regions; a city reformer in Yucatan, Carrillo Puerto, arouses village Indians to join his civil war for progress and freedom against landowners and townspeople; Marxists discover that revolution can be based on the peasants without waiting for the development of an industrial proletariat (Mitrany, 1952).

The conception of progress is itself an idea shaped by and expressive of one culture or civilization, that of the recent West.[16] What Toynbee and others have called the 'Westernization' of the world may be the spread of only parts of the ideas associated in the West with the word 'progress'. Not without investigation can it be safely assumed that the spread of Western ideas from cities carries into the countryside a new and Western value system emphasizing hard work, enterprise, a favorable view of social change and a central faith in material prosperity. In the cases of some of the peoples affected by modern urbanization these values may be already present. In other cases the apparent spread of progress may turn out, on closer examination, to be a return to ancient values different from those of the West. Nationalistic movements are in part a nostalgic turning back to local traditional life. We shall understand better the varieties and

15. For further discussion of these concepts of 'mood', 'aspiration' and 'policy' as they might figure in community studies, see Redfield (1955, ch. 7 'Little Community as a History').

16. See Kroeber (1948, secs. 127, 128); Singer (1900), for an examination of some of the evidence on this point for American Indian cultures. Also see Redfield (1950), especially ch. 8, 'Chan Kom, its ethos and success'. Recent material on cross-cultural comparisons of value systems will be found in Forde (1954), and in the forthcoming publications of the Harvard Values Study Project directed by Clyde Kluckhohn.

complexities of the relations today between city and country as we compare the values and world views of the modernizing ideologies, and those of the Little and Great Traditions of the cultures and civilizations that are affected by the modern West. It may be that such studies[17] will discover greater 'ambivalence' in the mood to modernize than we, here in the West, acknowledge; that the progressive spirit of Asia and Africa is not simply a decision to walk the road of progressive convictions that we have traversed, but rather in significant part an effort of the 'backward' peoples to recover from their disruptive encounters with the West by returning to the 'sacred centers' of their ancient indigenous civilizations.

17. Several such studies have been made. See, for example, Barnouw (1954); Mus (1952); Sarkisyanz (?1953); Shen-Yu Dai (1952).

References

AYYER, C. P. V. (n.d.), *Town Planning in the Ancient Dekkan*, with an Introduction by P. Geddes, Madras.

BARNOUW, V. (1954), 'The changing character of a Hindu festival', *Amer. Anthrop.*, February.

BROWN, W. N., *et al.* (1939), 'The beginnings of civilization', *J. Amer. Oriental Soc.*, sup. no. 4, December, pp. 3–61.

CHABOT, G. (1931), 'Les zones d'influence d'une ville', *Cong. int. Geog.*, vol. 3.

CHAUDHURI, N. C. (1951), *The Autobiography of an Unknown Indian*, Macmillan.

CHI LI (1928), *The Formation of the Chinese People*, Harvard University Press.

DICKINSON, R. E. (1951), *The West European City*, Routledge & Kegan Paul.

EBERHARD, W. (1937), *Early Chinese Cultures and Their Development*, Smithsonian Institution Annual Report, 1938.

FEI HSIAO-TUNG (1953), *China's Gentry, Essays in Rural–Urban Relations*, University of Chicago Press.

FORDE, D. (ed.) (1954), *African Worlds*, Oxford University Press for the International African Institute.

FROMM, E. (1941), *Escape from Freedom*, Holt Rinehart & Winston.

FRYER, D. W. (1953), 'The "million city" in southeast Asia', *Geog. Rev.*, vol. 43, October.

GADGIL, D. R. (1944), *The Industrial Revolution of India in Recent Times*, Oxford University Press.

GANN, T., and THOMPSON, J. E. (1931), *The History of the Maya*, New York.

GEDDES, P. (1947), *Patrick Geddes in India*, J. Tyrwhitt (ed.), Humphries.

GEORGE, P. (1952), *La Ville*, Paris.

HALLOWELL, P. (1937), 'Temporal orientations in Western and non-Western cultures', *Amer. Anthrop.*, vol. 39.

HARRIS, C. (1943), 'A functional classification of cities in the United States', *Geog. Rev.*, vol. 33.

HARRIS, C. (1945), 'Ethnic groups in cities of the Soviet Union', *Geog. Rev.*, vol. 35.

HAWLEY, H. A. (1950), *Human Ecology*, New York.

HILLER, (1941), 'Extension of urban characteristics into rural areas', *Rural Sociol.*, vol. 6.

JEFFERSON, M. (1931), 'Distribution of the world's city folk: a study in comparative civilization', *Geographia*.

JEFFERSON, M. (1939), 'The law of the primate city', *Geog. Rev.*, pp. 226–32.

JONES, A. H. M. (1940), *The Greek City from Alexander to Justinian*, Oxford University Press.

KIRCHHOFF, P. (1952), 'Four hundred years after: general discussions of acculturation, social change and the historical provenience of culture elements', in S. Tax *et al.* (eds.), *Heritage of Conquest*, Free Press.

KISSLING, H. J. (1955), 'The sociological and educational role of the Dervish orders in the Ottoman Empire', in G. E. von Grunebaum (ed.), *Unity and Variety in Muslim Civilization*, University of Chicago Press.

KNEEDLER, G. M. (1951), 'Functional types of cities', reprinted in P. K. Hatt and A. J. Reiss, Jr (eds.), *Reader in Urban Sociology*, Free Press.

KRAMRISCH, S. (1946), *The Hindu Temple*, Calcutta.

KROEBER, A. (1948), *Anthropology*, Harcourt.

KROEBER, A. (1953), 'The delimitation of civilizations', *J. hist. Ideas*, vol. 14.

LINTON BOGLE, J. M. (1929), *Town Planning in India*, Oxford University Press.

MANDELBAUM, D. G. (1939), 'The Jewish way of life in Cochin', *Jewish soc. Studies*, vol. 1.

MANDELBAUM, D. G. (1949) (ed.), 'Integrated social science research for India', *Planning Memo.*, University of California.

MASSON-OURSEL, P. (1916), 'La sophistique: étude de philosophie comparée', *Revue Metaphysique Morale*, vol. 23, pp. 343–62.

MITRANY, D. (1961), *Marx against the Peasant*, Collier.

MORLEY, S. G. (1946), *The Ancient Maya*, Stanford University Press.

MUDGETT *et al.* (n.d.), *Banaras: Outline of a Master Plan*, prepared by Town and Village Planning Office, Lucknow.

MUS, P. (1952), *Viet-Nam, histoire d'une guerre*, Paris.

NEHRU, J. (1946), *The Discovery of India*, John Day, New York.

PARK, R. E. (1952a), 'Magic, mentality and city life', reprinted in R. E. Park, *Human Communities*, Free Press.

PARK, R. E. (1952b), 'Newspaper circulation and metropolitan regions', reprinted in R. E. Park, *Human Communities*, Free Press.

PARK, R. E. (1952c), 'Symbiosis and socialization: a frame of reference for the study of society', reprinted in R. E. Park, *Human Communities*, Free Press.

PARK, R. E. (1952d), 'The urban community as a spatial pattern and a moral order', reprinted in R. E. Park, *Human Communities*, Free Press.

PATIL, D. (1946), *Cultural History of the Vaya Purana*, Poona.

PIRENNE, H. (1956), *Medieval Cities*, Doubleday.

RAMANAYYA, N. V. (1930), *An Essay of the Origin of the South Indian Temple*, Madras.

RAO, H. (n.d.), 'Rural habitation in India', *Quarterly J. Mythic Soc.*, vol. 14,

Record of the XXVIIth Meeting of the International Institute of Differing Civilizations (1952), Brussels.

REDFIELD, R. (1939), 'Primitive merchants of Guatemala', *Quarterly J. Inter-Amer. Relations*, vol. 1, no. 4, pp. 48–9.

REDFIELD, R. (1941), *The Folk Culture of Yucatan*, University of Chicago Press.

REDFIELD, R. (1950), *A Village that Chose Progress*, University of Chicago Press.

REDFIELD, R. (1953a), 'The natural history of the folk society', *Social Forces*, vol. 31, pp. 224–8.

REDFIELD, R. (1953b), *The Primitive World and its Transformations*, Cornell University Press.

REDFIELD, R. (1955), *The Little Community*, University of Chicago Press.

RIESMAN, D., *et al.* (1950), *The Lonely Crowd*, Yale University Press.

ROWLAND, B. (1953), *The Art and Architecture of India*, Penguin Books.

SARKISYANZ, E. (?1953), 'Russian *Weltanschauung* and Islamic and Buddhist messianism', doctoral dissertation, University of Chicago.

SHEN-YU DAI (1952), 'Mao Tse-Tung and confucianism', doctoral dissertation, University of Pennsylvania.

SIMMEL, G. (1950), 'The metropolis and mental life', reprinted in P. K. Hatt and A. J. Reiss (eds.), *Reader in Urban Sociology*.

SINGER, M. (1900), *Shame Cultures and Guilt Cultures*.

SOROKIN P., and ZIMMERMAN, C. (1929), *Principles of Rural–Urban Sociology*, Holt, Rinehart & Winston.

SPATE, O. H. K. (1942), 'Factors in the development of capital cities', *Geog. Rev.*, vol. 32, pp. 622–31.

SPATE, O. H. K., and AHMAD, E. (1950), 'Five cities of the Gangetic Plain: a cross-section of Indian cultural history', *Geog. Rev.*, vol. 40.

SPENCER, J. E. (1951), 'Changing Asiatic cities', *Geog. Rev.*, vol. 41.

TOYNBEE, A. (1950), *Greek Civilization and Character*, Beacon Press.

WIRTH, L. (1938), 'Urbanism as a way of life', reprinted in P. K. Hatt and A. J. Reiss (eds.), *Reader in Urban Sociology*, Free Press.

Part Five
'Them' – The Peasantry as an Object of Policies of the Modern State

Part Five begins with a number of short pronouncements on peasants which reveal something of the outsider's understanding of peasantry and peasant life. These views, with their tremendous discrepancies, underlie the attitudes, ideologies and policies directed towards the peasantry in the contemporary world. Reading 26, by Dore, is devoted to agrarian reform, while Huizer attempts to place this issue in relation to peasant political action as well as the U N sponsored programmes of community development. Myrdal concludes the collection of Readings by discussing possible optimal agricultural policies in contemporary societies with peasant majorities, i.e. the majority of mankind.

25 Peasantry in the Eyes of Others

Maxim Gorky

The Barbarians

Excerpts from M. Gorky, *On the Russian Peasantry*, Ladyzhnikov, 1922, pp. 4–21. Translated by Paula V. Harry.

Western man from his very childhood, from the moment he stands up on his hind legs, sees all around him the monumental results of the work of his forefathers. From the canals of Holland to the tunnels of the Italian Riviera and the vineyards of Vesuvius, from the great workshops of England to the mighty Silesian factories, the whole of Europe is densely covered by grandiose embodiments of the organizational will of man – the will which puts forward as its proud aim to subject the elemental forces of nature to the intelligent interests of man. The land is in the hands of man and man is truly its sovereign. The child of the West soaks up these impressions; a consciousness of the value of man and a respect for his work, together with a feeling of his own significance is raised in him, as heir to the marvel of the works and creations of his predecessors.

Such thoughts, such feelings and values cannot grow in the soul of the Russian peasant. The boundless plains on which the wooden, thatch-roofed villages crowd together have the poisonous peculiarity of emptying a man, of sucking dry his desires. The peasant has only to go out past the bounds of the village and look at the emptiness around him to feel in a short time that this emptiness is creeping into his very soul. Nowhere around can one see the results of creative labour. The estates of the landowners? But they are few and inhabited by enemies. The towns? But they are far and not much more cultured than the village. Round about lie endless plains and in the centre of them, insignificant tiny man abandoned on this dull earth for penal labour. And man is filled with the feeling of indifference killing his ability to think, to remember his past, to work out his ideas from experience. A historian of Russian culture, characterizing the peasantry, said of it 'a host of superstitions, and no ideas whatsoever'. This judgement is backed up by all the Russian folklore. [. . .]

The technically primitive labour of the countryside is incredibly heavy, the peasantry call it *strada* from the Russian verb *stradat* – to suffer. The burden of the work, linked to the insignificance of its results, deepens in the peasant the instinct of property, making him unresponsive to those views which place at the root of the sinfulness of man that very instinct. [. . .]

Even the memories of Pugachev [the leader of the major and most recent peasant-cossack rebellion] did not remain bright within the peasantry and memories of other less significant political achievements of the Russian people similarly faded.

It can be said about all this, in the words of a historian of the 'Time of Troubles' in Russian history, '. . . all these rebellions changed nothing, brought nothing new into the mechanism of the state, into the structure of understanding, into customs and inclinations . . .'.

To this judgement it is appropriate to add the conclusion of a foreigner who had closely observed the Russian people: 'This people has no historical memory. It does not know its past and even acts as if it does not want to know it.' [. . .]

But where is the good-natured, thoughtful Russian peasant, indefatigable searcher after truth and justice, who was so convincingly and beautifully depicted in the world of nineteenth-century Russian literature?

In my youth I searched for such a man across the Russian countryside and did not find him. I met there instead a tough, cunning realist who, when it was favourable to him, knew quite well how to make himself out as a simpleton. By nature the peasant is not stupid and knows it well. He has composed a multitude of wistful songs and rough, cruel stories, created thousands of proverbs embodying the experience of his difficult life.

He knows that 'The peasant is not stupid, it is the world which is the fool' and that 'The community [*mir*] is as powerful as water and as stupid as a pig'. He says 'Do not fear devils, fear people',

'Beat your own kind and then strangers will fear you.' He holds no high opinion of truth, 'Truth will not feed you', 'What is wrong with a lie if it makes you live well?' 'A truthful man is like a fool, both are harmful.' [. . .]

Those who took on themselves the bitter Herculean work of cleaning the Augean stables of Russian life I cannot consider 'tormentors of the people', from my point of view they are rather victims.

I say this from a strong conviction, based on experience, that the whole of the Russian intelligentsia for almost an entire century courageously tried to lift on to its feet the heavy Russian people lazily, carelessly, incapably slumped on its land – the entire intelligentsia is the victim of the historical backwardness of the people, which managed to live unbelievably wretchedly on a land of fairytale richness. The Russian peasant, whose common sense has now been awakened by the revolution, could say of its intelligentsia: 'stupid like the sun, works just as selflessly'.

[And in the future]. . . . The half-savage, stupid, heavy people of the Russian village and all those almost frightening people spoken of earlier, will die out and will be replaced by a new breed, a literate, reasonable, cheerful people. To my mind this will not mean a very 'nice and likeable Russian people' but will be at last a businesslike people, mistrustful and indifferent towards everything that does not directly bear on its needs. [. . .]

The town, the unquenchable fire of all pioneering thoughts, spring of irritating, not always comprehensible, events, will not quickly gain its just appreciation on the part of this man. He will not quickly understand it as a workshop, constantly producing new ideas, machines, goods, the aim of which is to brighten and beautify the life of the people.

Frantz Fanon

The Revolutionary Proletariat of our Times

Excerpts from Frantz Fanon, *The Wretched of the Earth*, Penguin Books, 1967, pp. 47–101, translated by Constance Farrington. First published in 1961.

The peasantry is systematically disregarded for the most part by the propaganda put out by the nationalist parties. And it is clear that in the colonial countries the peasants alone are revolutionary, for they have nothing to lose and everything to gain. The starving peasant, outside the class system, is the first among the exploited to discover that only violence pays. For him there is no compromise, no possible coming to terms; colonization and decolonization are simply a question of relative strength. [. . .]

The history of middle-class and working-class revolutions [in the West] has shown that the bulk of the peasants often constitutes a brake on the revolution. Generally in industrialized countries the peasantry as a whole are the least aware, the worst organized and at the same time the most anarchical element. They show a whole range of characteristics – individualism, lack of discipline, liking for money and propensities towards waves of uncontrollable rage and deep discouragement which define a line of behaviour that is objectively reactionary.

We have seen that the nationalist parties copy their methods from those of the Western political parties; and also, for the most part, that they do not direct their propaganda towards the rural masses. In fact, if a reasoned analysis of colonized society had been made, it would have shown them that the native peasantry lives against a background of tradition, where the traditional structure of society has remained intact, whereas in the industrialized countries it is just this traditional setting which has been broken up by the progress of industrialization. In the colonies, it is at the very core of the embryonic working class that you find individual behaviour. The landless peasants, who make up the *lumpen-proletariat*, leave the country districts, where vital statistics are just so many insoluble problems, rush towards the towns, crowd into tin-shack settlements, and try to make their way into the ports and cities founded by colonial domination. The bulk of the country people for their part continue to live within a rigid framework, and the extra mouths to feed have no other alternative than to emigrate towards the centres of population. The peasant who stays put defends his traditions stubbornly, and in a colonized society stands for the disciplined element whose interests lie in maintaining the social structure. It is true that this unchanging way of life, which hangs on like grim death to rigid social structures, may occasionally give birth to movements which are based on religious fanaticism or tribal wars. But in their spontaneous movements the country people as a whole remain disciplined and altruistic. The individual stands aside in favour of the community.

The country people are suspicious of the townsman. The latter dresses like a European; he speak the European's language, works with him, sometimes even lives in the same district; so he is considered by the peasants as a turncoat who has betrayed everything that goes to make up the national heritage. The townspeople are 'traitors and knaves' who seem to get on well with the occupying powers, and do their best to get on within the framework of the colonial system. This is why you often hear the country people say of town-dwellers that they have no morals. Here, we are not dealing with the old antagonism between town and country; it is the antagonism which exists between the native who is excluded from the advantages of colonialism and his counterpart who manages to turn colonial exploitation to his account.[. . .]

The militants fall back towards the countryside and the mountains, towards the peasant people. From the beginning, the peasantry closes in around them, and protects them from being pursued by the police. The militant nationalist who decides to throw in his lot with the country people instead of playing at hide-and-seek with the police in urban centres will lose nothing. The peasant's cloak will wrap him around with a gentleness and firmness that he never suspected. These men, who are in fact exiled to the backwoods, who are cut off from the urban background against which they had defined their ideas of the nation and of the political fight, these men have in fact become 'Maquisards'. Since they are obliged to move about the whole time in order to escape from the police, often at night so as not to attract attention, they will have good reason to wander through their country and to get to know it. The cafés are forgotten; so are the arguments about the next elections or the spitefulness of some policeman or other. Their ears hear the true voice of the country, and their eyes take in the great and infinite poverty of their people. They realize the precious time that has been wasted in useless commentaries upon the colonial regime. They finally come to understand that the change-over will not be a reform, nor a bettering of things. They come to understand, with a sort of bewilderment that will from henceforth never quite leave them, that political action in the towns will always be powerless to modify or overthrow the colonial regime.

These men get used to talking to the peasants. They discover that the mass of the country people have never ceased to think of the problem of their liberation except in terms of violence, in terms of taking back the land from the foreigners, in terms of national struggle, and of armed insurrection. It is all very simple. These men discover a coherent people who go on living, as it were, statically, but who keep their moral values and their devotion to the nation intact. They discover a people that is generous, ready to sacrifice themselves completely, an impatient people, with a stony pride. It is understandable that the meeting between these militants with the police on their track and these mettlesome masses of people, who are rebels by instinct, can produce an explosive mixture of unusual potentiality.

Julius K. Nyerere

Those Who Pay the Bill

Excerpt from Julius K. Nyerere, 'The Arusha Declaration',
Freedom and Socialism: Uhuru na Ujamaa, Oxford University
Press, 1968p, p. 242–3.

Our emphasis on money and industries has made us concentrate on urban development. We recognize that we do not have enough money to bring the kind of development to each village which would benefit everybody. We also know that we cannot establish an industry in each village and through this means effect a rise in the real incomes of the people. For these reasons we spend most of our money in the urban areas and our industries are established in the towns.

Yet the greater part of this money that we spend in the towns comes from loans. Whether it is used to build schools, hospitals, houses or factories, etc., it still has to be repaid. But it is obvious that it cannot be repaid just out of money obtained from urban and industrial development. To repay the loans we have to use foreign currency which is obtained from the sale of our exports. But we do not now sell our industrial products in foreign markets, and indeed it is likely to be a long time before our industries produce for export. The main aim of our new industries is 'import substitution' – that is, to produce things which up to now we have had to import from foreign countries.

It is therefore obvious that the foreign currency we shall use to pay back the loans used in the development of the urban areas will not come from the towns or the industries. Where, then, shall we get it from? We shall get it from the villages and from agriculture. What does this mean? It means that the people who benefit directly from development which is brought about by borrowed money are not the ones who will repay the loans. The largest proportion of the loans will be spent in, or for, the urban areas, but the largest proportion of the repayment will be made through the efforts of the farmers.

This fact should always be borne in mind, for there are various forms of exploitation. We must not forget that people who live in towns can possibly become the exploiters of those who live in the rural areas. All our big hospitals are in towns and they benefit only a small section of the people of Tanzania. Yet if we have built them with loans from outside Tanzania, it is the overseas sale of the peasants' produce which provides the foreign exchange for repayment. Those who do not get the benefit of the hospitals thus carry the major responsibility for paying for them. Tarmac roads, too, are mostly found in towns and are of especial value to the motor-car owners. Yet if we have built those roads with loans, it is again the farmer who produces the goods which will pay for them. What is more, the foreign exchange with which the car was bought also came from the sale of the farmers' produce. Again, electric lights, water pipes, hotels and other aspects of modern development are mostly found in towns. Most of them have been built with loans and most of them do not benefit the farmer directly, although they will be paid for by the foreign exchange earned by the sale of his produce. We should always bear this in mind.

Although when we talk of exploitation we usually think of capitalists, we should not forget that there are many fish in the sea. They eat each other. The large ones eat the small ones, and the small ones eat those who are even smaller. There are two possible ways of dividing the people in our country. We can put the capitalists and feudalists on one side, and the farmers and workers on the other. But we can also divide the people into urban dwellers on one side and those who live in the rural areas on the other. If we are not careful we might get to the position where the real exploitation in Tanzania is that of the town dwellers exploiting the peasants.

26 R. P. Dore

Land Reform and Japan's Economic Development –
A Reactionary Thesis

R. P. Dore, 'Land reform and Japan's economic development',
Developing Economies, Special Issue, vol. 3, 1965, no. 4, pp. 487–96.

There is general agreement among the students of Japan's economic development that agriculture's contribution to the task of building a strong industrial base was a considerable one. It provided export earnings and import substitutes which helped in acquiring the machinery and raw materials which had to be bought abroad. It managed a steady expansion of the supply of staple foods which enabled a growing town population to be fed reasonably cheap food. It contributed through the land tax a substantial portion of the funds which provided the infrastructure of communications, government and education, and through the profits of the landlords some of the capital which developed especially the small industries. And it was in part a growth in productivity which made this 'squeeze' possible without such a drastic lowering of rural living standards as to cause uncontrollable political instability.

Was this in part because of, or in spite of, the nature of the land tenure system? It has by now become a truism that one important factor determining the productivity of agriculture is the system of property institutions under which land is owned and used. The question which naturally arises, therefore, is this: granted that agriculture made a substantial contribution to Japan's economic growth, was it the best that it could have made? Or is it possible that under a different land tenure system it could have done more?

This question, like all the other 'if' questions about human history, can only be answered by guesses derived from comparison with other countries. For such comparisons it is useful to have a typology. The one I suggest below has no particular merit except that it seems to be applicable to a variety of situations and is a handy basis for generalization.

The typology is little more than a distinction between two types of land reforms based on the kind of landlord whose power and property is affected. The key is therefore the definition of the two types of landlord. The first is typically one who acquires control of a territory by military conquest or by infeudation – being allocated territory by a warrior chief who thereby secures his allegiance. At first he is lord and master in every sense; he draws produce from the cultivator by virtue of his monopoly of violence; political control and economic exploitation are one and indivisible and there is no conceptual distinction between rents and taxes.

At a later stage of development the autonomy and arbitrariness of his political power may become circumscribed by the development of a central state authority. The central government may claim the sole right to tax and the former feudal magnate now only draws a rent. He may still, however, exercise political power in his hereditary fief by ascriptive right, though he may exercise it through delegates, he himself living in the central capital and only occasionally visiting his estates for supervisory or ceremonial purposes.

The second type of landlord is characteristically one who achieves his position by *economic* means within the framework of a system of established political order; not by warfare or that milder type of warfare that is politics. Sometimes he is a merchant, sometimes a thrifty farmer who acquires land from the improvidence or misfortunes of others, sometimes a money-lender. He may also exercise some political power, but it is power exercised through the framework of a system of government in which he has no ascriptive right, only the power of manipulation gained by virtue of his superior wealth. Such landlords have smaller estates than the first kind, and they generally live near the land they own. They may, in Marxist terms, act as the rural wing of the bourgeoisie, a conservative political force which gains advantages for itself from contacts with the urban politicians, and provides the latter with a necessary basis of support in proto-democratic systems. They are not necessarily obstacles to all economic progress and can in some cases serve as the agents of economic development.

The next distinction follows logically from the first. What will be called a Stage I redistribution is one which expropriates, or in some way drastically reduces the power of, Type I landlords. A Stage II land redistribution is one which expropriates or weakens the second type of landlord.

For some countries the classification seems clearly apposite. One can pinpoint the two distinct historical events representing the two stages of land reform. In Czechoslovakia, Yugoslavia and other countries of the old Austro-Hungarian Empire the land reforms which took place after the First World War were Stage I reforms; those which came after the Second World War were Stage II reforms. In Russia one may take the land redistribution following the revolution as the first stage, and collectivization, destroying the power of the *kulaks*, as the second. There are other countries such as England where there has been no first-stage reform and where the Type I landlords have never disappeared. Their local political power has been whittled away to the point where only in the more remote areas of rural Scotland can the scions of noble families, such as Lord Home, claim a parliamentary seat almost as a hereditary right. Their economic hold over the land remains, however, though it is in no sense different from that of the Type II landlords – those who acquired their land by economic means, often by investing in small estates the profits derived from industry and commerce. (Already by the sixteenth century it is difficult to separate the two types of landlords, as witness the historians' disputes about the rise or fall of the 'gentry' or the 'aristocracy'.)

France, by contrast, quite clearly had a Stage I redistribution in the celebrated events which took place in 1789, but in neither France nor England has a Stage II redistribution taken place. Instead, in both countries, the Type II landlords who supported the bourgeois regimes of the nineteenth century were forced, as their political power waned, to accept tenancy reforms which redistributed income without redistributing the ownership of land. In these countries, and in England especially, industrialization *before* population growth created serious pressure on the land, and the ability of landlords to accept gradual reform (if only because they had already acquired substantial industrial interests too) has created a situation where the entrepreneurial tenant can be counted as a member of the prosperous middle class. In Ireland, on the other hand, greater population pressure, greater tenant distress and a more intransigent unwillingness of landlords to accept reform led, not to evolution, but to drastic changes which saw the virtual elimination of the Type I landlords in the space of a decade.

Again, there are countries where a first-stage land reform has only recently been carried out; India, for example, where the removal of the *jagadirs* and *zemindars* did not immediately affect the Type II landlords, and Iran where only the holders of whole villages were affected by the original land reform measure.

A new phenomenon in the modern world, however, is the accelerated spread of communications, education and political consciousness, one of the results of which is that the political demand for land reform can become irresistible in countries which are otherwise at a level of economic development at which, a century ago, effectively organized popular political demands of any kind would have been unthinkable. Hence the strong political pressure for a Stage II land reform in India, only a decade or so after the first. Hence the second wave of land reforms in Iran which is aimed, two years after the first, at the estates of the smaller landlords. Hence, too, countries where the land reform which has taken place has been in effect a telescoped Stage I plus Stage II operation, jumping from a structure of large 'feudal' holdings to atomized peasant proprietorship. Bolivia is an outstanding recent example.

If the reader still thinks that the typology has any validity he will have no doubt where to fit Japan into the picture. The Meiji Restoration and the creation of a centralized system of government dispossessed (though with handsome compensation) Japan's Type I landlords, the *diamio*. They remained wealthy, but their wealth was no longer in landed property. They almost entirely lost local political influence and became a metropolitan aristocracy, and although they were granted, to be sure, a place in the political system in the House of Peers, at no time was the House of Peers at the centre of political power.

This fact in itself was of considerable importance for Japan's industrialization. Those who controlled policy after the Meiji Restoration were not landed gentlemen but members of a bureaucracy who depended for their income on their salaries, and on the less formal income channels provided by their more or less corrupt relations with the new industrial class. They had, therefore, no personal interest in protecting agricultural incomes at the cost of slowing the growth of industry. They could, and did, maintain a high level of taxation on agriculture. There is a marked contrast here with the situation in, say, England, where the landed aristocracy, with strong personal agricultural interests, maintained their political influence until a relatively advanced stage of industrial development. It was not until the middle of the nineteenth century that the repeal of the Corn Laws marked the final emergence to political supremacy of industrial interests. Similarly, in a good many Latin American countries today the continued political power of a traditional landlord class (fortified by those who have urban wealth back into the purchase of landed estates and adopted traditional values) remains an obstacle to serious industrial development.

The removal of the *daimio* left a clear field for the Type II landlords, those smaller village landlords who had been acquiring control over land by economic means in the latter half of the Tokugawa period. The first decades of the new regime saw an extension of their power; various factors, but especially the operation of the new tax system, increased the amount of land which such landlords controlled, from about 30 to about 45 per cent of the total. They remained the dominant economic and political influence in the countryside until Japan's Stage II land reform put them out of business in 1947–49.

No one can seriously doubt that the Stage I land reform represented by the dispossession of the *daimio* was an essential pre-condition for Japan's development. The question whether or not the land tenure system after 1870 was the best one to promote that development resolves itself, therefore, into the question: could the Stage II land reform with advantage have come earlier?

Supposing that the Meiji government had insisted that the land certificates issued in the 1870s should always be given to the actual cultivator and that all other claims and liens should be ignored or compensated for; and supposing that it had set rigid limits to the area of land which any family might subsequently acquire by purchase; supposing, in other words, that the Stage I and Stage II land reforms had been telescoped into one, thus establishing immediately a small peasant holding system; would the growth of agricultural productivity have been faster, or agriculture's contribution to economic development in general greater?

There are some good grounds for answering 'no'. One might list them as follows:

1. These landlords were village landlords, themselves often farmers, with an understanding of agriculture and personal motives for improving their tenants' standards of husbandry. (Though rents were generally fixed rents, in produce, the tradition of rent reductions in years of bad harvest preserved elements of a share system.) Many of them, through experience as village headmen and contact with the *samurai* class, had developed Confucian ideas of paternal responsibility which meant that their economic interests were sometimes reinforced by a sense of moral duty to improve their tenants' production methods for the latter's own good. As a consequence they had the *motive* to use their economically-based political control of village society to improve agriculture.[1]

2. Secondly, they also were in a better position than other villagers to have the *knowledge* to do so. Being richer they had more leisure and travelled more. They brought their brides from further afield and consequently had wider kinship connexions. They could afford education and were sometimes the only literate

1. The literature available in English reflects only a fraction of the information available in the works of Japanese scholars, but a good general idea of the development of agriculture in Japan, and in particular of the role of the landlords, may be gained from the following: Dore (1959), Dore (1960), Johnston (1962), Nakamura (1965), Ogura (1963), Ohkawa and Rosovsky (1960), Sawada (1965) and Smith (1956).

members of their village. They were consequently in a better position to learn of superior methods practised elsewhere and to keep in touch with the national centres of technical innovation – as well as sometimes being inventors and experimenters themselves.

3. Many of the productive innovations in agriculture in this period required the creation of new formal organizations. Consolidated schemes for the reorganization of field sizes, irrigation and drainage systems certainly did. So did the creation of new marketing channels, of incentive-creating shows and competitions, of the primitive travelling-lecturer system of agricultural extension, and so on. Such organizations could be created much more easily in an authoritarian manner by use of the landlord's traditional power than they could have been if it had been necessary to persuade the majority of the villagers to come together to form such organizations on a footing of equality in a democratic manner.

4. The landlords' role as links in a communication system joining the villages to the centre of government was important for more than just the diffusion of agricultural improvements. They were interpreters of government policies without whom there might have been far more peasant uprisings and general political unrest that there in fact was. At the same time their own political ambitions forced the creation of local government systems which could be gradually expanded to meet increasing demands for political participation, whereas if there had been no landlord class to make demands which were of a nature moderate enough to be acceptable with modifications to the ruling Tokyo oligarchy, concessions might have been delayed and really revolutionary forces built up which might have destroyed the whole structure of administration. The landlords were particularly important as interpreters of the government's educational policy and often played a leading part in the building and expansion of schools. As village landlords they sent their own children to the village schools, and hence had a direct interest in them. Even when they became absentees, for one or two generations they maintained close links with their village, and the desire to maintain the 'prestige of the house' in the village where the family land

and graves were, prompted many of them not to begrudge taxes and contributions for village schools and public works.

5. The landlords commanded the 'agricultural surplus'. In their hands it was more effectively taxable. Moreover, many of them used their wealth in productive ways – in the education of their children and in investment in food-processing and other local industries. If this wealth had not been squeezed out of their tenants it would have been used for direct consumption; the overall rate of savings would have been lower and economic development slower.

6. By analogy one might argue from situations such as Bolivia where a telescope State I/Stage II land reform left the villages without small landlords and without a structure of local leadership, and where there seems to have been not only no economic development but in fact a decline in production, and administrative anarchy.

As against these, one might set the following arguments for the contrary point of view:

1. The landlords may have brought new ideas and techniques to the villages, but this advantage was cancelled out by the well-known drawbacks of a tenancy system; the fact that tenants, with only insecure tenure, had no motive for carrying out improvements with long-term effects, and the fact that the burden of rents kept them so poor that they could not afford the kind of investment in, for instance, fertilizers, which was most capable of bringing big increases in production.

2. It is debatable whether the tradition-sanctioned authority of the landlords was a necessary condition for creating the organizational structure necessary to improve agricultural practices. The tradition of village co-operation between equals is an old one in Japanese rural areas. There were villages, particularly in the commercially more developed areas of central Japan from Gifu to Hiroshima, where landlord influence was less strong and a more egalitarian type of village structure prevailed. These areas were not notably slow in developing the co-operative organization required for agricultural development, and there is no reason to

suppose that the more authoritarian villages could not have adapted to more egalitarian forms if the influence of the landlords was removed – as in fact they did after 1950.

3. The landlords may have invested some of the income they squeezed out of their tenants in productive ways, but they also consumed conspicuously, to some extent in luxury imported goods. If there had been greater equality of village incomes there might not have been as much local investment in commerce and industry, but there would have been a quicker and wider diffusion of popular education. Many more villagers might have sent their children to school for, say, six years instead of four.

4. The pre-emption of local formal political authority by the landlords was a loss, not a gain, for agriculture. As soon as they were allowed representation in the national Diet their main interest was directed towards reducing their tax burden. This pressure on the national budget slowed the growth of agricultural research and extension services and of the developmental subsidy system. If the voice of the villages in the Diet had been the voice of practising farmers these things would not have been neglected.

5. The 'political stability' of the countryside ensured by the landlords' power was also a loss rather than a gain. If the demand for political participation had built up to revolutionary proportions before concessions were contemplated and a real revolution had taken place, there might earlier have emerged a democratic political system with a government really devoted to the cause of popular welfare.

It is impossible to reach any definite conclusions on this matter. On balance it seems difficult to believe, given the level of violence associated even with middle-class politics and even in the 1920s and 1930s, that a regime of any stability or any power to plan economic development could have emerged from a successful popular revolution at any time in the Meiji period. It equally seems difficult to believe that organizational and technical innovation in the villages could have proceeded as fast without the backing of traditional landlord authority. I am inclined to believe that economic development would have been slower if there had been a Stage II land reform at any time before, say, 1900.

But the situation was already different by 1920. By then most farmers were literate and more capable both of informing themselves individually about new agricultural methods and of forming the organizations necessary to put them into practice. (As Galbraith, 1963, has recently said, 'Nowhere in the world is there an illiterate peasantry that is progressive. Nowhere is there a literate peasantry that is not.') More important, if the landlord's traditional authority *had* been put to productive purposes in the Meiji period, this was only because that authority was *accepted* by the tenants. By 1920 tenants were beginning to lose their deferential submissiveness – as the growing number of disputes over rents and the formation of tenant unions testify. Hence, by this time, the advantages of landlord control had all but disappeared. Only the disadvantages of poor incentives and tenant poverty remained. A Stage II reform at any time after 1920 would probably have hastened economic development, as well as conducing to a more satisfactory internal political structure (more satisfactory by our present-day values) and possibly modifying Japanese external policies as well.

There are two further comments worth making on this issue. The first concerns the evaluative implications of the fact – if it is a fact – that the Meiji landlords contributed to the cause of Japanese economic development. Japanese historians are inclined to write of the landlord system in the Meiji period as a social evil. In part this is a back-projection into the past of judgements about recent situations, but in so far as this is not the case, what would they make of the assertion that on balance economic development took place more rapidly with landlords than it would have done without them? One answer, which would probably be favoured by the majority, is that the assertion is wrong and that my summary of the balance between the two sets of arguments is at fault. There is, however, another answer. One can accept the assumption and still argue that a Stage II land reform was desirable at a very early stage. It may be granted that the landlords helped to hasten the pace of economic development, but this was done at the expense of miserable poverty on the part of tenants, and at the cost of preserving a system of social relations in the villages which was an affront to human dignity. It would have been better, it can be argued, to have improved the lot of the Meiji tenant even if this meant a slower pace of economic growth; even if it meant postponing the arrival of television sets in the villages from 1960 to 1980, to the generation of those tenants' great-grandchildren rather than their grandchildren. This is a perfectly valid argument. Economic growth is not the only end in life. Just how much sacrifice of personal welfare by the present generation is justified by how much improved welfare for future generations is a difficult value question which every development planner must face.

The second comment is this: none should try, without very drastic modifications, to draw from the history of Meiji Japan the conclusion that a small village landlord system is a beneficial factor in the initial stages of economic growth and seek to apply this as a 'lesson' to the situation of the developing countries today. It is inappropriate as a lesson from many points of view. The population growth rate in most of the developing countries is much higher than it was in Meiji Japan, thus adding a new dimension to the problem of rural development. Communications techniques have improved considerably, making less necessary the informal intermediate policy-interpreting function of the Meiji landlord. Many countries have less need to squeeze industrial capital out of the traditional agricultural sector, because of mineral revenues, foreign aid or the taxation of agricultural exports produced by capitalist plantations. Above all, the political revolution of the twentieth century – the new assumption that all governments ought to derive their power from electoral consent – together with the development of mass media in even poor countries, has created a political demand for land reform even in economies which are characterized by an almost wholly subsistence agriculture. What this means is that the traditional *acceptance* of landlord authority – a necessary condition for landlords to play the kind of useful role they played in Meiji Japan – has already been destroyed. Social relations in the villages have often reached a level of conflict similar to that of Japan in the 1920s, even though agricultural development may remain at Japan's 1870 level.

The trouble with these 'if' questions about history is not only that one can rarely arrive at satisfying answers. Even if one gets an answer it is rare that one can draw any simple 'lessons' from it for the solution of contemporary problems. For if there are some senses in which the countries of the world are moving in different directions – the poor perhaps getting relatively poorer and the rich relatively richer – there are other ways – in the accumulating stock of scientific knowledge and political ideas – in which the world as a whole moves on.

References

DORE, R. P. (1959), 'The Japanese landlord: good or bad?', *J. Asian Studies*, vol. 18, no. 2.

DORE, R. P. (1960), 'Agricultural improvement in Japan:1870–1900', *Econ. Devel. cult. Change*, October, part 2.

GALBRAITH, J. K. (1963), *Economic Development in Perspective*, Harvard University Press.

JOHNSTON, B. F. (1962), 'Agricultural development and economic transformation: a comparative study of the Japanese experience', *Food Res. Instit. Studies*, vol. 3, no. 3.

NAKAMURA, J. I. (1965), 'The growth of Japanese agriculture: 1875–1920', in W. W. Lockwood (ed.), *The State and Economic Enterprise in Modern Japan*, Princeton University Press.

OGURA, T. (1963), *Agricultural Development in Modern Japan*, Japan FAO Association.

OHKAWA, M., and ROSOVSKY, H. (1960), 'The role of agriculture in modern Japanese economic development', *Econ. Devel. cult. Change*, vol. 9, no. 1, pp. 43–67.

SAWADA, S. (1965), 'Innovation in Japanese agriculture', in W. W. Lockwood (ed.), *The State and Economic Enterprise in Modern Japan*, Japan FAO Association.

SMITH, T. C. (1956), 'Landlords and rural capitalists in the modernization of Japan', *J. econ. Hist.*, June.

27 Gerrit Huizer

Community Development, Land Reform and
Political Participation

Gerrit Huizer,[1] 'Community development, land reform and political
participation', *American Journal of Economics and Sociology*, vol. 28,
1969, no. 2, pp. 159–78.

The need to link community development programs with such
larger development measures as agrarian reform has been
stressed by the United Nations many times in the last few years
(United Nations, 1963a, para. 53; UN Economic and Social
Council, 1960, paras. 37–43; UN Food and Agricultural Organization, 1966, ch. 6). One reason is that it has become increasingly
obvious that community development programs often do not
have the desired success because of unresolved land tenure problems which, since they are regarded as fundamental by most
peasants, keep them from having confidence in and fully participating in government action (well intentioned as it may be).
'There are exceptions to this rule of course, but *latifundismo* (the
large estate system) is almost everywhere recognized to be not
only an economic problem but also a hindrance to community
development' (Gillin, 1949, pp. 182ff.). The effect of a static semi-
feudal social structure on people is recognized by social anthropologists as well as pragmatic agricultural technicians (see
Leonholdt, 1953, p. 7).

The author of this paper found confirmation of the fact when
he did village-level work in the Valle de la Esperanza in El Salvador in 1955, where he helped in the work of a sanitary drinking
water project and road improvement. The Valle de la Esperanza
is well known for its semi-feudal social structure (Adams, 1957,
p. 431). The adverse effects of this structure circumscribe efforts to
organize community activities.

Both the sanitation and road-improvement projects appeared

1. Although the author of this paper is employed by an agency of the
United Nations, the opinions expressed in it are personal and do not necessarily coincide with views officially held by the UN.

to be ideal community development efforts since they corresponded with strongly felt needs of the villagers who had to get water from contaminated wells some distance away and who suffered also when the rainy season made it difficult to reach even the nearest towns. In addition, both projects looked ideal with regard to contributions from the government. For the sanitary drinking water system several kilometers of pipes were being supplied by the government. The latter was also contributing technical supervision and help in collecting the water at a well in the nearby mountains. The villagers only had to contribute manual labor which, because of chronic underemployment in rural El Salvador, was abundantly available. A similar arrangement was offered for the road work. Initially the villagers did not respond actively, however.

Only after living in the community for several months (see Huizer, 1963, pp. 161ff.; 1965a; 1965b), and only after the people's confidence had been gained, did the author discover some of the factors that prevented their wholehearted participation in those useful projects.

The most striking factor certainly was distrust. Once a confidential relationship with the villagers had been established, they revealed their strong conviction that the sanitation project would not benefit them but would rather serve the local large landholder, whose big house was not far from the center of the village. In their experience, government employees and landlords always organized such things together. The people also resented having to work without pay while the officials who made them do so earned (compared with a rural day laborer) relatively high salaries. Most of these officials are, moreover, known to enjoy additional incomes as absentee landowners. Along with all these factors was the further one of those government agents (mostly engineers, but including the social educator who was an ex-Army major) treating the villagers, not as responsible citizens whose collaboration was sought with reasonable arguments, but as inferior beings who were merely to be told what they should do. This attitude was strongly resented by the villagers, but since no open opposition was tolerated, people withdrew in silence and simply did not show up for work.

The spirit of distrust and resentment was expressedly related to such past experiences as the bloody repression of a peasant revolt in 1932, still well remembered in 1955, although rarely mentioned and then only in a low voice at somebody's home.[2] It was said that thousands of peasants had been killed in those days and that since then public gatherings of more than five peasants were not allowed.[3] It is known that the formation of peasants' organizations in El Salvador is legally forbidden (Ambrosini, 1954, p. 16; Marroquín, 1959, pp. 371ff.). The terror still existing in rural areas could often be verified by the author when quiet, leisurely gatherings of people in the center of the village suddenly dispersed if a boy came running up to announce that a patrol of the national guards was approaching the village.

It will be clear that in this kind of authoritarian social climate to create an atmosphere favorable to voluntary cooperation is very difficult. 'When a village is differentiated in this way by divergence of economic interest, the general body of villagers may not be motivated to give free labor for the benefit of the privileged minority' (United Nations, 1963a, para. 105) and such is the case in many Latin American villages.

Distrust and suspicion were also the first responses encountered by agricultural extension students in the region of Turrialba in Costa Rica when they were sent into the villages to study the effectiveness of extension agencies there (Loomis *et al.*, 1953, p. 206). The directors of the study noted the importance of the attitude of the extension worker in overcoming such distrust, but they did not indicate much about the reasons for such distrust and its relation to the 'stratification in a class-system' which they found (by means of sociometric techniques) to exist in some of the villages (ibid., p. 48ff.).[4] In this respect the great advantages

2. Alejandro Dagoberto Marroquín indicated that in Panchimalco, the village in El Salvador which he studied in 1958, the same fear of the authorities existed (1959, pp. 324, 346 ff.).

3. According to Sergio Maturana (1963, p. 51) 17,000 peasants were killed in this repression. See also Marroquín (1959, p. 324).

4. The land tenure situation in Costa Rica has been characterized as follows: 'Even though Costa Rica is mentioned at times as a nation of small farmers, 9 per cent of its farms account for 71 per cent of the cultivated land' (Jones, 1962, p. 13).

of 'participant observation' and 'participant intervention' (Holmberg, 1955, pp. 23–6; Huizer, 1965a) as research techniques for discovering the deeper motivations may be stressed.

Among peasants in Southern Italy, a region that has much in common with Latin America, the author observed the same distrust and suspicion (Huizer, 1962). By way of an explanation for this situation, Edward Banfield speaks of what he calls 'amoral familism'.[5] Because of the predominance of a mentality which leads to 'political incapacity' (Banfield, 1958, p. 31) Banfield sees few chances for successful community development programs in Southern Italy (ibid., pp. 175ff.). Unfortunately he does not make clear statements regarding the causes of this 'amoral familism', nor suggestions for improvement in this respect. Some experimenting proved, however, that although 'amoral familism' was deeply rooted in Sicily, as well as in El Salvador, certain common undertakings could be organized in both places. It became clear that the 'political incapacity' of the peasants was related to the authoritarian and oppressive social climate and thus can be changed under proper circumstances. The slow but continuous growth of peasant organizations, although faced with violent action by the Mafia, which has killed thirty-three of the most vigorous peasant leaders since 1954, indicates that the situation is not as hopeless as Banfield suggests.[6]

Some experiments in which land reform measures have improved the social climate and thus created a favorable condition for co-operative effort and community development are described below.

In El Salvador the author became acquainted with one of the 'Fincas de Beneficio Proporcional' of the Instituto de Colonización Rural.[7] These are projects for resettling landless peasants on

5. Edward Banfield (1958, p. 85). In this work he indicates that the mentality of an 'amoral familist' is: 'Maximize the material, short-run advantage of the nuclear family; assume that all others will do likewise.'

6. For a description of the problems encountered when trying to stimulate development program in Sicily, see also Danilo Dolci (1960, 1963).

7. It is interesting to note that Maturana (1963, p. 51) sees a relationship between the creation of this institute and the peasant revolt that took place in 1932.

land belonging to the government, a sort of collective farm, managed initially by employees of the Institute but destined to be taken over eventually by the peasants themselves. Successful community development efforts have been carried out in this new, small settlement village. It was noted by the United Nations that this experiment was too limited and that any enlargement would probably find resistance from the large landowner class of El Salvador (Leonholdt, 1953, p. 57). It was also noted by the United Nations that: 'A common danger in the use of pilot projects is that of over-investment of personnel and funds to the extent that projects could not possibly be duplicated on a national scale' (United Nations, 1963a, para. 49).

Another rather small-scale but scientifically well-controlled experiment of the same sort has been carried out in the former *hacienda* (estate) Vicos in Peru, under the direction of social anthropologists and other technicians from Cornell University. Vicos, a rather typical Peruvian *hacienda* with about 300 Quechua-speaking Indian families attached to the land (but owning none of it), was taken over by the study group in 1952. At that time 'standards of living were at a bare minimum. Health and nutritional levels were extremely low. Educational facilities were almost completely lacking. Cooperation within the community was the exception rather than the rule, and resistance to the outside world was high. Attitudes toward life were static and pessimistic' (Holmberg, 1961, pp. 80–81; Vázquez, 1962). The purpose of the experiment was that of 'developing within the community independent and dynamic problem-solving and decision-making organizations which could gradually assume the responsibilities of leadership in public affairs in a rational and humane manner and along democratic lines' (Holmberg, 1961, p. 83). Many of the traditional abuses of the *hacienda* system were abolished and a new type of relationship, based on the principles of friendship and respect for human dignity, was created (Vázquez, 1962, p. 301). The inhabitants were also helped to improve their agriculture by means of an attractive credit system.

Between 1952 and 1957 the executive power over this *hacienda* was transferred little by little to the indigenous community.

Locally respected people were carefully selected and trained in bearing responsibility and settling conflicts. Decisions made by this group were discussed by the community as a whole. At the same time improvements in health and education were introduced and local people made responsible for such activities. The several groups organized to this effect gradually learned to assume greater responsibilities, so that in 1957 the management of the whole *hacienda* could practically be given over to an elected body of local leaders.

This case can be considered an example of slowly executed agrarian reform. The results were striking. Production of potatoes doubled between 1957 (when everything was still managed under the old system) and 1958, with only a third of the labor force working in the field. Production per man thus went up 600 per cent.

From these findings in the Vicos project, Holmberg concludes: 'While it is dangerous to draw general conclusions from a single instance of this kind, particularly one in which many intervening variables were obviously involved, nevertheless, the data from Vicos are not without theoretical significance. They tend to confirm a hypothesis long ago expressed by Marx, namely that the alienation of people from control over the means of production retards social and economic development' (1959, p. 9).

The effects of the Vicos experiment are well summarized by Harold Lasswell: 'Among the inhabitants of Vicos generations of oppression had created profound skepticism regarding the motives of any outsider, and particularly of the *padrone* (landlord). Hence the strategy of rapid intervention, and the dramatic abolition of old abuses at the very beginning of Cornell's intervention. The new revolution program was launched in a setting of surprise, incredulity, gratitude and hope' (1962, p. 117). That this drastic change of social climate in one place had a strong appeal in the surrounding region and led to unrest and awakening among the peasants and resistance from the side of the landlords who feared to lose their age-old privileges has been indicated by several anthropologists who participated in Cornell's experiment (Dobyns, Monge and Vázquez, 1962; Vázquez, 1962, p. 307).

The anthropologist Alain Dessaint, describing extensively the often socially disorganizing effects of the feudal *hacienda* and the plantation system on the indigenous population of Guatemala, notes a similar awakening influence of agrarian reform and other organizing efforts, carried out in the early fifties in Guatemala (Dessaint, 1962, p. 352). 'The period of reform, 1945–54, caused a change in the paternalistic relationship of owner toward worker, as the latter especially began to identify himself with nation-wide groups and movements' (Dessaint, 1962, p. 335).

Richard Adams also observed the influence of Guatemala's 1952–3 land redistribution measures (which were suspended in 1954[8]): 'Among its effects, the [Jacobo] Arbenz period destroyed any remnant of mutual interest between farm laborers and farm owners. The paternalism of the earlier pattern persists today mainly in the written provisions of the labor code. The farm labor groups are now acutely aware that a new type of relationship is possible between themselves and the cosmopolite local upper and middle classes. Similarly, the emergent middle mass is conscious of its own potential strength, once it has been consolidated through labor unions and similar organizations. It was the emergent middle class that generally gave dynamic impetus to the Arbenz programs' (Adams, 1961, p. 270).

The *1963 Report on the World Social Situation*, noted the 'explosive unrest in large parts of the countryside' and referring to the increasing strength of these forces remarked aptly, 'Such movements have not yet been objectively studied' (United Nations, 1964, pp. 25–6; see also Huizer, 1965b).

One of the better-known experiments in Latin America concerned with a large-scale combination of land reform, peasant organization, supervised credit and community development is the one which has been carried on since 1936 in the Comarca Lagunera, a cotton-producing region in the north of Mexico.

8. CIDA (1965, p. 45) indicates that after the change of government in 1954 most of the 100,000 peasant families who had benefited from the reform measures lost their lands again to the former large owners.

In spite of the agrarian legislation of 1917 the *hacienda* system still prevailed. The peasants, mostly workers attached to the cotton *haciendas*, were striking for better conditions and organized themselves to counteract the strike-breaking efforts by the large landholders. In 1936 these actions took such dramatic proportions that the national economy was threatened. President Lázaro Cárdenas then promised the peasants' organizations to apply Article 27 of the Mexican Constitution (concerning land reform) to the region which meant redistribution of most of the *haciendas* among peasant communities. 'It was not until the land-workers of La Laguna organized and acted for themselves that they were able to secure application of national laws to the region' (Senior, 1958, p. 66).

In order not to damage the existing production systems too much, the *haciendas* were converted into a number of collectively worked *ejidos*[9] and a number of legally allowed, maximum-size plots for the old proprietors and some of their employees.[10] The collective *ejidos* were run by the peasants and their leaders in collaboration with government technicians, especially those from the Ejido Credit Bank (Senior, 1958, p. 97). Within 45 days three-fourths of the irrigated land and one-fourth of the unirrigated but usable land in the region was turned over to 30,000 peasants organized into about 300 *ejidos*.

During the first four years after the reform, while Cárdenas was still President, great efforts were made to 'secure the participation of the *ejidatarios* themselves in all aspects of the new social structures in the region (Senior, 1958, p. 118). The organization department of the Ejido Bank, in consultation with

9. 'Land held in *ejido* tenure is the property of a town or village either for collective use or distribution among the inhabitants for cultivation in small plots, to which each individual has a right of occupancy and use so long as he keeps the land under cultivation. In colonial times villages had received grants of lands of this kind but during the nineteenth century had lost their landholdings to the owners of large estates. The restitution or grant of *ejido* land has thus involved the splitting up of the large *latifundia* and the return of the land to village ownership' (United Nations, 1954, p. 38, note 54).

10. Thus, e.g., the Tlahualilo *hacienda*, consisting of 46,630 hectares, half of which are cultivated, was divided into 13 *ejidos* and around 150 'small properties'. See Senior (1958, p. 93).

the more responsible peasant leaders, began to organize advisory committees of *ejidatarios*. Later this setup became more formalized and conventions were held in each zone of the region to elect members. Also a central committee was formed with zone delegates, each of whom was responsible for a certain field in the communities in his zone. Such fields were: education (help in building schools, help in organizing night schools, the encouragement of sports, obtaining community support for school gardens, etc.), agriculture (the stimulation, in collaboration with agronomists, of all kinds of improvements), health (the promotion of public health activities in the communities, street cleaning, etc.). It is interesting to note the participation of women, strongly encouraged by President Cárdenas, in all kinds of activities. So 'the most outstanding cooperative successes in the region have been registered by 61 women's groups, running corn-grinding machines' (ibid, p. 129).

Although the phrase 'community development' was never used, the program executed in the Laguna region may well be considered to fall within the internationally accepted definition of the phrase.[11]

The whole program was given legal status in 1939 under the name Central Union of Collective Credit Societies. 'The first flush of enthusiasm among the peasants gave a tremendous advantage to the Central Union. It seemed obvious to everyone that "one for all and all for one" was a slogan that would bring results' (Senior, 1958, pp. 124–5). But gradually the high morale of the early days declined. Personality difficulties, mistakes made during the redistribution of land, defalcations by several minor

11. 'The term "community development" has come into international usage to connote the process by which the efforts of the people themselves are united with those of governmental authorities to improve the economic, social, and cultural conditions of communities, to integrate these communities into the life of the nation and to enable them to contribute fully to national progress. This complex of processes is then made up of two essential elements: the participation of the people themselves in efforts to improve their level of living with as much reliance as possible on their own initiative; and the provision of technical and other services in ways which encourage initiative, self-help and mutual help and make these more effective. It is expressed in programs designed to achieve a wide variety of specific movements' (see United Nations, 1960b, paras. 1, 2).

officials, decreasing support from the national government during the presidential terms following that of Cárdenas, changes in the policy of the Ejido Bank (more stress on purely economic gains), several years of drought that exhausted the irrigation scheme, rivalry among peasant groups, increasing population pressure and many other factors are considered responsible for this decline. Careful evaluation of the influence of each of these factors should be undertaken. An indicator that occasionally has been used for this purpose is productivity or 'expanded output' (United Nations, 1960a, ch. 2).

While as we have seen in the Vicos case that productivity per hectare went up significantly after the reforms, the cotton yield in the Laguna region showed strong fluctuations (probably depending on the irrigation water available) both before and after the changes of 1936. The productivity of wheat per hectare declined after the first four years of the reform had passed.[12]

It has also been noted that while productivity in the *ejidal* sector of the Laguna region has fallen, it rose in the private sector.[13] Senior demonstrates that the decisive factor for this is not a constant (the *ejidal* form of agricultural organization) but great number of variables (Senior, 1958, p. 193). There are also exceptions. In some *ejidos*, like Tlahualilo, production after the reform went up steadily. Whetten sees as the two main reasons for the lack of success of most collective *ejidos:* (1) the lack of adequate local leadership, and (2) lack of discipline (1948, pp. 212–14). He also notes a tendency toward assignment of individual parcels to *ejidatarios* as a solution to the problem of low productivity. For the individually worked *ejidos* of the Bajio

12. Senior (1958, table 5, p. 71 and table 7, p. 79). He also notes, however, the 'more equal distribution of profits among resident workers', which benefits the Mexican economy, while 'formerly few individuals spent all the profits in the capitals of European countries or elsewhere' (ibid., p. 238).

13. Senior (1958, p. 189). In the Bajio region, where land reform did not promote collective *ejidos*, like in the Laguna region, but *ejidos* that were parceled out individually among *ejidatarios*, a similar fact, private farmers doing better than *ejidatarios*, has been noted by Carlos Manuel Castillo (1956, especially ch. 9). Mr Castillo also indicated many other fields, e.g. education (pp. 63 ff.), in which the *ejidatarios* are at a disadvantage, as compared with the private farmers.

region, in Central Mexico, however, Castillo distinguishes structural and functional problems in the *ejidas* organization that have much in common with the reasons for the failure of many collective *ejidos* in the Comarca Lagunera. He stresses the need for administrative efficiency and the necessity of creating instruments of collective action that help the community to solve all kinds of problems and integrate itself into the national political system, thus improving some of the aspects of the *ejido* which do not conform to modern criteria of efficiency (1956, p. 156).

He indicated as a 'structural problem' the centralized decision making by the agencies in the regions where land reform has been carried out, which creates a material and psychological climate in which both the individual *ejidatario* and the community are not capable of acting for themselves even in relatively simple situations (p. 159). The paternalistic attitude of the central organizations hinders the social evolution of the *ejidos* (p. 160).

These facts are related to the 'functional problems', especially the need to stimulate training of local leaders to organize group action and the need to spread in a more balanced way the responsibilities within the *ejidos* (p. 162).

The same thing is true of the Laguna region. Senior indicates that, notwithstanding the increased 'well-being'[14] of the peasants, especially after the initial years, 'the education of the *ejidatarios* themselves in a manner to involve in "problem solving" has been neglected in a most irresponsible manner' (1958, p. 198).

On several other occasions the paternalism of government

14. Although the United Nations' Second Report on *Progress in Land Reform* (1956, p. 135), indicates about the reforms in the Laguna district: 'the effect of these measures on the well-being of the rural population is not measurable', an attempt to evaluate this aspect with modern techniques of the social sciences may now be worthwhile. Clarence Senior, who participated many years in several projects carried out in the region, says about 'well-being': 'It is towards this goal value that the Laguna experiment has made the most progress. Much of the advance is now past quantifying. One thinks for example of numerous reports of eyewitnesses and participants in whippings of field workers only a few months before the expropriations; of houses destroyed and peons driven off *haciendas* only a few years before 1936. One remembers hundreds of meetings in which men and women vibrated with a new dignity and determination to work hard and make a success of the "land which is now ours"' (1958, p. 195).

employees and its disastrous effects on the self-help activity of people has been noted in the Laguna region (as regards self-help housing, see Kelly, 1953, p. 6). One of the explanations given by Whetten is that, because of lack of good personnel, the Ejido Bank recruited many of the former employees of the old *haciendas* (1948, p. 225). A problem related to this paternalism is the fact that some of the leaders arising from among the peasants start dominating and even exploiting their followers once they are in a position of power. This is a rather widespread but barely investigated aspect of rural life in Mexico, called *caciquismo*.

Carlos Manuel Castillo characterizes such problems and the needed processes of solution as highly political (1956, p. 160). But they certainly are at the same time a task for community development, as the United Nations has said: 'While motivation adds the dimension of popular enthusiasm to getting needed things done, the quality and the impact of popular effort must be safeguarded through good organization' (United Nations, 1963a, para. 83).

Over the last few years various United Nations' publications have indicated how community development, peasant organizations and land reform can be related at various stages of development. In the initial stage of agrarian reform there are two ways by which community development can strengthen the land reform process, as noted by the U N Economic and Social Council (1962, para. 69):

First, land tenure reform legislation is seldom enacted until a groundswell of opinion (such as community development programs can help to generate) has arisen in the countryside in favor of such reform. Second, local support by the people concerned is needed for enforcement of land tenure legislation after it is enacted, since otherwise it is likely to remain a dead letter because of opposition from entrenched interests.

In the United Nations' Third Report on *Progress in Land Reform* (1962, ch. 6, para. 14), these two potential tasks for community development were further elaborated:

Community development programs are well adapted to help create such a groundswell. In a number of instances such programs existed for some years before land tenure reforms, even in the restricted legal sense, were instituted, and have demonstrated their ability to help bring into being the conditions that make viable land reform possible. They have done this essentially by educating the rural people about the possibilities and by enabling them to find spokesmen, an organization, the beginning of organizing competence and of the habit of working through organizations. The reform laws were then in large part initiated and their passage assured, by the community itself.

After laws have been passed, many illiterate peasants have been ignorant of their new rights. Even where fairly adequate means of public education have been available, a lack of strong peasant organizations in rural areas has helped landowners to disregard legislation, or to get around it. The presence of such strong community organizations, at the local level, on the other hand, has turned the tide in favor of enforcement (para. 17).

For Latin America, with its large number of landless peasants, various techniques were recommended to secure enforcement of tenure reform legislation:

One of the most promising approaches to integration of agrarian reform and community development may be through legislative encouragement of group rather than individual applications for land, and democratic election of representatives of the applicants. This may create a focus for community activity and common interest among landless laborers and others among whom community organization is usually very weak. It would provide the kind of pressures for enforcement needed to overcome the resistance of landowners, and might lead to effective national organization and political representation of the rural population. It would lead naturally to more permanent forms of community organization and to initiative in dealing with government agencies once the land was allocated – without in itself, however, implying collective ownership or use of the land (para. 34).

As examples of this type of community development, the report lists the local farm unions and peasant leagues in Venezuela which are now organized into a National Peasant Federation (para. 43).

In Venezuela the Labor Law of July 1936, made rural unionization possible (Powell, 1964, p. 4). Political leaders who had been in exile for many years had returned to Venezuela after the death of President Gómez in December, 1935. They relied upon labor organizations and peasant unions to organize political support. According to the study by John Powell, between 1936 and 1945, 77 peasant syndicates with 6279 members were formed against many odds. Between 1945 and 1948, during the presidency of Rómulo Betancourt, the formation and legalization of the peasant unions was simplified, so that 515 syndicates with 43,302 members were organized (p. 7). The unions were brought together in the Federación Campesina (FCV) with Ramón Quijada as its first president:

Quijada, a tough man among tough men, had worked his way up as a *campesino* organizer from Sucre state during the period from 1936 to 1945 when union activities were often considered illegal by local governments, dangerous by local landlords, politically subversive by many military and national guard commandants, and suppressed accordingly (p. 8).

Between 1948 and 1958 under President Pérez Jiménez, peasant organization was again made extremely difficult. The peasant movement continued in a clandestine way, however, and after the fall of Pérez Jiménez rose again:

Lands which had been opened to the peasants under the Acción Democrática government in 1945–8, and from which they had been forcibly evicted by the forces of the dictatorship, were invaded spontaneously under the urging of many militant local *campesino* leaders (p. 11).

At the First Campesino Congress in 1959 in Caracas, Quijada was elected to reconstitute the Federación Campesina again, but an internal struggle within Acción Democrática brought about a purge of Quijada and his group at the Second Campesino Congress in 1962 (p. 11).

The impressive growth of the peasant movement after 1958, Powell believes, resulted from the concrete local objectives it pursued (pp. 15–25). The peasants saw in the Federación an instrument for rural communities to get things done. Among the concerns of the local syndicates were credit from the Banco Agrícola y Pecuario and requests for land, as well as such items as housing, drinking water, educational and medical facilities.

Apparently well-organized and coordinated invasions of lands (Taylor, 1960, paras. 86, 87) brought, in certain areas, a rapid execution of land reform measures by the National Agrarian Institute (Instituto Agrario Nacional), as stipulated by the Agrarian Reform Law promulgated on 3 March 1960.

An illustration of how reform and community development are integrated is seen in La Julia-Jubo Dulce, in the state of Aragua, a pilot project with which the author is acquainted. The success of the settlement was partly due to a strong rural organization, built up since 1948. This local peasant union accelerated the execution of the land reform law in the community and some surrounding places through a well-planned and nonviolent invasion of the lands to be affected according to the criteria of the law. A United Nations evaluation mission noted that CORDIPLAN (Oficina Nacional de Coordinación y Planificación) has successfully created a common nucleus of living which, together with the efforts of the Federación, are integrating the formerly scattered and isolated peasants into public life (United Nations, 1963b, para. 36). In some of the states where CORDIPLAN'S community development program has operated successfully, such as Aragua and Carabobo (CORDIPLAN, 1965), the peasant unions have been active longer than in other places (Powell, 1964, p. 2). The Ministry of Labor subsidizes 85 per cent of the Federación's budget and the National Agrarian Institute covers another 10 per cent (ibid., pp. 80–81). According to Powell, the Federación has 'a political payoff to the parties in the form of rural votes and community-*campesino* payoff in the form of the goods and services provided in the government's agrarian reform program' (ibid., p. 71).

Besides the official support that the Federación enjoyed for many years, the relative success of the movement might be explained by the charismatic leadership which helped to integrate the many local unions into a national organization, along with the fact that the unions were established against many odds. Sociologists have noted the greater cohesion that may grow within groups, especially labor unions, when they are threatened from the outside (Coser, 1956).

Although peasant organizations have existed in many countries, their political implications have kept many sociologists and community development workers from giving them serious study. These implications cannot be avoided, however, since a greater participation of rural communities in the life of the nation is the objective of community development. Certain changes in the power structure have to be brought about where this structure is still rigid. As Gillin (1949, p. 206) notes:

Extremes of class and relative lack of education for the great mass of the people have often prevented anything approaching democratic participation by the bulk of the population; the majority of the people did not know how to take part in political affairs and the upper class would not permit them to do so, anyway.

To be nurtured and to grow, the peasant groups must receive political support of a nonpartisan character 'strong enough to inspire people with new hope, to overcome the inertia and fragmentation of traditional bureaucracies, and to transform the attitudes and working habits of public personnel' (United Nations, 1959, paras. 41–2). However, it will be seen that in practice all kinds of political forces enter the scene. The Secretary General of the United Nations (1965, para. 78) noted in this respect:

It has been argued that although in Latin America land reform is not normally introduced as an integral part of comprehensive social and political change, it is, nevertheless, an explosive force, unpredictable and revolutionary, to the extent that a certain amount of violence, unrest and disorder is unavoidable and even necessary, for successful reform measures, the initiation of which is likely to create further disturbing or unsettling elements. Not only is there a reciprocally influential relationship between land reform and other forms of economic change, especially industrialization, but land reform has also become a subject of vast and often unrealizable promises by many political parties who, by espousing its cause – at least verbally – may make some powerful enemies, but will make numerous friends. This political potential of land reform measures appears to have been recognized, moreover, by those external interests which urge on many developing countries the introduction of land reform, whether as an integral part of major institutional change or as a means of avoiding such radical change.

It is well known that large landowners at times have expressed opposition to consistent community development programs or even education of rural workers (Loomis *et al.*, 1953, p. 98; Paulson, 1964, pp. 26, 47). Certain limited community improvement projects may be realized. However, as long as *haciendas* retain their traditional dominance over *minifundio* settlements within rural localities, the proportion of 'community' self-help in the latter can have only limited and precarious achievements. Such a program may even serve as a device to excuse evasion of the central issue of land tenure.

Political implications of effective rural organization and popular participation have been studied in several ILO country reports, such as those on El Salvador (Ambrosini, 1954, p. 16). They have also been the subject of representations to the Inter-American Conference of Ministers of Labor in Bogota in May 1963. Union spokesmen disclosed to the ministers that none of the important Latin American countries (Brazil, Bolivia, Colombia, Chile, Mexico, Peru and Venezuela) were making serious efforts to fulfill one of the conditions of the Alliance for Progress, namely to have free labor union representatives participate in national planning. In some countries they even met with a deliberate effort to exclude such representatives (Unión Panamericana, 1963, pp. 172–3).

It was probably for the above reason that some paragraphs of the Declaration of Cundinamarca and recommendations of this Inter-American Conference of Ministers of Labor explicitly requested that Latin American governments recognize the right of agricultural workers to organize labor unions freely (pp. 260–68, para. 32), and also stimulate the active participation of organized workers in national development planning on all levels.

In commenting on the problem of gaining effective power, Charles Anderson (1965, p. 27) noted:

Latin American governments are quite responsive to those privileged interests that can formulate 'appropriate' demands for state action and bring them to the attention of policy-makers in a compelling way.

Rather, the problem is that few mechanisms exist to 'link' large sectors of the population to the decision-making process, to make their interests known to policy-makers and to reinforce these interests with real political power that can affect the conditions of political survival. Another way of putting this is that public decisions in Latin America are often taken under circumstances of acute ignorance as to what is actually going on in society.

To overcome this problem and in order to promote a 'gradualist' development strategy, Anderson proposed that 'political activism' be an essential part of the development policy. This includes community development[15] and, if needed, even certain forms of civil disobedience:

... for a peasant movement, constantly seeking representational access to decision makers, and having exhausted procedural remedies, to occupy unused lands, held in private property only for purposes of speculation, may be a most suitable political tactic. This is particularly true where a strong legal presumption in favor of the 'social function' of property exists. . . .[16]

The need for and effectiveness of the various approaches in this field will be different from one country to another, although there are some basic considerations, as expressed at the 1966 World Land Reform Conference (United Nations Food and Agricultural Organization, 1966, p. 15):

It was observed that, in some countries, legal obstacles and sometimes violent oppression against peasant organizations had impeded any movement of this nature. In some countries, the peasants rely on such dramatic actions as hunger marches or peaceful invasions of expropriable land. Obstacles impeding the formation and activities of peasant organizations need to be removed, and complete liberty for

15. Anderson (1965, pp. 39–40), where as 'forms of organization appropriate to reform-mongering' are mentioned 'clientele groups', organization of cooperatives, community development programs, political party organization, peasant syndicates.

16. Anderson (1965, p. 38). An interesting example in this respect can be found in the principles and activities of FANAL (Federación Agraria Nacional), the peasant organization in Colombia which closely collaborates with the U N assisted community development program Acción Comunal. FANAL organized various invasions of unused public or private lands, supported by its 'moral advisor', Father Vicente Andrade, S.J., who wrote a leaflet to that effect (1963, especially p. 14).

independent peasant organizations to unite in their best interests needs to be guaranteed.

Because of the obstacles to their effective participation in politics, the peasants have expressed their demands in ways that have generally been of a spontaneous and at times more or less violent nature. Though frequently nonviolent methods of action were also successful. It is not an exaggeration to say that in most areas where effective land reform has taken place, it has taken place due to direct action methods applied by organized peasant groups after the legal approach had proved hopeless. Spectacular examples are the activities of the peasant unions during 1952–3 in Bolivia, particularly in the Cochabamba area (Patch, 1961). Widely publicized also was the action of the peasant federation in the late fifties and early sixties in the Valle de La Convención in the Cuzco area in Peru. This movement, strongly opposed by intransigent landowners, became increasingly radical under the leadership of Hugo Blanco in a later stage (Craig, 1969). In addition to armed force, a special land reform decree for the area was promulgated in order to calm down the movement. But in spite of this, in 1963 about 300,000 indigenous peasants occupied lands in different areas of the Peruvian highlands, lands which they claimed had been theirs for years (CIDA, 1966).

Around 1958 similar movements took place in the northwestern states of Mexico, organized by the independent leftist peasant organization headed by Jacinto López. This movement made such an impact that the government stepped up its land distribution program in the country as a whole (Huizer, 1968–9). In the north-west of Mexico some vast foreign estates, such as the Cananea Cattle Company, left untouched in circumvention of the Mexican Constitution, were expropriated and transformed into collective cattle *ejidos*.

These different cases have at least one factor in common. The movements took place in areas which, and among peasants who, were comparatively 'modernized'. The Cochabamba region in Bolivia is among the most prosperous of the country, thanks to a highly commercialized agriculture. In the Valle de La Convención in Peru the local peasants had made some progress through the cultivation of coffee. But in both instances the traditional rural elite tried to maintain its economic, social and political position of power through an intransigent attitude toward the peasantry. In the north-west of Mexico the situation was somewhat different. The modernization process was more spectacular. Large areas of land, brought under irrigation as part of vast development projects, had been distributed to commercial farmers for the production of cash crops. In earlier years land reform legislation had been changed to provide that landholdings of less than 300 hectares of irrigated cash crop land (741 acres) could not be expropriated. Circumventing the law, many new proprietors were able to retain tracts of several times this amount. The boom in commercial farming resulted in considerable 'conspicuous consumption' by the growing middle classes in the towns of the area. This contrasted strongly with the low levels of living of the peasantry, which had hoped to obtain land through the reform program but which had seen this hope fade, even though their claims were legally recognized. This area, considered by Charles Erasmus to be an example of development of a kind desired by US policy – through the rise of a middle class mobilized by the emulative force of 'conspicuous consumption'[17] – experienced, probably because of the new contrasts created through such policy, considerable popular upheaval since the late fifties, of which the invasions mentioned above formed a part.

The relative success of the agrarian reform and community development efforts in areas where peasant participation in strong movements preceded the reform measures, such as in the cases of the collective cattle *ejidos* established in Cananea[18] and the coffee producers cooperatives founded with the peasants in La Convención, indicates that non-traditional forms of conflict solution and political participation may be a worthwhile field for study and experimentation.

17. Erasmus (1961). It is surprising that Erasmus, who was present in the area when the mass invasions took place on various occasions, only mentions these facts in two minor paragraphs (p. 220 and p. 263), in a book which deals with the implications of rural development.

18. Concerning the success of the Cananea collective *ejidos*, see Eckstein (1966, pp. 165–8).

References

ADAMS, R. N. (1957), *Cultural Surveys of Panama, Nicaragua, Guatemala, El Salvador, Honduras*, Pan American Sanitary Bureau.

ADAMS, R. N. (1961), 'Social change in Guatemala and US policy', in R. N. Adams *et al.*, *Social Change in Latin America Today*, Vintage.

AMBROSINI, J. (1954), *Informe al gobierno de El Salvador sobre los asalariados agricolas*, International Labour Organization.

ANDERSON, C. W. (1965), 'Reform-mongering and the uses of political power', *Interamer. econ. Aff.*, vol. 19, no. 2.

ANDRADE, V. (1963), *Juicio moral sobre la invasión de tierras*, Publicaciones de la Federación Agraria Nacional, no. 3, Colombia.

BANFIELD, E. (1958), *The Moral Basis of Backward Society*, Free Press.

CASTILLO, C. M. (1956), 'La economía agricola en la región del Bajío', *Problemas Agricolas e Industriales de México*, vol. 8, nos. 3–4.

CIDA (1965), *Guatemala: tenencia de la tierra y desarrollo socio-económico del sector agricola*, Unión Panamericana, Washington.

CIDA (1966), *Perú: tenencia de la tierra y desarrollo socio-económico del sector agrícola*, Unión Panamericana, Washington.

CORDIPLAN (1965), *Logros tangibles e intangibles del desarrollo de la comunidad en Venezuela, 1960–1964*, separata 1, cuadro no. 12.

COSER, L. A. (1956), *The Functions of Social Conflict*, Free Press.

CRAIG, W. W. (1969), 'The peasant movement of La Convención', in H. A. Landsberger (ed.), *Peasant Movements in Latin America*, Cornell University Press.

DESSAINT, A. (1962), 'Effects of the *hacienda* and plantation systems on Guatemala's indians', *América Indígena*, vol. 22, no. 4.

DOBYNS, H. B., MONGE, C., and VÁZQUEZ, M. C. (1962), 'Summary of technical–organizational progress, and reaction to it', *Human Organization*, vol. 21, no. 2.

DOLCI, D. (1960), *Outlaws of Partinico*, MacGibbon & Kee.

DOLCI, D. (1963), *Waste*, MacGibbon & Kee.

ECKSTEIN, S. (1966), *El ejido colectivo en Mexico*, Fondo de Cultura Económica, Mexico.

ERASMUS, C. J. (1961), *Man Takes Control*, University of Minnesota Press.

GILLIN, J. (1949), '*Mestizo* America', in R. Linton (ed.), *Most of the World*, Columbia University Press.

HOLMBERG, A. R. (1955), 'Participant intervention in the field', *Human Organization*, vol. 14, no. 1.

HOLMBERG, A. R. (1959), 'Land tenure and planned social change: a case from Vicos, Peru', *Human Organization*, vol. 18, no. 1.

HOLMBERG, A. R. (1961), 'Changing community attitudes and values in Peru: a case study in guided change', in R. Adams *et al.*, *Social Change in Latin America Today*, Vintage.

HUIZER, G. (1962), 'Some community development problems in Partinico, western Sicily', *Int. Rev. Community Devel.*, no. 10.

HUIZER, G. (1963), 'A community development experience in a Central American village', *Int. Rev. Community Devel.*, no. 12.

HUIZER, G. (1965a), 'Evaluating community development at the grassroots: some observations on methodology', *América Indígena*, vol. 25, no. 3.

HUIZER, G. (1965b), 'Some notes on community development and rural social research', *América Latina*, vol. 8, no. 3, pp. 128–44.

HUIZER, G. (1968–9), 'Peasant organization in the process of agrarian reform in Mexico', *Studies compar. int. Devel.*, vol. 4, no. 6.

JONES, E. (1962), *Revisión de unas reformas agrarias*, Instituto Interamericano de Ciencias Agrícolas, Turrialba, Costa Rica.

KELLY, I. (1953), 'Informe preliminar del proyecto de habitación en La Laguna, ejido El Cuije, cercano a Torreón, Coahuila', Instituto de Asuntos Interamericanos, Mexico, mim.

LASSWELL, H. D. (1962), 'Integrating communities in more inclusive systems, *Human Organization*, vol. 21, no. 2.

LEONHOLDT, F. (1953), *The Agricultural Economy of El Salvador*, report for the UNTA mission to El Salvador.

LOOMIS, C. P., *et al.* (1953), *Turrialba: Social Systems and the Introduction of Change*, Free Press.

MARROQUIN, A. D. (1959), *Panchimalco: investigación sociológica*, San Salvador, Editorial Universataria.

MATURANA, S. (1963), *Los problemas de tenencia de la tierra en los paises de Centroamérica*, FAO/CAIS/63.

PATCH, R. W. (1961), 'Bolivia: US assistance in a revolutionary setting', in R. Adams *et al.*, *Social Change in Latin America Today*, Vintage.

PAULSON, B. H. (1964), 'Local political patterns in northeast Brazil', a community case study, Land Tenure Center, University of Wisconsin, mim.

POWELL, J. D. (1964), 'Preliminary report on the Federación Campesina de Venezuela – origins, organization, leadership and role in the agrarian reform program', Land Tenure Center, Wisconsin, mim.

SENIOR, C. (1958), *Land Reform and Democracy*, University of Florida Press.

TAYLOR, P. S. (1960), *Venezuela: A Case Study of Relationships between Community Development and Agrarian Reform*, United Nations.

United Nations (1954), *Progress in Land Reform*, E.2526.

United Nations (1956), *Progress in Land Reform*, second report, E/2930.

United Nations (1959), *Public Administration Aspects of Community Development Programs*, ST/TAO/M/14.

United Nations (1960a), *Community Development and Economic Development*, part 1, E/CN. 11/540, Bangkok.

United Nations (1960b), *Community Development and Related Services*, E/2931, annex 3.

United Nations (1962), *Progress in Land Reform*, third report, ST/SOA/49.

United Nations (1963a), *Community Development and National Development*, report by an *ad hoc* group of experts, E/CN. 5/379/Rev. 1.

United Nations (1963b), *Report of a Community Development Evaluation Mission to Venezuela*, TAO/VEN/15.

United Nations (1964), *Report on the World Social Situation, 1963*, E/CN. 5/375/add. 2.

United Nations (1965), *The Impact of Land Reform on Economic and Social Development*, note by the Secretary General, E/CN.5/386.

United Nations Economic and Social Council (1960), *Report of the Fifteenth Session of the Social Commission*, official records thirty-sixth session, supplement no. 12, E/3769.

United Nations Economic and Social Council (1962), Report of the thirty-fourth session, E/3603.

United Nations Economic and Social Council (1967), *Land Reform*, Report of the 1966 World Land Reform Conference, E/4298.

United Nations Food and Agricultural Organization (1966), World Land Reform Conference, Working Party Reports, General Rapporteur's Report and Resolutions, RU:WLR/66/T.

Unión Panamericana (1963), 'Conferencia interamericana de Ministros de Trabajo sobre la Alianza para el Progreso', *Revista Interamericana de Ciencias Sociales*, second series, vol. 2, no. 2.

VÁZQUEZ, M. C. (1962), 'Cambios socio–económicos en una hacienda andina del Perú', *América Indígena*, vol. 22, no. 4, pp. 297–312.

WHETTEN, N. (1948), *Rural Mexico*, University of Chicago Press.

28 Gunnar Myrdal

Paths of Development

Excerpts from Gunnar Myrdal, 'Paths of development', *New Left Review*, no. 36, 1966, pp. 65–74.

The first question I want to raise is that of the priority to be given to industry and agriculture in the under-developed countries' present situation.

It is a fact that intellectuals in under-developed countries largely pin their hopes on industrialization; and I want to emphasize from the start that this article should not be construed as implying that under-developed countries must not do their utmost to build up industry as fast as possible.[1]

The need for this is particularly pressing in countries with a high population/land ratio. A country like India, whose population will double before the turn of the century, cannot in the long run hope to raise the dismally low living standards of its masses unless a very much higher proportion of its labour force is employed in industry. This is true regardless of whatever progress is made in Indian agriculture. More generally, without the under-developed countries' progressive industrialization, it will be impossible to prevent the ever-widening income gap between

1. I want also to make clear that in an article dealing with such a vast subject, my remarks are necessarily limited to a few bare essentials, and even these have had to be simplified to an extent that allows no space for substantiation, differentiation or qualification. I have also had to exclude from my analysis those small areas of the world where under-developed countries have oil and other resources, for which the demand is rapidly rising because of the advanced nations' development. I omit these not because their problems are uninteresting or unimportant, but because the vast majority of people in the under-developed world have no access to such resources. I should add, finally, that most of my detailed knowledge is of South Asia.

rich and poor countries from continuing to grow as it has done for a century.

This long-term trend is reason enough for the under-developed countries to give prominence to industrialization in their development plans. But even so, a few points need to be made. To begin with, for many future decades, even a much more rapid process of industrialization than that achieved by most underdeveloped countries will not provide sufficient employment for the under-utilized labour force in these countries. This is so because the additional labour demand created by industrialization is a function not only of the speed of industrial growth but of the low level from which it starts.

If, as is often obviously rational, investment capital and human resources (both of which will always be limited, even if the developed countries provide much more assistance than at present) are to a large extent put into fully modern, fairly large-scale industries, the additional labour demand will be small. Furthermore, when industrialization implies rationalization of earlier, more labour-intensive industries, and when these can no longer compete with the new industries, the net effect on labour demand may be negative: in this case industrialization releases more labour than it employs. From this point of view industrial development for export and for import-substitution has an advantage in addition to those usually recognized. But no under-developed country can industrialize exclusively along these lines. This implies that in the early stages of industrialization there are always 'backwash' effects which decrease, wipe out or even reverse the efforts to create new employment.

In a study of development in the Central Asian Republics of the Soviet Union undertaken by the Secretariat of the Economic Commission for Europe, it was found that, despite heavy industrialization, the labour force employed in manufacturing decreased for more than two decades until the industrial base became so large that its continuingly rapid advance brought about a correspondingly large increase in demand for labour. Similarly, a comparison of the census figures for 1950 and 1960 in India – a country which not only promoted industrialization but steered it into import-substitution while protecting its traditional manufacturing – shows that industrialization had hardly any effect at all on the proportion of the labour force earning its livelihood from agriculture.

The Population Explosion

The fact that for many future decades industrialization will not create much additional net employment in under-developed countries starting from a small industrial base, must now be considered in conjunction with the fact that over the same period the labour force in all under-developed countries will increase by more than 2 per cent a year, and in some countries by very much more. In this connexion it should be noted that a decrease in the birth-rate, especially a gradual one, has no effect on the size of the labour force for fifteen years, and only a very minor effect for at least three decades.

At this point it is worth noting that not only will there *not* be a spontaneous decrease in fertility in the under-developed countries, but that such a decrease could be brought about only by a policy of government-sponsored family planning; in no country as yet has such a policy been pursued with sufficient effectiveness to bring substantial results. Moreover, the increasing percentage of young in the under-developed countries' populations implies a tremendous momentum towards higher birth-rates. Even if a policy to spread birth-control can have little effect on the size of the labour force for three decades, it has none the less immediate and beneficial effects on age distribution and, consequently, on the level of *per capita* income, savings potentiality and labour productivity. To press for such a policy is therefore of the utmost importance and urgency. But it is entirely beside the point to equate, as is only too often done, the problem of population increase with the problem of 'finding employment' for the coming generation, for whom the increase in the labour force is a given quantity, almost entirely independent of what happens to fertility.

The conclusion is evident: if, for several decades, little or even no new employment can be generated by industrialization, while the certainty remains that the labour force will increase by between 2 per cent and 4 per cent annually, then the greater part of this increase in the labour force must remain outside industry, mainly in agriculture. At this point I may be excused for expressing my surprise that these simple facts have not been recognized by economists who constantly refer to industrialization as the means by which the increased labour force in underdeveloped countries can be employed outside agriculture; indeed, they often talk about decreasing the labour force presently employed in agriculture. The other spread-effects generally considered in discussions which take industrialization as the dynamic force in an under-developed country's economy are thought to operate by raising the level of technical interest and knowledge, mobility, readiness for experiment and change, enterprise and rationality even outside industry. Unfortunately, these spread-effects are again a function of the levels already reached in these areas. The experience of many under-developed countries in the colonial era, in which great spurts of industrialization produced strange and isolated enclaves, should be warning enough that these effects are likely to be small. There is a danger, it seems to me, that, in their efforts to pursue industrialization, many under-developed countries are achieving the same result of building small enclaves within a much bigger economy that remains backward and stagnant. What I am asking for, in other words, is a much larger plan – a plan designed to encompass effective agricultural planning and reform.

Agricultural Development

I want to repeat that these remarks are not an argument against industrializing as rapidly as possible. If anything they are an argument for starting as soon as possible and proceeding as fast as possible in order the sooner to reach the end of the transitional period – that long period during which industrialization does not significantly serve to create employment and its spread-effects remain minimal. But awareness of these facts should be an encouragement to make serious efforts in other directions. This is particularly necessary in the present conditions of underdevelopment when everything must be done to prevent industrial development being frustrated and finally aborted. Indeed, in the absence of such development plans on a wider front, even the most strenuous attempts to industrialize will most probably not prevent increasing misery, particularly in the poorer countries. Agriculture is by far the largest sector in the economies of all under-developed countries. Normally more than half – and in most under-developed countries anything up to 80 per cent – of the total population earn their living from the land. The immediate cause of poverty, and thus of under-development, in these countries is the extremely low productivity of labour in agriculture. It is a dangerous illusion to believe that there can be any significant economic development in these countries without radically raising the productivity of agricultural labour.

Given the two facts of an increase in the labour force – which we can safely predict will continue to the end of this century – and of an unchanging, if not actually decreasing demand for labour caused by industrialization, we cannot avoid coming to an important policy conclusion. This is that any realistic agricultural policy must reckon on a tremendous increase in the agricultural labour force. During the considerable period in which industrialization creates only insignificant new employment, that part of the agricultural labour surplus which takes refuge from agrarian poverty and oppression by moving to the cities will be characterized by the same under-utilization of labour as in agriculture: it will go mostly into petty trading and services of various sorts, or will swell the number of odd-job seekers, unemployed and beggars. Urbanization on any scale in under-developed countries unfortunately does not, and cannot, equal industrialization.

The conclusion that planning must take into account a very rapid increase of the agrarian labour force becomes a more serious challenge in face of the fact that the present labour force is under-utilized on a vast scale – a situation that is popularly termed 'under-employment'. Rational agricultural policy must therefore be directed towards more intensive utilization of an under-employed labour force that is constantly and rapidly increasing. We might note in passing that this is a necessity which for various reasons none of the now highly-developed countries faces or ever faced during its development. Again, I am surprised that this obvious conclusion is so seldom stressed.

Land Reform

In a short article I cannot examine the implications of this conclusion for agricultural planning, except to point out that successful agricultural development requires an entirely new technology in the under-developed countries. As yet no scientific basis, founded on intensive research, and taking into account the climatic conditions in the tropical and sub-tropical zones of most under-developed countries, has been elaborated.

These countries, and the rest of humanity with them, cannot afford to fail in the task of achieving a more intensive use of a rapidly increasing under-employed agrarian labour force. There is, however, one ray of hope: the present productivity of land in the under-developed countries is exceedingly low. There must, therefore, be means by which a very great increase in labour input and efficiency can raise yields per acre by much more proportionally than the increase in efficient labour input.

When we have reached this point in awareness, we have to face the fact that the main blockage to such an advance is political and institutional. In many under-developed countries power is in the hands of reactionaries who have, or believe they have, an interest in preventing those changes in land-ownership and tenancy that would allow the peasantry to become conscious of – and change – their lot. Even in those countries with enlightened national leaders, landlords, money-lenders and other middlemen frequently use their power locally to subvert legislative reforms. And the peasants, sunk in apathy, ignorance and superstition which their poverty not only causes but maintains, do not protest because of their very apathy.

About this there is general agreement. The FAO has studied the problem, and resolutions for land reform and similar measures are constantly being passed by the Economic and Social Council and the UN's General Assembly. But in practice little is accomplished in most under-developed countries. With the steady increase in the agrarian labour force – which, without rapid economic development, is itself causing increased inequality – an extremely dangerous situation is developing. The reluctance among many agricultural experts really to press the issue, their tendency to evade it by taking refuge in technological questions, is equally dangerous. This is another practice which stems from colonial traditions. The F A O Freedom from Hunger Campaign has underlined the extremely low productivity of labour and land in the under-developed countries. Countries with populations of hundreds of millions, such as India and Pakistan – both of which have more than two-thirds of their labour force employed in agriculture – are on a sub-optimal level of nutrition and are increasingly dependent on American charity to feed themselves. Food production in South Asia as a whole has, in recent decades, swung from surplus to deficit. The tragic experiences in Latin America in the post-war period, its major inflations and its retarded development, are not unrelated to the fact that vested interests have so far blocked most of the major agrarian reforms on which agricultural development – and its beneficial or retardatory effects on industrial development – depends.

The F A O has calculated that close to one-half of the world's population suffers from hunger or crippling malnutrition or both – and this half lives in the under-developed countries. Within these countries the masses of the under-nourished are peasants. Taking into account future increases in population, the F A O calculates that total food supplies must be doubled by 1980 and trebled by 2000 to provide a reasonable level of nutrition for the world's population. My own studies lead me to believe that this is an under-estimate rather than the contrary.

Two things are clear. First, most of this increase in food production must take place in the under-developed countries, which implies a sharp swing against the present curve of their agrarian development. Second, failure to reach this goal implies a world catastrophe whose import is terrifying.

Superficial Planning

It is in this light that we can see the danger of considering industrialization as a cure-all for the problems of under-development. The danger is all the greater because this belief serves vested interests (and many wishful thinkers) with an excuse for not facing up to the real and difficult problems involved. If the image of industrialization can be put forward as the essential requirement for what wishful thinking calls the 'take-off' to 'self-sustaining' growth, then these interests need not concern themselves either with the failure to change economic and social conditions on the land, or with the failure to increase agrarian productivity. It is much easier to construct factories often with foreign aid in capital and technicians, than to change social and economic agrarian conditions and the attitudes to life and work of millions of poverty-stricken peasants. And since no one can be against industrialization, this reinforces the arguments of those in positions of influence in the under-developed world who often have direct personal interests in industrialization.

This mode of thought is encouraged by the tendency to superficial planning which can be observed in the prejudiced and careless reasoning about priorities. The facts I have pointed to, and the conclusions I have reached, move me, in any discussion about priorities in these terms, to give first priority to agriculture. But this mode of reasoning assumes that there is a choice in which the answers are mutually exclusive. This assumption is on the whole false or, at least, only partly true.

First, the necessary institutional reforms are costly neither in scarce capital resources nor in foreign exchange. Many of the necessary investments in agriculture are, moreover, highly labour-intensive which would mobilize under-utilized labour for all sorts of permanent improvements of the land. There has been much talk about this but little action. Similarly, efforts to raise the levels of education, health and hygiene do not require heavy expenditure of capital or foreign exchange. These efforts in most under-developed countries have bordered on the feeble, even when considered exclusively from the point of view of productivity, i.e. in their potential effectiveness in relieving the peasantry of its apathy and traditional irrationality. To the extent that these and other reforms require the investment of capital and foreign exchange, such investment serves industrialization – the construction of factories producing fertilizers and agricultural machinery – as well as being necessary to any rational development plan and being highly productive.

For those few under-developed countries that have reached more advanced forms of planning and have emphasized the need for industrialization, the conclusion of my analysis at this point is, *not* that they should have chosen otherwise, but that they should direct this emphasis to maximal advantage for agricultural development, which is of paramount importance for the success or failure of their economic development. My main conclusion, however, is that industrialization alone is insufficient. Even more important is that the problem of raising – rapidly and radically – the productivity of labour and land be squarely faced. If this issue is relegated, if it is given no more than second 'priority', then this type of planning is inviting its own defeat, however successful temporarily it is in constructing a few factories.

[In the subsequent part the author discusses the intrinsic lack of equality in the position of the so-called 'developing societies' in the world market and the necessity to counter it by 'a double standard of morality in regard to commercial and financial policies – one, which for once, gives licence to the weaker instead of the stronger'. *Ed.*]

It must not be forgotten that the overwhelming bulk of under-developed countries' exports is of traditional exports, and that the greater part of these consists of agricultural products which make up about 70 per cent of their total exports. It is an illusion to believe that any substantial improvement can be made in the under-developed countries' international trading position without tackling the problem of *defending their markets for traditional exports* which, for years and probably decades, will constitute the bulk of what they have to sell.

The main cause of the under-developed countries' worsening international trade position lies in a falling-off in the growth of demand for their traditional exports, and in particular for agricultural products. To the extent that this has been due to low income-elasticity of demand and technological change, the trend is irreversible. But in some part it is caused by fiscal levies, which keep down consumption even of such tropical products as coffee whose imports do not compete with domestic production, and by other forms of protection which directly or indirectly are detrimental to these exports.

Two things can be asked of the advanced industrial nations

which are themselves in the process of rapid development and therefore should be able to take them in their stride. First, that they be prepared to eliminate all purely fiscal duties and taxes on the under-developed countries' exports. Second, that they lower and finally eliminate the protective trade barriers they have erected which, directly or indirectly, limit demand for imports from the under-developed countries. It must be recognized that the advanced nations may need a transitional period to meet this latter demand - though not the former - as it implies a shrinkage of domestic production. In the long run, such structural adjustments for the use of their own labour force and productive capacity would accord with their rational interests, since it is not generally to their advantage to tie up resources in these sectors of production.

A further point I wish to stress is the extreme importance of increasing multilateralization - at least to the degree of the FAO's aid in food and other agricultural products to the under-developed countries - so that present or potential surplus countries are *protected, indeed encouraged, to produce agricultural products for this type of export*. Their productive potentialities may otherwise remain unutilized, particularly when their natural customers are other under-developed countries which are short of foreign exchange. Aid in agricultural products from the US and other rich countries inevitably tends to destroy their markets. They are not in a position to give away their exports. The rational solution would be to give the new experimental agency for agricultural surplus disposal, created by the FAO, the funds to pay such countries for their exports, even if these are in turn given away as aid to other under-developed countries.

Although the policies I have briefly recommended are in the interests of the advanced nations - interests which can only be reinforced by the international tensions created by the continual frustration of the under-developed countries' efforts to develop - the advanced nations cannot be expected to carry out these policies because of rationality and idealism. Pressure from the under-developed countries themselves is necessary. As this pressure becomes increasingly vocal, rationality will come to play a part in the policy-making of the advanced nations. But the pressure must be reasoned and accurately directed at all the important issues. Only then will new and effective policies be formulated to end the under-developed countries' struggle for development.

Further Reading

The division of references corresponds closely but not exactly to the chapter headings in the Reader. Only English-language sources are included.

Systematic text books

B. Galeski, *Rural Sociology*, Manchester University Press, 1971.

E. R. Wolf, *Peasants*, Prentice-Hall, 1966.

General readers

P. M. Back (ed.), *Peasants in the Modern World*, University of New Mexico Press, 1969.

G. Dalton (ed.), *Tribal and Peasant Economies*, Natural History Press, 1967.

J. M. Potter, G. M. Foster and M. M. Diaz (eds.), *Peasant Societies: A Reader*, Little, Brown, 1967.

P. A. Sorokin, F. F. Zinnerman and C. J. Golpin (eds.), *Systematic Source Book in Rural Sociology*, Russell & Russell, 1965.

Of this list the Readers by Potter *et al.* and Dalton are particularly comprehensive.

General: the peasant social structure

I. Ajarni, 'Social classes, family demographic characteristics and mobility in three Iranian villages', *Sociologia Ruralis*, vol. 9, 1969, no. 1. Differentiation and socio-economic mobility in rural society.

R. Dumont, 'Lands Alive', *Monthly Review Press*, 1965. A discussion of the social conditions in a wide variety of rural societies all round the world.

L. A. Fallers, 'Are African cultivators to be called peasants?', *Current Anthrop.*, vol. 2, April 1961, no. 2. Relevant to general discussion of peasantry as a specific social structure.

Fei Hsiu-Tung, 'Peasantry and gentry', *Amer. J. Sociol.*, vol. 52, 1946, pp. 1–17. An excellent discussion of peasantry and traditional landowners in China prior to industrialization.

G. M. Foster, 'Interpersonal relations in peasant society', *Human Organisation*, vol. 19, 1960. Critical analysis of Redfield's studies of a small community.

S. H. Franklin, 'Reflection on peasantry', *Pacific Viewpoint*, vol. 3, 1962. General discussion of peasantry as a social structure.

J. M. Halpern, *The Changing Village Community*, Prentice-Hall, 1967.

R. H. Hilton, 'Manor, serfdom and villeinage', in *Encyclopaedia Britannica*, An important discussion of peasantry and traditional landowners in Western Europe.

G. C. Homans, *English Villagers of the Thirteenth Century*, Harvard University Press, 1942. A first-class inquiry into peasantry and traditional landowners.

M. E. Opler, 'The extensions of an Indian village', *J. Asian Studies*, vol. 16, 1956, no. 1.

A. Pearse, *The Latin American Peasant*, Pall Mall Press, 1970.

R. Redfield, *The Little Community* and *Peasant Society and Culture*, University of Chicago Press, 1965. Two long essays discussing respectively the specific characteristics of small communities and the generic characteristics of peasantry in various places and periods.

H. Rosenfeld, 'Property, kinship and power in the marriage system of an Arab village', in J. Peristiany (ed.), *Contribution to Mediterranean Sociology*, Mouton, 1968.

A. M. Shaw and M. N. Strinwas, 'The myth of the self-sufficiency of the Indian village', *Economic Weekly*, September 1960. Discussion of the external social links (political, economic and cultural) of a contemporary village community.

R. Stavenhagen, 'Changing functions of the community in underdeveloped countries', *Sociologia Ruralis*, vol. 4, 1964, no. 3–4.

E. R. Wolf, 'Types of Latin American peasantry: a preliminary discussion', *Amer. Anthrop.*, vol. 57, 1955. Discussion of regional sub-types of peasant social structure.

Peasant economy

S. Barraclough, and A. Domike, 'Agrarian structure in the Latin American countries', *Land Economics*, vol. 62, 1966. A comprehensive discussion with a particular stress on land tenure and land reform.

C. S. Belshaw, *Traditional Exchange and Modern Markets*, Prentice-Hall, 1965.

I. H. Boeke, *Economics and Economic Policy of Dual Societies*, Institute of Pacific Relations, 1953. A discussion of peasantry with a particular stress on peasant economy in the framework of colonial and post-colonial society.

A. V. Chayanov (1925), *Organizatsiya krest'yanskogo khozyaistva*. Translated as *The Theory of Peasant Economy*, D. Thorner, R. E. F. Smith and B. Kerblay (eds.), Irwin, 1966. The major statement of thought and theory of the school which treats peasant economy as qualitatively specific.

R. Firth, 'Indo-Pacific economic systems,' *Inter. soc. Sci. Bulletin*, vol. 6, 1954, pp. 400–410. The impact of the extension of money and market relations on the peasant economy.

R. Firth and B. S. Jamey (eds.), *Capital, Saving and Credit in Peasant Societies*, Allen & Unwin, 1964. A statement of views that the peasant economy is essentially similar to the capitalist one and is to be treated in the same conceptual framework.

G. Gertz, *Agricultural Involution*, University of California Press, 1963. The interrelation of geographical and cultural aspects of agriculture.

M. Lipton, 'The theory of the optimising peasant', *J. devel. Studies*, April 1968. A discussion stressing the essential similarity between peasant and capitalist economies.

H. H. Mann, *The Social Framework of Agriculture: India, the Middle East, England*, edited by D. Thorner, Verry, 1967.

S. Mintz, 'Internal market systems as mechanisms of social articulation', in V. F. Ray (ed.), *Proceedings of the 1959 Annual Spring Meeting of the American Ethnological Society*, University of Wisconsin Press, 1959.

S. Mintz, 'Peasant markets', *Scient. Amer.*, vol. 2/2, 1960.

M. Nash, *Primitive and Peasant Economic Systems*, Chandler Publishing Co., 1966. A systematic discussion stressing the specific character of peasant economy.

K. Polanyi, C. M. Arensberg and H. W. Parsons (eds.), *Trade and Market in the Early Empires*, Free Press, 1957. In the relevant sections, an illuminating discussion of the place of trade and market in the development of human society.

G. W. Skinner, 'Marketing and social structure in rural China', *J. Asian Studies*, vol. 24, 1964.

D. Warriner, *Economics of Peasant Farming*, Oxford University Press, 1939. A somewhat dated but still very good discussion of the comparative problems of peasant economies, in a form readily comprehensible by non-economists.

Numerous basic issues involved in peasant economy are dealt with in the Reader by G. Dalton, *Tribal and Peasant Economies*.

Peasant political action

H. Alavi, 'Peasantry and revolution', *The Socialist Register 1965*, Merlin Press. An attempt to analyse comparatively the position of various groups of peasantry in political action.

M. Bequiri, *Peasantry in Revolution*, Cornell University Press, 1966. Particularly interesting in its discussion of leadership in peasant societies.

E. J. Hobsbawm, *Primitive Rebels*, Praeger, 1963. Forms of peasant rebellion in the nineteenth and twentieth centuries.

E. Jacoby, *Agrarian Unrest in South Asia*, Asia Publishing House, 1961. A discussion of the background and the forms of revolt and tensions involved in agrarian problems.

A. A. Landsberger, 'The role of peasant movements and revolts in development: an analytical framework', *Inter. Instit. Labour Studies*, bulletin 4, February 1968.

J. Lopreato and J. E. Saltzman, 'Descriptive models of peasant society: a reconciliation from southern Italy', *Human Organisation*, vol. 27, 1968. Class structure in rural society.

D. Mitrany, *Marx against the Peasant*, Collier, 1961. A selection of ideological treatments of peasantry by political theorists, mainly Marxists.

Barrington Moore, Jr, *Social Origins of Dictatorship and Democracy*, Beacon Press, 1966; Penguin Books, 1969. An illuminating discussion of the impact of power relations in the countryside on the political development of the contemporary world.

J. Petras and M. Zeitlin, 'Agrarian radicalism in Chile', *Brit. J. Sociol.*, vol. 19, 1968, no. 3, pp. 254–70. A comparative analysis of legal political action in rural society.

R. Stavenhagen (ed.), *Agrarian Problems and Peasant Movements in Latin America*, Doubleday, 1970.

A. L. Stinchcaulse, 'Agricultural enterprise and rural class relations', *Amer. J. Sociol.*, vol. 67, 1961–2, pp. 165–76. Classes in rural society.

P. Worsley, *The Third World*, Weidenfeld & Nicolson, 1967. A discussion of Populism approached as an ideology typical of the mainly peasant 'developing societies'.

Peasant culture

E. C. Banfield, *The Moral Basis of a Backward Society*, Free Press, 1958. Family self-centredness and suspicion as the major cultural features of southern Italian peasant society.

G. M. Foster, 'The peasants and the image of limited good', *Amer. Anthrop.*, vol. 62, 1965, no. 2. A basic discussion of the specific peasant cognition of reality as determined by the essentially finite and limited supply of earthly goods and the life of a small community.

A. Lopreto, 'Interpersonal relations in peasant society, a peasant view', *Human Organisation*, vol. 21, 1962, no. 1, pp. 21–4.

A. Pawelczynska, 'Urbanisation and industrialisation as factors promoting the acceptance of urban cultural patterns by the rural areas', *Polish sociol. Bull.*, vol. 2, 1964, pp. 116–33.

A. Pearse, 'The intrumentality of education systems', *Transactions of the Sixth World Congress of Sociology*, vol. 2.

R. Trouton, *Peasant Renaissance in Yugoslavia, 1900–50*, Routledge & Kegan Paul, 1952. The spread of education and its impact on the social structure of Yugoslav villages.

A. J. Wichers, '"Amoral familism", reconsidered', *Sociologia Ruralis*, vol. 4, 1964, pp. 167–81. A criticism of Banfield – 'amoral familism' as a reflection of the suppression of peasantry by the local land owning classes.

Contemporary agricultural reform and development

G. Arrighi and J. S. Saul, 'Socialism and economic development in tropical Africa', *J. mod. Afr. Studies*, vol. 6, 1968. A good discussion of the alternative ways of growth in the main rural African societies.

R. P. Dore, *Land Reform in Japan*, Oxford University Press, 1959.

R. Dumont, *False Start in Africa*, Deutsch, 1966.

C. Erasmus, 'The upper limits of peasantry and agrarian reform: Bolivia, Venezuela and Mexico compared', *Ethnology*, vol. 6, 1967, no. 4.

G. Huizer, 'Community development, land reform and political participation', *Amer. J. Econ. Sociol.*, vol. 28, 1969, no. 2.

A. Iwanska, 'The impact of agricultural reform on a Mexican Indian village, *Sociologus, N. F.*, vol. 15, 1965, pp. 54–67.

E. H. Jacoby, *Interrelation Between Agrarian Reform and Agricultural Development*, FAO, Rome. 1951.

E. H. Jacoby, *Man and Land: The Fundamental Issue in Development*, Deutsch, 1970.

D. Warriner, *Land Reform in Principle and Practice*, Clarendon Press, 1969.

P. Worsley (ed.), *Two Blades of Grass: Rural Co-operation in 'Developing Societies'*, Manchester University Press, 1971.

Some monographs on specific peasant societies

H. Ammar, *Growing Up in an Egyptian Village*, Routledge & Kegan Paul, 1954.

C. M. Arensberg, *The Irish Countrymen*, Macmillan, 1937.

E. Fel, and T. Hofer, *Proper Peasants* (Hungarian Peasants), Wenner-Gren Foundation, N.Y., 1968.

R. Firth, *Malayan Fishermen: Their Peasant Economy*, Kegan Paul, 1946.

H. W. Hutchinson, *Village and Plantation Life in Northwestern Brazil*, University of Washington Press, 1957.

M. Marriott (ed.), *Village India: Studies in the Little Community*, University of Chicago Press, 1955.

P. Mayer, *Townsmen or Tribesmen* (African worker-peasants), Oxford University Press, 1961.

J. Myrdal, *Report from a Chinese Village*, Heinemann, 1965; Penguin Books, 1967.

M. Nash, *The Golden Road to Modernity: Village Life in Contemporary Burma*, Wiley, 1965.

J. Steward (ed.), *The People of Puerto Rico*, University of Illinois Press, 1956.

S. Tax, *Penny Capitalism: A Guatemalan Indian Economy*, Smithsonian Institution, 1953.

E. Wolf, *Sons of the Shaking Earth* (Peru), University of Chicago Press, 1959.

C. K. Yang, *A Chinese Village in Early Communist Transition*, MIT Press, 1959.

Also see the studies by Stirling (Turkey), Robinson (pre-revolutionary Russia), Ayrout (Egypt), Franklin (contemporary Europe), excerpts of which are published in this Reader.

Acknowledgements

During the course of the preparation of this Reader a large correspondence was received which has profoundly influenced its content and form. I would like to express my thanks to all those who offered their help and advice:

Hamza A. Alavi (W. Pakistan – IDS, Brighton), Orlando Fals-Borda (Colombia – RISA, Geneva), R. Buve (University of Leiden), A. K. Constandse (Agricultural University of Wageningen), Ronald P. Dore (IDS, Brighton), Vojislav Duric (University of Novi Sad), Mathew Edel (MIT), Ray Emerson (University of East Anglia), Raymond Firth (LSE – University of Hawaii), Shephard Forman (University of Indiana), Harvey Franklin (University of Victoria, Wellington), Boguslaw Galeski (PAN, Warsaw), Margaret Haswell (University of Oxford), Pedro F. Hernandes (Louisiana State University), Rodney H. Hilton (University of Birmingham), G. P. Hirsch (University of Oxford), Eric J. Hobsbawm (Birkbeck College, London), Tomas Hofer (Budapest), Gerrit Huizer (Mexico – IILS, Geneva, Eric H. Jacoby (FAO – IIES, Stockholm), Jeremy Kemp (University of Oxford), Harry A. Landsberger (University of N. Carolina), Varda Langholtz (London), Michael Levy (Rio de Janiero – University of Manchester), Joseph Lopreato (University of Texas), Simon Mitchell (University of Glasgow), Gunnar Myrdal (IIES, Stockholm), Sutti Ortiz (LSE, London), Andrew Pearse (Santiago de Chile – St Antony's, Oxford), Vlado Puljiz (University of Zagreb), Ignacy Sachs (EPHE, Paris), John Saul (University College, Dar-es-Salaam), Robert E. F. Smith (University of Birmingham), M. M. Srinwas (University of Delhi), Henri H. Stahl (University of Bucharest), Rudolfo Stavenhagen (Mexico – IILS, Geneva), Elizabeth P. Taylor (AU, Cairo – University of York), Joan Thirsk (St Hilda's, Oxford), Daniel Thorner (EPHE, Paris), K. E. Wadekin, (IPWTH, Achen), Doreen Warriner (University of London), W. F. Wertheim (University of Amsterdam), Erich R. Wolf (University of Michigan), Peter Worsley (University of Manchester).

I am particularly grateful to Susan J. Robertshaw for her advice, assistance and patience. I would also like to express my thanks for the technical help provided by CREES, University of Birmingham.

Permission to reprint the Readings in this volume is acknowledged from the following sources:

Reading 1	Dover Publications Inc.
Reading 2	Clarendon Press
Reading 3	Weidenfeld & Nicolson Ltd and John Wiley & Sons Inc.
Reading 4	Beacon Press
Reading 5	American Anthropological Association and Eric R. Wolf
Reading 6	Andrew Pearse
Reading 7	Latin American Center for Research in the Social Sciences and Ernest Feder
Reading 8	Associated Book Publishers Ltd
Reading 9	John S. Saul
Reading 10	European Society for Rural Sociology and Boguslaw Galeski
Reading 11	Associated Book Publishers Ltd
Reading 12	Basile Kerblay
Reading 13	University of Texas Press and Manning Nash
Reading 14	Macmillan Co.
Reading 15	Polish Academy of Sciences and Boguslaw Galeski
Reading 16	Mouton & Co.
Reading 17	Clarendon Press
Reading 18	Lawrence & Wishart Ltd
Reading 19	*Sociological Review*
Reading 20	UNESCO
Reading 21	Polish Academy of Sciences
Reading 22	The British Association for the Advancement of Science and Frederick G. Bailey
Reading 23	Sutti Ortiz
Reading 24	University of Chicago Press
Reading 25 (ii)	Granada Publishing Ltd and Grove Press Inc.
Reading 25 (iii)	Oxford University Press
Reading 26	Asian Economic Research Institute and R. P. Dore
Reading 27	*American Journal of Economics and Sociology* and Gerrit Huizer
Reading 28	*New Left Review*

Author Index

Subject Index

Acculturation, 16, 54, 76
Accumulation
  capitalist, 219, 220–21, 224
  primitive, 220–23
  socialist, 219–20, 223, 224, 225
Africa
  capitalist farming in, 107, 108,
    109–10, 111, 112, 113
  cash-cropping in, 108–9, 111,
    112
  centres of labour demand in, 108
  colonialism in, 106–8, 111, 112
  cultural identifications in, 109
  definition of peasants in, 103–9
  environmental potential in,
    108–9, 112–13
  heterogenetic cities in, 342, 347
  indigenous elite and bourgeoisie
    in, 108, 109, 110, 310
  migrant farmers in, 107, 111, 112
  migrant labourers in, 107, 111,
    112
  pastoralists in, 105, 147
  political consciousness in, 110,
    261
  population pressures in, 110, 111
  primitive agriculturalists in,
    106–8
  proletarianization in, 107, 110,
    111
  regional markets in, 173
  'sacred centers' in, 362
  tenant farmers in, 112
  tribal consciousness in, 110, 113
  see also Egypt; Ghana;
    Southern Rhodesia;
    Tanzania
Agricultural
  communities, 115–16, 129
  economists, 15, 99

economy, 189, 207, 323
education, 189, 196, 383
enterprises,
  advantages of large-scale, 158
  capitalist, 109
  effect of large-scale, 249
  industrial enterprise and, 115,
    143–4, 249
  occupational structure in, 180,
    189, 195
  organization of, 117–23, 136,
    187
  specialization in, 132
  village community and, 123–6
entrepreneurs, 78, 103, 122, 154,
  186, 198
exports, 387
innovation, 318, 383
manufacture, 133–4
productivity, 142, 145, 149, 150,
  190, 197, 377
proletariat, 110
proletarization of, 158
reform, 132, 135, 389, 392, 395,
  400–404, 408, 418
revolution, 245
schools, 194, 196
science, 142, 194, 197
services, 196
structure, 71
surplus, 384, 421
Agriculture
  aim, 141
  as an occupational division, 180
  capitalist, 132, 154, 209
  commercial, 74, 147, 407–8
  choice of type, 146–8
  economic surplus, 249
  effect of high-density
    population on, 145

Little Tradition in, 348, 353, 355, 359, 362
market in, 340–41, 342
modern colonial, 347
nationalism in, 349–50, 361
primary urbanization of, 344–7, 348–9, 350–51, 352–3, 358
rural-urban integration and, 356, 358
secondary urbanization of, 345–7, 348, 349–51, 352, 356, 358, 360
social structure in, 349–50
Clans, 49, 203, 287
Code Napoléon, 231, 234
Cognition systems, 326, 332
Cognitive maps, 300–302
future in, 299, 313–15
leadership in, 306–12, 316
mediators in, 308–12
outsiders in, 303–6, 308, 312
time in, 299, 313–16, 317
Collective farming, 116, 118, 119–20, 125, 128–33, 135, 187, 215
see also Communes; *Ejidos*; Kolkhoz
Colombia, 86, 324–6, 328, 405
Colonialism
exploitation, 220, 222, 223
in Africa, 106–8, 111
in India, 210–11
in Indonesia, 210
political activity under, 372–3, 374
mentioned, 329, 415
see also Mexico
Common land, 41, 45, 58, 174, 216, 294, 329
see also Land, access to
Communal land *see* Common land
Communes, 34, 116, 215, 241, 269
see also Collective farming; *Ejidos*
Community development programmes

definition, 397
in Costa Rica, 391–2
in El Salvador, 389–91, 392–3
in Guatemala, 395
in Italy, 392
in Mexico, 395–400, 408
in Peru, 394–5, 407
in Venezuela, 401–3
political activity and, 392, 395–6, 401–7, 408
Community-orientated groups *see* Mexico
Compadrazgo, 66
Confucius, 348, 352, 382
Congo, 238
Consumer
behaviour, 127
demands, 155–7
determined aims, 32
labour enterprises, 30
needs, 15, 30, 241, 250, 341
Co-operatives
advantages of, 76, 83
competitive power of, 156
in China, 215
in Japan, 384
in Tanzania, 113
mentioned, 198
Cora Indians, 163–5
CORDIPLAN, 403
Corn Laws, 381
Costa Rica, 391
Costume *see* Dress
Crafts, craftsmen
in China, 215
industrial competition and, 215, 250
Indian, 163, 164, 167–8, 169
in Japan, 214
in Poland, 291, 293
in Russia, 32, 34, 178–9
in Turkey, 39
landless, 16, 291, 293
supplementary employment, 32, 34, 178–9, 205, 214, 215, 323
mentioned, 45, 169, 339, 349

Kabylia, 271
Kan-ch'ing, 66
Kibbutz, 115–16, 129
Kinship, 38, 100, 164, 203, 246, 264, 281, 303, 305, 310
  see also Family
Kolkhoz, 16, 119
Kozaks, 16
Kulaks, 151, 375

Labour, labourers, agricultural
  demand, 101, 107, 108–9, 147
  dis-utility of, 151
  division of, 16, 31, 99, 119, 132, 187, 230, 242, 304
  efficiency, 149, 291, 293, 373, 417
  eviction of, 94–5
  free, 94, 95, 164–5, 168, 205, 329, 391
  in under-developed countries, 412–15, 416, 417–18, 419
  landless,
    cultural values and, 291
    in Africa, 113
    in Latin America, 84, 93
    in Poland, 291, 293
    in villages, 100
    landlords and, 84, 268
    migration of, 373
    marginal, 55, 151
    migrant, 109, 112, 294
    occupational attitudes, 187–90
    on collectives, 119
    on estates, 70, 85–92, 97, 121, 205, 209
    on industrial farms, 117, 131
    on plantations, 70, 93, 162–3, 210, 265
    oppression of, 89, 90–91
    organization of, 89, 90–91, 95, 97
    part-time, 92, 99, 101, 102, 178, 250
    productivity of, 416–17, 420
    professionalization of, 189, 195
    reserve, 70
    resident, 56, 57, 93, 398

  rural-urban migration, 84, 93, 96, 266, 270
  seasonal, 92, 147, 265, 296
  shortages, 101, 143
  social division, 183, 184, 185, 188, 194
  see also Cash-workers; Family; Indians; Wages
Labour–consumer balance, 153
Labour unions *see* Unions
Ladino, 168, 170, 175
Laguna, 398, 399, 400
Land
  access to, 66, 69, 84, 94, 266
  consolidation, 125
  fragmentation, 189, 233
  grants, 211
  improvements, 153–4
  investment in, 59, 129
  peasants and, 80, 105, 240–41
  purchase, 58–9, 131, 153, 174, 192
  redistribution, 61, 127, 150, 379, 395, 397, 407
  reform, 75, 213, 266, 379, 380–82, 384, 407
  shortage of, 295, 325, 326
  source of power, 83–4, 90
  tenure, 83–4, 92, 97, 111, 287, 377, 381, 391
  utilization, 92, 147, 241
  see also Community development; Under-developed countries
Landlords, landowners,
  absentee, 86, 88–9, 94, 124, 378, 383, 390
  attitudes of, 89, 91–2, 206, 207, 378
  definition of, 378–9
  economic development and, 89, 378–9, 381, 387
  in China, 215, 268
  in El Salvador, 391, 393
  in England, 379–80
  in India, 211, 380
  in Indonesia, 210

National-oriented groups, 50–53, 57–8, 60–62, 64, 65–6
'Native purchase', 111
Near East, 337
Nehru, Jawarhalal, 354
Neo-colonialism, 314
Nigeria, 343
Nippur, 346
Nkrumah, Kwame, 112
Nomads see Tribal-nomads
Normandy, 142
North America, 337
  see also United States of America

Oaxaca, 162, 168, 169, 172
Ocotlan, 169
Occupational structure, 125, 134, 188, 193, 195, 197, 198
Oriente province, 269, 271
Orissa, 299, 301, 309–10
Oxchuc Indians, 328–30
Oyabun-kobun, 66

Páez Indians, 324–5, 327–8, 330, 334
Pakistan, 418
Panajachel, 166, 172, 174
Panajacheleños Indians, 166
Paraguay, 203
Parental authority, 24–5, 47, 286, 326
Parent-child relationships, 24, 73, 120, 281, 288
Pastoral economy, 142
Pastoralists, 105, 142, 147, 266
Paternal authority, 24, 281, 288, 326
Patriarchy, 31, 120, 122, 281, 287, 329
Patzcuaro, Lake, 168, 169
Peasant culture
  anonymity in, 282, 286
  basic conditions for, 281–2
  conservatism in, 278–9, 281
  definition of, 323

disintegration of, 16, 287, 295–8, 349
education and, 280, 296, 297
feudalism and, 280, 290, 295–6, 297
in historical perspective, 292–3
in primitive societies, 280
integrated with cities, 352–62
mediators in, 308–12
'of repression', 331
role of magic in, 281, 284, 285, 288–90
role of religion in, 285–6, 290, 296
sociability in, 284–6
success in, 314, 315, 316
traditional, concept of, 277–80
transmission of, 277–80, 282–4, 295, 296, 353
villages and, 296–8, 293–5
used to define 'peasant', 323, 324, 326, 327
  see also Africa; Culture; Indians
Peasant economy, 99–100, 104–5, 150–59, 202–17, 253, 323–4
Peasant households,
  characteristics, 30
  definition of, 205–7, 208–9
  Indian, 171, 174
  in Japan, 213–14
  in Poland, 25–9
  in Tsarist Russia, 30–34
  stability of, 240
  mentioned, 32, 212, 230, 240–41
Peasant league, 83, 401
  see also Unions
Peasant syndicates, 406
Peasants, peasantry
  alienation of resources, 224, 268
  anarchism of, 272–3, 372
  bondage of, 209
  characteristics of, 238–9, 255, 327, 330, 372–4, 419
  conservatism of, 46, 112, 231, 269, 281
  decapitalization of, 78

definitions of, 104–6, 238–45,
251, 254–5, 322–6, 333
dependence of, 75, 79, 268
deterioration of, 80, 84
dispossession of, 70, 95–6
duality of, 253–4
effect of incorporate drive on,
71–3, 75, 79–80
emancipation of, 209, 213, 293,
297
exploitation and oppression of,
90–91, 94–5, 206–7, 231–2,
281–2, 292, 376, 391–2
general type of, 14
in frontier areas, 270–71
in historical context, 245–51,
292–3
in industrializing societies, 246,
248–9, 252–3
institutional role of, 77–8
isolation of, 70, 77, 230, 369,
403
integration of, 16, 351, 403
labour-exporting, 108, 109, 112
leadership of, 257, 259, 261,
306–13, 384, 393, 403
marginal groups, 15–16
'middle', 77, 252, 269–70
mobility of, 179, 269, 271
motivations of, 191–2
nationalism in, 373–4
organization of, 372, 392, 400,
402–3, 405–6
political action of
guerrilla warfare, 260
guided action, 257–8
local riots, 258
in Algeria, 259, 264, 269, 271
in China, 259, 264, 268, 269,
271
in Cuba, 264, 269, 271
in France, 229, 231, 232–3
in Mexico, 259, 264, 268,
269–71
in Poland, 296–7
invasions by, 402, 403, 406–8
in Venezuela

poverty of, 230, 233, 234, 235,
250, 331, 417, 419
pre-industrial, 244–5
see also Farmers; Labour;
Peonage
Peiping, 342, 343, 346
Peonage, peons, 18, 210, 268,
324, 399
Peru, 57, 96, 331, 393, 407
Plantations, 93, 108, 112, 162–3,
210, 211, 213, 383
Poland, 25, 192–3, 250, 277,
285–7, 290, 295, 297–8
Polytheism, 356
Popoluca, 169, 175, 176
Population,
explosion, 250, 265, 414–15, 418
density, 145, 240
in Algeria, 265
in China, 215, 265
in Cuba, 265
in India, 250–51, 412, 418
in Japan, 213–14, 380
in Latin America, 92
in Mexico, 57, 211, 265, 389
in Pakistan, 418
in Russia, 265
in Vietnam, 265
pressure on land, 110, 111, 329,
380, 389, 412
mentioned, 72, 102, 142
Primitive
agriculturalists, 103, 105, 106,
108
communities, 345
economy, 141, 149, 202, 322, 323
societies, 45–6, 348
Pueblos, 163
Puerto, Carrillo, 361

Quezaltengo, 166, 167, 168
Quijada, Ramón, 402

Recession, 127
Redemption payments, 266
Regional marketing system,
161–2, 165–74, 176